protest, dissent and the supreme court

Robert L. Cord

Winthrop Publishers, Inc.
Cambridge, Massachusetts

193322

ii

TO MARGUERITE J. FISHER,
STUART GERRY BROWN,
*and all the other very special
people who care.*

contents

War Protest As Disorderly Conduct:

2. political association and participation as freedom of expression

3. the courtroom and political expression

The Contempt Power And Free Expression Outside The Courtroom Case:

4. protest and public property

5. protest and private property

introduction

This book is about dissent and dissenters in the United States. It is about real people, with different points of view—from each other and from government—protesting public policy. It is about the Supreme Court of the United States and its continuing concern for the preservation of the freedom of individuals and groups of all political coloration to dissent. It is about an ongoing problem of American democracy or any constitutional society that seeks *in fact* to limit the exercise of governmental power; the reconciliation of individual freedom and majority rights when they collide.

Perhaps the foregoing is a bit too abstract. *Specifically*, what is this book about?

First, it is about dissent against the war involvements of the United States government. *Second*, it is about many diverse associational and individual acts of protest as types of freedom of expression. *Third*, this book is about the constitutional right to criticize governmental officials without fear of criminal action being brought by the state or a private suit for damages in a libel or slander suit. *Fourth*, the book raises problems concerning the conflict between guaranteed courtroom procedural rights, like the rights of counsel and confrontation of your accusers, and the current attempt by some persons accused of crime to turn their trials into public podiums for denouncing the American political, economic, and social system.

Finally, this book raises the constitutional questions and the political and social implications arising from protests against racism in the United States. Cases involving segregation in privately owned restaurants and demonstrations to end racial discrimination in general are presented in depth.

This book also attempts to provide the reader with an introduction to a somewhat "mysterious" institution—the United States Supreme Court. It seeks to explain briefly the functions of the Court; where its cases come from; what its powers and limitations are; how opinions get written; and how the Court generally fits into the American constitutional and judicial systems.

This book also provides thought-provoking questions after each case in the hope that they will provide the student with a meaningful and long-range understanding of the right of dissent in America. The questions are a very important part of each case study and this book. They challenge the serious student to analyze the problem, and formulate *reasons* for his judgment.

There is, in addition, a glossary of legal terms and Latin phrases at the end of the book.

Lastly, and most importantly: the initial chapters, the introductory essays, the lengthy excerpts of the cases themselves, and the questions after each case are designed to stimulate the reader to gain *a greater understanding of what constitutional democratic government is all about*. The awareness of the importance of freedom of expression, which includes wide latitudes for legal dissent and protest within the political system, is, I believe, crucial to that understanding.

Not too long ago, a candid young President of the United States, admitting an error of his Administration, noted that success has many fathers— failure is always an orphan. It is appropriate for me to reverse this proposition. If there is some merit in what I have consigned to these pages, in all candor, it belongs to the legion of teachers, colleagues, friends, and students who have contributed to my intellectual and personal development. If there are faults herein, the parentage resides with me.

For many ideas, much tolerance, and plentiful encouragement, I am particularly indebted to my friends and colleagues Irene A. Nichols, David W. Barkley, Minton F. Goldman, Walter S. Jones, Jr., James A. Medeiros. Margaret Elizabeth O'Leary, and R. Gregg Wilfong of Northeastern University and Morton J. Horwitz and Arthur E. Sutherland of the Harvard Law School. Appreciation is also due my junior colleague at Northeastern, H. Kennedy Hudner, for undertaking without complaint many tedious tasks.

Throughout the preparation of the manuscript many helpful suggestions were made by Professors Gordon Baker, University of California at Santa Barbara, David Danielski of Yale, Samuel Krislov, University of Minnesota, and Martin Shapiro, Harvard University. In addition, I am grateful to Jim Murray and Muriel Harman of Winthrop Publishers for doing many of the important things.

Finally, a purely personal note. There are many in my life who have contributed much to make it an acceptable enterprise. The debt I owe to Evelyn L. Cord, Arleen R. Cord, Richard H. Cord, Anna Lewis, Emanuel Lewis, Gerald E. Bouchoux, James L. Sheldon, Norma Pallocco, Ann Rath, Thomas J. Kerr IV, Ann Hayes, Barbara Barkley, John Vorenberg, and Michael O. Sawyer can never be calculated. Knowing them, they would not even acknowledge its existence.

ROBERT L. CORD
Cambridge, Massachusetts

If a nation expects to be ignorant and free . . .
it expects what never was and never will be.

—*Thomas Jefferson*

To sin by silence when they should protest
makes cowards of men.

—*Abraham Lincoln*

PROTEST, DISSENT AND THE SUPREME COURT

one. freedom of expression and american democracy

Is individual freedom diminishing in the United States? How are protest and dissent important to a democracy? Can draft card burning be constitutionally upheld? Can burning the flag? Is picketing "symbolic free speech?" How is a demonstration on public property constitutionally distinguished from a demonstration on private property? What is "private" property? Which modes of human expression are "free?"

It is important to gain an understanding of the degree of liberty which exists to dissent openly from government policy without fear of official retribution. And, in the last forty years, no formal governmental institution has been more important to the preservation of individual and collective dissent than the United States Supreme Court. Its opinions are the primary sources for defining community rights as opposed to individual rights in almost every area of human endeavor in our society.

The struggle to maintain basic democratic freedoms in any society is an ongoing one. There was no generation of Americans who secured the liberties of this country forever. Those liberties which we now have—relatively speaking—are susceptible to erosion or termination. Many freedoms important to the advance of democratic constitutional government have not even been fully realized. Liberties in a nation—any nation—are constantly in jeopardy from some of the people most of the time, and from all of the people some of the time. Frequently, freedoms are threatened or denied by those in government, in associations, or individuals in society, who act in the belief that they are preserving democracy.

The character of a nation depends on its institutions, the philosophy that permeates them, and the commitment of the people to preserve those institutions. Dissent is risky business unless a society is committed to its right to exist, its utility or worth, and its being a legitimate act of good citizenship. In a highly pluralistic society such as the United States, with its many religious and cultural inputs, races, ethnic backgrounds, sectional problems, political views of the nation and the world, schools of ethics and concepts of morality, diversity necessarily exists. This diversity can be a great source of alternatives, or it can be an endless source of internal problems and dissension. In this country it has been both.

Why does a democratic society make a commitment to the free exchange of ideas anyway? What is so valuable about the freedom to speak and print when many irresponsible and dangerous ideas will be uttered and printed as a consequence? In short, what is so sacred about the freedom of expression? And doesn't its constitutional protection exact from society a great price?

One should approach these questions by initially recognizing that a social commitment to the protection of freedom of expression—which oftentimes includes falsehoods and odious opinions—is costly indeed but has nevertheless been consistently defended by the Supreme Court as an essential downpayment of a free and progressive society. The members of the First Congress, who drafted what later became the First Amendment and who submitted it to the States for ratification were willing to meet that cost because they—like the Constitutional ratifying conventions before them—understood the utility and desirability of limiting the power of government to interfere with freedom of thought and expression.

Essentially, the First Amendment, with its many prohibitions on government, protects the freedom to think, to believe, and to communicate. It is difficult to overemphasize the importance of these rights to a rational decision-making process. Defending the importance of the First Amendment, Judge Learned Hand wrote that it "presupposes that right conclusions are more likely to be gathered out of a multitude of tongues, than through any kind of authoritative selection. To many this is, and always will be, folly; but we have staked upon it our all." [*United States* v. *Associated Press*, 52 F. Supp. 362.]

Mr. Justice Holmes' minority opinion in *Abrams* v. *United States*, 250 U.S. 616 (1919), had developed earlier the argument for the social utility of a wide latitude of freedom of expression and dissent from orthodoxy in a manner most reminiscent of John Stuart Mill's eloquent brief in *On Liberty*.

Mill reasoned that any man's opinion on social problems and their possible resolution would contain either much value or truth, little truth, or no value at all. In each instance, he believed that the community would be better served by the expression of the opinion.

If a man's speech contained a great deal of truth, the community would lose that truth if it silenced him or created a repressive atmosphere making him fearful of expressing his ideas. Obviously there can be little human progress when people are afraid to utter unorthodox opinions because there is concern that it will lead to physical or social retribution. Societies which create an atmosphere of tolerance for unorthodox views will be those which will benefit from the value later found to be contained therein.

But what if, as in the second instance, a man's opinion does not contain much value but only a little "truth?" What if his ideas are not of great utility to society in resolving its many problems—ought he to be guaranteed the right to speak because it is in the community's interest? Mill reasoned that even if a man's opinion contained only a few useful ideas, society would still profit from hearing him speak because it would be diminished if the expression of his limited insights were discouraged. Therefore, even where there is a very limited amount to be gained by the expression of opinion, society could not realize even that small gain if a repressive atmosphere existed.

But what if there is no truth at all in an opinion? How could its expression possibly benefit society? Why ought freedom of expression to be guaranteed in that instance?

It must, of course, be recognized that it is not possible to assess the value of an opinion before it is uttered. But even if it could be determined *before the fact* that an opinion *contained* no valuable content whatsoever, Mill argued that, that fact notwithstanding, the expression of an "apparently worthless" opinion still served a useful purpose after all. Against the expression of foolish opinions current social "truths" can be measured and their value can be more easily appreciated. Mill concluded that whatever the content of an opinion—whether it contained many or no valuable ideas—*the very expression of the opinion itself* must serve a useful function in society.

What makes Mill's argument so intriguing is that *he does not* argue that freedom of expression should be guaranteed to the individual *primarily* because of some social commitment to human dignity. Mill put in paramount position the proposition that freedom of expression in any society is necessary and makes good sense if people are to test contemporary orthodoxies against new ideas even though unorthodox opinion may appear foolish, odious, and perhaps even threatening.

Justice Brandeis extended Mill's analysis in a similar but more comprehensive justification for freedom of expression in his concurring opinion in *Whitney* v. *California*, 247 U.S. 357 (1927). Brandeis wrote in 1927:

> Those who won our independence believed that the final end of the state was to make men free to develop their faculties; and that in its government the deliberative forces should prevail over the arbitrary. They valued liberty both as an end and as a means. They believed liberty to be the secret of happiness and courage to be the secret of liberty. They believed that freedom to think as you will and to speak as you think are means indispensable to the discovery and spread of political truth; that without free speech and assembly discussion would be futile; that with them, discussion affords ordinarily adequate protection against the dissemination of noxious doctrine; that the greatest menace to freedom is an inert people; that public discussion is a

political duty; and that this should be a fundamental principle of the American government. They recognized the risks to which all human institutions are subject. But they knew that order cannot be secured merely through fear of punishment for its infraction; that it is hazardous to discourage thought, hope and imagination; that fear breeds repression; that repression breeds hate; that hate menaces stable government; that the path of safety lies in the opportunity to discuss freely supposed grievances and proposed remedies; and that the fitting remedy for evil counsels is good ones. Believing in the power of reason as applied through public discussion, they eschewed silence coerced by law—the argument of force in its worst form. Recognizing the occasional tyrannies of governing majorities, they amended the Constitution so that free speech and assembly should be guaranteed.

Brandeis in *Whitney* further indicated that men "feared witches" and thus burned women. The horror of this proposition gets back to the root of Holmes' dissent in *Abrams*. Holmes warned us that today's "truths" are tomorrow's fictions. Through the conflict of competing ideas, Holmes reminded us, free men approach the best *available* test of the validity of "supposed truths." The competition of ideas did not guarantee the emergence of truth, but rather, society's search for truth and value was a continuing experiment.

In the late 1930's when the Holmes and Brandeis position as to the importance of freedom of expression became the commitment of a majority of the Supreme Court, there emerged a judicial doctrine known as the "preferred position of the First Amendment." In brief, this doctrine elevated the guarantees of the First Amendment over other constitutionally protected rights. The rationale for the preferred position of the First Amendment was succinctly stated by Mr. Justice Cardozo in *Palko* v. *Connecticut*, 302 U.S. 319 (1937). Reflecting on the importance of freedom of thought and speech he wrote, "Of that freedom one may say that it is the matrix, the indispensable condition, of nearly every other form of freedom."

Constitutionally Protected and Unprotected Speech

With great care the United States Supreme Court has tried to differentiate between those modes of expression and communication which are constitutionally protected by the First Amendment and those which are not. Justice Holmes in his unanimous opinion for the Court in *Frohwerk* v. *United States*, 249 U.S. 204 (1919), clearly indicated that certain uses of language were never historically considered constitutionally protected speech:

> With regard to the argument [that all speech whatever its nature was constitutionally protected] we think it necessary to add to what has been said in *Schenck* v. *United States*, . . . only that the First Amendment while prohibiting legislation against free speech as such cannot have been, and obviously was not intended to give immunity for every possible use of language. *Robertson* v. *Baldwin*, 165 U.S. 275 (1897). We venture to believe that neither Hamilton nor Madison, nor any other competent person then or later, ever supposed that to make criminal the counselling of a murder within the jurisdiction of Congress would be an unconstitutional interference with free speech.

This general principle was also held to be true of the constitutional guarantee of press, assembly, and all other forms of communication.

In sum, the Supreme Court has consistently held that all that may ·be spoken or printed should *not* be *indiscriminately* thought of as constitutionally protected speech or press. The use of certain words, in definite contexts, with specific intentions, may constitute action which can be outlawed by Congress and/or the state legislatures. These classifications historically include slander and libel, obscenity, conspiracy or a plot to commit a crime, the advocacy of criminal behavior with the intent of stirring people to action, and "fighting-words" which are likely to provoke the "average man" to an immediate breach of the peace. In contradistinction, oral or printed expression of opinion, discussion of social problems, and even *abstract* advocacy of criminal behavior has been considered constitutionally protected speech or press.

In several important cases, the Supreme Court has attempted to clarify which classification of words (spoken or printed) fail to come under the constitutional protection of free speech or press. Mr. Justice Roberts' opinion of the Court in *Cantwell* v. *Connecticut*, 310 U.S. 296 (1940), represented part of this effort. He sought to distinguish between the use of language which would be constitutionally punishable under a local breach of the peace statute and that which would not:

> . . . One may, however, be guilty of the offense [breach of the peace] if he commits acts or makes statements likely to provoke violence and disturbing of good order, even though no such eventuality be intended. Decisions to this effect are many but examination discloses that, in practically all, the provocative language which was held to amount to a breach of the peace consisted of profane, indecent, or abusive remarks directed to the person of the hearer. Resort to epithets or personal abuse is not in any proper sense communication of information or

opinion safeguarded by the Constitution, and its punishment as a criminal act would raise no question under that instrument.

In *Chaplinsky* v. *New Hampshire*, 315 U.S. 568 (1942), the Supreme Court unanimously upheld New Hampshire's legislative authority to forbid the addressing in a public place, of anyone, with "offensive, derisive, or annoying" words—"face-to-face words plainly likely to cause a breach of the peace by the addressee" or "words likely to cause an average addressee to fight"—and sustained Chaplinsky's conviction for having called a city marshal a "damned racketeer" and a "damned Fascist." Mr. Justice Murphy wrote:

> There are certain well-defined and narrowly limited classes of speech, the prevention and punishment of which have never been thought to raise any Constitutional problem. These include the lewd and obscene, the profane, the libelous, and the insulting or "fighting" words—those which by their very nature inflict injury or tend to incite an immediate breach of the peace. It has been well observed that such utterances are no essential part of any exposition of ideas, and are of such slight social value as a step to truth that any benefit derived from them is clearly outweighed by the social interest in order and morality.

In each of these instances, that language considered to be constitutionally unprotected speech, has had insufficient social quality to redeem it from legislative prohibition or criminal sanction.

Also, language which advocated criminal behavior *with the intent of inciting people to criminal action* has been held to be beyond the protection of the First Amendment's guarantee. But language which merely advocates crime *in the abstract* has been differentiated by the Court from advocacy of *criminal action* and has been generally protected as beyond legislative punishment.

In *Dennis* v. *United States*, 341 U.S. 494 (1951), Mr. Chief Justice Vinson distinguished between abstract advocacy of crime and advocacy of criminal action. This distinction had been made by the judge, for the jury, in the original Federal District Court trial. Indicating that the Smith Act of 1940, under which twelve high-level members of the American Communist Party had been convicted for, among other things, "knowingly and willfully" organizing to advocate and to teach "the duty and necessity of overthrowing and destroying the Government of the United States by force and violence," the Chief Justice wrote that "the Smith Act is directed at advocacy not discussion." Vinson stressed that:

> . . . [T]he trial judge properly charged the jury that they could not convict if they found the petitioners did "no more than pursue peace-

ful studies and discussions or teaching and *advocacy* [Editor's emphasis.] in the realm of ideas." . . .

. . .

"In further construction and interpretation of the statute I charge you that it is not the abstract doctrine of overthrowing or destroying government by unlawful means which is denounced by this law, but the teaching and advocacy of action for the accomplishment of that purpose, by language reasonably and ordinarily calculated to incite persons to such action. . . ."

Justice Harlan, delivering the opinion of the Court in *Yates* v. *United States*, 354 U.S. 298 (1957), made this same dichotomy when the Supreme Court, for the second time, upheld the constitutionality of the Smith Act's "advocacy clause."

The distinction between advocacy of abstract doctrine and advocacy directed at *promoting unlawful action* [Editor's emphasis.] is one that has been consistently recognized in the opinions of this Court. . . . This distinction was heavily underscored in *Gitlow* v. *New York*, 268 U.S. 652 (1925), in which the statute involved was nearly identical with the one now before us, and where the Court, despite the narrow view there taken of the First Amendment, said:
"The statute does not penalize the utterance or publication of abstract 'doctrine' or academic discussion having no quality of incitement to concrete action. . . . It is not the abstract 'doctrine' of overthrowing organized government by unlawful means which is denounced by the statute, but the advocacy of action for the accomplishment of that purpose. . . ."

The Court has held also that libel is not constitutionally protected speech. *Beauharnais* v. *Illinois*, 343 U.S. 250 (1952), brought before the Supreme Court the constitutionality of an Illinois statute which made it illegal to produce, sell, or exhibit pictures, lithographs, plays, etc. which portrayed any class of citizens of a particular race, creed, color, or religion in a contemptuous or derisive manner. The Illinois legislature, in passing the law, had hoped to cool somewhat the existing racial tensions in their state. Characterizing it as a "group libel" statute, Mr. Justice Frankfurter for the Court upheld the Illinois act and dismissed the constitutional challenge because "libelous utterances" were not "within the area of constitutionally protected speech. . . ."

Five years later in *Roth* v. *United States*, 354 U.S. 476 (1957), the Supreme Court dealt squarely with the issue of constitutional protection for obscenity. Going beyond the immediate issue of whether or not obscenity was constitutionally protected speech the Court eloquently advanced anew the rationale used from the days of the Framers to the present to distinguish between "protected and unprotected speech." Justice Brennan, in the opinion of the Court, wrote:

> The guaranties of freedom of expression in effect in 10 of the 14 States which by 1792 had ratified the Constitution, gave no absolute protection for every utterance. Thirteen of the 14 States provided for the prosecution of libel, and all of those States made either blasphemy or profanity, or both, statutory crimes. . . .
>
> . . . At the time of the adoption of the First Amendment, obscenity law was not as fully developed as libel law, but there is sufficiently contemporaneous evidence to show that obscenity, too, was outside the protection intended for speech and press.
>
> *The protection given speech and press was fashioned to assure unfettered interchange of ideas for the bringing about of political and social changes desired by the people.* [Editor's emphasis.] This objective was made explicit as early as 1774 in a letter of the Continental Congress to the inhabitants of Quebec:
>
> "The last right we shall mention regards the freedom of the press. The importance of this consists, besides the advancement of truth, science, morality, and arts in general, in its diffusion of liberal sentiments on the administration of Government, its ready communication of thoughts between subjects, and its consequential promotion of union among them, whereby oppressive officers are shamed or intimidated, into more honourable and just modes of conducting affairs." [1 *Journals of the Continental Congress* 108 (1774).]
>
> All ideas having even the slightest redeeming social importance— *unorthodox ideas, controversial ideas, even ideas hateful to the prevailing climate of opinion* [Editor's emphasis.]—have the full protection of the guaranties, unless excludable because they encroach upon the limited area of more important interests. But implicit in the history of the First Amendment is the rejection of obscenity as utterly without redeeming social importance. This rejection for that reason is mirrored in the universal judgment that obscenity should be restrained, reflected in the international agreement of over 50 nations, in the obscenity laws of all of the 48 States, and in the 20 obscenity laws enacted by the Congress from 1842 to 1956. . . .
>
> We hold that obscenity is not within the area of constitutionally protected speech or press.

Before moving to another point it should be noted that the value-judgment as to whether some specific expression—be it spoken words, printed words, picketing, pictures, or burning a draft card, etc.—is constitutionally protected communication or falls within an unprotected classification and is thus punishable, is one which a jury and/or judge must decide in specific cases with a detailed set of facts following an indictment for violation of some relatively explicit statute. In all these cases the burden of proof is on the state to prove that what is alleged by the defendant to be constitutionally protected freedom of expression is, in fact, some type of communication which has no constitutional immunity.

As we have noted, no formal governmental institution has been more consistently concerned with the defense of individual liberties in the past forty years than has the United States Supreme Court. The rights of the majority, or an individual who projects conventional views are seldom placed in jeopardy in *any* society. One of the "acid tests" of the degree of freedom which *in fact* exists in a society is the way in which its institutions of power treat dissenters. The cases in this book are, to some degree, an indication of how committed American society is, *in reality*, to individual political liberty.

two. the supreme court in the american system of government

The Supreme Court: Constitutional Arbiter and Highest Federal Court

"Good Evening, My Fellow Citizens," the President of the United States began, "For a few minutes this evening I want to speak to you about the serious situation that has arisen in Little Rock."

Dwight D. Eisenhower explained that he had specifically flown to the "house of Lincoln, of Jackson, and of Wilson" from his summer retreat in Rhode Island to underscore the importance of what he was about to say to the American people:

> In that city, under the leadership of demagogic extremists, disorderly mobs have deliberately prevented the carrying out of proper orders from a Federal Court. Local authorities have not eliminated that violent opposition and, under the law, I yesterday issued a Proclamation calling upon the mob to disperse.
>
> This morning the mob again gathered in front of the Central High School of Little Rock, obviously for the purpose of again preventing the carrying out of the Court's order relating to the admission of Negro children to that school.
>
> Whenever normal agencies prove inadequate to the task and it becomes necessary for the Executive Branch of the Federal Government to use its powers and authority to uphold Federal Courts, the President's responsibility is inescapable.

In accordance with that responsibility, I have today issued an Executive Order directing the use of troops under Federal authority to aid in the execution of Federal law at Little Rock, Arkansas. This became necessary when my Proclamation of yesterday was not observed, and the obstruction of justice still continues.

It is important that the reasons for my action be understood by all our citizens.

As you know, the Supreme Court of the United States has decided that separate public educational facilities for the races are inherently unequal and therefore compulsory school segregation laws are unconstitutional.

Our personal opinions about the decision have no bearing on the matter of enforcement; the responsibility and authority of the Supreme Court to interpret the Constitution are very clear. Local Federal Courts were instructed by the Supreme Court to issue such orders and decrees as might be necessary to achieve admission to public schools without regard to race—and with all deliberate speed.[1]

And so, American troops were sent to an American city, by a President of the United States to execute the orders of Federal courts which followed the constitutional interpretation of the United States Supreme Court.

The Governor of Arkansas had a different interpretation of the Federal Constitution. U.S. troops were not to enter his state to establish order unless either he or the Arkansas Legislature called for them under Article IV Section 4. Since that was not the case, the Governor concluded that the federal troops were present in Little Rock illegally and unconstitutionally.

Months later, *Cooper* v. *Aaron*, 358 U.S. 1 (1958), specifically raised the incident at Little Rock which, the Supreme Court said, involved "a claim by the Governor and Legislature of a State that there is no duty on state officials to obey federal court orders resting on this Court's considered interpretation of the United States Constitution." The Court's opinion went on to explain that "the Governor and Legislature of Arkansas" proceeded upon the premise that they were not bound by "our holding in *Brown* v. *Board of Education*," the desegregation decision of 1954.

Rejecting these contentions in an unprecedented unanimously signed opinion in *Cooper*, the Nation's High Tribunal employed the most unequivocal terms to define its own role in the American constitutional system:

Article VI of the Constitution makes the Constitution the "supreme Law of the Land." In 1803, Chief Justice Marshall, speaking for a unanimous Court, referring to the Constitution as "the fundamental

1. From the Radio & T.V. address of President Eisenhower of September 24, 1957, *Public Papers of the Presidents of the United States: Dwight D. Eisenhower*, 1957 (Washington, D.C.: Government Printing Office, 1958).

and paramount law of the nation," declared in the notable case of *Marbury* v. *Madison,* 1 Cranch 137, 177, 2 L.Ed. 60, that "It is emphatically the province and duty of the judicial department to say what the law is." This decision declared the basic principle that the federal judiciary is supreme in the exposition of the law of the Constitution, and that principle has ever since been respected by this Court and the Country as a permanent and indispensable feature of our constitutional system. *It follows that the interpretation of the Fourteenth Amendment enunciated by this Court in the Brown case is the supreme law of the land,* and Art. VI of the Constitution makes it of binding effect on the States "any Thing in the Constitution or Laws of any State to the Contrary notwithstanding." Every state legislator and executive and judicial officer is solemnly committed by oath taken pursuant to Art. VI,§3 "to support this Constitution. . . ." [Editor's emphasis.]

"The Supreme Court *is* the Constitution," Professor Felix Frankfurter used to tell his Harvard law students. As final interpreter of the Constitution none could reject the proposition that, in the last analysis, the words of Charles Evans Hughes rang true: "The Constitution is what the judges say it is."

Since there are fifty-one court systems interpreting the Constitution in cases daily, the practical need for a unitary interpretation by the Supreme Court is essential to harmonize the diversity of such a decentralized national judicial system. Or are we to have fifty-one Federal Constitutions?

Nevertheless, even with this vastly conceded authority of constitutional interpretation, the Supreme Court must rely on the Executive department to implement its decisions as the episode in Little Rock illustrates. It relies on the Congress for funds and for its continued broad appellate jurisdiction. It relies on its non-political image with the American public to preserve it from expedient political assaults which might have momentary popular appeal.

It is important to note that although the Supreme Court may declare what the Constitution commands or requires, its interpretations are not self-executing. Many years have passed since the *Brown* decision declared racially segregated schools unconstitutional, yet segregation still exists in many public schools. Contrary to other Supreme Court interpretations some school districts still include worship exercises at the beginning of each day in violation of the First and Fourteenth Amendments. In short, the vast power to declare what is the "supreme Law of the Land" does not carry with it the power to make all citizens—private as well as those in positions of public trust—respect it and abide by it.

In addition to its role as final interpreter of the Constitution, the Supreme Court is the court of last appeal in all federal cases which do not involve constitutional questions (i.e., bankruptcy cases, anti-trust suits, suits between states on common water rights, etc.). The High Court also performs a rather important parallel function in the federal court system which almost every state supreme court performs in the state system. It is the supervisory court of the federal judicial system. (The federal judicial system includes over 90 district courts of original jurisdiction; 11 circuit courts of appeals; and several special courts such as the United States Court of Claims, the United States Court of Military Appeals, the United States Court of Customs and Patent Appeals and the Tax Court of the United States.) As such the Supreme Court, from time to time, announces rules of procedure to be followed in civil and criminal cases in the eleven federal circuits into which the United States and its territories are divided. Thus, in addition to being the court of finality for all federal constitutional questions, the Supreme Court is the court of finality for non-constitutional federal questions, such as bankruptcy cases, etc.; and also acts in supervisory capacity over the entire federal court system.

The Jurisdiction of the Supreme Court

The Third Article of the Constitution provides for the establishment of the federal judiciary. According to its language it would seem that the only federal court which had to be established under the new Constitution of 1789 was the United States Supreme Court.

Article III, Section I of the Constitution provides that "the *judicial power* of the United States shall be vested in one Supreme Court, [this appears mandatory] and in such inferior courts as the Congress may, from time to time ordain and establish." [This seems optional and depends on Congressional discretion.] The Article reads as follows:

> SECTION 1. The judicial power of the United States, shall be vested in one supreme court, and in such inferior courts as the Congress may, from time to time, ordain and establish. The judges, both of the supreme and inferior courts, shall hold their offices during good behavior, and shall, at stated times, receive for their services a compensation, which shall not be diminished during their continuance in office.

Pursuant to this Constitutional section, the First Congress passed the Judiciary Act of 1789 which provided for lower federal courts, intermediate federal appeals courts, the number of justices who shall sit on the Supreme Court (a Chief Justice and 5 Associate Justices) and when the various courts would meet and conduct their business (the terms of the courts). This act, in defining the business of the federal courts, was little more than an enabling statute distributing the jurisdiction assigned to the judicial power of the United States in Article III, Section 2.

The jurisdiction of the Supreme Court (i.e., the authority by which the Court and its judicial officers hear and decide cases) is explicitly discussed in Article III, Section 2, of the Constitution, as follows:

SECTION 2. The judicial power shall extend to all cases, in law and equity, arising under this Constitution, the laws of the United States, and treaties made, or which shall be made under their authority; to all cases affecting ambassadors, other public ministers and consuls; to all cases of admiralty and maritime jurisdiction; to controversies between two or more states, *between a state and citizens of another state*, between citizens of different states, between citizens of the same state, claiming lands under grants of different states, and between a state, or the citizens thereof, and foreign states, *citizens or subjects.*

In all cases affecting ambassadors, other public ministers and consuls, and those in which a state shall be party, the supreme court shall have original jurisdiction. In all the other cases before-mentioned, the supreme court shall have appellate jurisdiction, both as to law and fact, with such exceptions, and under such regulations as the Congress shall make.

The trial of all crimes, except in cases of impeachment, shall be by jury; and such trial shall be held in the state where the said crimes shall have been committed; but when not committed within any state, the trial shall be at such place or places as the Congress may by law have directed.

The Supreme Court is both a court of original jurisdiction (i.e., some cases may be initially tried there) and an appellate court (i.e., a court which hears cases successfully appealed from decisions in lower courts).

According to the Constitution, the Supreme Court has original jurisdiction in "all cases affecting ambassadors, other public ministers and consuls, and those in which a state shall be a party." This does not mean that such cases *must* be initially tried in the Supreme Court but that they *may* be initially tried there if the Court agrees to hear them. Other courts in the country share jurisdiction over these types of cases with the Supreme Court; this sharing is referred to as "concurrent jurisdiction." Therefore, although the Supreme Court has original jurisdiction in the types of cases mentioned above it is not exclusive jurisdiction and other courts—state and federal— have concurrent jurisdiction over some of these cases.

The original jurisdiction of the Supreme Court can only be altered by Constitutional amendment. It cannot be diminished where it is constitutionally specified and it cannot be enlarged except by amendment since the Supreme Court, in the famous case of *Marbury* v. *Madison* 1 Cranch 137 (1803), held that Congress cannot alter the Court's original jurisdiction by Federal law:

If it had been intended to leave it in the discretion of the legislature to apportion the judicial power between the supreme and inferior courts according to the will of that body, it would certainly have been useless to have proceeded further than to have defined the judicial power, and the tribunals in which it should be vested. The subsequent part of the section is mere surplusage, is entirely without meaning, if such is to be the construction. *If congress remains at liberty to give this court appellate jurisdiction, where the constitution has declared their jurisdiction shall be original; and original jurisdiction where the constitution has declared it shall be appellate; the distribution of jurisdiction, made in the constitution, is form without substance. . . .* [Editor's emphasis.]

It cannot be presumed that any clause in the constitution is intended to be without effect; and, therefore, such a construction is inadmissible, unless the words require it.

The Supreme Court's appellate jurisdiction (i.e., cases it may hear and decide on appeal from lower state and federal courts) also mentioned in Article III, Section 2 of the U.S. Constitution extends to all the cases which fall within the judicial power of the United States with the exception of those over which it has original jurisdiction or which Congress may exclude from its appellate authority. Congress may determine by statute the breadth of cases which the Supreme Court may hear on appeal from lower courts. The present statutory appellate jurisdiction of the Supreme Court established by the Congress is so broad as to embrace virtually every federal question (i.e., questions involving either a federal law, a treaty, or the U.S. Constitution) and diversity of citizenship cases (i.e., where citizens of different states are suing each other). The Supreme Court's statutory jurisdiction (original and appellate) and how it may be appropriately exercised is set forth in the *United States Code*, Title 28.

How Cases Get to the Supreme Court

As we have mentioned, the United States has fifty-one (51) court systems, fifty state and one federal system. Each of these systems may hear federal cases (i.e., cases which raise federal questions as defined above). Federal courts do not decide purely state questions (i.e., questions which *do not in any way* involve a federal law, treaty, or the U.S. Constitution). *Purely state questions* are decided with finality in the state courts and may not be appealed to the U.S. Supreme Court or any other federal court. However, those cases in state courts which involve both state and federal questions are appealable to the Supreme Court once all the appeals in the state court system have been exhausted. Therefore, the U.S. Supreme Court is literally besieged each year to review thousands of cases—all raising interesting and important federal questions—coming from the 50 highest state courts and from the eleven federal circuits.

However, the justices can only hear, deliberate over, and write opinions for a limited number of cases. In order for the Court to exercise either its original or appellate jurisdiction over a case, four justices must vote in secret conference to accept the case. If four justices concur on the acceptance of a case it will be brought before the Court either through permission to file a case in original jurisdiction, or by issuance of a writ of *certiorari* or a writ of appeal. (See glossary.) It should be emphasized that in all instances, it is the justices of the Supreme Court who determine which cases they shall hear. With the exception of the relatively few cases that come before the Court under a writ of appeal, the justices also determine which cases they shall decide.

Before the justices decide whether or not to hear a case, lengthy briefs (i.e., written arguments as to the issues and why the case should be heard) are printed and submitted to the Court from both contending parties and any other parties who are granted permission to do so as a "friend of the Court" (i.e., *amicus curiae*, See glossary.) The justices then meet in secret conference and determine by vote which cases shall be *heard.* These are put on the Court's calendar. No written records are kept of any of the Court's conferences and the justices, who meet completely alone, consider it a basic canon of their high office that the conference remain secret. This is also true of the conferences which discuss the cases the Court has accepted and which negotiate the opinions finally produced and published.

How Opinions are Written

After the written briefs are received and reviewed by the Court, the cases accepted are scheduled for oral argument before the justices. The attorneys for the contending parties are alloted a specified amount of time to present their arguments and the justices are free to interrupt with questions.

Following these presentations, the justices argue the case among themselves in conference and take a preliminary vote to determine the initial disposition of the Court. If the Chief Justice finds himself on the side of the majority he will write or assign to an allied justice the task of writing the preliminary draft of the opinion of the Court. (There can be no opinion of the Court unless a majority of the voting justices, assuming a quorum [any six justices] is present and voting, and agree on the reasoning in a particular opinion as well as to how the case should be decided.)

If the Chief Justice is with the minority, the senior associate justice with the majority performs the task of assignment of the opinion of the Court. All of the justices are perfectly free to write their own separate opinions in each case whether or not they join in the opinion of the Court.

After the preliminary draft of the Court's opinion is written it is circulated to all the justices so that they can make a final determination as to whether or not they want to join it. Individual dissenting opinions and concurring opinions do not have to be circulated, but frequently are, and often are joined by some of the other members of the Court. The majority is never at a loss to know what the dissenters are likely to write since most of the arguments are advanced orally in the early conferences about the case.

In some cases there may be no opinion of the Court. This might occur when a majority agree as to how to decide a case but cannot agree on a single statement as to why it should be decided in that way. In such cases there appears at the beginning of the first opinion: "Mr. Justice 'A' announced the *judgment* of the Court in an opinion in which Justices 'X', 'Y' and 'Z' joined." The other opinions follow but a majority would be voting similarly on the *disposition* of the case.[2] In the event of a tie vote, the decision of the lower court would stand.

Self-Imposed Limitations on Federal Judicial Power

Since the U.S. Constitution is considered a document limiting power as well as granting it, the Supreme Court has held that the judicial power is limited in its exercise due to various constitutional provisions.

In *Marbury* v. *Madison*, 1 Cranch 137 (1803), the Court indicated that the judicial authority of the United States cannot be invoked to require a member of the executive branch of authority to perform a purely discretionary act. To do so, the Court implied, would be to encroach upon executive prerogative and invade the separation of powers—an essential doctrine of the written Constitution. From this case and *Kendall* v. *United States*, 12 Peters 524 (1838), which elaborates on this point, the doctrine of "political question" is developed. Succinctly stated, the Supreme Court has held that some constitutional questions are not within its judicial province to decide because they involve a clash with another coordinate branch of the national government and would necessitate a violation of the separation of powers theory. [See *Baker* v. *Carr*, 369 U.S. 186 (1962), for a recent amplification of this point.]

In addition to not deciding "political questions" the Supreme Court has historically developed a whole series of self-limiting rules which were summarized by Mr. Justice Brandeis in his concurring opinion in *Ashwander* v. *T.V.A.*, 297 U.S. 288 (1936):

The Court developed, for its own governance in the cases confessedly within its jurisdiction, a series of rules under which it has avoided

2. For an explanation of the terms "concurring opinion," "dissenting opinion," and *"Per Curiam* opinion," see the glossary.

passing upon a large part of all the constitutional questions pressed upon it for decision. They are:

1. The Court will not pass upon the constitutionality of legislation in a friendly, non-adversary, proceeding, declining because to decide such questions "is legitimate only in the last resort, and as a necessity in the determination of real, earnest and vital controversy between individuals. It never was the thought that, by means of a friendly suit, a party beaten in the legislature could transfer to the courts an inquiry as to the constitutionality of the legislative act. . . ."

2. The Court will not "anticipate a question of constitutional law in advance of the necessity of deciding it. . . ." It is not the habit of the court to decide questions of a constitutional nature unless absolutely necessary to a decision of the case. . . ."

3. The Court will not "formulate a rule of constitutional law broader than is required by the precise facts to which it is to be applied. . . ."

4. The Court will not pass upon a constitutional question although properly presented by the record, if there is also present some other ground upon which the case may be disposed of. This rule has found most varied application. Thus, if a case can be decided on either of two grounds, one involving a constitutional question, the other a question of statutory construction or general law, the Court will decide only the latter. . . .

5. The Court will not pass upon the validity of a statute upon complaint of one who fails to show that he is injured by its operation. . . .

6. The Court will not pass upon the constitutionality of a statute at the instance of one who has availed himself of its benefits. . . .

7. "When the validity of an act of the Congress is drawn in question, and even if a serious doubt of constitutionality is raised, it is a cardinal principle that this Court will first ascertain whether a construction of the statute is fairly possible by which the question may be avoided. . . ."

Trends in the Court's Business

In recent years the Supreme Court has spent a large part of its time dealing with the problems which arise from the relationship of the individual and the national and/or state government. Unlike the period 1789–1865 when the relationship of the states to the federal government was of paramount concern; or the period after the Civil War to 1937 when the relationship between business and government had primacy; today the personal liberties of the Bill of Rights and the Fourteenth Amendment constitute the primary focus of the Supreme Court's activities. All of the cases in this book are examples of that concern.

After 1937 and the Court's acceptance of the constitutionality of an expanded governmental role in economic affairs, there was increased attention in constitutional litigation to develop substantive and procedural rights, regarded as inherent in the concept of due process of law. In some instances it is difficult to distinguish clearly between a substantive and procedural right. Generally speaking, substantive constitutional rights are those which, by their nature, tend to limit the legislative goals that constitutional government may legitimately pursue. As with most procedural rights, substantive guarantees in the U.S. Constitution are framed in negative terminology. Hence the substantive freedom of religious worship flows from the prohibition on Congress that it "shall make no law respecting an establishment of religion or prohibiting the free exercise thereof. . . ." In contrast, procedural rights are those which limit the methodology of constitutional government as it seeks to discharge its executive, legislative, and judicial functions. For instance, the conviction of an alleged lawbreaker which was obtained by the state without adherence to the procedures limiting the state and consequently protecting the accused is an example of a violation of procedural due process.

The emerging relationship being developed through the 1930's, 1940's, 1950's and 1960's between the Bill of Rights and the Fourteenth Amendment related to this new focus in constitutional law. The next section of this chapter traces the historical evolution of that relationship.

The Bill of Rights and the States

Today, by virtue of the restraining nature of the due process clause of the Fourteenth Amendment, all of the liberties of the First Amendment; the Fourth Amendment guarantee against unreasonable searches and seizures, together with the exclusionary rule; the Fifth Amendment guarantee against double jeopardy; the Fifth Amendment privilege against self-incrimination accompanied by the "no comment rule"; the Fifth Amendment just compensation clause; the Sixth Amendment right to a speedy and public trial, the right of confrontation, the right of compulsory process, and the effective assistance of counsel; the Eighth Amendment's cruel and unusual punishment clause; and the right of privacy derived from Amendments One, Four, Five, and Nine, have in some form or another been held to be enforceable against the states.

The following is a brief historical account of how the "nationalization" of *most* of the Bill of Rights guarantees has occurred.

The Barron Doctrine

When the initial eight amendments became part of the Federal Constitution in 1791, it was understood that they constituted prohibitions on the federal government only. Indeed, many of the state ratifying conventions had formed them as a condition for their ratifying the original body of the Constitution. However, it was not clear whether the Bill of Rights also constituted limitations on state authority. The Supreme Court initially addressed itself to this question in the celebrated case of *Barron* v. *Baltimore*, 7 Peters 247, (1833).

Barron, who owned a wharf, sued the City of Baltimore for compensation resulting from what he claimed was a taking of his property for a public purpose. The city, in paving its streets, diverted the water of several streams which carried large amounts of sand and deposited them around Barron's wharf. The sand deposits made the area around the wharf so shallow that ships were unable to approach it for the loading and unloading of cargo.

Barron's constitutional claim assumed that the Fifth Amendment obligated the states (and their creations such as the City of Baltimore) to provide just compensation when they took private property for a public purpose. Mr. Chief Justice John Marshall, speaking for the Court, dismissed the case as beyond the Court's jurisdiction in that it did not present a valid federal question. The *Barron* claim failed to qualify as a federal question, Marshall held, because the Fifth Amendment had to be understood as a restraint *solely* upon the national government. The Court's opinion further implied that Amendments One through Eight were not conceived of as limitations on state power. State authority was to be principally limited by the State Constitution:

> The Constitution was ordained and established by the people of the United States for themselves, for their own government and not for the government of the individual States. Each State established a constitution for itself and in that constitution provided such limitations and restrictions on the powers of its particular government as its judgment dictated. The people of the United States formed such a government for the United States as they supposed best adapted to their situation, and best calculated to promote their interests. The powers they conferred on this government were to be exercised by itself; and if expressed in general terms, are naturally, and, we think, necessarily applicable to the general government created by the instrument. They are limitations on power granted in the instrument itself; not of distinct governments framed by different persons and for different purposes.
>
> If these propositions be correct, the Fifth Amendment must be understood as restraining the power of the general government, not as applicable to the States.

Initially then, the Supreme Court construed the prohibitions of the Bill of Rights narrowly.

If there was any doubt as to the clear meaning of the *Barron* decision, it should have been dispelled by the Court's decision, in *Permoli* v. *New Orleans*, 3 Howard 589 (1845). Permoli, a Catholic priest, had been fined $50.00 for violation of a New Orleans health ordinance forbidding the exposure of dead persons in a public place. Officiating at a funeral, the priest had exposed and blessed the deceased. He claimed the ordinance was passed in violation of the First Amendment. The Supreme Court, speaking through Mr. Justice Catron, held that the First Amendment did not protect state citizens from intrusion into their religious life by state authority:

> The ordinances complained of must violate the Constitution or laws of the United States, or some authority exercised under them; if they do not we have no power by the 25th section of the Judiciary Act to interfere. *The Constitution makes no provision for protecting the citizens of the respective States in their religious liberties; this is left to the State Constitutions and laws: nor is there any inhibition imposed by the Constitution of the United States....* [Editor's emphasis.]
>
> In our judgment, the question presented by the record is exclusively of state cognizance, and equally so in the old States and the new ones; and that the writ of error must be dismissed.

The constitutional principles had thus been set and the precedents provided. The Federal Bill of Rights did not in any way legally limit the authority of the states. The prohibitions of Amendments One through Eight were binding on federal power alone. In sum, the *Barron* doctrine held that these Amendments were simply not relevant to the exercise of state governmental power.

After the passage of the Fourteenth Amendment (1868), new attempts were made to apply the limitations of the Federal Bill of Rights to the states. The two clauses of section one (of the Fourteenth Amendment) that served as the principal vehicles for these new attempts at "nationalization" of the Bill of Rights were the "privileges or immunities" clause, and the "due process" clause.

The Privileges or Immunities Clause

In the *Slaughter-House Cases*, 16 Wallace 36 (1873), the first to reach the Supreme Court requiring an interpretation of the Fourteenth Amendment, the hopes for a broad construction of the privileges or immunities clause were dealt a blow from which they have not to this day recovered. The appellants, who were butchers in New Orleans, challenged the constitutionality of a Louisiana statute which conferred exclusive slaughtering rights in the state on a newly chartered slaughter-house company. It was claimed that the state law creating the monopoly violated the privileges and immunities of U.S. citizens engaged in the butchering business.

Mr. Justice Miller in the opinion of a narrowly divided Court (5–4) indicated that the dual citizenship recognized by the first section of the Amendment conferred diverse rights upon Americans. An individual residing in a state had rights which flowed from his state citizenship as well as rights which flowed from his U.S. citizenship. However, only the latter was protected from state intrusion by the privileges or immunities clause. Emphatically, Justice Miller rejected the proposition that the privileges or immunities clause had shifted the responsibility for the protection of civil liberties from the states to the federal government as follows:

> . . . Was it the purpose of the 14th Amendment, by the simple declaration that no state should make or enforce any law which shall abridge the privileges and immunities of citizens of the United States, to transfer the security and protection of all the civil rights which we have mentioned, from the states to the Federal Government? And where it is declared that Congress shall have the power to enforce that article, was it intended to bring within the power of Congress the entire domain of civil rights heretofore belonging exclusively to the states?
>
> .   .   .
>
> We are convinced that no such results were intended by the Congress which proposed these amendments, nor by the legislatures of the states, which ratified them.

In short, the majority of the Court did not see the Fourteenth Amendment as changing the pattern established under the *Barron* case. The civil liberties of most Americans continued to be guaranteed primarily by the state constitutions because those liberties, the Court declared, derived from state citizenship.

The dissenting opinions reflected the theory that the privileges and immunities designated for federal protection by this Fourteenth Amendment clause were "those which of right belong to the citizens of all free governments." The implications were that many of these immunities corresponded with those specified in the Bill of Rights. This theory was subsequently rejected several times by the Court and has never been given the sanction of a majority.

The fact that the Supreme Court had, since 1873, rejected the claim of the interrelationship between the Bill of Rights and the privileges or immunities clause so often led Mr. Justice Cardozo in *Palko* v. *Connecticut*, 302 U.S. 319 (1937), to dismiss that assertion with but one terse sentence.

Due Process under the Fourteenth Amendment

Initially, the Fourteenth Amendment's due process clause did not fare any better as a vehicle by which the guarantees of the Bill of Rights would become enforceable against the states.

Prior to the adoption of the Fourteenth Amendment, the due process clause of the Fifth Amendment had been the subject of little litigation. That clause had been generally recognized as a guarantee only in the narrow sense that the Congress was required to provide due process for the enforcement of law. The sole notable exception to this early restrictive interpretation of due process appears to have been in the *Dred Scott* case, 19 Howard 393 (1857), where the Court held the Missouri Compromise of 1850 unconstitutional as depriving persons of their property (slaves) without due process of law.

In light of the foregoing, it is not surprising that Mr. Justice Miller in *Davidson* v. *New Orleans*, 96 U.S. 97 (1878), expressed amazement at the breadth of the prohibitions which claimants before the Court now urged in the name of due process:

> It is not a little remarkable that while this provision has been in the Constitution of the United States, as a restraint upon the authority of the Federal government, for nearly a century, and while during all that time, the manner in which the powers of that government have been exercised has been watched with jealousy, and criticism in all its branches, this special limitation upon its powers has rarely been invoked in the judicial forum or the more enlarged theatre of public discussion. But while it has been part of the Constitution, as a restraint upon the power of the States, only a very few years, the docket of this Court is crowded with cases in which we are asked to hold that State courts and State legislatures have deprived their own citizens of life, liberty, or property without due process of law. There is here abundant evidence that there exists some strange misconception of the scope of this provision as found in the Fourteenth Amendment.

The Miller commentary on the departure from the conventional interpretation of the clause is the more comprehendible when one recalls that the Fourteenth Amendment clause is an exact copy of the Fifth Amendment statement, and was considered to carry the same meaning. That this point had great importance for the Court is abundantly clear in the landmark case of *Hurtado* v. *California*, 110 U.S. 516, (1884).

The Hurtado Case: A Narrow
Construction of Fourteenth Amendment
Due Process

Hurtado was indicted for murder in California by means of an *information*. He was tried in a California county court, found guilty, and was sentenced to death. His appeal from conviction eventually reached the U. S. Supreme Court, where the conviction was challenged as a violation of his right to indictment by grand jury protected from federal encroachment by the Fifth Amendment and now equally protected from state invasion by the due process clause of the Fourteenth Amendment.

Rejecting this assertion, Mr. Justice Matthews speaking for the Court removed any doubt that the Court was about to accept the nationalization of the Bill of Rights via the due process clause with less reluctance than it had accepted similar claims under the privileges or immunities clause, as follows:

> The same words are contained in the Fifth Amendment. That article makes specific and express provisions for perpetuating the institution of the grand jury, so far as it relates to prosecutions, for the more aggravated crimes under the laws of the United States. It declares that "no person shall be held to answer for a capital or otherwise infamous crime, unless on a presentment or indictment of a grand jury, except in cases arising in the land or naval forces, or in the militia when in actual service in time of war or public danger; nor shall any person be subject for the same offence to be twice put in jeopardy of life or limb; nor shall he be compelled in any criminal case to be a witness against himself." It then immediately adds: "nor be deprived of life, liberty, or property without due process of law." According to a recognized canon of interpretation, especially applicable to formal and solemn instruments of Constitutional law, we are forbidden to assume, without clear reason to the contrary, that any part of this most important amendment is superfluous. The natural and obvious inference is, that in the sense of the Constitution, "due process of law" was not meant or intended to include, *ex ui termini*, the institution and procedure of a grand jury in any case. The conclusion is equally irresistible, that when the same phrase was employed in the Fourteenth Amendment to restrain the action of the States, it was used in the same sense and with no greater extent; and that if in the adoption of that Amendment it had been part of its purpose to perpetuate the institution of the grand jury in all the States, it would have embodied, as did the Fifth Amendment, express declarations to that effect. . . .

The logical extension of Justice Matthew's rule of construction in *Hurtado* led to the conclusion that none of the procedural or substantive freedoms specifically mentioned in Amendments One through Eight were included in the due process clause or else there was wordiness in the U. S. Constitution.

Within sixteen years after its ratification, the Court had explicitly rejected two attempts to make the Fourteenth Amendment a successful vehicle through which the prohibitions of the Bill of Rights would be enforced against the states. Many subsequent cases raised allied questions which allowed the Court to continue to speak its collective mind about the relationship between the Fourteenth Amendment and the Bill of Rights. Its position on the prohibitions of the Bill of Rights remained the same as in *Barron* v. *Baltimore, supra.* The passage of the Fourteenth Amendment apparently had not affected the *Barron* doctrine:

> That the first ten Articles of Amendment were not intended to limit the powers of the state governments in respect to their own people, but to operate on the National Government alone, was decided more than a half century ago, and that decision has been steadily adhered to since . . . [*Spies* v. *Illinois*, 123 U.S. 131 (1887).]

The cases which followed these precedents seem too numerous to indicate anything other than that this constitutional controversy was settled. As late as 1922 in *U.S.* v. *Lanza*, 260 U.S. 377, the Court had invoked the *Barron* case to hold that "the Fifth Amendment, like all the other guarantees in the first eight amendments, applied only to proceedings by the Federal Government."

The Emergence of Substantive Due Process

The *Hurtado* case, however, did not preclude the due process clause of the Fourteenth Amendment from taking on a greater substantive content than had previously been identified with its Fifth Amendment counterpart. Simultaneous with the many decisions reaffirming the *Hurtado* denial of any relationship between the "liberty" of the Fourteenth Amendment and the substantive specific guarantees of the Bill of Rights; the Supreme Court in other cases *accepted* the contention that there were substantive economic freedoms under the Fourteenth Amendment's protection.

In the hope of curtailing certain corporate abuses and making private enterprise more socially responsible, some states had established regulatory commissions to supervise intrastate rail rates, and had enacted laws guaranteeing reasonable minimal standards for production and conditions of employment. The *laissez-faire* economic philosophy, prevalent in America during the late nineteenth century, found expression in United States Supreme Court decisions which struck at the constitutionality of these legislative and administrative attempts to regulate private enterprise and property.

Taken together these decisions established a category of substantive rights understood to be "liberties" guaranteed by the due process clause of the Fourteenth Amendment. The constitutional precedents for a substantive rights concept attributed to a due process clause—unique and novel in the *Dred Scott* case—became commonplace as many judicial opinions were written to support *laissez-faire* philosophy against state economic regulatory legislation after the turn of the twentieth century.

In retrospect, it seems clear that the substantive economic liberties entrusted to the Fourteenth Amendment's care were only a step away from the substantive liberties of speech and press.

A "Settled" Constitutional Principle Eroded: The Demise of the Barron Doctrine

In 1925 the Court handed down the precedent shattering opinion which first related some of the substantive liberties of the First Amendment to the Fourteenth Amendment. The persistent efforts to relate the Bill of Rights to the states over the preceding fifty years resulted in what was to develop into a constitutional revolution in federal-state relations.

In *Gitlow* v. *New York*, 268 U.S. 652 (1925), the Court charted a new course in the interpretation of the Fourteenth Amendment due process clause, which would eventually sweep away most of the rationale and nullify the holding of the *Hurtado* decision. All the earlier decisions to the contrary notwithstanding, Mr. Justice Sanford held:

> For present purposes we may and do assume that freedom of speech and of the press—which are protected by the First Amendment from abridgement by Congress—are among the fundamental personal rights and "liberties" protected by the Due Process Clause of the Fourteenth Amendment from impairment by the states. We do not regard the incidental statement in *Prudential Insurance Company* v. *Cheek*, 259 U.S. 530, that the Fourteenth Amendment imposes no restrictions on the states concerning freedom of speech, as determinative of this question.

As Mr. Justice Brennan was to put it almost thirty years later, the Court "initiated a series of decisions which today hold immune from state invasion every First Amendment protection for the cherished rights of mind and spirit—the freedoms of speech, press, religion, assembly, association, and petition for redress of grievances."

In the *Gitlow* case Justice Sanford was in effect saying that because freedom of speech and press are fundamental liberties, they are part of the "liberty" protected from abridgement by the due process clause of the Fourteenth Amendment. Thus, the term "liberty" in the Fourteenth Amendment's due process clause was, for the first time, understood to embrace some of the specific fundamental liberties protected by the First Amendment from federal invasion. As the Brennan reference above indicates, the fundamental liberties of the Fourteenth Amendment soon grew in number.

In *Near* v. *Minnesota*, 283 U.S. 697 (1931), the "assumption" of *Gitlow* became fixed constitutional law:

> . . . It is no longer open to doubt that the liberty of the press and of speech is within the liberty safeguarded by the due process clause of the Fourteenth Amendment from invasion by state action. . . .

Six years later in *DeJonge* v. *Oregon*, 299 U.S. 353 (1937), Mr. Chief Justice Hughes, speaking for the Court, added the right of peaceful assembly to the growing list of fundamental liberties in the Fourteenth Amendment:

> Freedom of speech and of the press are fundamental rights which are safeguarded by the due process clause of the Fourteenth Amendment of the Federal Constitution. . . . The right of peaceable assembly is a right cognate to those of free speech and free press and is equally fundamental.

In *Cantwell* v. *Connecticut*, 310 U.S. 296 (1940), the Court further supplemented the list of fundamental rights with the two-fold religious guarantees of the First Amendment.

If the right of association was not clearly considered fundamental as an incident of the right of assembly, it acquired an autonomous fundamental status as a basic right in *N.A.A.C.P.* v. *Alabama*, 357 U.S. 449 (1958).

> . . . It is beyond debate that freedom to engage in association for the advancement of beliefs and ideas is an inseparable aspect of the "liberty" assured by the Due Process Clause of the Fourteenth Amendment, which embraces freedom of speech.*

The list of rights enforced against the states through the due process clause was not exhausted, however, when all of the liberties protected by the First Amendment were applied. Many procedural rights considered

[*Editor's Note: the right of association is discussed in depth in the introduction to Part II.]

essential to the concept of justice and to due process itself were also ranked as fundamental by the Court and thus became binding on the states.

Initially, the assistance of counsel in capital cases [*Powell* v. *Alabama*, 287 U.S. 45 (1932)] and eventually in all serious criminal cases was applied [*Gideon* v. *Wainwright*, 372 U.S. 335 (1963)]. The right of an individual to be secure in his home from unreasonable searches and seizures was added in *Wolf* v. *Colorado*, 338 U.S. 25 (1949):

> The security of one's privacy against arbitrary intrusion by the police —which is at the core of the Fourth Amendment—is basic to a free society. It is therefore implicit in "the concept of ordered liberty" and as such enforceable against the States through the Due Process Clause. . . .

The exclusionary rule, which prohibited the admission into evidence of illegally seized materials, was subsequently applied to the states by *Mapp* v. *Ohio*, 367 U.S. 643 (1961).

The Eighth Amendment's ban on cruel and unusual punishment was unequivocally added to the list of fundamental liberties in *Robinson* v. *California*, 370 U.S. 660 (1962):

> . . . But, in the light of contemporary human knowledge, a law which made a criminal offense of such a disease [dope addiction] would doubtless be universally thought to be an infliction of cruel and unusual punishment in violation of the Eighth and Fourteenth Amendments.

Setting aside several previous holdings, the Court in *Malloy* v. *Hogan*, 378 U.S. 1 (1964), made the privilege against self-incrimination enforceable against the states:

> We hold today that the Fifth Amendment's exception from compulsory self-incrimination is also protected by the Fourteenth Amendment against abridgement by the States. . . .

During the October 1964 term, *Griffin* v. *California*, 380 U.S. 609, held that the "no-comment" rule was an essential part of the privilege against self-incrimination and enforceable against the states. The "no-comment" rule had been operative in the federal courts and generally precluded the prosecutor or the judge from commenting to the jury about the failure of a defendant to take the stand in a proceeding against him. It prohibited the jury from drawing inferences of guilt from a defendant's invocation of the Fifth Amendment privilege.

Earlier that same term in *Pointer* v. *Texas*, 380 U.S. 400 (1965), the

High Tribunal announced that the Sixth Amendment right of confrontation applied to the states:

> . . . We hold that petitioner was entitled to be tried in accordance with the protection of the confrontation guarantee of the Sixth Amendment, and that that guarantee, like the right against compelled self-incrimination, is "to be enforced against the States under the Fourteenth Amendment according to the same standards that protect those personal rights against federal encroachment. . . ."

A somewhat more nebulous "right to privacy" was also added to the list of the fundamental liberties in *Griswold* v. *Connecticut*, 381 U.S. 479 (1965), which struck down a Connecticut state statute prohibiting the use of contraceptive drugs or instruments as contravening the guarantees of the Fourteenth Amendment.

Continuing the Court's recent accelerated trend of deflecting specific Bill of Rights guarantees against the states, in 1967 the Sixth Amendment's right to a speedy trial [*Klopfer* v. *North Carolina*, 386 U.S. 213] and the guarantee that a defendant shall have the right of "compulsory process for obtaining witnesses in his favor" were held binding in state criminal cases because of the due process protection of the Fourteenth Amendment [*Washington* v. *Texas*, 388 U.S. 14 (1967)].

The following year, in *Duncan* v. *Louisiana*, 391 U.S. 145 (1968), the Court ruled that the Fourteenth Amendment due process clause obligated the states to provide the same "right of jury trial in all criminal cases which —were they to be tried in a federal court—would come under the Sixth Amendment guarantee."

Finally, at the end of the October 1968 term, the High Court, overruling its previous holdings in *Palko* v. *Connecticut, supra,* and *Brock* v. *North Carolina*, 344 U.S. 424 (1953), held in *Benton* v. *Maryland*, 395 U.S. 784 (1969), that the double jeopardy prohibition of the Fifth Amendment applied to the states through the Fourteenth Amendment.

It should be reemphasized that *not all* of the provisions of Amendments One through Eight are enforceable against the states. The controversy about the relationship of the remaining particulars of the Bill of Rights and the Fourteenth Amendment continues. Still to be determined is whether all of the Bill of Rights guarantees, in all their particulars and with all their vitality, circumscribe state governmental actions in *precisely* the same way as they limit federal authority. The basic purpose of this section has not been to exhaust those questions, but rather to trace briefly the legal evolution of the relationship between the Bill of Rights and legitimate state governmental power. This was partially in order to provide a historical perspective; partially to set forth the shifting legal facts governing that relationship; and finally to indicate that law—even constitutional law— is not able to be reduced to static formulation.

1. war protestation as freedom of expression

1. **Introductory Essay**

2. **The Early Cases:**

   Schenck v. *U.S.*, 249 U.S. 47 (1919): "The Anti-Conscription Case."
   Abrams v. *U.S.*, 250 U.S. 616 (1919): "The Anti-Archangel Expedition Case."

3. **The Anti-war "Symbolic Speech" Cases:**

   United States v. *O'Brien*, 391 U.S. 367 (1968): "The Draft Card Burning Case."
   Tinker v. *Des Moines*, 393 U.S. 503 (1969): "The Black Armband Case."

4. **The Draft Re-classification Cases:**

   Oestereich v. *Selective Service Board*, 393 U.S. 233 (1968): "The Divinity Exemption Case."
   Gutknecht v. *U.S.*, 396 U.S. 295 (1970): "The Speed-up Induction Case."

5. **War Protest As Disorderly Conduct:**

   Bachellar v. *Maryland*, 397 U.S. 564 (1970): "The Recruitment Station 'Lay-in' Case."

1. war protestation as freedom of expression

Can you legally burn your draft card? Can you be reclassified I-A for turning in your draft card at a war protest rally? Can you legally be conscripted without a formal declaration of war? What constitutes "symbolic free speech"?

All of the cases in section I have at least two things in common. First, they involve the use of First and Fourteenth Amendment rights by private persons to protest and dissent from various government war commitments (the first two involve World War I, the rest, the Vietnam conflict). Second, they ultimately present the Supreme Court with the task of developing standards by which the latitude of serious political protest and dissent can be measured against the valid war-making powers constitutionally entrusted to the federal government. The consideration of these problems has demanded of the Supreme Court a search for values essential to a society that at the same time is both capable of dealing with crisis and striving to maintain free expression.

In the *Schenck* case, Schenck was convicted under the Espionage Act of 1917 for, among other things, attempting to obstruct draft recruitment with pamphlets sent through the mail to several thousand inductees. Although there was no evidence that he was successful, the Supreme Court unanimously sustained his conviction because it held that Schenck's actions, in time of war, created a "clear and present danger" of interference with conscription —a valid legislative function.

The "Clear and Present Danger" Test

Even that speech which is constitutionally protected must, under certain conditions and circumstances, be subject to governmental restriction and, in extreme cases, prohibition. Because great social value has been placed on the utility of free speech the Supreme Court in *Schenck* v. *United States, supra,* developed a test which had the potential of making governmental interference with constitutionally protected speech an exception rather than a rule. In *Schenck,* Justice Holmes advanced a judicial "rule of thumb" by which constitutionally protected speech *in normal times* may in times of crisis be punishable under a somewhat vague but valid Congressional enactment. Schenck's protest against the conscription of World War I, Holmes implied, would be tolerable and constitutionally guaranteed under ordinary circumstances but the guarantee of free speech must of necessity be narrowed *when events dictate* that its exercise may create a "clear and present danger" of a substantive evil that the national legislature had a constitutional right to prevent. Schenck's protest was viewed as creating a "clear and present danger" of interference with conscription. Since conscription is a logical outgrowth of the delegated Congressional authority under Article I, Section 8 of the Constitution to raise and support armies, this was considered a threat to a legitimate legislative power.

As with spoken words, the *Schenck* case emphasized that the constitutionally protected right of dissent was not absolutely guaranteed under the First Amendment and indeed depended—to a great degree—upon value-judgments made by jurists as to the *imminency of evils* from which the legislature had been empowered to protect the community.

The *Abrams* case—also of World War I vintage—presented a somewhat different question. There, a split Supreme Court (7-2) found Abrams guilty of interfering with the "war effort" by protesting United States expeditions into Soviet Russia. The "war effort" protected by the statute which Abrams was said to be guilty of violating was clearly one which was concerned with the conflict with the Central Powers (i.e., Germany, Austro-Hungary, Turkey, etc.), of which Soviet Russia was not one.

The dissent by Holmes and Brandeis vigorously opposed the majority on the grounds that Abrams, a Communist, had *not demonstrated intent* to violate the statute and interfere with any aspect of the *declared* war effort. For them, therefore, his indictments under the statute could not be legally sustained. Furthermore, since Abrams was ineffectual in interfering with production for the declared war against Germany there was no demonstrated proof that his printed speech was grave enough to constitute a "clear and present danger" of the substantive evil of hampering munitions production. In his dissent, Justice Holmes decried the majority opinion as one which condoned needless repression of unorthodox political opinion simply because it was unorthodox.

The *O'Brien* case and the *Tinker* case, apart from the fact that both reflect political dissent against United States involvement in the undeclared "war" in Vietnam, raise the interesting question as to whether *physical manifestations of protest* can be legally viewed as protected symbolic speech under the First and Fourteenth Amendments and further, if so, to what extent?

In the *O'Brien* case, an overwhelming Court majority (7-1) through Chief Justice Warren rejected David O'Brien's burning of his draft card as a constitutionally protected act of "symbolic speech" for essentially two reasons. First, the Federal Act which prohibits destruction of draft cards does not have as its purpose the suppression of dissent or the abridgment of free speech but instead is designed to protect an essential part of a reasonable and elaborate system to facilitate universal male conscription in the United States. Second, O'Brien, although sincere in his action, had available to him other modes of legally guaranteed expression through which he could have denounced the federal government's war policy without encumbering its constitutionally implied authority to implement the delegated authority of raising an army.

The lone dissent by Mr. Justice Douglas questioned the assumption by the majority that Congress can constitutionally conscript young men into the service when there has been no *formal* declaration of war against another nation. Douglas believed that question—the extent, if any, of the power of Congress to conscript in the absence of a Constitutional declaration of war— is one which must first be examined before any judgment can be made as to the validity of any federal statute implementing what is presumably a constitutional "peace time" draft.

Neither the majority opinion nor the single concurring opinion of Mr. Justice Harlan seemed to question the constitutional validity of "symbolic speech," when properly employed. But which physical actions are "symbolic speech?" In *Tinker* v. *Des Moines*, Mr. Justice Fortas in the opinion of the Court addressed himself to that question.

The Tinker children, who wore black armbands to school to protest the hostilities in Victnam, were sent home and suspended from school pending their return without the armbands. In the *Tinker* case, the Supreme Court made clear that this type of "symbolic speech" is "akin to pure speech" and as such falls under the constitutional protection of free expression. The majority opinion in *Tinker* can be differentiated from that of *O'Brien* inasmuch as no valid governmental function is shown to be threatened or disrupted by the wearing of the armbands. Although the school authorities claimed that they feared disruption, the thrust of the Court's opinion indicated that there was no evidence which justified this invasion of individual expression.

The dissents of Mr. Justice Black and Mr. Justice Harlan were more concerned with what they deemed an apparent assumption by the Supreme Court of power over local school decisions than with the substantive question concerning "symbolic speech." Taken together the *O'Brien* and *Tinker* decisions indicated that the Supreme Court considered physical actions which indicated political protest to be constitutionally protected expressions of dissent unless they clearly interfered with a valid governmental function.

In the *Oestereich* case, the Supreme Court dealt with the punishment of war dissent by the novel manner of draft reclassification. James Oestereich, a divinity student who had according to Federal law been classified IV-D by his Selective Service Board in Wyoming, returned his draft card to the government as a protest against the American military involvement in Vietnam. His subsequent reclassification as I-A and an order to report for induction was appealed and rejected by the local Draft Board because they had declared him a delinquent under another section of the Selective Service Regulations for failing to have his draft card in his possession. The Majority opinion by Mr. Justice Douglas vigorously attacked the action of the local Board as "lawless" in that it retaliated against Oestereich for his unpopular political views by denying to him an exemption to which he was entitled by federal law because he dared to exercise his freedom of political expression guaranteed by the Constitution.

The dissent by Mr. Justice Stewart, joined by Justices Brennan and White, ignored the issue of reclassification as "prematurely" raised. Unlike Douglas, who believed that the procedures and reasons used by a Draft Board for reclassifying a registrant were subject to judicial scrutiny before induction,the Dissenters interpreted the Selective Service Act narrowly as to preclude judicial review of this type of issue until after Oestereich had been inducted. Since they did not believe the substantive statutory or constitutional question was properly before them, they expressed no opinion about the validity of the local Draft Board's actions.

Following the *Oestereich* precedent, the Supreme Court in *Gutknecht* v. *United States* overwhelmingly reversed a speed-up by the local Draft Board of the induction of a war protest student after having declared him delinquent for leaving his draft card on the steps of the Federal Building in Minneapolis. The majority warned that statutory punishments, such as the classification of delinquency, which are not clearly constrained by legislative guidelines and which are basically provided for those who fail to register, may not be interpreted and applied to constrict the political liberties protected by the Constitution.

The *Bachellar* case raised still another question regarding the scope of freedom of expression and war protest. Donald Bachellar was convicted of "disorderly conduct" on a public street while protesting against the Vietnam War in front of an Army recruitment center in Baltimore, Maryland. Mr. Justice Brennan speaking for a unanimous Supreme Court indicated that where a trial judge's instructions to a jury were so broad as to create the possibility that the defendant could be convicted on a disorderly conduct charge for exercising his constitutionally protected right to express publicly opinions that may be offensive to some of the hearers, the convictions must be reversed. This case represented a recent, clear and unequivocal endorsement by the nation's High Tribunal as to the importance of free expression in public places. We will examine how the Supreme Court continues to uphold the right of free expression in public places in Part IV.

It is important to note in concluding the introduction to the cases on war protestation, that in the *Tinker* case, the *Oestereich* case, the *Gutknecht* case, and the *Bachellar* case, the power of state authority against unpopular dissenters was invoked at the level of authority on which the average citizen was most likely to be a direct participant in the decision-making process (e.g., local school boards, local draft boards, and local juries). It was left to the highest judicial level—the United States Supreme Court—to reverse the suppression of political war protest in all of these cases.

SCHENCK v. UNITED STATES

249 U.S. 47; 39 S. Ct. 247; 63 L.Ed. 470 (1919)

MR. JUSTICE HOLMES *delivered the opinion of the court.*

This is an indictment in three counts. The first charges a conspiracy to violate the Espionage Act of June 15, 1917, chap. 30, §3, 40 Stat. at L. 217, 219, by causing and attempting to cause insubordination, etc., in the military and naval forces of the United States, and to obstruct the recruiting and enlistment service of the United States, when the United States was at war with the German Empire; to wit, that the defendant wilfully conspired to have printed and circulated to men who had been called and accepted for military service under the Act of May 18, 1917, a document set forth and alleged to be calculated to cause such insubordination and obstruction. The count alleges overt acts in pursuance of the conspiracy, ending in the distribution of the document set forth. The second count alleges a conspiracy to commit an offense against the United States; to wit, to use the mails for the transmission of matter declared to be nonmailable by title 12, §2, of the Act of June 15, 1917, to wit, the above-mentioned document, with an averment of the same overt acts. The third count charges an unlawful use of the mails for the transmission of the same matter and otherwise as above. The defendants were found guilty on all the counts. They set up the First Amendment to the Constitution, forbidding Congress to make any law abridging the freedom of speech or of the press, and bringing the case here on that ground, have argued some other points also of which we must dispose.

It is argued that the evidence, if admissible, was not sufficient to prove that the defendant Schenck was concerned in sending the documents. According to the testimony Schenck said he was general secretary of the Socialist party and had charge of the Socialist headquarters from which the documents were sent. He identified a book found there as the minutes of the executive committee of the party. The book showed a resolution of August 13, 1917, that 15,000 leaflets should be printed on the other side of one of them in use, to be mailed to men who had passed exemption boards, and for distribution. Schenck personally attended to the printing. On August 20 the general secretary's report said, "Obtained new leaflets from the printer and started work addressing envelopes," etc.; and there was a resolve that Comrade Schenck be allowed $125 for sending leaflets through the mail. He said that he had about fifteen or sixteen thousand printed. There were files of the circular in question in the inner office which he said were printed on the other side of the one-sided circular and were there for distribution. Other copies were proved to have been sent through the mails to drafted men. Without going into confirmatory details that were proved, no reasonable man could doubt that the defendant Schenck was largely instrumental in sending the circulars about. As to the defendant Baer, there was evidence that she was a member of the executive board and that the minutes of its transactions were hers. The argument as to the sufficiency of the evidence that the defendants conspired to send the documents only impairs the seriousness of the real defense. . . .

The document in question, upon its first printed side, recited the 1st section of the Thirteenth Amendment, said that the idea embodied in it was violated by the Conscription Act, and that a conscript is little better than a convict. In impassioned language it intimated that conscription was despotism in its worst form and a monstrous wrong against humanity, in the interest of Wall Street's chosen few. It said: "Do not submit to intimidation"; but in form at least confined itself to peaceful measures, such as a petition for the repeal of the act. The other and later printed side of the sheet was headed, "Assert Your Rights." It stated reasons for alleging that anyone violated the Constitution when he refused to recognize "your right to assert your opposition to the draft," and went on: "If you do not assert and support your rights, you are helping to deny or disparage rights which it is the solemn duty of all citizens and residents of the United States to retain." It described the arguments on the other side as coming from cunning politicians and a mercenary capitalist press, and even silent consent to the Conscription Law as helping to support an infamous conspiracy. It denied the power to send our citizens away to foreign shores to shoot up the people of other lands, and added that words could not express the condemnation such cold-blooded ruthlessness deserves, etc., etc., winding up, "You must do your share to maintain, support, and uphold the rights of the people of this country." Of course the document would not have been sent unless it had been intended to have some effect and we do not see what effect it could be expected to have upon persons subject to the draft except to influence them to obstruct the carrying of it out. The defendants do not deny that the jury might find against them on this point.

But it is said, suppose that that was the tendency of this circular, it is protected by the First Amendment to the Constitution. Two of the strongest expressions are said to be quoted respectively from well-known public men. It well may be that the prohibition of laws abridging the freedom of speech is not confined to previous restraints, although to prevent them may have been the main purpose, as intimated in *Patterson* v. *Colorado*, 205 U.S. 454, 462. We admit that in many places and in ordinary times the defendants, in saying all that was said in the circular, would have been within their constitutional rights. But the character of every act depends upon the circumstances in which it is done. *Aikens* v. *Wisconsin*, 195 U.S. 194, 205, 206. The most stringent protection of free speech would not protect a man in falsely shouting fire in a theater, and causing a panic. It does not even protect a man from an injunction against uttering words that may have all the effect of force. *Gompers* v. *Buck's Stove & Range Co.*, 221 U.S. 418, 439. The question in every case is whether the words used are used in such circumstances and are of such a nature as to create a clear and present danger that they will bring about the substantive evils that Congress has a right to prevent. It is a question of proximity and degree. When a nation is at war many things that might be said in time of peace are such a hindrance to its effort that their utterance will not be endured so long as men fight, and that no Court could regard them as protected by any constitutional right. It seems to be admitted that if an actual obstruction of the recruiting service were proved, liability for words that produced that effect might be enforced. The Statute of 1917, in §4, punishes conspiracies to obstruct as well as actual obstruction. If the act, (speaking, or circulating a paper,) its tendency and the intent with which it is done, are the same, we perceive no ground for saying that success alone warrants making the act a crime. . . .

Judgments affirmed.

QUESTIONS

1. In the *Schenck* case does Mr. Justice Holmes believe that what Schenck printed and distributed would be protected by the First Amendment guarantee in ordinary times? How do you arrive at your conclusion? Do you think that what Schenck did should ever be protected under the Constitution? Why or why not?

2. On the basis of the facts of the case, do you think that Schenck and his activities represented a real likelihood of interference with the draft? If yes—how do you arrive at this conclusion? If no—what is the justification for holding that he constituted a "clear and present" danger of interference with conscription and ought to be punished under the law?

3. Do you think "words" ought to ever be treated as having the effect of force? If yes—when? If no—why not? Are words always harmless?

4. If you were a member of the Supreme Court in this case, would you vote with Holmes or would you dissent? If you would dissent, what would be your justification(s)?

5. What perils for freedom of speech, if any, do you see in a judicial rule, such as the "clear and present danger" test?

ABRAMS v. UNITED STATES

250 U.S. 616; 40 S. Ct. 17; 63 L.Ed. 1173 (1919)

MR. JUSTICE CLARKE *delivered the opinion of the court.*

On a single indictment, containing four counts, the five plaintiffs in error, hereinafter designated the defendants, were convicted of conspiring to violate provisions of the Espionage Act of Congress (§3, Title I, of Act approved June 15, 1917, as amended May 16, 1918, 40 Stat. 553).

Each of the first three counts charged the defendants with conspiring, when the United States was at war with the Imperial Government of Germany, to unlawfully utter, print, write and publish: In the first count, "disloyal, scurrilous and abusive language about the form of Government of the United States;" in the second count, language "intended to bring the form of Government of the United States into contempt, scorn, contumely and disrepute;" and in the third count, language "intended to incite, provoke and encourage resistance to the United States in said war." The charge in the fourth count was that the defendants conspired "when the United States was at war with the Imperial German Government, . . . unlawfully and wilfully, by utterance, writing, printing and publication, to urge, incite and advocate curtailment of production of things and products, to wit, ordnance and ammunition, necessary and essential to the prosecution of the war." The offenses were charged in the language of the act of Congress.

It was charged in each count of the indictment that it was a part of the conspiracy that the defendants would attempt to accomplish their unlawful purpose by printing, writing and distributing in the City of New York many copies of a leaflet or circular, printed in the English language, and of another printed in the Yiddish language, copies of which, properly identified, were attached to the indictment.

All of the five defendants were born in Russia. They were intelligent, had considerable schooling, and at the time they were arrested they had lived in the United States terms varying from five to ten years, but none of them had applied for naturalization. Four of them testified as witnesses in their own behalf and of these, three frankly avowed that they were "rebels," "revolutionists," "anarchists," that they did not believe in government in any form, and they declared that they had no interest whatever in the Government of the United States. The fourth defendant testified that he was a "socialist" and believed in "a proper kind of government, not capitalistic," but in his classification the Government of the United States was "capitalistic."

It was admitted on the trial that the defendants had united to print and distribute the described circulars and that five thousand of them had been printed and distributed about the 22d day of August, 1918. The group had a meeting place in New York City, in rooms rented by defendant Abrams, under an assumed name, and there the subject of printing the circulars was discussed about two weeks before the defendants were arrested. The defendant Abrams, although not a printer, on July 27, 1918, purchased the printing outfit with which the circulars were printed and installed it in a basement room where the work was done at night. The circulars were distributed some by throwing them from a window of a building where one of the defendants was employed and others secretly, in New York City.

The defendants pleaded "not guilty," and the case of the Government consisted in showing the facts we have stated, and in introducing in evidence copies of the two printed circulars attached to the indictment, a sheet entitled "Revolutionists Unite for Action," written by the defendant Lipman, and found on him when he was arrested, and another paper, found at the headquarters of the group, and for which Abrams assumed responsibility.

Thus the conspiracy and the doing of the overt acts charged were largely admitted and were fully established.

On the record thus described it is argued, somewhat faintly, that the acts charged against the defendants were not unlawful because within the protection of that freedom of speech and of the press which is guaranteed by the First Amendment to the Constitution of the United States, and that the entire Espionage Act is unconstitutional because in conflict with that Amendment.

This contention is sufficiently discussed and is definitely negatived in *Schenck* v. *United States* and *Baer* v. *United States*, 249 U.S. 47; and in *Frohwerk* v. *United States*, 249 U.S. 204.

.   .   .

The first of the two articles attached to the indictment is conspicuously headed, "The Hypocrisy of the United States and her Allies." After denouncing President Wilson as a hypocrite and a coward because troops were sent into Russia, it proceeds to assail our Government in general, saying:

"His [the President's] shameful, cowardly silence about the intervention in Russia reveals the hypocrisy of the plutocratic gang in Washington and vicinity."

It continues:

"He [the President] is too much of a coward to come out openly and say: 'We capitalistic nations cannot afford to have a proletarian republic in Russia.'"

Among the capitalistic nations Abrams testified the United States was included.

Growing more inflammatory as it proceeds, the circular culminates in:

"The Russian Revolution cries: Workers of the World! Awake! Rise! Put down your enemy and mine!

"Yes! friends, there is only one enemy of the workers of the world and that is CAPITALISM."

This is clearly an appeal to the "workers" of this country to arise and put down by force the Government of the United States which they characterize as their "hypocritical," "cowardly" and "capitalistic" enemy.

It concludes:

"Awake! Awake, you Workers of the World!"

"REVOLUTIONISTS."

The second of the articles was printed in the Yiddish language and in the translation is headed, "Workers —Wake up." After referring to "his Majesty, Mr. Wilson, and the rest of the gang; dogs of all colors!", it continues:

"Workers, Russian emigrants, you who had the least belief in the honesty of *our* Government," which defendants admitted referred to the United States Government, "must now throw away all confidence, must spit in the face the false, hypocritic, military propaganda which has fooled you so relentlessly, calling forth your sympathy, your help, to the prosecution of the war."

The purpose of this obviously was to persuade the persons to whom it was addressed to turn a deaf ear to patriotic appeals in behalf of the Government of the United States, and to cease to render it assistance in the prosecution of the war.

It goes on:

"With the money which you have loaned, or are going to loan them, they will make bullets not only for the Germans, but also for the Workers Soviets of Russia. *Workers in the ammunition factories, you are producing bullets, bayonets, cannon, to murder not only the Germans, but also your dearest, best, who are in Russia and are fighting for freedom.*"

It will not do to say, as is now argued, that the only intent of these defendants was to prevent injury to the Russian cause. Men must be held to have intended, and to be accountable for, the effects which their acts were likely to produce. Even if their primary purpose and intent was to aid the cause of the Russian Revolution, the plan of action which they adopted necessarily involved, before it could be realized, defeat of the war program of the United States, for the obvious effect of this appeal, if it should become effective, as they hoped it might, would be to persuade persons of character such as those whom they regarded themselves as addressing, not to aid government loans and not to work in ammunition factories, where their work would produce "bullets, bayonets, cannon" and other munitions of war, the use of which would cause the "murder" of Germans and Russians.

Again, the spirit becomes more bitter as it proceeds to declare that—

"America and her Allies have betrayed (the Workers). Their robberish aims are clear to all men. The destruction of the Russian Revolution, that is the politics of the march to Russia.

"*Workers, our reply to the barbaric intervention has to be a general strike! An open challenge* only will let the Government know that not only the Russian Worker fights for freedom, but also *here in America lives the spirit of Revolution.*"

This is not an attempt to bring about a change of administration by candid discussion, for no matter what may have incited the outbreak on the part of the defendant anarchists, the manifest purpose of such a publication was to create an attempt to defeat the war plans of the Government of the United States, by bringing upon the country the paralysis of a general strike, thereby arresting the production of all munitions and other things essential to the conduct of the war.

.   .   .

That the interpretation we have put upon these articles, circulated in the greatest port of our land, from which great numbers of soldiers were at the time taking ship daily, and in which great quantities of war supplies of every kind were at the time being manufactured for transportation overseas, is not only the fair interpretation of them, but that it is the meaning which their authors consciously intended should be conveyed by them to others is further shown by the additional writings found in the meeting place of the defendant group and on the person of one of them. One of these circulars is headed: "Revolutionists! Unite for Action!"

After denouncing the President as "Our Kaiser" and the hypocrisy of the United States and her Allies, this article concludes:

"Socialists, Anarchists, Industrial Workers of the World, Socialists, Labor party men and other revolutionary organizations *Unite for action* and let us save the Workers' Republic of Russia!

"*Know you lovers of freedom that in order to save the Russian revolution, we must keep the armies of the allied countries busy at home.*"

Thus was again avowed the purpose to throw the country into a state of revolution if possible and to thereby frustrate the military program of the Government.

The remaining article, after denouncing the President for what is characterized as hostility to the Russian revolution, continues:

"We, the toilers of America, who believe in real liberty, shall *pledge ourselves*, in case the United States will participate in that bloody conspiracy against Russia, *to create so great a disturbance that the autocrats of America shall be compelled to keep their armies at home, and not be able to spare any for Russia.*"

It concludes with this definite threat of armed rebellion:

"If they will use arms against the Russian people to enforce their standard of order, *so will we use arms*, and they shall never see the ruin of the Russian Revolution."

These excerpts sufficiently show, that while the immediate occasion for this particular outbreak of lawlessness, on the part of the defendant alien anarchists, may have been resentment caused by our Government sending troops into Russia as a strategic operation against the Germans on the eastern battle front, yet the plain purpose of their propaganda was to excite, at the supreme crisis of the war, disaffection, sedition, riots, and, as they hoped, revolution, in this country for the purpose of embarrassing and if possible defeating the military plans of the Government in Europe. . . . Thus it is clear not only that some evidence but that much persuasive evidence was before the jury tending to prove that the defendants were guilty as charged in both the third and fourth counts

of the indictment and under the long established rule of law hereinbefore stated the judgment of the District Court must be
Affirmed.

MR. JUSTICE HOLMES *dissenting.*

This indictment is founded wholly upon the publication of two leaflets which I shall describe in a moment. The first count charges a conspiracy pending the war with Germany to publish abusive language about the form of government of the United States, laying the preparation and publishing of the first leaflet as overt acts. The second count charges a conspiracy pending the war to publish language intended to bring the form of government into contempt, laying the preparation and publishing of the two leaflets as overt acts. The third count alleges a conspiracy to encourage resistance to the United States in the same war and to attempt to effectuate the purpose by publishing the same leaflets. The fourth count lays a conspiracy to incite curtailment of production of things necessary to the prosecution of the war and to attempt to accomplish it by publishing the second leaflet to which I have referred.

The first of these leaflets says that the President's cowardly silence about the intervention in Russia reveals the hypocrisy of the plutocratic gang in Washington. It intimates that "German militarism combined with allied capitalism to crush the Russian revolution"—goes on that the tyrants of the world fight each other until they see a common en-

emy—working class enlightenment, when they combine to crush it; and that now militarism and capitalism combined, though not openly, to crush the Russian revolution. It says that there is only one enemy of the workers of the world and that is capitalism; that it is a crime for workers of America, &c., to fight the workers' republic of Russia, and ends "Awake! Awake, you Workers of the World. Revolutionists." A note adds "It is absurd to call us pro-German. We hate and despise German militarism more than do you hypocritical tyrants. We have more reasons for denouncing German militarism than has the coward of the White House."

The other leaflet, headed "Workers—Wake Up," with abusive language says that America together with the Allies will march for Russia to help the Czecko-Slovaks in their struggle against the Bolsheviki, and that this time the hypocrites shall not fool the Russian emigrants and friends of Russia in America. It tells the Russian emigrants that they now must spit in the face of the false military propaganda by which their sympathy and help to the prosecution of the war have been called forth and says that with the money they have lent or are going to lend "they will make bullets not only for the Germans but also for the Workers Soviets of Russia," and further, "Workers in the ammunition factories, you are producing bullets, bayonets, cannon, to murder not only the Germans, but also your dearest, best, who are in Russia and are fighting for freedom." It then appeals to the same Russian emigrants at some length not to consent to the "inquisitionary expedition to Russia," and says that the destruction of the Russian revolution is "the politics of the march to Russia." The leaflet winds up by saying "Workers, our reply to this barbaric intervention has to be a general strike!," and after a few words on the spirit of revolution, exhortations not to be afraid, and some usual tall talk ends "Woe unto those who will be in the way of progress. Let solidarity live! The Rebels."

No argument seems to me necessary to show that these pronunciamentos in no way attack the form of government of the United States, or that they do not support either of the first two counts. What little I have to say about the third count may be postponed until I have considered the fourth. With regard to that it seems too plain to be denied that the suggestion to workers in the ammunition factories that they are producing bullets to murder their dearest, and the further advocacy of a general strike, both in the second leaflet, do urge curtailment of production of things necessary to the prosecution of the war within the meaning of the Act of May 16, 1918, c. 75, 40 Stat. 553, amending §3 of the earlier Act of 1917. But to make the conduct criminal that statute requires that it should be "with intent by such curtailment to cripple or hinder the United States in the prosecution of the war." It seems to me that no such intent is proved.

I am aware of course that the word intent as vaguely used in ordinary legal discussion means no more than knowledge at the time of the act that the consequences said to be intended will ensue. Even less than that will satisfy the general principle of civil and criminal liability. A man may have to pay damages, may be sent to prison, at common law might be hanged, if at the time of his act he knew facts from which common experience showed that the consequences would follow, whether he individually could foresee them or not. But, when words are used exactly, a deed is not done with intent to produce a consequence unless that consequence is the aim of the deed. It may be obvious, and obvious to the actor, that the consequence will follow, and he may be liable for it even if he regrets it, but he does not do the act with intent to produce it unless the aim to produce it is the proximate motive of the specific act, although there may be some deeper motive behind.

It seems to me that this statute must be taken to use its words in a strict and accurate sense. They would be absurd in any other. A patriot might think that we were wasting money on aeroplanes, or making more cannon of a certain kind than we needed, and might advocate curtailment with success, yet even if it turned out that the curtailment hindered and was thought by other minds to have been obviously likely to hinder the United States in the prosecution of the war, no one would hold such conduct a crime. I admit that my illustration does not answer all that might be said but it is enough to show what I think and to let me pass to a more important aspect of the case. I refer to the First Amendment to the Constitution that Congress shall make no law abridging the freedom of speech.

I never have seen any reason to doubt that the questions of law that alone were before this Court in the cases of *Schenck, Frohwerk* and *Debs,* 249 U.S. 47, 204, 211, were rightly decided. I do not doubt for a moment that by the same reasoning that would justify punishing persuasion to murder, the United States constitutionally may punish speech that produces or is intended to produce a clear and imminent danger that it will bring about forthwith certain substantive evils that the United States constitutionally may seek to prevent. The power undoubtedly is greater in time of war than in time of peace because war opens dangers that do not exist at other times.

But as against dangers peculiar to war, as against others, the principle of the right to free speech is always the same. It is only the present danger of immediate evil or an intent to bring it about that warrants Congress in setting a limit to the expression of opinion where private rights are not concerned. Congress certainly cannot forbid all effort to change the mind of the country. Now nobody can suppose that the surreptitious publishing of a silly leaflet by an unknown man, without more, would present any immediate danger that its opinions would hinder the success of the government arms or have any appreciable tendency to do so. Publishing those opinions for the very purpose of obstructing however, might indicate a greater danger and at any rate would have the quality of an attempt. So I assume that the second leaflet if published for the purposes alleged in the fourth count might be punishable. But it seems pretty clear to me that nothing less than that would bring these papers within the scope of this law. An actual intent in the sense that I have explained is necessary to constitute an attempt, where a further act of the same individual is required to complete the substantive crime, for reasons given in *Swift & Co.* v. *United States,* 196 U.S. 375, 396. It is necessary where the success of the attempt depends upon others because if that intent is not present the actor's aim may be accomplished without bringing about the evils sought to be checked. An intent to prevent interference with the revolution in Russia might have been satisfied without any hindrance to carrying on the war in which we were engaged.

I do not see how anyone can find the intent required by the statute in any of the defendants' words. The second leaflet is the only one that affords even a foundation for the charge, and there, without invoking the hatred of German militarism expressed in the former one, it is evident from the beginning to the end that the only object of the paper is to help Russia and stop American intervention there against the popular government—not to impede the United States in the war that it was carrying on. To say that two phrases taken literally might import a suggestion of conduct that would have interference with the war as an indirect and probably undesired effect seems to me by no means enough to show an attempt to produce that effect.

I return for a moment to the third count. That charges an intent to provoke resistance to the United States in its war with Germany. Taking the clause in the statute that deals with that in connection with the other elaborate provisions of the act, I think that resistance to the United States means some forcible act of opposition to some proceeding of the United States in pursuance of the war. I think the intent must be the specific intent that I have described and for the reasons that I have given I think that no such intent was proved or existed in fact. I also think that there is no hint at resistance to the United States as I construe the phrase.

In this case sentences of twenty years imprisonment have been imposed for the publishing of two leaflets that I believe the defendants had as much right to publish as the Government has to publish the Constitution of the United States now vainly invoked by them. Even if I am technically wrong and enough can be squeezed from these poor and puny anonymities to turn the color of legal litmus paper; I will add, even if what I think the necessary intent were shown; the most nominal punishment seems to me all that possibly could be inflicted, unless the defendants are to be made to suffer not for what the indictment alleges but for the creed that they avow—a creed that I believe to be the creed of ignorance and immaturity when honestly held, as I see no reason to doubt that it was held here, but

which, although made the subject of examination at the trial, no one has a right even to consider in dealing with the charges before the Court.

Persecution for the expression of opinions seems to me perfectly logical. If you have no doubt of your premises or your power and want a certain result with all your heart you naturally express your wishes in law and sweep away all opposition. To allow opposition by speech seems to indicate that you think the speech impotent, as when a man says that he has squared the circle, or that you do not care whole-heartedly for the result, or that you doubt either your power or your premises. But when men have realized that time has upset many fighting faiths, they may come to believe even more than they believe the very foundations of their own conduct that the ultimate good desired is better reached by free trade in ideas—that the best test of truth is the power of the thought to get itself accepted in the competition of the market, and that truth is the only ground upon which their wishes safely can be carried out. That at any rate is the theory of our Constitution. It is an experiment, as all life is an experiment. Every year if not every day we have to wager our salvation upon some prophecy based upon imperfect knowledge. While that experiment is part of our system I think that we should be eternally vigilant against attempts to check the expression of opinions that we loathe and believe to be fraught with death, unless they so imminently threaten immediate interference with the lawful and pressing purposes of the law that an immediate check is required to save the country. I wholly disagree with the argument of the Government that the First Amendment left the common law as to seditious libel in force. History seems to me against the notion. I had conceived that the United States through many years had shown its repentance for the Sedition Act of 1798, by repaying fines that it imposed. Only the emergency that makes it immediately dangerous to leave the correction of evil counsels to time warrants making any exception to the sweeping command, "Congress shall make no law . . . abridging the freedom of speech." Of course I am speaking only of expressions of opinion and exhortations, which were all that were uttered here, but I regret that I cannot put into more impressive words my belief that in their conviction upon this indictment the defendants were deprived of their rights under the Constitution of the United States.

MR. JUSTICE BRANDEIS *concurs with the foregoing opinion.*

QUESTIONS

1. In *Abrams* v. *United States* do you agree with the majority opinion that a man must be held accountable for the consequences of his acts even though he did not intend the results? If you agree with Justice Clarke about this do you think that a man who accidentally kills someone ought to be charged with murder?

2. After having read excerpts of Abram's pamphlets are you of the opinion that he was abstractly advocating interference with munitions productions or was he advocating interference with the quality of incitement likely to produce a munitions production stoppage? What are your justifications for your opinion? *How do you* differentiate *abstract* advocacy from advocacy *of action?*

3. Should the constitutional right of expression protect the type of ideas that Abrams advanced in his pamphlets? Why or why not? Of what benefit, if any, are they to society?

4. Do you think that only expressions which are of benefit to society ought to be constitutionally protected? Why or why not? If you reject this criterion to determine what expressions shall be legally protected, what standard, if any, would you substitute? How do you justify your position?

5. Do you think Holmes' positions in *Schenck* and *Abrams* are reconcilable? If not, why not? If so, why? Was Schenck a greater danger to the war effort than Abrams? How?

UNITED STATES v. O'BRIEN

391 U.S. 367; 88 S. Ct. 1673; 20 L.Ed. 2d 672 (1968)

MR. CHIEF JUSTICE WARREN *delivered the opinion of the Court.*

I.

On the morning of March 31, 1966, David Paul O'Brien and three companions burned their Selective Service registration certificates on the steps of the South Boston Courthouse. A sizable crowd, including several agents of the Federal Bureau of Investigation, witnessed the event.[1] Immediately after the burning, members of the crowd began attacking O'Brien and his companions. An FBI agent ushered O'Brien to safety inside the courthouse. After he was advised of his right to counsel and to silence, O'Brien stated to FBI agents that he had burned his registration certificate because of his beliefs, knowing that he was violating federal law. He produced the charred remains of the certificate, which, with his consent, were photographed.

For this act, O'Brien was indicted, tried, convicted, and sentenced in the United States District Court for the District of Massachusetts.[2] He did not contest the fact that he had burned the certificate. He stated in argument to the jury that he burned the certificate publicly to influence others to adopt his antiwar beliefs, as he put it, "so that other people would reevaluate their positions with Selective Service, with the armed forces, and reevaluate their place in the culture of today, to hopefully consider my position."

The indictment upon which he was tried charged that he "wilfully and knowingly did mutilate, destroy, and change by burning . . . [his] Registration Certificate (Selective Service System Form No. 2); in violation of Title 50, App., United States Code, Section 462(b)." Section 462(b) is part of the Universal Military Training and Service Act of 1948. Section 462(b)(3), one of six numbered subdivisions of § 462(b), was amended by Congress in 1965, 79 Stat. 586 (adding the words italicized below), so that at the time O'Brien burned his certificate an offense was committed by any person,

> "who forges, alters, *knowingly destroys, knowingly mutilates,* or in any manner changes any such certificate . . . ." (Italics supplied.)

[*Editor's note: Throughout the book the numbered footnotes are reproduced from the text quoted, without change of number.*]

1. At the time of the burning, the agents knew only that O'Brien and his three companions had burned small white cards. They later discovered that the card O'Brien burned was his registration certificate, and the undisputed assumption is that the same is true of his companions.

2. He was sentenced under the Youth Correction Act, 18 U.S.C. § 5010(b), to the custody of the Attorney General for a maximum period of six years for supervision and treatment.

In the District Court, O'Brien argued that the 1965 Amendment prohibiting the knowing destruction or mutilation of certificates was unconstitutional because it was enacted to abridge free speech, and because it served no legitimate legislative purpose. The District Court rejected these arguments, holding that the statute on its face did not abridge First Amendment rights, that the court was not competent to inquire into the motives of Congress in enacting the 1965 Amendment, and that the Amendment was a reasonable exercise of the power of Congress to raise armies.

On appeal, the Court of Appeals for the First Circuit held the 1965 Amendment unconstitutional as a law abridging freedom of speech. At the time the Amendment was enacted, a regulation of the Selective Service System required registrants to keep their registration certificates in their "personal possession at all times." . . . Wilful violations of regulations promulgated pursuant to the Universal Military Training and Service Act were made criminal by statute. . . . The Court of Appeals, therefore, was of the opinion that conduct punishable under the 1965 Amendment was already punishable under the nonpossession regulation, and consequently that the Amendment served no valid purpose; further, that in light of the prior regulation, the Amendment must have been "directed at public as distinguished from private destruction." On this basis, the Court concluded that the 1965 Amendment ran afoul of the First Amendment by singling out persons engaged in protests for special treatment. The Court ruled, however, that O'Brien's conviction should be affirmed under the statutory provision, 50 U.S.C. App. § 462(b) (6), which in its view made violation of the nonpossession regulation a crime, because it regarded such violation to be a lesser included offense of the crime defined by the 1965 Amendment.[6]

The Government petitioned for *certiorari*, in No. 232, arguing that the Court of Appeals erred in holding the statute unconstitutional, and that its decision conflicted with decisions by the Court of Appeals for the Second and Eighth Circuits upholding the 1965 Amendment against identical constitutional challenges. . . . We granted the Government's petition to resolve the conflict in the circuits. . . . We hold that the 1965 Amendment is constitutional both as enacted and as applied. We therefore vacate the judgment of the Court of Appeals and reinstate the judgment and sentence of the District Court. . . .

When a male reaches the age of 18, he is required by the Universal Military Training and Service Act to

---

6. The Court of Appeals nevertheless remanded the case to the District Court to vacate the sentence and resentence O'Brien. In the Court's view, the district judge might have considered the violation of the 1965 Amendment as an aggravating circumstance in imposing sentence. The Court of Appeals subsequently denied O'Brien's petition for a rehearing, in which he argued that he had not been charged, tried, or convicted for nonpossession, and that nonpossession was not a lesser included offense of mutilation or destruction. *O'Brien* v. *United States*, 376 F.2d 538, 542 (C.A. 1st Cir. 1967).

register with a local draft board. He is assigned a Selective Service number, and within five days he is issued a registration certificate (SSS Form No. 2). Subsequently, and based on a questionnaire completed by the registrant, he is assigned a classification denoting his eligibility for induction, and "[a]s soon as practicable" thereafter he is issued a Notice of Classification (SSS Form No. 110). This initial classification is not necessarily permanent, and if in the interim before induction the registrant's status changes in some relevant way, he may be reclassified. After such a reclassification, the local board "as soon as practicable" issues to the registrant a new Notice of Classification.

Both the registration and classification certificates are small white cards, approximately 2 by 3 inches. The registration certificate specifies the name of the registrant, the date of registration, and the number and address of the local board with which he is registered. Also inscribed upon it are the date and place of the registrant's birth, his residence at registration, his physical description, his signature, and his Selective Service number. The Selective Service number itself indicates his State of registration, his local board, his year of birth, and his chronological position in the local board's classification record.

The classification certificate shows the registrant's name, Selective Service number, signature, and eligibility classification. It specifies whether he was so classified by his local board, an appeal board, or the President. It contains the address of his local

board and the date the certificate was mailed.

Both the registration and classification certificates bear notices that the registrant must notify his local board in writing of every change in address, physical condition, and occupational, marital, family, dependency, and military status, and of any other fact which might change his classification. Both also contain a notice that the registrant's Selective Service number should appear on all communications to his local board.

Congress demonstrated its concern that certificates issued by the Selective Service System might be abused well before the 1965 Amendment here challenged. The 1948 Act, 62 Stat. 604, itself prohibited many different abuses involving "any registration certificate, . . . or any other certificate issued pursuant to or prescribed by the provisions of this title, or rules or regulations promulgated hereunder" . . . [It] was unlawful (1) to transfer a certificate to aid a person in making false identification; (2) to possess a certificate not duly issued with the intent of using it for false identification; (3) to forge, alter, "or in any manner" change a certificate or any notation validly inscribed thereon; (4) to photograph or make an imitation of a certificate for the purpose of false identification; and (5) to possess a counterfeited or altered certificate. . . . In addition, as previously mentioned, regulations of the Selective Service System required registrants to keep both their registration and classification certificates in their personal possession at all times. . . .

By the 1965 Amendment, Congress added to § 12(b) (3) of the 1948 Act the provision here at issue, subjecting to criminal liability not only one who "forges, alters, or in any manner changes" but also one who "knowingly destroys, [or] knowingly mutilates" a certificate. We note at the outset that the 1965 Amendment plainly does not abridge free speech on its face, and we do not understand O'Brien to argue otherwise. Amended § 12(b) (3) on its face deals with conduct having no connection with speech. It prohibits the knowing destruction of certificates issued by the Selective Service System, and there is nothing necessarily expressive about such conduct. The Amendment does not distinguish between public and private destruction, and it does not punish only destruction engaged in for the purpose of expressing views. . . . A law prohibiting destruction of Selective Service certificates no more abridges free speech on its face than a motor vehicle law prohibiting the destruction of drivers' licenses, or a tax law prohibiting the destruction of books and records.

O'Brien nonetheless argues that the 1965 Amendment is unconstitutional in its application to him, and is unconstitutional as enacted because what he calls the "purpose" of Congress was "to suppress freedom of speech." We consider these arguments separately.

II.

O'Brien first argues that the 1965 Amendment is unconstitutional as applied to him because his act of burning his registration certificate was protected "symbolic speech" within the First Amendment. His argument is that the freedom of expression which the First Amendment guarantees includes all modes of "communication of ideas by conduct," and that his conduct is within this definition because he did it in "demonstration against the war and against the draft."

We cannot accept the view that an apparently limitless variety of conduct can be labelled "speech" whenever the person engaging in the conduct intends thereby to express an idea. However, even on the assumption that the alleged communicative element in O'Brien's conduct is sufficient to bring into play the First Amendment, it does not necessarily follow that the destruction of a registration certificate is constitutionally protected activity. This Court has held that when "speech" and "nonspeech" elements are combined in the same course of conduct, a sufficiently important governmental interest in regulating the nonspeech element can justify incidental limitations on First Amendment freedoms. To characterize the quality of the governmental interest which must appear, the Court has employed a variety of descriptive terms: compelling; substantial; subordinating; paramount; cogent; strong. Whatever imprecision inheres in these terms, we think it clear that a government regulation is sufficiently justified if it is within the constitutional power of the government; if it furthers an important or substantial governmental interest; if the governmental interest is unrelated to the suppression of free expression;

and if the incidental restriction on alleged First Amendment freedom is no greater than is essential to the furtherance of that interest. . . .

The constitutional power of Congress to raise and support armies and to make all laws necessary and proper to that end is broad and sweeping. . . . The power of Congress to classify and conscript manpower for military service is "beyond question." *Lichter* v. *United States, supra,* 334 U.S. at 756, 68 S.Ct. at 1302; *Selective Draft Law Cases, supra.* Pursuant to this power, Congress may establish a system of registration for individuals liable for training and service, and may require such individuals within reason to cooperate in the registration system. The issuance of certificates indicating the registration and eligibility classification of individuals is a legitimate and substantial administrative aid in the functioning of this system. And legislation to insure the continuing availability of issued certificates serves a legitimate and substantial purpose in the system's administration.

O'Brien's argument to the contrary is necessarily premised upon his unrealistic characterization of Selective Service certificates. He essentially adopts the position that such certificates are so many pieces of paper designed to notify registrants of their registration or classification, to be retained or tossed in the wastebasket according to the convenience or taste of the registrant. Once the registrant has received notification, according to this view, there is no reason for him to retain the certificates. O'Brien

notes that most of the information on a registration certificate serves no notification purpose at all; the registrant hardly needs to be told his address and physical characteristics. We agree that the registration certificate contains much information of which the registrant needs no notification. This circumstance, however, leads not to the conclusion that the certificate serves no purpose but that, like the classification certificate, it serves purposes in addition to initial notification. Many of these purposes would be defeated by the certificates' destruction or mutilation. Among these are:

1. The registration certificate serves as proof that the individual described thereon has registered for the draft. The classification certificate shows the eligibility classification of a named but undescribed individual. Voluntarily displaying the two certificates is an easy and painless way for a young man to dispel a question as to whether he might be delinquent in his Selective Service obligations. Correspondingly, the availability of the certificates for such display relieves the Selective Service System of the administrative burden it would otherwise have in verifying the registration and classification of all suspected delinquents. Further, since both certificates are in the nature of "receipts" attesting that the registrant has done what the law requires, it is in the interest of the just and efficient administration of the system that they be continually available, in the event, for exam-

ple, of a mix-up in the registrant's file. Additionally, in a time of national crisis, reasonable availability to each registrant of the two small cards assures a rapid and uncomplicated means for determining his fitness for immediate induction, no matter how distant in our mobile society he may be from his local board.

2. The information supplied on the certificates facilitates communication between registrants and local boards, simplifying the system and benefiting all concerned. To begin with, each certificate bears the address of the registrant's local board, an item unlikely to be committed to memory. Further, each card bears the registrant's Selective Service number, and a registrant who has his number readily available so that he can communicate it to his local board when he supplies or requests information can make simpler the board's task in locating his file. Finally, a registrant's inquiry, particularly through a local board other than his own, concerning his eligibility status is frequently answerable simply on the basis of his classification certificate; whereas, if the certificate were not reasonably available and the registrant were uncertain of his classification, the task of answering his questions would be considerably complicated.

3. Both certificates carry continual reminders that the registrant must notify his local board of any change of address, and other specified changes in his status. The smooth functioning of the system requires that local boards be continually aware of the status and whereabouts of registrants, and the destruction of certificates deprives the system of a potentially useful notice device.

4. The regulatory scheme involving Selective Service certificates includes clearly valid prohibitions against the alteration, forgery or similar deceptive misuse of certificates. The destruction or mutilation of certificates obviously increases the difficulty of detecting and tracing abuses such as these. Further, a mutilated certificate might itself be used for deceptive purposes.

The many functions performed by Selective Service certificates establish beyond doubt that Congress has a legitimate and substantial interest in preventing their wanton and unrestrained destruction and assuring their continuing availability by punishing people who knowingly and wilfully destroy or mutilate them. And we are unpersuaded that the pre-existence of the nonpossession regulations in any way negates this interest.

. . .

Equally important, a comparison of the regulations with the 1965 Amendment indicates that they protect overlapping but not identical governmental interests, and that they reach somewhat different classes of wrongdoers. The gravamen of the offense defined by the statute is the deliberate rendering of certificates unavailable for the various purposes which they may serve. Whether registrants keep their certificates in their personal possession at all times, as required by the regulations, is of no particular concern under the 1965

Amendment, as long as they do not mutilate or destroy the certificates so as to render them unavailable. Although as we note below we are not concerned here with the nonpossession regulations, it is not inappropriate to observe that the essential elements of nonpossession are not identical with those of mutilation or destruction. Finally, the 1965 Amendment, like § 12(b) which it amended, is concerned with abuses involving *any* issued Selective Service certificates, not only with the registrant's own certificates. The knowing destruction or mutilation of someone else's certificates would therefore violate the statute but not the nonpossession regulations.

We think it apparent that the continuing availability to each registrant of his Selective Service certificates substantially furthers the smooth and proper functioning of the system that Congress has established to raise armies. We think it also apparent that the Nation has a vital interest in having a system for raising armies that functions with maximum efficiency and is capable of easily and quickly responding to continually changing circumstances. For these reasons, the Government has a substantial interest in assuring the continuing availability of issued Selective Service certificates. . . .

...The governmental interest and the scope of the 1965 Amendment are limited to preventing a harm to the smooth and efficient functioning of the Selective Service System. When O'Brien deliberately rendered unavailable his registration certificate, he wilfully frustrated this governmental interest. For this noncommu-

nicative impact of his conduct, and for nothing else, he was convicted.

The case at bar is therefore unlike one where the alleged governmental interest in regulating conduct arises in some measure because the communication allegedly integral to the conduct is itself thought to be harmful. In *Stromberg* v. *People of State of California*, 283 U.S. 359, 51 S.Ct. 532, 75 L.Ed. 1117 (1931), for example, this Court struck down a statutory phrase which punished people who expressed their "opposition to organized government" by displaying "any flag, badge, banner, or device." Since the statute there was aimed at suppressing communication it could not be sustained as a regulation of noncommunicative conduct. . . .

In conclusion, we find that because of the Government's substantial interest in assuring the continuing availability of issued Selective Service certificates, because amended § 462(b) is an appropriately narrow means of protecting this interest and condemns only the independent noncommunicative impact of conduct within its reach, and because the noncommunicative impact of O'Brien's act of burning his registration certificate frustrated the Government's interest, a sufficient governmental interest has been shown to justify O'Brien's conviction.

III.

O'Brien finally argues that the 1965 Amendment is unconstitutional as enacted because what he calls the "purpose" of Congress was "to suppress freedom of speech." We reject this argument because under settled principles the purpose of Congress, as O'Brien uses that term, is not a basis for declaring this legislation unconstitutional.

It is a familiar principle of constitutional law that this Court will not strike down an otherwise constitutional statute on the basis of an alleged illicit legislative motive. . . .

Inquiries into congressional motives or purposes are a hazardous matter. When the issue is simply the interpretation of legislation, the Court will look to statements by legislators for guidance as to the purpose of the legislature, because the benefit to sound decision-making in this circumstance is thought sufficient to risk the possibility of misreading Congress' purpose. It is entirely a different matter when we are asked to void a statute that is, under well-settled criteria, constitutional on its face, on the basis of what fewer than a handful of Congressmen said about it. What motivates one legislator to make a speech about a statute is not necessarily what motivates scores of others to enact it, and the stakes are sufficiently high for us to eschew guesswork. We decline to void essentially on the ground that it is unwise legislation which Congress had the undoubted power to enact and which could be reenacted in its exact form if the same or another legislator made a "wiser" speech about it.

.   .   .

IV.

Since the 1965 Amendment to § 12(b) (3) of the Universal Military Training and Service Act is constitutional as enacted and as applied, the Court of Appeals should have affirmed the judgment of conviction entered by the District Court. Accordingly, we vacate the judgment of the Court of Appeals, and reinstate the judgment and sentence of the District Court. . . .

It is so ordered.

MR. JUSTICE MARSHALL *took no part in the consideration or decision of these cases.*

MR. JUSTICE HARLAN, *concurring.*

The crux of the Court's opinion, which I join, is of course its general statement, . . . that:

"a government regulation is sufficiently justified if it is within the constitutional power of the government; if it furthers an important or substantial governmental interest; if the governmental interest is unrelated to the suppression of free expression; and if the incidental restriction on alleged First Amendment freedom is no greater than is essential to the furtherance of that interest."

I wish to make explicit my understanding that this passage does not foreclose consideration of First Amendment claims in those rare instances when an "incidental" restriction upon expression, imposed by a regulation which furthers an "important or substantial" governmental interest and satisfies the Court's other criteria, in practice has the effect of entirely preventing a "speaker" from reaching a significant audience with whom he could not otherwise lawfully communicate. This is not such a case, since O'Brien manifestly could have conveyed his message in many ways other than by burning his draft card.

MR. JUSTICE DOUGLAS, *dissenting.*

The Court states that the constitutional power of Congress to raise and support armies is "broad and sweeping" and that Congress' power "to classify and conscript manpower for military service is 'beyond question.'" This is undoubtedly true in times when, by declaration of Congress, the Nation is in a state of war. The underlying and basic problem in this case, however, is whether conscription is permissible in the absence of a declaration of war.* That question has not been briefed nor was it presented in oral argument; but it is, I submit, a question upon which the litigants and the country are entitled to a ruling. I have discussed in *Holmes* v. *United States*, post, 391 U.S. p. 936, 88 S.Ct. p. 1835, the nature of the legal issue and it will be seen from my dissenting opinion in that case that this Court has never ruled on the question. It is time that we made a ruling. This case should be put down for reargument and heard with *Holmes* v. *United States* and with *Vondon Hart* v. *United States*, post, 391 U.S. p. 956, 88 S.Ct. p. 1851, 20 L.Ed.2d p. 871, in which the Court today denies *certiorari*. . . .

QUESTIONS

1. Does O'Brien argue that the 1965 Amendment to the Selective Service Act is unconstitutional as applied to him or in all its applications (on its "face")? How does he justify the position that he takes? What do you think of his argument? Justify your agreement or disagreement.

2. What is the Court's reasoning for dismissing O'Brien's contention that Congress had as its purpose the suppression of freedom of speech when it enacted the 1965 Amendment to the Selective Service Act?

---

*Neither of the decisions cited by the majority for the proposition that Congress' power to conscript men into the armed services is "'beyond question'" concerns peacetime conscription. As I have shown in my dissenting opinion in *Holmes v. United States*, post, 391 U.S. 936, 88 S.Ct. p. 1835, 20 L.Ed.2d 856, the *Selective Draft Law Cases*, 245 U.S. 366, 38 S.Ct. 159, 62 L.Ed. 349, decided in 1918, upheld the constitutionality of a conscription act passed by Congress more than a month after war had been declared on the German Empire and which was then being enforced in time of war. *Lichter v. United States*, 334 U.S. 742, 68 S.Ct. 1294, 92 L.Ed. 1694, concerned the constitutionality of the Renegotiation Act, another wartime measure, enacted by Congress over the period of 1942–1945 (*id.*, at 745, n. 1, 68 S.Ct. at 1297) and applied in that case to excessive war profits made in 1942–1943 (*id.*, at 753, 68 S.Ct. at 1300). War had been declared, of course, in 1941 (55 Stat. 795). The Court referred to Congress' power to raise armies in discussing the "background" (*ibid*) of the Renegotiation Act, which it upheld as a valid exercise of the War Power.

3. Do you think physical actions such as burning a draft card, whatever the motive, ought to be equated with speech? If yes—why? If not, why not?

4. If you equate some physical action with constitutionally protected speech, how would you determine when the two are able to be equated and when they are not? What criteria would you develop to determine this difference? Has the Supreme Court developed any criteria in this case which may be of help?

5. Apart from your feeling about David O'Brien's actions and beliefs, if you were a member of the Supreme Court in 1968, how do you think you would have cast your vote? Why?

TINKER *v.* DES MOINES

393 U.S. 503; 89 S. Ct. 733; 21 L.Ed. 2d 731 (1969)

MR. JUSTICE FORTAS *delivered the opinion of the Court.*

Petitioner John F. Tinker, 15 years old, and petitioner Christopher Eckhardt, 16 years old, attended high schools in Des Moines. Petitioner Mary Beth Tinker, John's sister, was a 13-year-old student in junior high school.

In December 1965, a group of adults and students in Des Moines, Iowa, held a meeting at the Eckhardt home. The group determined to publicize their objections to the hostilities in Vietnam and their support for a truce by wearing black armbands during the holiday season and by fasting on December 16 and New Year's Eve. Petitioners and their parents had previously engaged in similar activities, and they decided to participate in the program.

The principals of the Des Moines schools became aware of the plan to wear armbands. On December 14, 1965, they met and adopted a policy that any student wearing an armband to school would be asked to remove it, and if he refused he would be suspended until he returned without the armband. Petitioners were aware of the regulation that the school authorities adopted.

On December 16, Mary Beth and Christopher wore black armbands to their schools. John Tinker wore his armband the next day. They were all sent home and suspended from school until they would come back without their armbands. They did not return to school until after the planned period for wearing armbands had expired—that is, until after New Year's Day.

This complaint was filed in the United States District Court by petitioners, through their fathers, under § 1983 of Title 42 of the United States Code. It prayed for an injunction restraining the defendant school officials and the defendant members of the board of directors of the school district from disciplining the petitioners, and it sought nominal damages. After an evidentiary hearing the District Court dismissed the complaint. It upheld the constitutionality of the school authorities' actions on the ground that it was reasonable in order to prevent disturbance of school discipline. 258 F.Supp. 971 (1966). The court referred to but expressly declined to follow the Fifth Circuit's holding in a similar case that prohibition of the wearing of symbols like the armbands cannot be sustained unless it "materially and substantially interfere[s] with the requirements of appropriate discipline in the operation of the school." *Burnside* v. *Byars*, 363 F.2d 744, 749 (1966).

On appeal, the Court of Appeals for the Eighth Circuit considered the case *en banc*. The court was equally divided, and the District Court's decision was accordingly affirmed, without opinion. 383 F.2d 988 (1967). We granted *certiorari*, 390 U.S. 942, 88 S.Ct. 1050, 19 L.Ed.2d 1130 (1968).

I.

The District Court recognized that the wearing of an armband for the purpose of expressing certain views is the type of symbolic act that is within the Free Speech Clause of the First Amendment. . . . As we shall discuss, the wearing of armbands in the circumstances of this case was entirely divorced from actually or potentially disruptive conduct by those participating in it. It was closely akin to "pure speech" which, we have repeatedly held, is entitled to comprehensive protection under the First Amendment. . . .

First Amendment rights, applied in light of the special characteristics of the school environment, are available to teachers and students. It can hardly be argued that either students or teachers shed their constitutional rights to freedom of speech or expression at the schoolhouse gate. This has been the unmistakable holding of this Court for almost 50 years. In *Meyer* v. *Nebraska*, 262 U.S. 390, 43 S.Ct. 625, 67 L.Ed. 1042 (1923), and *Bartels* v. *Iowa*, 262 U.S. 404, 43 S.Ct. 628, 67 L.Ed. 1047 (1923), this Court, in opinions by Mr. Justice McReynolds, held that the Due Process Clause of the Fourteenth Amendment prevents States from forbidding the teaching of a foreign language to young students. Statutes to this effect, the Court held, unconstitutionally interfere with the liberty of teacher, student, and parent. . . .

In *West Virginia State Board of Education* v. *Barnette, supra,* this Court held that under the First Amendment, the student in public school may not be compelled to salute the flag. . . .

On the other hand, the Court has repeatedly emphasized the need for affirming the comprehensive authority of the States and of school authorities, consistent with fundamental constitutional safeguards, to prescribe and control conduct in the schools. . . . Our problem lies in the area where students in the exercise of First Amendment rights collide with the rules of the school authorities.

II.

The problem presented by the present case does not relate to regulation of the length of skirts or the type of clothing, to hair style or deportment. . . . It does not concern aggressive, disruptive action or even group demonstrations. Our problem involves direct, primary First Amendment rights akin to "pure speech."

The school officials banned and sought to punish petitioners for a silent, passive, expression of opinion, unaccompanied by any disorder or disturbance on the part of petitioners. There is here no evidence whatever of petitioners' interference, actual or nascent, with the school's work or of collision with the rights of other students to be secure and to be let alone. Accordingly, this case does not concern speech or action that intrudes upon the work of the school or the rights of other students.

Only a few of the 18,000 students in the school system wore the black armbands. Only five students were suspended for wearing them. There is no indication that the work of the school or any class was disrupted. Outside the classrooms, a few students made hostile remarks to the children wearing armbands, but there were no threats or acts of violence on school premises.

The District Court concluded that the action of the school authorities was reasonable because it was based upon their fear of a disturbance from the wearing of the armbands. But, in our system, undifferentiated fear or apprehension of disturbance is not enough to overcome the right to freedom of expression. Any departure from absolute regimentation may cause trouble. Any variation from the majority's opinion may inspire fear. Any word spoken, in class, in the lunchroom or on the campus, that deviates from the views of another person, may start an argument or cause a disturbance. But our Constitution says we must take this risk, *Terminiello* v. *Chicago*, 337 U.S. 1, 69 S.Ct. 894, 93 L.Ed. 1131 (1949); and our history says that it is this sort of hazardous freedom—this kind of openness—that is the basis of our national strength and of the independence and vigor of Americans who grow up and live in this relatively permissive, often disputatious society.

In order for the State in the person of school officials to justify prohibition of a particular expression of opinion, it must be able to show that its action was caused by something more than a mere desire to avoid the discomfort and unpleasantness that always accompany an unpopular viewpoint. Certainly where there is no finding and no showing that the exercise of the forbidden right would "materially and substantially interfere with the requirements of appropriate discipline in the operation of the school," the prohibition cannot be sustained. . . .

In the present case, the District Court made no such finding, and our independent examination of the record fails to yield evidence that the school authorities had reason to anticipate that the wearing of the armbands would substantially interfere with the work of the school or impinge upon the rights of other students. Even an official memorandum prepared after the suspension that listed the reasons for the ban on wearing the armbands made no reference to the anticipation of such disruption.[3]

On the contrary, the action of the school authorities appears to have been based upon an urgent wish to avoid the controversy which might result from the expression, even by the silent symbol of armbands, of opposition to this Nation's part in the conflagration in Vietnam.[4] It is revealing, in this respect, that the meeting at which the school principals decided to issue the contested regulation was called in response to a student's statement to the journalism teacher in one of the schools that he wanted to write an article on Vietnam and have it published in the school paper. . . .

It is also relevant that the school authorities did not purport to prohibit the wearing of all symbols of political or controversial significance. The record shows that students in some of the schools wore buttons relating to national political campaigns, and some even wore the Iron Cross, traditionally a symbol of nazism. The order prohibiting the wearing of armbands did not extend to these. Instead, a particular symbol —black armbands worn to exhibit opposition to this Nation's involvement in Vietnam—was singled out for prohibition. Clearly, the prohibition of expression of one particular opinion, at least without evidence that it is necessary to avoid material and substantial interference with school work or discipline, is not constitutionally permissible.

In our system, state-operated schools may not be enclaves of totalitarianism. School officials do not possess absolute authority over their students. Students in school as well as out of school are "persons" under our Constitution. They are possessed of fundamental rights which the State must respect, just as they themselves must respect their obligations to the State. In our system, students

---

3. The only suggestions of fear of disorder in the report are these:

"A former student of one of our high schools was killed in Viet Nam. Some of his friends are still in school and it was felt that if any kind of a demonstration existed, it might evolve into something which would be difficult to control.

"Students at one of the high schools were heard to say they would wear arm bands of other colors if the black bands prevailed."

Moreover, the testimony of school authorities at trial indicates that it was not fear of disruption that motivated the regulation prohibiting the armbands; the regulation was directed against "the principle of the demonstration" itself. School authorities simply felt that "the schools are no place for demonstrations," and if the students "didn't like the way our elected officials were handling things, it should be handled with the ballot box and not in the halls of our public schools."

4. The District Court found that the school authorities, in prohibiting black armbands, were influenced by the fact that "[t]he Viet Nam war and the involvement of the United States therein has been the subject of a major controversy for some time. When the arm band regulation involved herein was promulgated, debate over the Viet Nam war had become vehement in many localities. A protest march against the war had been recently held in Washington, D.C. A wave of draft card burning incidents protesting the war had swept the country. At that time two publicized draft card burning cases were pending in this Court. Both individuals supporting the war and those opposing it were quite vocal in expressing their views." 258 F.Supp., at 972–973.

may not be regarded as closed-circuit recipients of only that which the State chooses to communicate. They may not be confined to the expression of those sentiments that are officially approved. In the absence of a specific showing of constitutionally valid reasons to regulate their speech, students are entitled to freedom of expression of their views. . . .

...In *Keyishian* v. *Board of Regents*, 385 U.S. 589, 603, 87 S.Ct. 675, 683, 17 L.Ed. 2d 629, Mr. Justice Brennan, speaking for the Court, said:

> " 'The vigilant protection of constitutional freedom is nowhere more vital than in the community of American schools.' *Shelton* v. *Tucker*, [364 U.S. 479, 487, 81 S.Ct. 247, 5 L.Ed.2d 231]. The classroom is peculiarly the 'marketplace of ideas.' The Nation's future depends upon leaders trained through wide exposure to that robust exchange of ideas which discovers truth 'out of a multitude of tongues, [rather] than through any kind of authoritative selection'. . . ."

The principle of these cases is not confined to the supervised and ordained discussion which takes place in the classroom. The principal use to which the schools are dedicated is to accommodate students during prescribed hours for the purpose of certain types of activities. Among those activities is personal intercommunication among the students. This is not only an inevitable part of the process of attending school. It is also an important part of the educational process. A student's rights therefore, do not embrace merely the classroom hours. When he is in the cafeteria, or on the playing field, or on the campus during the authorized hours, he may express his opinions, even on controversial subjects like the conflict in Vietnam, if he does so "[without] materially and substantially interfering with . . . appropriate discipline in the operation of the school" and without colliding with the rights of others. *Burnside* v. *Byars, supra*, 363 F. 2d at 749. But conduct by the student, in class or out of it, which for any reason—whether it stems from time, place, or type of behavior—materially disrupts classwork or involves substantial disorder or invasion of the rights of others is, of course, not immunized by the constitutional guaranty of freedom of speech. . . .

Under our Constitution, free speech is not a right that is given only to be so circumscribed that it exists in principle but not in fact. Freedom of expression would not truly exist if the right could be exercised only in an area that a benevolent government has provided as a safe haven for crackpots. The Constitution says that Congress (and the States) may not abridge the right to free speech. This provision means what it says. We properly read it to permit reasonable regulation of speech-connected activities in carefully restricted circumstances. But we do not confine the permissible exercise of First Amendment rights to a telephone booth or the four corners of a pamphlet, or to supervised and ordained discussion in a school classroom.

If a regulation were adopted by school officials forbidding discussion of the Vietnam conflict, or the expression by any student of opposition to it anywhere on school property except as part of a prescribed classroom exercise, it would be obvious that the regulation would violate the constitutional rights of students, at least if it could not be justified by a showing that the students' activities would materially and substantially disrupt the work and discipline of the school. . . . In the circumstances of the present case, the prohibition of the silent, passive "witness of the armbands," as one of the children called it, is no less offensive to the constitution's guaranties.

As we have discussed, the record does not demonstrate any facts which might reasonably have led school authorities to forecast substantial disruption of or material interference with school activities, and no disturbances or disorders on the school premises in fact occurred. These petitioners merely went about their ordained rounds in school. Their deviation consisted only in wearing on their sleeve a band of black cloth, not more than two inches wide. They wore it to exhibit their disapproval of the Vietnam hostilities and their advocacy of a truce, to make their views known, and by their example, to influence others to adopt them. They neither interrupted school activities nor sought to intrude in the school affairs or the lives of others. They caused discussion outside of the classrooms, but no interference with work and no disorder. In the circumstances, our Constitution does not permit officials of the State to deny their form of expression. . . .

Reversed and remanded.

MR. JUSTICE STEWART, *concurring.**

Although I agree with much of what is said in the Court's opinion, and with its judgment in this case, I cannot share the Court's uncritical assumption that, school discipline aside, the First Amendment rights of children are co-extensive with those of adults. . . . "[A] State may permissibly determine that, at least in some precisely delineated areas, a child—like someone in a captive audience—is not possessed of that full capacity for individual choice which is the presupposition of First Amendment guarantees." . . .

MR. JUSTICE BLACK, *dissenting.*

The Court's holding in this case ushers in what I deem to be an entirely new era in which the power to control pupils by the elected "officials of state supported public schools . . ." in the United States is in ultimate effect transferred to the Supreme Court. The Court brought this particular case here on a petition for *certiorari* urging that the First and Fourteenth Amendments protect the right of school pupils to express their political views all the way "from kindergarten through high school." . . .

As I read the Court's opinion it relies upon the following grounds for holding unconstitutional the judgment of the Des Moines school offi-

*[Editor's note: MR. JUSTICE WHITE, who joined the opinion of the Court, wrote an additional concurring opinion, which is omitted.]

cials and the two Courts below. First the Court concludes that the wearing of armbands is "symbolic speech" which is "akin to pure speech" and therefore protected by the First and Fourteenth Amendments. Secondly, the Court decides that the public schools are an appropriate place to exercise "symbolic speech" as long as normal school functions are not "unreasonably" disrupted. Finally, the Court arrogates to itself, rather than to the State's elected officials charged with running the schools, the decision as to which school disciplinary regulations are "reasonable."

. . . While I have always believed that under the First and Fourteenth Amendments neither the State nor Federal Government has any authority to regulate or censor the content of speech, I have never believed that any person has a right to give speeches or engage in demonstrations where he pleases and when he pleases. This Court has already rejected such a notion. In *Cox* v. *Louisiana*, 379 U.S. 536, 85 S.Ct. 453, 13 L.Ed.2d 471 (1964), for example, the Court clearly stated that the rights of free speech and assembly "do not mean that anyone with opinions or beliefs to express may address a group at any public place and at any time." . . .

While the record does not show that any of these armband students shouted, used profane language or were violent in any manner, a detailed report by some of them shows their armbands caused comments, warnings by other students, the poking of fun at them, and a warning by an older football player that other, nonprotesting students had

better let them alone. There is also evidence that the professor of mathematics had his lesson period practically "wrecked" chiefly by disputes with Beth Tinker, who wore her armband for her "demonstration." Even a casual reading of the record shows that this armband did divert students' minds from their regular lessons, and that talk, comments, etc., made John Tinker "self-conscious" in attending school with his armband. While the absence of obscene or boisterous and loud disorder perhaps justifies the Court's statement that the few armband students did not actually "disrupt" the classwork, I think the record overwhelmingly shows that the armbands did exactly what the elected school officials and principals foresaw it would, that is, took the students' minds off their classwork and diverted them to thoughts about the highly emotional subject of the Vietnam war. And I repeat that if the time has come when pupils of state-supported schools, kindergarten, grammar school or high school, can defy and flaunt orders of school officials to keep their minds on their own school work, it is the beginning of a new revolutionary era of permissiveness in this country fostered by the judiciary. . . .

. . . The truth is that a teacher of kindergarten, grammar school, or high school pupils no more carries into a school with him a complete right to freedom of speech and expression than an anti-Catholic or anti-Semitic carries with him a complete freedom of speech and religion into a Catholic church or Jewish synagogue. Nor does a person carry with him into the United States Senate or House, or to the Supreme Court, or any other court, a complete constitutional right to go into those places contrary to their rules and speak his mind on any subject he pleases. It is a myth to say that any person has a constitutional right to say what he pleases, where he pleases, and when he pleases. Our Court has decided precisely the opposite. See, e. g., *Cox* v. *Louisiana,* 379 U.S. 536, 555, 85 S.Ct. 453, 464, 13 L.Ed. 2d 471; *Adderley* v. *Florida,* 385 U.S. 39, 87 S.Ct. 242, 17 L.Ed. 149.

In my view, teachers in state-controlled public schools are hired to teach there. . . . [C]ertainly a teacher is not paid to go into school and teach subjects the State does not hire him to teach as a part of its selected curriculum. Nor are public school students sent to the schools at public expense to broadcast political or any other views to educate and inform the public. The original idea of schools, which I do not believe is yet abandoned as worthless or out of date, was that children had not yet reached the point of experience and wisdom which enabled them to teach all of their elders. It may be that the Nation has outworn the old-fashioned slogan that "children are to be seen not heard," but one may, I hope, be permitted to harbor the thought that taxpayers send children to school on the premise that at their age they need to learn, not teach.

.   .   .

. . . And as I have pointed out before, the record amply shows that public protest in the school classes against the Vietnam war "distracted from that singleness of purpose which the state (here Iowa) desired to exist in its public educational institutions." . . . But even if the record were silent as to protests against the Vietnam war distracting students from their assigned class work, members of this Court, like all other citizens, know, without being told, that the disputes over the wisdom of the Vietnam war have disrupted and divided this country as few other issues ever have. Of course students, like other people, cannot concentrate on lesser issues when black armbands are being ostentatiously displayed in their presence to call attention to the wounded and dead of the war, some of the wounded and the dead being their friends and neighbors. It was, of course, to distract the attention of other students that some students insisted up to the very point of their own suspension from school that they were determined to sit in school with their symbolic armbands.

Change has been said to be truly the law of life but sometimes the old and the tried and true are worth holding. The schools of this Nation have undoubtedly contributed to giving us tranquility and to making us a more law-abiding people. Uncontrolled and uncontrollable liberty is an enemy to domestic peace. We cannot close our eyes to the fact that some of the country's greatest problems are crimes committed by the youth, too many of school age. School discipline, like parental discipline, is an integral and important part of training our children to be good citizens—to be better citizens. Here a very small number of students have crisply and summarily refused to obey a school order designed to give pupils who want to learn the opportunity to do so. One does not need to be a prophet or the son of a prophet to know that after the Court's holding today that some students in Iowa schools and indeed in all schools will be ready, able, and willing to defy their teachers on practically all orders. This is the more unfortunate for the schools since groups of students all over the land are already running loose, conducting break-ins, sit-ins, lie-ins, and smash-ins. Many of these student groups, as is all too familiar to all who read the newspapers and watch the television news programs, have already engaged in rioting, property seizures and destruction. They have picketed schools to force students not to cross their picket lines and have too often violently attacked earnest but frightened students who wanted an education that the picketers did not want them to get. Students engaged in such activities are apparently confident that they know far more about how to operate public school systems than do their parents, teachers, and elected school officials. It is no answer to say that the particular students here have not yet reached such high points in their demands to attend classes in order to exercise their political pressures. Turned loose with law suits for damages and injunctions against their teachers like they are here, it is nothing but wishful thinking to imagine that young, immature students will not soon believe it is their right to control the schools rather than the right of the States that col-

lect the taxes to hire the teachers for the benefit of the pupils. This case, therefore, wholly without constitutional reasons in my judgment, subjects all the public schools in the country to the whims and caprices of their loudest-mouthed, but maybe not their brightest, students. I, for one, am not fully persuaded that school pupils are wise enough, even with this Court's expert help from Washington, to run the 23,390 public school systems in our 50 States. I wish, therefore, wholly to disclaim any purpose on my part, to hold that the Federal Constitution compels the teachers, parents, and elected school officials to surrender control of the American public school system to public school students. I dissent.

MR. JUSTICE HARLAN, *dissenting.*

I certainly agree that state public school authorities in the discharge of their responsibilities are not wholly exempt from the requirements of the Fourteenth Amendment respecting the freedoms of expression and association. At the same time I am reluctant to believe that there is any disagreement between the majority and myself on the proposition that school officials should be accorded the widest authority in maintaining discipline and good order in their institutions. To translate that proposition into a workable constitutional rule, I would, in cases like this, cast upon those complaining the burden of showing that a particular school measure was motivated by other than legitimate school concerns—for example, a desire to prohibit the expression of an unpopular point of view, while permitting expression of the dominant opinion.

Finding nothing in this record which impugns the good faith of respondents in promulgating the arm band regulation, I would affirm the judgment below.

QUESTIONS

1. Is a classroom a proper place for a student to register his political views about the war in Vietnam? Would every classroom be a proper place (i.e., a mathematics class)?

2. If a student may wear an armband or engage in some type of symbolic expression of his political views in a classroom, is he also within his rights to speak his views or circulate leaflets in class? Why or why not?

3. If the two should conflict, where, if at all, would you draw the line between a student's right to express his political beliefs in class and the other students right to learn unimpeded the subject matter of that course? Who should draw that line? What is your justification(s) for drawing the line where you have?

4. Would you object to having a student wear a swastika armband to class to express his *sincerely* held anti-semitic convictions or a Ku Klux Klan badge indicating he subscribed to white supremacy? Why or why not? How about a big button that says "Black is Best" or "Fuck S.D.S." or "Birchism = Americanism"?

5. Is this decision reconcilable with the one in the *O'Brien* case? Why do you think it is? Why not? Why is a majority of the Supreme Court willing to conclude "symbolic speech" is constitutionally protected in this case, when it seems they hold to the contrary in the *O'Brien* case?

OESTEREICH v. SELECTIVE SERVICE SYSTEM BD. #11, CHEYENNE, WYOMING

393 U.S. 233; 89 S. Ct. 414; 21 L.Ed. 2d 402 (1968)

MR. JUSTICE DOUGLAS *delivered the opinion of the Court.*

Petitioner is enrolled as a student at a theological school preparing for the ministry and was accordingly classified as IV–D by the Selective Service Board. Section 6(g) of the Selective Service Act, 50 U.S.C. App. § 456(g), gives such students exemption from training and service under the Act.[1] He returned his registration certificate to the Government, according to the complaint in the present action, "for the sole purpose of expressing dissent from the participation by the United States in the war in Vietnam." Shortly thereafter his Board declared him delinquent (1) for failure to have the registration certificate in his possession, and (2) for failure to provide the Board with notice of his local status. The Board thereupon changed his IV–D classification to I–A. He took an administrative appeal and lost and was ordered to report for induction.

At that point he brought suit to restrain his induction. The District Court dismissed the complaint, 280 F.Supp. 78, and the Court of Appeals affirmed. . . .

As noted, § 6(g) of the Act states that "students preparing for the ministry" in qualified schools "shall be exempt from training and service" under the Act. Equally unambiguous is § 10(b) (3) of the Military Selective Service Act of 1967, 81 Stat. 100, which provides that there shall be no preinduction judicial review "of the classification or processing of any registrant,"[4] judicial review being limited to a defense in a criminal prosecution or, as the Government concedes, to *habeas corpus* after induction.[5] . . . If we assume, as we must for present purposes, that petitioner is entitled to a statutory exemption as a divinity student, by what authority can the Board withhold it or withdraw it and make him a delinquent?

In 1967 Congress added a provision concerning the immediate service of a "prime age group" after expiration of their deferment, stating that they were the first to be inducted "after delinquents and volunteers." 50 U.S.C. App. § 456(h) (1). Congress has also made criminal the knowing failure or neglect to perform any duty prescribed by the rules or regulations of the Selective Service System. 50 U.S.C. App. § 462(a). But Congress did not de-

1. Section 6(g) reads as follows:
"Regular or duly ordained ministers of religion, as defined in this title, and students preparing for the ministry under the direction of recognized churches or religious organizations, who are satisfactorily pursuing full-time courses of instruction in recognized theological or divinity schools, or who are satisfactorily pursuing full-time courses of instruction leading to their entrance into recognized theological or divinity schools in which they have been pre-enrolled shall be exempt from training and service (but not from registration) under this title."
4. Section 10(b) (3) reads as follows:
"No judicial review shall be made of the classification or processing of any registrant by local boards, appeal boards, or the President, except as a defense to a criminal prosecution instituted under section 12 of this title, after the registrant has responded either affirmatively or negatively to an order to report for induction, or for civilian work in the case of a registrant determined to be opposed to participation in war in any form: *Provided* That such review shall go to the question of the jurisdiction herein reserved to local boards, appeal boards, and the President only when there is no basis in fact for the classification assigned to such registrant."
5. S. Rep. No. 209, 90th Cong., 1st Sess., p. 10.
"A registrant who presents himself for induction may challenge his classification by seeking a writ of *habeas corpus* after his induction. If the registrant does not submit to induction, he may raise as a defense to a criminal prosecution the issue of the legality of the classification." . . .

fine delinquency; nor did it provide any standards for its definition by the Selective Service System. Yet Selective Service, as we have noted, has promulgated regulations governing delinquency and uses them to deprive registrants of their statutory exemption, because of various activities and conduct and without any regard to the exemptions provided by law.

We can find no authorization for that use of delinquency. Even if Congress had authorized the Boards to revoke statutory exemptions by means of delinquency classifications, serious questions would arise if Congress were silent and did not prescribe standards to govern the Boards' actions. There is no suggestion in the legislative history that, when Congress has granted an exemption and a registrant meets its terms and conditions, a Board can nonetheless withhold it from him for activities or conduct not material to the grant or withdrawal of the exemption. So to hold would make the Boards freewheeling agencies meting out their brand of justice in a vindictive manner.

Once a person registers and qualifies for a statutory exemption, we find no legislative authority to deprive him of that exemption because of conduct or activities unrelated to the merits of granting or continuing that exemption. The Solicitor General confesses error on the use by Selective Service of delinquency proceedings for that purpose.

We deal with conduct of a local Board that is basically lawless. It is no different in constitutional implications from a case where induction of an ordained minister or other clearly exempt person is ordered (a) to retaliate against the person because of his political views or (b) to bear down on him for his religious views or his racial attitudes or (c) to get him out of town so that the amorous interests of a Board member might be better served. . . . In such instances, as in the present one, there is no exercise of discretion by a Board in evaluating evidence and in determining whether a claimed exemption is deserved. The case we decide today involves a clear departure by the Board from its statutory mandate. To hold that a person deprived of his statutory exemption in such a blatantly lawless manner must either be inducted and raise his protest through *habeas corpus* or defy induction and defend his refusal in a criminal prosecution is to construe the Act with unnecessary harshness. As the Solicitor General suggests, such literalness does violence to the clear mandate of § 6(g) governing the exemption. Our construction leaves § 10(b) (3) unimpaired in the normal operations of the Act.

. . . Since the exemption granted divinity students is plain and unequivocal and in no way contested here,[7] and since the scope of the statutory delinquency concept is not broad enough to sustain a revocation of what Congress has granted as a

---

7. We would have a somewhat different problem were the contest over, say, the quantum of evidence necessary to sustain a Board's classification. Then we would not be able to say that it was plain on the record and on the face of the Act that an exemption had been granted and there would therefore be no clash between § 10(b) (3) and another explicit provision of the Act.

statutory right, or sufficiently buttressed by legislative standards, we conclude that pre-induction judicial review is not precluded in cases of this type.

We accordingly reverse the judgment and remand the case to the District Court where petitioner must have the opportunity to prove the facts alleged and also to demonstrate that he meets the jurisdictional requirements of 28 U.S.C. § 1331. *Reversed.*

MR. JUSTICE HARLAN, *concurring in the result.*

. . .

At the outset, I think it is important to state what this case does and does not involve. Petitioner does not contend that the Selective Service System has improperly resolved factual questions, or wrongfully exercised its discretion, or even that it has acted "without any basis in fact," as that phrase is commonly used in this area of law. . . . He asserts, rather, that the procedure pursuant to which he was reclassified and ordered to report for induction— a procedure plainly mandated by the System's self-promulgated published regulations, 32 CFR, part 1642—is unlawful. Specifically, he asserts that the delinquency reclassification scheme is not authorized by any statute, that it is inconsistent with his statutory exemption as a ministerial student, 50 U.S.C. App. § 456(g), and that, whether or not approved by Congress, the regulations are facially unconstitutional.

The pivotal language of § 10(b) (3), for present purposes, is the statute's proscription of pre-induction judicial review "of the classifi-cation or processsing of any registrant . . . ." I take the phrase "classification or processing" to encompass the numerous discretionary, factual, and mixed law-fact determinations which a Selective Service board must make prior to issuing an order to report for induction. I do not understand that phrase to prohibit review of a claim, such as that made here by petitioner, that the very statutes or regulations which the board administers are facially invalid.

. . .

Congress' decision to defer judicial review of such decisions by the Selective Service boards until after induction was, I believe, responsive to two major considerations. *First,* because these determinations are of an individualized and discretionary nature, a reviewing court must often examine board records and other documentary evidence, hear testimony, and resolve controversies on a sizeable record. . . .

Second, the registrant has been afforded, prior to his induction, the opportunity for a hearing and administrative appeals within the Selective Service System. 32 CFR, parts 1624–1627. It is properly presumed that a registrant's board has fully considered all relevant information presented to it, and that it has classified and processed him regularly, and in accordance with the applicable statutes and regulations. . . .

These factors are significantly altered where the registrant contends that the procedure employed by the board is invalid on its face.

First, such a claim does not invite the court to review the factual and discretionary decisions inherent in the "classification or processing" of registrants, and does not, therefore, present opportunity for protracted delay. . . .

Second, a challenge to the validity of the administrative procedure itself not only renders irrelevant the presumption of regularity, but presents an issue beyond the competence of the Selective Service boards to hear and determine. Adjudication of the constitutionality of congressional enactments has generally been thought beyond the jurisdiction of administrative agencies. . . .

To withhold pre-induction review in this case would, thus, deprive petitioner of his liberty without the prior opportunity to present to *any* competent forum—agency or court—his substantial claim that he was ordered inducted pursuant to an unlawful procedure. Such an interpretation of § 10(b) (3) would raise serious constitutional problems,[6] and is not indicated by the statute's history, language, or purpose. On the foregoing basis I agree that § 10(b) (3) does not forbid pre-induction review in this instance.

Because both the District Court and the Court of Appeals passed on the merits of petitioner's challenge to the delinquency reclassification regulations, this issue is ripe for our consideration. Whatever validity the procedure may have under other circumstances, I agree that the delinquency reclassification of petitioner for failure to possess his registration certificate is inconsistent with petitioner's conceded statutory exemption as a student of the ministry.

MR. JUSTICE STEWART, *with whom* MR. JUSTICE BRENNAN *and* MR. JUSTICE WHITE *join, dissenting.*

It is clear that in enacting § 10(b) (3) of the Military Selective Service Act of 1967, Congress intended to specify the exclusive methods by which the determinations of selective service boards may be judicially reviewed. Since under the terms of that provision the present suit is plainly premature, I would affirm the judgment of the Court of Appeals.

Section 10(b) (3) provides in pertinent part as follows:

> "No judicial review shall be made of the classification or processing of any registrant by local boards, appeal boards, or the President, except as a defense to a criminal prosecution instituted under section 12 of this title, after the registrant has responded either affirmatively or negatively to an order to report for induction. . . ."

It is unquestioned that the overriding purpose of this provision was "to prevent litigious interruptions of procedures to provide necessary military manpower." To be sure, the provision is somewhat inartistically drawn, but its background and legislative history clearly resolve whatever difficulties might otherwise be presented by the imprecision of the draftsman's language.

In interpreting the less explicit terms of predecessor statutes, this

---

6. It is doubtful whether a person may be deprived of his personal liberty without the prior opportunity to be heard by some tribunal competent fully to adjudicate his claims. . . .

Court had established the general rule that draft classifications could not be judicially reviewed prior to the time a registrant was to be inducted. Review was held to be proper only when challenges to such determinations were raised either (1) in defense to a criminal prosecution following a refusal to be inducted, or (2) in *habeas corpus* proceedings initiated after induction. . . .

. . .

Thus there can be no doubt that § 10(b) (3) was designed to permit judicial review of draft classifications only in connection with criminal prosecutions or *habeas corpus* proceedings. Today, however, the Court holds that § 10(b) (3) does not mean what it says in a case like this, where it is "plain on the record and on the face of the Act that an exemption ha[s] been granted." In such a case, it is said, there is a "clash" between the exemption and the provisions of § 10(b) (3). With all respect, I am simply unable to perceive any "clash" whatsoever. Exemptions from service are substantive, while § 10(b) (3) is purely procedural, specifying *when* substantive rights may be asserted. How the Court can conclude that the provisions of § 10(b) (3) somehow do "violence to" the divinity student exemption is a mystery to me.

The only other reason the Court offers for its casual disregard of § 10(b) (3) is the suggestion that obedience to the statute would lead to "unnecessary harshness." But if the statute is constitutional, we have no power to disregard it simply because we think it is harsh. That is a judgment for Congress, not for us. And the Court does not question the law's constitutionality. To the contrary, the constitutionality of § 10(b) (3) is upheld this very day in *Clark v. Gabriel*, 393 U.S. 256, 89 S.Ct. 424, 21 L.Ed.2d 418, in reaffirmation of several previous decisions in which this Court has enunciated and applied the rule against pre-induction review of selective service determinations.

. . .

I respectfully dissent.

QUESTIONS

1. Why does the majority opinion express concern over the lack of legislative standards provided by Congress to govern local Draft Boards in applying the "delinquency section" of the Selective Service Act? What is wrong, if anything, with Draft Boards providing their own guidelines for determining if a registrant is "delinquent" and ought to be reclassified?

2. Do you think this majority opinion by Justice Douglas is hard to reconcile with the Court's opinion in *O'Brien* in that, in both cases, failure to have the draft card—whether because it is burned or given away—impairs the functioning of the Selective Service System as outlined in the *O'Brien* case?

3. Why shouldn't Oestereich be classified as "delinquent" since there are many other ways of protesting the war in Vietnam without violating his Selective Service duties?

4. Do you think special exemptions for divinity students constitutes an "unfair" discrimination against atheists? Isn't such an exemption a violation of the First Amendment requirement that "Congress shall make no law respecting an establishment of religion. . ."? Justify your opinion.

5. Aren't all "conscientious objection" classifications similarly a violation of the First Amendment? Why yes? Why no?

GUTKNECHT v. UNITED STATES

396 U.S. 295; 90 S. Ct. 506; 24 L.Ed. 2d 532 (1970)

MR. JUSTICE DOUGLAS *delivered the opinion of the Court.*

This case presents an important question under the Military Selective Service Act of 1967. 62 Stat. 604, as amended, 65 Stat. 75, 81 Stat. 100.

Petitioner registered with his Selective Service Local Board and was classified I–A. Shortly thereafter he received a II–S (student) classification. In a little over a year he notified the Board that he was no longer a student and was classified I–A. Meanwhile he had asked for an exemption as a conscientious objector. The Board denied that exemption, reclassifying him as I–A, and he appealed to the State Board. While that appeal was pending, he surrendered his registration certificate and notice of classification by leaving them on the steps of the Federal Building in Minneapolis with a statement explaining he was opposed

to the war in Vietnam. That was on October 16, 1967. On November 22, 1967, his appeal to the State Board was denied. On November 27, 1967, he was notified that he was I–A.

On December 20, 1967, he was declared delinquent by the local board. On December 26, 1967, he was ordered to report for induction on January 24, 1968. He reported at the induction center, but in his case the normal procedure of induction was not followed. Rather, he signed a statement, "I refuse to take part or all [*sic*] of the prescribed processing." Thereafter he was indicted for wilfully and knowingly failing and neglecting "to perform a duty required of him" under the Act. He was tried without a jury, found guilty, and sentenced to four years' imprisonment. *United States* v. *Gutknecht*, D.C., 283 F.Supp. 945. His conviction was affirmed by the Court of Appeals. 8 Cir., 406 F.2d

494. The case is here on a petition for a writ of *certiorari*, 394 U.S. 997, 89 S.Ct. 1595, 22 L.Ed.2d 775.

I.

Among the defenses tendered at the trial was the legality of the delinquency Regulations which were applied to petitioner. It is that single question which we will consider.

By the Regulations promulgated under the Act a local board may declare a registrant to be a "delinquent" whenever he

"has failed to perform any duty or duties required of him under the selective service law other than the duty to comply with an Order to Report for Induction (SSS Form No. 252) or the duty to comply with an Order to Report for Civilian Work and Statement of Employer (SSS Form No. 153). . . ." 32 CFR § 1642.4.

In this case, petitioner was declared a delinquent for failing to have his registration certificate (SSS Form No. 2) and current classification notice (SSS Form No. 110) in his personal possession at all times, as required by 32 CFR §§ 1617.1 and 1623.5 respectively.

The consequences of being declared a delinquent under § 1642.4 are of two types: (1) Registrants who have deferments or exemptions may be reclassified in one of the classes available for service, I–A, I–A–O, or I–O, whichever is deemed applicable. 32 CFR § 1642.12. (2) Registrants who are already classified I–A, I–A–O, or I–O, and those who are reclassified to such a status, will be given first priority in the order of call for induction, requiring them to be called even ahead of volunteers for induction. 32 CFR § 1642.13. The latter consequence deprives the registrant of his previous standing in the order of call as set out in 32 CFR § 1631.7.[1]

. . .

II.

There is a preliminary point which must be mentioned and that is the suggestion that petitioner should have taken an administrative appeal from the order declaring him "delinquent" and that his failure to do so bars the defense in the criminal prosecution.

The pertinent Regulation is 32 CFR § 1642.14, which gives a delinquent who "is classified in or reclassified into Class I–A, Class I–A–O or Class I–O" three rights:

(a) the right to a personal appearance, upon request, *"under the same circumstances as in any other case";*

(b) the right to have his classification reopened *"in the discretion of the local board";* and

---

1. Under the terms of 32 CFR § 1631.7 (a). (1) in effect at the time of petitioners trial, the first in line for induction were "Delinquents who have attained the age of 19 years in the order of their dates of birth with the oldest being selected first." That provision has been included in the new § 1631.7 (a) promulgated after the random system of selection, discussed hereafter, was adopted.

(c) the right to an appeal *"under the same circumstances and by the same persons as in any other case."*

The right to a personal appearance "in any other case" is covered by 32 CFR § 1624.1(a). That section gives the right to "every registrant *after his classification is determined by the local board"* provided a request is made therefor within 30 days. The action taken against this petitioner, however, did not involve classification. The term "classification" is used exclusively in the Regulations to refer to classification in one of the classes determining availability for service, *e. g.,* I–A, I–O. See 32 CFR Pts. 1621–1623. "Delinquency" is not such a classification, and a registrant is "declared" a delinquent, *not* "classified" as a delinquent. . . .

*The right to reopen his classification is also irrelevant to petitioner as he is not attacking his classification, but only his accelerated induction.**

The right to appeal "in any other case" is covered by 32 CFR § 1626.2 (a). That section provides that "the registrant . . . may appeal to an appeal board *from the classification of a registrant by the local board."*

Again, since petitioner was not classified in conjunction with his delinquency, but only had his induction accelerated, it would mean that he did not have the right to an appeal under the Regulations. We are not advised in any authoritative way, that this interpretation of the Regulations is contrary to the administrative construction of them or to the accepted practice.

* [*Editor's Note: Emphasis added.*]

III.

We come then to the merits. The problem of "delinquency" goes back to the 1917 Act. . . . The present "delinquency" Regulations with which we are concerned stem from the 1948 Act.

The Regulations issued under the 1948 Act were substantially identical to the present delinquency regulations. . . .

.   .   .

Oestereich involved a case where a divinity school student with a statutory exemption and a IV–D classification was declared "delinquent" for turning in his registration certificate to the government in protest to the war in Vietnam. His Board thereupon reclassified him as I–A. After he exhausted his administrative remedies, he was ordered to report for induction. At that point he brought suit in the District Court for judicial review of the action by the Board. We held that under the unusual circumstances of the case, pre-induction judicial review was permissible prior to induction and that there was no statutory authorization to use the "delinquency" procedure to deprive a registrant of a statutory exemption. We said:

"There is no suggestion in the legislative history that, when Congress has granted an exemption and a registrant meets its terms and conditions, a Board can nonetheless withhold it from him for activities or conduct not material to the grant or withdrawal of the exemption. So to hold would make the Boards free-wheeling agencies meting out their brand of justice in a vindictive manner.

"Once a person registers and qualifies for a statutory exemption, we find no legislative authority to deprive him of that exemption because of conduct or activities unrelated to the merits of granting or continuing that exemption." 393 U.S., at 237, 89 S.Ct. at 416.

The question in the instant case is different because no "exemption," no "deferment," no "classification" in the statutory sense is involved. "Delinquency" was used here not to change a classification but to accelerate petitioner's induction from the third category to the first; and it was that difference which led the Court of Appeals to conclude that what we said in *Oestereich* was not controlling here.

Deferment of the order of call may be the bestowal of great benefits; and its acceleration may be extremely punitive. As already indicated, the statutory policy is the selection of persons for training and service "in an impartial manner." 50 U.S.C. App. § 455(a) (1). That is the only express statutory provision which gives specific content to that phrase. That section does permit people registered at one time to be selected "before, together with, or after" persons registered at a prior time. Moreover, those who have not reached the age of 19 are given a deferred position in the order of call. But those variations in the phrase "in an impartial manner" are of no particular help in the instant case, except to underline the concern of

Congress with the integrity of that phrase.

We know from the legislative history that, while Congress did not address itself specifically to the "delinquency" issue, it was vitally concerned with the order of selection, as well as with exemptions and deferments. Thus in 1967 a Conference Report brought House and Senate together against the grant of power to the President to initiate "a random system of selection"—a grant which, it was felt, would preclude Congress from "playing an affirmative role" in the constitutional task of "raising armies." H.Rep. No. 346, *supra,* at 9–10. It is difficult to believe that with that show of resistance to grant of a more limited power, there was acquiescence in the delegation of a broad, sweeping power to Selective Service to discipline registrants through the "delinquency" device.

The problem of the order of induction was once more before the Congress late in 1969. Section 5(a) (2) of the 1967 Act, 50 U.S.C. App. § 455(a) (2) provided:

"Notwithstanding the provisions of paragraph (1) of this subsection, the President in establishing the order of induction for registrants within the various age groups found qualified for induction shall not effect any change in the method of determining the relative order of induction for such registrants within such age groups as has been heretofore established and in effect on the date of enactment of this paragraph, unless authorized by law enacted after the date of enactment of the Military Selective Service Act of 1967."

While § 5(a) (2) gave the President authority to designate a prime age group for induction, it required him to select from the oldest first within the group. S.Rep. No. 91–531, 91st Cong., 1st Sess., p. 1. The Act of November 26, 1969, 83 Stat. 220, repealed § 5(a) (2) pursuant to a request of the President that a random system of selection be authorized. See S.Rep. No. 91–531, *supra,* pp. 3–4; H.R.Rep. No. 91–577, 91st Cong., 1st Sess., pp. 2, 9.[5] The random system has now been put in force.[6] It applies of course only prospectively. But its legislative history, as well as the concern of the Congress that the order in which registrants are inducted be achieved "in an impartial manner," emphasizes a deep concern by Congress with the problems of the order of induction as well as with those of exemptions, deferments, and classifications.

While § 5(a) (1) provides that "there shall be no discrimination against any person on account of race or color," 50 U.S.C. App. §

455(a) (1), there is no suggestion that as respects other types of discrimination the Selective Service has free-wheeling authority to ride herd on the registrants using immediate induction as a disciplinary or vindictive measure.

The power under the regulations to declare a registrant "delinquent" has no statutory standard or even guidelines. The power is exercised entirely at the discretion of the local board. It is a broad, roving authority, a type of administrative absolutism not congenial to our law-making traditions. In *Kent* v. *Dulles,* 357 U.S. 116, 128–129, 78 S.Ct. 1113, 1119–1120, 2 L.Ed.2d 1204, we refused to impute to Congress the grant of "unbridled discretion" to the Secretary of State to issue or withhold a passport from a citizen "for any substantive reason he may choose." . . . Where the liberties of the citizen are involved, we said that "we will construe narrowly all delegated powers that curtail or dilute them." . . . The Director of Selective Service described the "delinquency" regulations as designed "to prevent, wherever possible, prosecutions for minor in-

---

5. And see 115 Cong.Rec., October 29, 1969, p. H 10255 *et seq., ibid.* October 30, 1969, pp. H 10301 *et seq.,* H 10313 *et seq., ibid.* November 19, 1969, p. S 14632 *et seq.*

6. The random selection was established by the President through Proclamation 3945, on November 26, 1969. 34 Fed.Reg. 19017 (November 29, 1969).

7. "The escalation of the United States military involvement in Vietnam increased the draft calls, and there was an upsurge of public demonstrations in protest. Some of these protests took the form of turning 'draft' cards in to various public officials of the Department of Justice, the State or National Headquarters of Selective Service System, or directly to local boards. By

agreement with the Department of Justice, registrants who turned in cards (as contrasted to those who burned cards) were not prosecuted under section 12(a) of the Military Selective Service Law of 1967, but were processed administratively by the local boards. In many instances, the local boards determined that a deferment of such registrant was no longer in the national interest, and he was reclassified 1-A delinquent for failure to perform a duty required of him under the Act, namely retaining in his possession the Registration Card and current Notice of Classification card." Hershey, Legal Aspects of Selective Service 46–47 (1969).

fraction of rules" during the selective service processing.[7] We search the Act in vain for any clues that Congress desired the Act to have punitive sanctions apart from the criminal prosecutions specifically authorized. Nor do we read it as granting personal privileges which may be forfeited for transgressions which affront the local board. If federal or state laws are violated by registrants, they can be prosecuted. If induction is to be substituted for these prosecutions, a vast rewriting of the Act is needed. Standards would be needed by which the legality of a declaration of "delinquency" could be judged. And the regulations, when written, would be subject to the customary inquiries as to infirmities on their face or in their application, including the question whether they were used to penalize or punish the free exercise of constitutional rights.
Reversed.

MR. CHIEF JUSTICE BURGER *concurs in the result reached by the Court generally for the reasons set out in the separate opinion of* MR. JUSTICE STEWART.

MR. JUSTICE WHITE *joins the opinion of the Court insofar as it holds that Congress has not delegated to the President the authority to promulgate the delinquency regulations involved in this case.*

MR. JUSTICE HARLAN, *concurring.*

I join the Court's opinion with the following observations. First, as I see it, nothing in the Court's opinion prevents a selective service board, under the present statute and existing regulations, from classifying as I–A a registrant who fails to provide his board with information essential to the determination of whether he qualifies for a requested exemption or deferment. . . . I assume, of course, that under this regulation a board has no authority to keep a registrant classified I–A once it has information which justifies some lower classification.

Second, I think it entirely possible that consistent with our opinion today the President might promulgate new regulations, restricted in application to cases in which a registrant fails to comply with a duty essential to the classification process itself, that provide for accelerated induction under the existing statute. However, in order to avoid those punitive features now found to be unauthorized under existing legislation, any new regulations would have to give to a registrant being subjected to accelerated induction the right (like a person held in civil contempt) to avoid any sanction by future compliance. In other words, while existing legislation does not authorize the use of accelerated induction to punish past transgressions, it may well authorize acceleration to encourage a registrant to bring himself into compliance with rules essential to the operation of the classification process.

MR. JUSTICE STEWART, *concurring in the judgment.*

I do not reach the question whether Congress has authorized the delinquency regulations, because even under the regulations the petitioner's conviction cannot stand. After the petitioner's local board declared him delinquent, he had 30 days as a matter of right to seek a personal appearance before the board and to take an appeal from its ruling. Yet the board gave him no chance to assert either of those rights. Instead, it ordered him to report for induction only five days after it had mailed him a notice of the delinquency declaration.

The local board thus violated the very regulations it purported to enforce. Those provisions seek to induce Selective Service registrants to satisfy their legal obligations by presenting them with the alternative prospect of induction into the armed forces. The personal appearance and appeal are critical stages in the delinquency process. They enable the registrant declared delinquent by his local board to contest the factual premises on which the delinquency declaration rests, to correct his oversight if the breach of duty has arisen merely from neglect, or to purge himself of his delinquency if his violation has been willful. In any event, the regulatory objective is remedial. The board's authority to reclassify a registrant based on his delinquency and to accelerate his induction is analogous to the age-old power of the courts to pronounce judgments of civil contempt. In each case the subject of the order "carries the keys . . . in his own pocket" to the termination of the order's effect.

· · ·

Accordingly, even though the regulations seem to say that such reopening and removal lie within the discretion of the local board, the Government agrees that the board would abuse its discretion if it refused such remedial relief to a registrant who breached his duty inadvertently or carelessly, or who sought to correct the breach, even if originally willful, and to return to compliance with his obligations. But the Government argues that in this case the petitioner cannot avail himself of these provisions in the delinquency regulations, because he made no effort to correct his delinquency. The fact is that the petitioner's local board never gave him a chance to purge his delinquency. It declared him a delinquent on December 20, 1967, sent him a notice to that effect the next day, and five days later ordered him to report for induction, more than two weeks before the expiration of the petitioner's time to seek a personal appearance or take an appeal. In these circumstances the petitioner's failure to seek his local board's advice on what he should do, as suggested by the delinquency notice, does not detract from the force of his attack upon the validity of his criminal conviction.

The Government also argues that the petitioner was not prejudiced by the local board's departure from the prescribed regulatory routine because when he was declared delinquent he was already classified I–A. But the Court of Appeals noted that the petitioner's induction date was advanced as a result of the declaration, and the Government concedes that since the petitioner was only 20 years old at the time, it is unlikely that he would have been called at such an early date had he not been declared a delinquent. That the petitioner might eventually have been called—by no means a certainty, given the variations in draft calls and the possibility that he might subsequently have qualified for a deferment or exemption—does not mean he cannot complain that he was ordered to report for induction earlier than he should have been.

Finally, it is said that the petitioner had no right to a personal appearance before the local board and an appeal from its ruling because its delinquency declaration did not entail his removal into Class I–A from some other category. Since the petitioner was already I–A, the argu-

ment runs, his local board never "reclassified" him; it just shifted him from a lower to the highest category within the I–A order of call. . . . The regulation, recognizing that the status of the registrant prior to his being declared delinquent and placed at the head of the order of call is irrelevant to the delinquency process, ensures that all registrants declared delinquent will enjoy the same rights of personal appearance and appeal without regard to their previous status.

Because the challenged regulations afford the petitioner procedural rights that his local board never gave him a chance to exercise, I would reverse the judgment of conviction.

QUESTIONS

1. What relationship does the constitutional grant of legislative authority to Congress have to the question of which agent of power develops standards to define "delinquency" under Selective Service?

2. Do you agree with Justice Harlan that nothing in the *Gutknecht* opinion—which he joined—prevents Congress from legislating the speed up of inductions to punish people who hamper the operation of the Selective Service System?

3. Should Congress and/or the local Draft Boards have the power to speed up induction for being "delinquent" *in a case* like *Gutknecht*? Is the "delinquency" classification being used here to restrict constitutionally protected dissent and, if so, isn't this repressive? What is your opinion on these questions? Justify your position.

4. Speculate about the long-run implications for any society which allows a young man to violate the law in order to protest against the war when he has other means of protest legally available to him.

5. What similarities and what differences do you see between the *Oestereich* and *Gutknecht* cases?

BACHELLAR v. MARYLAND

397 U.S. 564; 90 S. Ct. 1312; 25 L.Ed. 2d 570 (1970)

MR. JUSTICE BRENNAN *delivered the opinion of the Court.*

A jury in Baltimore City Criminal Court convicted petitioners of violating Md.Code Ann., Art. 27, § 123 (1967),[1] which prohibits "acting in a disorderly manner to the disturbance of the public peace, upon any public street . . . in any [Maryland] city. . . ."[2] The prosecution arose out of a demonstration protesting the Vietnam War which was staged between 3 and shortly after 5 o'clock on the afternoon of March 28, 1966, in front of a United States Army recruiting station located on a downtown Baltimore street. The Maryland Court of Special Appeals rejected petitioners' contention that their conduct was constitutionally protected under the First and Fourteenth Amendments and affirmed their convictions. 3 Md.App. 626, 240 A.2d 623 (1968). The Court of Appeals of Maryland denied *certiorari* in an unreported order. We granted *certiorari*, 396 U.S. 816, 90 S.Ct. 109, 24 L.Ed.2d 68 (1969). We reverse.

The trial judge instructed the jury that there were alternative grounds upon which petitioners might be found guilty of violating § 123. The judge charged, first, that a guilty verdict might be returned if the jury found that petitioners had engaged in "the doing or saying or both of that which offends, disturbs, incites or tends to incite a number of people gathered in the same area." The judge also told the jury that "[a] refusal to obey a policeman's command to move on when not to do so may endanger the public peace, may amount to disorderly conduct."[3] So

1. The trial in the Criminal Court was *de novo* upon appeal from a conviction in the Municipal Court of Baltimore. The Criminal Court judge sentenced each petitioner to 60 days in jail and a $50 fine.

2. The statute was amended in 1968 but without change in the operative language involved in this case. See Md.Code Ann., Art. 27, § 123(c) (1969 Supp.).

3. Both elements of the instruction were based on the Maryland Court of Appeals' construction of § 123 in *Drews v. Maryland*, 224 Md. 186, 192, 167 A.2d 341, 343–344 (1961), vacated and remanded on other grounds, 378 U.S. 547, 84 S.Ct. 1900, 12 L.Ed.2d 1032 (1964), reaffirmed on remand, 236 Md. 349, 204 A.2d 64 (1964), appeal dismissed and *cert.* denied, 381 U.S. 421, 85 S.Ct. 1576, 14 L.Ed.2d 693 (1965). The instruction was "that disorderly conduct is the doing or saying or both

of that which offends, disturbs, incites or tends to incite a number of people gathered in the same area. It is conduct of such nature as to affect the peace and quiet of persons who may witness it and who may be disturbed or provoked to resentment because of it. A refusal to obey a policeman's command to move on when not to do so may endanger the public peace, may amount to disorderly conduct."

The trial judge refused to grant petitioners' request that the jury be charged to disregard any anger of onlookers that arose from their disagreement with petitioners' expressed views about Vietnam. For example, the judge refused to instruct the jury that "if the only threat of public disturbance arising from the actions of these defendants was a threat that arose from the anger of others who were made angry by their disagreement with the defendants' instructed, the jury returned a general verdict of guilty against each of the petitioners.

. . .

Baltimore law enforcement authorities had advance notice of the demonstration, and a dozen or more police officers and some United States marshals were on hand when approximately 15 protesters began peacefully to march in a circle on the sidewalk in front of the station. The marchers carried or wore signs bearing such legends as: "Peasant Emancipation, Not Escalation," "Make Love not War," "Stop in the Name of Love," and "Why are We in Viet Nam?" The number of protesters increased to between 30 and 40 before the demonstration ended. A crowd of onlookers gathered nearby and across the street. From time to time some of the petitioners and other marchers left the circle and distributed leaflets among and talked to persons in the crowd. The lieutenant in charge of the police detail testified that he "overheard" some of the marchers debate with members of the crowd about "the Viet Cong situation," and that a few in the crowd resented the protest; "[o]ne particular one objected very much to receiving the circular." However, the lieutenant did not think that the situation constituted a disturbance of the peace. He testified that "[a]s long as the peace was not disturbed I wasn't doing anything about it."

Clearly the wording of the plac-

ards was not within that small class of "fighting words" which, under *Chaplinsky* v. *New Hampshire*, 315 U.S. 568, 574, 62 S.Ct. 766, 770, 86 L.Ed. 1031 (1942), are "likely to provoke the average person to retaliation, and thereby cause a breach of the peace," nor is there any evidence that the demonstrators' remarks to the crowd constituted "fighting words." Any shock effect caused by the placards, remarks and peaceful marching must be attributed to the content of the ideas being expressed, or to the onlookers' dislike of demonstrations as a means of expressing dissent. But "[i]t is firmly settled that under our Constitution the public expression of ideas may not be prohibited merely because the ideas are themselves offensive to some of their hearers," . . . or simply because bystanders object to peaceful and orderly demonstrations. Plainly nothing that occurred during this period could constitutionally be the grounds for conviction under § 123. Indeed, the State makes no claim that § 123 was violated then.

We turn now to the events which occurred shortly before and after 5 o'clock. The petitioners had left the marchers after half past 3 to enter the recruiting station. There they had attempted to persuade the sergeant in charge to permit them to display their antiwar materials in the station or in its window fronting on the sidewalk. The sergeant had told them that Army regulations forbade him

expressed views concerning Viet Nam, or American involvement in Viet Nam, you must acquit these defendants. And if you have a reasonable doubt whether the anger of those other persons was occasioned by

their disagreement with defendants' views on Viet Nam, rather than by the conduct of defendants in sitting or staying on the street, you must acquit these defendants."

to grant such permission. The six thereupon staged a sit-in on chairs and a couch in the station.[4] A few minutes before 5 o'clock the sergeant asked them to leave, as he wanted to close the station for the day. When petitioners refused, the sergeant called on United States marshals who were present in the station to remove them. After deputizing several police officers to help, the marshals undertook to eject the petitioners.[5]

There is irreconcilable conflict in the evidence as to what next occurred. The prosecution's witnesses testified that the marshals and the police officers "escorted" the petitioners outside, and that the petitioners thereupon sat or lay down, "blocking free passage of the sidewalk." The police lieutenant in charge stated that he then took over and three times ordered the petitioners to get up and leave. He testified that when they remained sitting or lying down, he had each of them picked up bodily and removed to a patrol wagon. In sharp contrast, defense witnesses said that each petitioner was thrown bodily out the door of the station and landed on his back, that petitioners were not positioned so as to block the sidewalk completely, and that no police command was given to them to move away; rather, on the contrary, that as some of them struggled to get to their feet, they were held

down by the police officers until they were picked up and thrown into the patrol wagon. The evidence is clear, however, that while petitioners were on the sidewalk, they began to sing "We Shall Overcome" and that they were surrounded by other demonstrators carrying antiwar placards. Thus, petitioners remained obvious participants in the demonstration even after their expulsion from the recruiting station.[6] A crowd of 50–150 people, including the demonstrators, was in the area during this period.

The reaction of the onlookers to these events was substantially the same as that to the earlier events of the afternoon. The police lieutenant added only that two uniformed marines in the crowd appeared angry and that a few other bystanders "were debating back and forth about Bomb Hanoi and different things and I had to be out there to protect these people because they wouldn't leave." Earlier too, however, some of the crowd had taken exception to the petitioners' protest against the Vietnam war.

On this evidence, in light of the instructions given by the trial judge, the jury could have rested its verdict on any of a number of grounds. The jurors may have found that petitioners refused "to obey a policeman's command to move on when not to do so [might have endangered] the public peace." Or they may have

---

4. Petitioners' conduct in the station is not at issue in this case, since the State did not prosecute them for their conduct in that place.

5. The local police officers were deputized as marshals because their local police powers did not extend to the federally operated recruiting station.

6. The defense evidence indicated that petitioners were on the sidewalk after their removal from the recruiting station for only five minutes. A prosecution witness testified that they were there for 15 or 20 minutes.

relied on a finding that petitioners deliberately obstructed the sidewalk, thus offending, disturbing and inciting the bystanders.[7] Or the jurors may have credited petitioners' testimony that they were thrown to the sidewalk by the police and held there, and yet still have found them guilty of violating § 123 because their anti-Vietnam protest amounted to "the doing or saying . . . of that which offends, disturbs, incites, or tends to incite a number of people gathered in the same area." Thus, on this record, we find that petitioners may have been found guilty of violating § 123 simply because they advocated unpopular ideas. Since conviction on this ground would violate the Constitution, it is our duty to set aside petitioners' convictions.

. . .

On this record, if the jury believed the State's evidence, petitioners' convictions could constitutionally have rested on a finding that they sat or lay across a public sidewalk with the intent of fully blocking passage along

it, or that they refused to obey police commands to stop obstructing the sidewalk in this manner and move on. See, *e. g., Cox* v. *Louisiana* (I), 379 U.S., at 554–555, 85 S.Ct., at 464–465; *Shuttlesworth* v. *Birmingham*, 382 U.S. 87, 90–91, 86 S.Ct. 211, 213–214, 15 L.Ed.2d 176 (1965). It is impossible to say, however, that either of these grounds was the basis for the verdict. On the contrary, so far as we can tell, it is equally likely that the verdict resulted "merely because [petitioners' views about Vietnam were] themselves offensive to some of their hearers." *Street* v. *New York, supra,* 394 U.S., at 592, 89 S.Ct. at 1366. Thus, since petitioners' convictions may have rested on an unconstitutional ground, they must be set aside.

The judgment of the Maryland Court of Special Appeals is reversed and the case is remanded for further proceedings not inconsistent with this opinion. It is so ordered.

Judgment reversed and case remanded.

QUESTIONS

1. Should a city have the legislative authority to enact "breach of the peace" statutes? What are the justifications for them? Don't these types of ordinances invariably conflict with rights of assembly and speech? Do you feel that "parade permits" conflict equally with the rights of assembly and speech?

2. Do you think that freedom of expression should include the right of

7. Maryland states in its brief, at 41–42, that "[o]bstructing the sidewalk had the legal effect under these circumstances of not only constituting a violation of . . . § 123 . . . but also of Article 27, § 121 of the Maryland Code, obstructing free passage." Had the State wished to ensure a jury finding on the obstruction question, it could have prosecuted petitioners under § 121, which specifically punishes "[a]ny person who shall wilfully obstruct or hinder the free passage of persons passing along or by any public street or highway. . . ."

blocking an entrance way to a recruitment station? Why not, if this is a dramatic way of drawing attention to your "anti-war" position?

3. In this case, do you think the Supreme Court was deliberately trying to avoid the important issues concerning the protest at the station and consequently decided the case on a legal technical point, i.e., the charge to the jury?

4. If you were on the Supreme Court how much "physical behavior" would you urge be tolerated before the constitutionally protected right of dissent has been surpassed? What justifications and standards do you have for your position? How do you arrive at your conclusion?

5. Assuming all of the "facts" claimed by the state are correct, do you think it is a wise decision to reverse the convictions assuming the judge's charge was overbroad? Shouldn't people who deliberately violate the law be punished even if there is some technical error? Why do you think yes? Why no?

2. political association and participation as freedom of expression

1. Introductory Essay

2. The Political Association Cases:

   Bond v. *Floyd*, 385 U.S. 116 (1966): "The Legislative Qualifications Case."
   U.S. v. *Robel*, 389 U.S. 258 (1967): "The Communists In Government Case."
   Brandenburg v. *Ohio*, 395 U.S. 444 (1969): "The Ku Klux Klan Rally Case."

3. Individual Acts Of Political Participation Cases:

   Whitehill v. *Elkins*, 389 U.S. 54 (1967): "The Loyalty Oath Case."
   Pickering v. *Board of Education*, 391 U.S. 563 (1968): "The Letter To The Editor Case."
   Street v. *New York*, 394 U.S. 576 (1969): "The Flag Burning Case."

2. political association and participation as freedom of expression

Can a member of the Communist Party work in a defense plant? Are government employees obligated to take loyalty oaths to the United States irrespective of their wording? Can an elected State Legislator be constitutionally denied his office for making public statements critical of U.S. foreign policy? Is it a crime to be a member of the Communist Party or the Ku Klux Klan?

The Emergence of the Right of Association

The First Amendment, as such, does not *specifically* provide for freedom of association or political participation. These rights are derived from the more explicit First Amendment guarantees to speak, to practice one's religion, to print, to assemble, and to petition the government about grievances. They have also, by virtue of the Fourteenth Amendment's due process clause, been restrictive of state authority. (See Chapter Two).

In 1937 in *DeJonge* v. *Oregon*, 299 U.S. 353, the Supreme Court recognized that "the right of peaceful assembly is a right related to those of free speech and free press and is equally fundamental." It followed, said the Court, that "the very idea of a republican form of government implies a right on the part of its citizens to meet peaceably for consultation in respect to public affairs [association for political purposes] and to petition for a redress of grievances." Even more explicit on this point was the Supreme Court's 1958 declaration in *N.A.A.C.P.* v. *Alabama*, 357 U.S. 449 that:

... It is beyond debate that freedom to engage in association for the advancement of beliefs and ideas is an inseparable aspect of the "liberty" assured by the Due Process Clause of the Fourteenth Amendment, which embraces freedom of speech.

Of course, a consistent tenet of constitutional interpretation in this country has been that no legal right is or can be absolutely guaranteed in practice. Discussing what appeared to be an absolute prohibition on legislative interference with religious practice the Supreme Court in *Cantwell* v. *Connecticut, supra,* emphasized this principle:

... The First Amendment declares that Congress shall make no law respecting an establishment of religion or prohibiting the free exercise thereof. ... The Constitutional inhibition of legislation on the subject has a double aspect. ... [T]he Amendment embraces two concepts— freedom to believe and freedom to act. The first is absolute but, in the nature of things the second cannot be. Conduct remains subject to regulation for the protection of society. ...

Consequently, freedom of association under certain circumstances may be conditioned or regulated if social circumstances demand. Conditioning and regulating certain types of associations does not necessarily end these freedoms but may serve to accommodate the valid interests of society and the liberties of the individual when they appear to be in conflict.

The Registration Cases

In *Bryant* v. *Zimmerman*, 278 U.S. 63 (1928) the Supreme Court upheld a New York statute requiring that any association, which was not incorporated and which demanded an oath as a condition of membership, file with state authorities copies of its ". . . constitution, by-laws, rules, regulations and oath of membership, together with *a roster of its membership* and a list of officers for the current year." [Editor's emphasis.] The court held that the New York law pursued a valid state end (that of keeping track of potential terrorists) because of the nature of the organizations required to register. (Bryant was a member of the Ku Klux Klan.) The Klan's activities differentiated it from other organizations in the state which did not preach or resort to violence and intimidation. In essence, the Supreme Court's opinion held that requiring registration of certain organizations was not necessarily an unconstitutional interference with the right of association because the state was pursuing a valid end and membership lists were a reasonable means to that end. The Court also held that the New York law had a reasonable basis for differentiating organizations like the Klan from other associations in society; and was not, in the last analysis, forbidding the association of Klansmen or the joining of the Klan.

Employing this same line of reasoning the Supreme Court in 1958 rejected Alabama's attempt to coerce the N.A.A.C.P. to register. [*N.A.A.C.P.* v. *Alabama, supra.*] In this case the N.A.A.C.P. was, after much legal maneuvering, asked to submit a membership list to the State Attorney General along with its corporate charter to determine whether it was a "foreign" corporation transacting intrastate commerce under an Alabama Statute which required all "foreign" commercial corporations to designate a place of business and an agent to receive legal process. The Supreme Court held that while it was not unusual for a state to require "foreign" business corporations to register an agent to receive legal process, there was no reasonable relationship between the submission of a general membership list and the determination of whether the N.A.A.C.P. was such a corporation under the Alabama Act. The Court reasoned that the list was not essential to the state's judgment about the status of the N.A.A.C.P., given the atmosphere of intimidation in Alabama for known members of the N.A.A.C.P. The Court held that the requirement of a membership list *in this instance* would unreasonably burden the freedom of association protected by the Fourteenth Amendment.

Freedom of Association and the Communist Party

Employing the *Bryant* principle once again, the Supreme Court in 1961 upheld Congress' right to require registration and membership lists of Communist organizations.

In 1950, overriding President Truman's veto, the 81st Congress had passed the Subversive Activities Control Act which, among other things, provided that after investigation by a Subversive Activities Control Board (SACB), an organization declared to be a "Communist-action" or "Communist-front" group by the SACB could be required to register their general membership with the U.S. Attorney General's office. The registration was to be certified by the leadership of the groups.

Following an investigation by the newly-established SACB, the Communist Party was ordered to register under the 1950 Statute. The Party challenged the registration order and the Statute as violations of the First Amendment. After a decade in the federal courts, a narrowly divided (5-4) Supreme Court sustained the registration provisions of the Subversive Activities Control Act in *Communist Party* v. *Subversive Activities Control Board,* 367 U.S. 1 (1961).

The Court's opinion by Mr. Justice Frankfurter dealt only with the narrow question of whether the requirement of registering an organization, as such, necessarily violated the guarantees of the First Amendment. In rejecting the contention that a registration requirement must violate the freedoms of speech and association, Justice Frankfurter conceded that this type of governmental regulation "may in some circumstances affront the constitutional guarantee of freedom of expression." But Justice Frankfurter went on to explain: "The present statute does not, of course, attach the registration requirement to the incident of speech, but to the incidents of foreign domination and of operation to advance the objectives of the world Communist movement. . . ."

Noting that Congress on the basis of its detailed investigations "has found that there exists a world Communist movement, foreign-controlled whose purpose it is by whatever means necessary to establish totalitarian dictatorship in the countries throughout the world," Frankfurter reminded the Court that "it was the nature of the organization regulated, and hence the danger involved in its covert operation, which justified [the New York Statute] and caused us to distinguish between the *Bryant* case" and the *N.A.A.C.P.* case.

Despite this government victory in 1961, neither the Communist Party nor any other organization has ever registered under the Act of 1950. This fact is due to an interesting chain of legal events which grew out of the apparent conflict between the "membership clause" of the Smith Act of 1940 and the Fifth Amendment guarantee against compulsory self-incrimination.

Shortly after the decision in *Communist Party* v. *Subversive Activities Control Board, supra,* two cases were announced by the Court which upheld the constitutionality of the "membership clause" of the Smith Act [18 *United States Code,* sec. 2385]. In *Scales* v. *United States,* 367 U.S. 203 (1961), a 5-4 opinion of the Court by Mr. Justice Harlan affirmed the conviction of Scales, chairman of the North and South Carolina districts of the Communist Party, for "holding of knowing membership in any organization which advocates the overthrow of the [Federal] Government by force or violence." That same day the Court again, through Mr. Justice Harlan, reversed the conviction of an upstate New York Communist Party member in *Noto* v. *United States,* 367 U.S. 290 (1961). Justice Harlan differentiated the two cases by stressing that the Smith Act *does not* make illegal membership in any organization but only membership which is initiated or continued after one learns about the illegal activities of the organization. Scales, said the Court's majority, was proven to be an "active" member of the Party and not merely a "nominal passive" member. As a leader of the Party he had "knowledge of the Party's illegal advocacy and a specific intent to bring about violent overthrow 'as speedily as circumstances would permit.'" Unconvinced that the government proved more than "mere" Communist Party membership in the *Noto* trial, the Court reversed that conviction. Harlan stressed in the *Scales* case that the Smith Act could not make *mere* association or membership in an organization illegal without infringing on the First Amendment freedoms.

These two decisions by the Supreme Court eventually served to "take the teeth out of" the registration ruling. Since the Communist Party could only be registered effectively by its leadership, the admission of leadership in a signed affidavit registering the Party might lead to an incriminating admission in light of the *Scales* decision. Thus, the leaders of the Communist Party could validly claim their Fifth Amendment right against compulsory self-incrimination and refuse to register the Party without being contemptuous of even a court order to do so. (Legitimate invocation of a constitutional right is not a contemptuous action.)

In a sense the four dissenters (Chief Justice Warren and Justice Brennan, Douglas and Black) in the *Subversive Activities Control Board* case prevailed. In separate dissenting opinions, they had all pointed out that the organization registration section of the Subversive Activities Control Act of 1950 violated the Fifth Amendment because the leadership, by being compelled to register their organization, would have to expose themselves to possible subsequent criminal prosecution under the Smith Act of 1940.

Another section of the Subversive Activities Control Act, making it mandatory for individual members of organizations designated as subversive by the SACB to register, was subsequently held unconstitutional as a violation of the Fifth Amendment by a unanimous opinion [Justice White not participating] in *Albertson* v. *Subversive Activities Control Board*, 382 U.S. 70 (1965).

Evaluated together these cases made the registration sections—for organizations and individuals—"dead letters" and in effect nullified the most important features of the Subversive Activities Control Act. Although the Supreme Court conceded that registration, as such, was not necessarily an unconstitutional interference with the First Amendment right of political association, the cases discussed above indicate clearly that there is no practical way of forcing registration of "subversive" organizations or suspected "subversive" persons consistent with the Fifth Amendment guarantee against compulsory self-incrimination.

The *Scales* and *Noto* cases are important for another reason entirely unrelated to the registration provisions of the Act of 1950. They established constitutional protection for the right of membership in or association with the Communist Party and similar organizations. They prohibited the drawing of an indiscriminate inference of illegality from the *mere act of membership* in or association with such groups. Proof of membership in these groups did not, in itself, constitute any crime under the Smith Act or any other law of the United States. According to the *Scales* and *Noto* cases, it would violate the First Amendment's guarantee of freedom of association to make such a sweeping indiscriminate legislative or judicial judgment. Proof of membership plus proof of knowledge of subversive or criminal activities or intent to bring them about must be established in a trial to sustain a conviction under the Smith Act's "membership clause."

The Political Association and
Individual Political Participation
Cases

The cases of *Bond* v. *Floyd*, 385 U.S. 116 (1966), *United States* v. *Robel*, 389 U.S. 258 (1967), and *Brandenburg* v. *Ohio*, 395 U.S. 444 (1969), involved the exercise of political expression in concert with others.

In *Bond*, Julian Bond, a legally elected representative to the Georgia Legislature was excluded from membership because of his association with the Student Non-violent Coordinating Committee (SNCC) and his subscription to a SNCC policy statement on the war in Vietnam. A unanimous Supreme Court speaking through Mr. Chief Justice Warren, pointed out that Mr. Bond was working for change within the constitutional system and indeed was willing to swear his allegiance to both the United States and Georgia Constitutions and held that the Georgia Legislature had acted unconstitutionally in excluding Julian Bond. Noting that people in political life may have even a greater obligation, if not right, to speak out on political and social issues, the Court refused to allow the Georgia Legislature to use its right to judge the qualifications of its own membership in such a way as to reduce the political dialogue guaranteed by the First and Fourteenth Amendments.

In the *Robel* case, the unfulfilled registration order against the American Communist Party by the SACB played a significant part. The opinion of the Court by Chief Justice Warren held that the section of the Subversive Activities Control Act of 1950 which prohibited members of Communist-action groups to work in any defense facility if the group was under a registration order [Section 5 (a) (1) (D)] was unconstitutional. The Court argued that this section indiscriminately prejudged all members of these organizations and amounted to "no work" because of guilt by mere association. This, the majority argued, was incompatible with the First Amendment. Robel, a Communist Party member, was a machinist for many years at a shipyard under contract with the United States Government, before he was fired because of his membership in the Communist Party.

The dissent by Mr. Justice White, joined by Mr. Justice Harlan, pointed out that there was no guaranteed First Amendment right of association as such and that even if there were one it would not be absolute but could be reasonably conditional. The justices argued further that the section of the Subversive Activities Control Act in question did not bar Robel from either continuing his association with the Communist Party or from working elsewhere. Justice White also found it a bit inconsistent that the majority opinion would confine Robel's work in defense establishments to "non-sensitive" jobs.

In the last association case, Clarence Brandenburg was convicted of advocating criminal syndicalism in violation of an Ohio law. In a *Per Curiam* decision the Supreme Court invalidated the law as failing to distinguish between abstract advocacy (protected constitutional speech) and advocacy of incitement (unprotected speech). Brandenburg, a leader of the Ku Klux Klan, had expressed some strong opinions at a Klan rally about taking revenge on the leaders of the United States for suppression of the "white Caucasian race."

In a concurring opinion, Mr. Justice Douglas, joined by Justice Black, launched a strong attack on the "clear and present danger" test and its great potential—from their point of view—to restrict constitutionally protected free speech. [Both Douglas and Black also joined the *Per Curiam* opinion of the Court.]

It is interesting to note how Douglas employed principles from cases which protected Communist's right to free speech and association to make his points in this case concerning speech for a member of the Klan. Perhaps the methodology of open political dialogue is truly distinct from any one political ideology.

Whitehill v. *Elkins*, 389 U.S. 54 (1967), *Pickering* v. *Board of Education*, 391 U.S. 563 (1968), and *Street* v. *New York*, 394 U.S. 576 (1969), all involved some individual act of political participation or conviction. In the *Whitehill* case, Howard Whitehill was dismissed from his teaching job at the University of Maryland for refusing to sign a loyalty oath. The opinion of the Court held that although a state may set reasonable employment conditions for its employees, it may not require a broad loyalty oath that might possibly snare an unsuspecting employee who was deceived by the vagueness of the oath.

The dissent, written by Mr. Justice Harlan and joined by Justices Stewart and White, disagreed that the oath was vague and implied that the majority was simply using this argument as a façade to cover their own aversion to loyalty oaths for state employees. It implied that in principle they continued to affirm the right of the state to draft and impose a "narrow" oath.

In the *Pickering* case, Marvin Pickering was dismissed from his high school teaching job because he wrote a letter criticizing the school budget to the local newspaper. In an opinion by Mr. Justice Marshall, the Supreme Court reversed his dismissal and overwhelmingly held that unless recklessly false statements were made, a teacher's exercise of his right to speak on public and professional issues cannot constitute constitutionally permissible grounds for dismissal from public employment.

Lastly, the *Street* case involved the burning of an American flag on a public street in New York City as a "symbolic" protest against the shooting of Black civil rights leader, James Meredith. Sidney Street was arrested for violating a city ordinance which prohibited, among other things, "the mutilation, destruction, or any other act whether by words or deeds which cast contempt on the flag of the United States." In a narrowly divided opinion of the Court (5-4) Mr. Justice Harlan reversed the conviction because of the broadness of the charge to the jury which would have allowed Street's conviction for harmless words. There were four separate dissents (Warren, Black, White and Fortas) which accused the majority of avoiding the substantive question (i.e., the right to burn a flag) and of hiding behind the legal technicality of the charge to the jury.

It is hoped that these cases illustrate the High Court's efforts to prevent the "guilt of criminal activity" from mere association with politically unpopular organizations. Further, some of these cases should establish the commitment of the justices to prevent the harassment of individuals who exercise their legitimate constitutional rights in a manner which *needlessly* frightens many in society.

BOND v. FLOYD

385 U.S. 116; 87 S. Ct. 339; 17 L.Ed. 2d 235 (1966)

MR. CHIEF JUSTICE WARREN *delivered the opinion of the Court.*

The question presented in this case is whether the Georgia House of Representatives may constitutionally exclude appellant Bond, a duly elected Representative, from membership because of his statements, and statements to which he subscribed, criticizing the policy of the Federal Government in Vietnam and the operation of the Selective Service laws. An understanding of the circumstances of the litigation requires a complete presentation of the events and statements which led to this appeal.

Bond, a Negro, was elected on June 15, 1965, as the Representative to the Georgia House of Representatives from the 136th House District. Of the District's 6,500 voters, approximately 6,000 are Negroes. Bond defeated his opponent, Malcolm Dean, Dean of Men at Atlanta University, also a Negro, by a vote of 2,320 to 487.

On January 6, 1966, the Student Nonviolent Coordinating Committee, a civil rights organization of which Bond was then the Communications Director, issued the following statement on American policy in Vietnam and its relation to the work of civil rights organizations in this country:

"The Student Nonviolent Coordinating Committee has a right and a responsibility to dissent with United States foreign policy on an issue when it sees fit. The Student Nonviolent Coordinating Committee now states its opposition to United States' involvement in Viet Nam on these grounds:

"We believe the United States government has been deceptive in its claims of concern for freedom of the Vietnamese people, just as the government has been deceptive in claiming concern for the freedom of colored people in such other countries as the Dominican Republic, the Congo, South Africa, Rhodesia and in the United States itself.

"We, the Student Nonviolent Coordinating Committee, have been involved in the black people's struggle for liberation and self-determination in this country for the past five years. Our work, particularly in the South, has taught us that the United States government has never guaranteed the freedom of oppressed citizens, and is not yet truly determined to end the rule of terror and oppression within its own borders.

"We ourselves have often been victims of violence and confinement executed by United States government officials. We recall the numerous persons who have been murdered in the South because of their efforts to secure their civil and human rights, and whose murderers have been allowed to escape penalty for their crimes.

"The murder of Samuel Young in Tuskegee, Ala., is no different than the murder of peasants in Viet Nam, for both Young and Vietnamese sought, and are seeking, to secure the rights guaranteed them by law. In each case, the United States government bears a great part of the responsibility for these deaths.

"Samuel Young was murdered because United States law is not being enforced. Vietnamese are murdered because the United States is pursuing an aggressive policy in violation of international law. The United States is no respecter of persons or law when such persons or laws run counter to its needs and desires.

"We recall the indifference, suspicion and outright hostility with which our reports of violence have been met in the past by government officials.

"We know that for the most part, elections in this country, in the North as well as the South, are not free. We have seen that the 1965 Voting Rights Act and the 1964 Civil Rights Act have not yet been implemented with full federal power and sincerity.

"We question, then, the ability and even the desire of the United States government to guarantee free elections abroad. We maintain that our country's cry of 'preserve freedom in the world' is a hypocritical mask behind which it squashes liberation movements which are not bound, and refuse to be bound, by the expediences of United States cold war policies.

"We are in sympathy with, and support, the men in this country who are unwilling to respond to a military draft which would compel them to contribute their lives to United States aggression in Viet Nam in the name of the 'freedom' we find so false in this country.

"We recoil with horror at the inconsistency of a supposedly 'free' society where responsibility to freedom is equated with the responsibility to lend oneself to military aggression. We take note of the fact that 16 per cent of the draftees from this country are Negroes called on to stifle the liberation of Viet Nam, to preserve a 'democracy' which does not exist for them at home.

"We ask, where is the draft for the freedom fight in the United States?

"We therefore encourage those Americans who prefer to use their energy in building democratic forms within this country. We believe that work in the civil rights movement and with other human relations organizations is a valid alternative to the draft. We urge all Americans to seek this alternative, knowing full well that it may cost them lives—as painfully as in Viet Nam."

On the same day that this statement was issued, Bond was interviewed by telephone by a reporter from a local radio station, and, although Bond had not participated in drafting the statement, he endorsed the statement in these words:

"Why, I endorse it, first, because I like to think of myself as a pacifist and one who opposes that war and any other war and eager and anxious to encourage people not to participate in it for any reason that they choose; and secondly, I agree with this statement because of the reason set forth in it—because I think it is sorta hypocritical for us to maintain that we are fighting for liberty in other places and we are not guaranteeing liberty to citizens inside the continental United States.

. . . .

"Well, I think that the fact that the United States Government fights a war in Viet Nam, I don't think that I as a second class citizen of the United States have a requirement to support that war. I think my responsibility is to oppose things that I think are wrong if they are in Viet Nam or New York, or Chicago, or Atlanta, or wherever."

When the interviewer suggested that our involvement in Vietnam was because "if we do not stop Communism there that it is just a question of where will we stop it next," Bond replied:

"Oh, no, I'm not taking a stand against stopping World Communism, and I'm not taking a stand in favor of the Viet Cong. What I'm saying that is, first, that I don't believe in that war. That particular war. I'm against all war. I'm against that war in particular, and I don't think people ought to participate in it. Because I'm against war, I'm against the draft. I think that other countries in the World get along without a draft—England is one—and I don't see why we couldn't, too.

. . .

". . . I'm not about to justify that war, because it's stopping International Communism, or whatever—you know, I just happen to have a basic disagreement with wars for whatever reason they are fought—. . . . [F]ought to stop International Communism, to promote International Communism, or for whatever reason. I oppose the Viet Cong fighting in Viet Nam as much as I oppose the United States fighting in Viet Nam. I happen to live in the United States. If I lived in North Viet Nam I might not have the same sort of freedom of expression, but it happens that I live here—not there."

The interviewer also asked Bond if he felt he could take the oath of office required by the Georgia Constitution, and Bond responded that he saw nothing inconsistent between his statements and the oath. Bond was also asked whether he would adhere to his statements if war were declared on North Vietnam and if his statements might become treasonous. He replied that he did not know "if I'm strong enough to place myself in a position where I'd be guilty of treason."

Before January 10, 1966, when the Georgia House of Representatives was scheduled to convene, a petition challenging Bond's right to be seated was filed by 75 House members. This petition charged that Bond's statements gave aid and comfort to the enemies of the United States and Georgia, violated the Selective Service laws, and tended to bring discredit and disrespect on the House. The petition further contended that Bond's endorsement of the SNCC statement "is totally and completely repugnant to and inconsistent with the mandatory oath prescribed by the Constitution of Georgia for a member of the House of Representatives to take before taking his seat." For the same reasons, the petition asserted that Bond could not take an oath to support the Constitution of the United States. When Bond appeared at the House on January 10 to be sworn in, the clerk refused to administer the oath to him until the issues raised in the challenge petition had been decided.

Bond filed a response to the challenge petition in which he stated his willingness to take the oath and argued that he was not unable to do so in good faith. He further argued that the challenge against his seating had been filed to deprive him of his First Amendment rights, and that the challenge was racially motivated. A special committee was appointed to report on the challenge, and a hearing was held to determine exactly what Bond had said and the intentions with which he had said it.

At this hearing, the only testimony given against Bond was that which he himself gave the committee. Both the opponents Bond had defeated in becoming the Representative of the 136th District testified to his good character and to his loyalty to the United States. A recording of the interview which Bond had given to the reporter after the SNCC statement was played, and Bond was called to the stand for cross-examination. He there admitted his statements and elaborated his views. He stated that he concurred in the SNCC

statement "without reservation," and, when asked if he admired the courage of persons who burn their draft cards, responded:

"I admire people who take an action, and I admire people who feel strongly enough about their convictions to take an action like that knowing the consequences that they will face, and that was my original statement when asked that question.

.   .   .

"I have never suggested or counseled or advocated that any one other person burn their draft card. In fact, I have mine in my pocket and will produce it if you wish. I do not advocate that people should break laws. What I simply try to say was that I admired the courage of someone who could act on his convictions knowing that he faces pretty stiff consequences."

.   .   .

The special committee concluded in its report to the House that Bond's endorsement of the SNCC statement and his supplementary remarks showed that he "does not and will not" support the Constitutions of the United States and of Georgia, that he "adheres to the enemies of the State of Georgia" contrary to the State Constitution, that he gives aid and comfort to the enemies of the United States, that his statements violated the Selective Service Act, 50 U.S.C. § 462, and that his statements "are reprehensible and are such as tend to bring discredit to and disrespect of the House." On the same day the House adopted the committee report without findings and without further elaborating Bond's lack of qualifications, and resolved by a vote of 184 to 12 that "Bond shall not be allowed to take the oath of office as a member of the House of Representatives and that Representative-Elect Julian Bond shall not be seated as a member of the House of Representatives."

Bond then instituted an action in the District Court for the Northern District of Georgia for injunctive relief and a declaratory judgment that the House action was unauthorized by the Georgia Constitution and violated Bond's rights under the First Amendment. A three-judge District Court was convened under 28 U.S.C. § 2281. All three members of the District Court held that the court had jurisdiction to decide the constitutionality of the House action because Bond had asserted substantial First Amendment rights. On the merits, however, the court was divided.

Judges Bell and Morgan, writing for the majority of the court, addressed themselves first to the question of whether the Georgia House had power under state law to disqualify Bond based on its conclusion that he could not sincerely take the oath of office. They reasoned that separation of powers principles gave the Legislature power to insist on qualifications in addition to those specified in the State Constitution. The majority pointed out that nothing in the Georgia Constitution limits the qualifications of the legislators to those expressed in the constitution.

Having concluded that the action of the Georgia House was authorized by state law, the court considered whether Bond's disqualification violated his constitutional right of freedom of speech. It reasoned that the decisions of this Court involving particular state political offices supported an attitude of restraint in which the principles of separation of powers and federalism should be balanced against the alleged deprivation of individual constitutional rights. On this basis, the majority below fashioned the test to be applied in this case as being whether the refusal to seat Bond violated procedural or what it termed substantive due process. The court held that the hearing which had been given Bond by the House satisfied procedural due process. As for what it termed the question of substantive due process, the majority concluded that there was a rational evidentiary basis for the ruling of the House. It reasoned that Bond's right to dissent as a private citizen was limited by his decision to seek membership in the Georgia House. Moreover, the majority concluded, the SNCC statement and Bond's related remarks went beyond criticism of national policy and provided a rational basis for a conclusion that the speaker could not in good faith take an oath to support the State and Federal Constitutions:

"A citizen would not violate his oath by objecting to or criticizing this policy or even by calling it deceptive and false as the statement did.

"But the statement does not stop with this. It is a call to action based on race; a call alien to the concept of the pluralistic society which makes this nation. It aligns the organization with '. . . colored people in such other countries as the Dominican Republic, the Congo, South Africa, Rhodesia. . . .' It refers to its involvement in the 'black people's struggle for liberation and self-determination. . . .' It states that 'Vietnamese are murdered because the United States is pursuing an aggressive policy in violation of international law.' It alleges that Negroes, referring to American servicemen, are called on to stifle the liberation of Viet Nam.

"The call to action, and this is what we find to be a rational basis for the decision which denied Mr. Bond his seat, is that language which states that SNCC supports those men in this country who are unwilling to respond to a military draft."[2]

Chief Judge Tuttle dissented. He reasoned that the question of the power of the Georgia House under the State Constitution to disqualify a Representative under these circumstances had never been decided by the state courts, and that federal courts should construe state law, if possible, so as to avoid unnecessary federal constitutional issues. Since Bond satisfied all the stated qualifications in the State Constitution, Chief Judge Tuttle concluded that his disqualification was beyond the power of the House as a matter of state constitutional law.

Bond appealed directly to this Court from the decision of the District Court under 28 U.S.C. § 1253. While this appeal was pending, the Governor of Georgia called a special election to fill the vacancy caused by

Bond's exclusion. Bond entered this election and won overwhelmingly. The House was in recess, but the Rules Committee held a hearing in which Bond declined to recant his earlier statements. Consequently, he was again prevented from taking the oath of office, and the seat has remained vacant. Bond again sought the seat from the 136th District in the regular 1966 election, and he won the Democratic primary in September 1966, and won an overwhelming majority in the election of November 8, 1966.

The Georgia Constitution sets out a number of specific provisions dealing with the qualifications and eligibility of state legislators. These provide that Representatives shall be citizens of the United States, at least 21 years of age, citizens of Georgia for two years, and residents for one year of the counties from which elected. The Georgia Constitution further provides that no one convicted of treason against the State, or of any crime of moral turpitude, or a number of other enumerated crimes may hold any office in the State. Idiots and insane persons are barred from office, and no one holding any state or federal office is eligible for a seat in either house. The State Constitution also provides:

"Elections, returns, etc.; disorderly conduct.—Each House shall be the judge of the election, returns, and qualifications of its members and shall have power to punish them for disorderly behavior, or misconduct, by censure, fine, imprisonment, or

2. *Id.*, at 344.

expulsion, but no member shall be expelled, except by a vote of two-thirds of the House to which he belongs."9

These constitute the only stated qualifications for membership in the Georgia Legislature and the State concedes that Bond meets all of them. The Georgia Constitution also requires Representatives to take an oath stated in the Constitution:

> *"Oath of members.*—Each senator and Representative, before taking his seat, shall take the following oath, or affirmation, to-wit: 'I will support the Constitution of this State and of the United States, and on all questions and measures which may come before me, I will so conduct myself, as will, in my judgment, be most conducive to the interests and prosperity of this State.' "10

The State points out in its brief that the latter part of this oath, involving the admonition to act in the best interests of the State, was not the standard by which Bond was judged.

The State does not claim that Bond refused to take the oath to support the Federal Constitution, a requirement imposed on state legislators by Art. VI, cl. 3, of the United States Constitution: . . .

Instead, it argues that the oath provisions of the State and Federal Constitutions constitute an additional qualification. Because under state law

the legislature has exclusive jurisdiction to determine whether an elected Representative meets the enumerated qualifications, it is argued that the legislature has power to look beyond the plain meaning of the oath provisions which merely require that the oaths be taken. This additional power is said to extend to determining whether a given Representative may take the oath with sincerity. The State does not claim that it should be completely free of judicial review whenever it disqualifies an elected Representative; it admits that, if a State Legislature excluded a legislator on racial or other clearly unconstitutional grounds, the federal (or state) judiciary would be justified in testing the exclusion by federal constitutional standards. But the State argues that there can be no doubt as to the constitutionality of the qualification involved in this case because it is one imposed on the State Legislatures by Article VI of the United States Constitution. Moreover, the State contends that no decision of this Court suggests that a State may not ensure the loyalty of its public servants by making the taking of an oath a qualification of office. Thus the State argues that there should be no judicial review of the legislature's power to judge whether a prospective member may conscientiously take the oath required by the State and Federal Constitutions.

We are not persuaded by the State's attempt to distinguish, for purposes of our jurisdiction, between an exclusion alleged to be on racial

---

9. Georgia Const., Art. 3, § 7 (§ 2–1901 Ga.Code Ann.).

10. Georgia Const., Art. 3, § 4 (§ 2–1605 Ga.Code Ann.).

grounds and one alleged to violate the First Amendment. The basis for the argued distinction is that, in this case, Bond's disqualification was grounded on a constitutional standard —the requirement of taking an oath to support the Constitution. But Bond's contention is that this standard was utilized to infringe his First Amendment rights, and we cannot distinguish, for purposes of our assumption of jurisdiction, between a disqualification under an unconstitutional standard and a disqualification which, although under color of a proper standard, is alleged to violate the First Amendment.

We conclude as did the entire court below that this Court has jurisdiction to review the question of whether the action of the Georgia House of Representatives deprived Bond of federal constitutional rights, and we now move to the central question posed in the case—whether Bond's disqualifications because of his statements violated the free speech provisions of the First Amendment as applied to the States through the Fourteenth Amendment.

The State argues that the exclusion does not violate the First Amendment because the State has a right, under Article VI of the United States Constitution, to insist on loyalty to the Constitution as a condition of office. . . . [W]e do not quarrel with the State's contention that the oath provisions of the United States and Georgia Constitutions do not violate the First Amendment. But this requirement does not authorize a majority of state legislators to test the sincerity with which another duly elected legislator can swear to uphold the Constitution. Such a power could be utilized to restrict the right of legislators to dissent from national or state policy or that of a majority of their colleagues under the guise of judging their loyalty to the Constitution. Certainly there can be no question but that the First Amendment protects expressions in opposition to national foreign policy in Vietnam and to the Selective Service system. The State does not contend otherwise. But it argues that Bond went beyond expressions of opposition, and counseled violations of the Selective Service laws, and that advocating violation of federal law demonstrates a lack of support for the Constitution. The State declines to argue that Bond's statements would violate any law if made by a private citizen, but it does argue that even though such a citizen might be protected by his First Amendment rights, the State may nonetheless apply a stricter standard to its legislators. We do not agree.

Bond could not have been constitutionally convicted under 50 U.S.C. § 462(a), which punishes any person who "counsels, aids, or abets another to refuse or evade registration."[12] Bond's statements were at

---

12. The pertinent provisions of § 462(a) are as follows:

"[A]ny person who shall knowingly make, or be a party to the making, of any false statement or certificate regarding or bearing upon a classification or in support of any request for a particular classification, for service under the provisions of this title . . . , or rules, regulations, or directions made pursuant thereto, or who otherwise evades or refuses registration or service in the armed forces or any of the requirements

worst unclear on the question of the means to be adopted to avoid the draft. While the SNCC statements said "We are in sympathy with, and support, the men in this country who are unwilling to respond to a military draft," this statement alone cannot be interpreted as a call to unlawful refusal to be drafted. Moreover, Bond's supplementary statements tend to resolve the opaqueness in favor of legal alternatives to the draft, and there is no evidence to the contrary. On the day the statement was issued, Bond explained that he endorsed it "because I like to think of myself as a pacifist and one who opposes that war and any other war and eager and anxious to encourage people not to participate in it for any reason that they choose." In the same interview, Bond stated categorically that he did not oppose the Vietnam policy because he favored the Communists; that he was a loyal American citizen and supported the Constitution of the United States. He further stated "I oppose the Viet Cong fighting in Viet Nam as much as I oppose the United States fighting in Viet Nam." At the hearing before the Special Committee of the Georgia House, when asked his position on persons who burned their draft cards, Bond replied that he admired the courage of persons who "feel

strongly enough about their convictions to take an action like that knowing the consequences that they will face." When pressed as to whether his admiration was based on the violation of federal law, Bond stated:

"I have never suggested or counseled or advocated that any one other person burn their draft card. In fact, I have mine in my pocket and will produce it if you wish. I do not advocate that people should break laws. What I simply try to say was that I admired the courage of someone who could act on his convictions knowing that he faces pretty stiff consequences."

Certainly this clarification does not demonstrate any incitement to violation of law. No useful purpose would be served by discussing the many decisions of this Court which establish that Bond could not have been convicted for these statements consistently with the First Amendment. . . . Nor does the fact that the District Court found the SNCC statement to have racial overtones constitute a reason for holding it outside the protection of the First Amendment. In fact the State concedes that there is no issue of race in the case.

The State attempts to circumvent

of this title . . . , or who knowingly counsels, aids, or abets another to refuse or evade registration or service in the armed forces or any of the requirements of this title . . . , or of said rules, regulations, or directions . . . or any person or persons who shall knowingly hinder or interfere or attempt to do so in any way, by force or violence or otherwise, with the administration of this title . . . , or the

rules or regulations made pursuant thereto, or who conspires to commit any one or more of such offenses, shall, upon conviction in any district court of the United States of competent jurisdiction, be punished by imprisonment for not more than five years or a fine of not more than $10,000, or both such fine and imprisonment. . . ."

the protection the First Amendment would afford to these statements if made by a private citizen by arguing that a State is constitutionally justified in exacting a higher standard of *loyalty* from its legislators than from its citizens. Of course, a State may constitutionally require an oath to support the Constitution from its legislators which it does not require of its private citizens. But this difference in treatment does not support the exclusion of Bond, for while the State has an interest in requiring its legislators to swear to a belief in constitutional processes of government, surely the oath gives it no interest in limiting its legislators' capacity to discuss their views of local or national policy. The manifest function of the First Amendment in a representative government requires that legislators be given the widest latitude to express their views on issues of policy. The central commitment of the First Amendment, as summarized in the opinion of the Court in *New York Times* v. *Sullivan*, 376 U.S. 254, 270, 84 S.Ct. 710, 721, 11 L.Ed.2d 686 (1964), is that "debate on public issues should be uninhibited, robust, and wide-open." We think the rationale of the *New York Times* case disposes of the claim that Bond's statements fell outside the range of constitutional protection. Just as erroneous statements must be

protected to give freedom of expression the breathing space it needs to survive, so statements criticizing public policy and the implementation of it must be similarly protected. The State argues that the *New York Times* principle should not be extended to statements by a legislator because the policy of encouraging free debate about governmental operations only applies to the citizen-critic of his government. We find no support for this distinction in the *New York Times* case or in any other decision of this Court. The interest of the public in hearing all sides of a public issue is hardly advanced by extending more protection to citizen-critics than to legislators. Legislators have an obligation to take positions on controversial political questions so that their constituents can be fully informed by them, and be better able to assess their qualifications for office; also so they may be represented in governmental debates by the person they have elected to represent them. We therefore hold that the disqualification of Bond from membership in the Georgia House because of his statements violated Bond's right of free expression under the First Amendment. . . .

The decision of the District Court is reversed.

Reversed.

QUESTIONS

1. Do you think a man who holds public office should have to bear greater responsibility for the things he says in public than an ordinary citizen? Why or why not?

2. Why should a man who is duly elected to public office have to swear allegiance to any system of government or any Constitution? Justify your answer. If the people who elected him think swearing allegiance to Constitutions are important won't they remove him from office? Isn't his behavior primarily their business since he is their representative?

3. On what grounds have the Georgia legislature or any legislature, including the two houses of the U.S. Congress, the right to refuse to seat a man duly elected by his constituency to represent them? Justify your position.

4. Do you think the fact that Bond was Black played a part in the legislature's determination not to seat him? Why or why not?

5. Should a state legislature or any legislature have the authority or be given the right to judge the sincerity with which an elected official takes his oath of office? If yes, what standards would you use to judge his sincerity? If not, why isn't this question of sincerity important for you?

UNITED STATES v. ROBEL

389 U.S. 258; 88 S. Ct. 419; 19 L.Ed. 2d 508 (1967)

MR. CHIEF JUSTICE WARREN *delivered the opinion of the Court.*

This appeal draws into question the constitutionality of § 5(a) (1) (D) of the Subversive Activities Control Act of 1950, 50 U.S.C. § 784(a) (1) (D),[1] which provides that, when a Communist-action organization[2] is under a final order to register, it shall be unlawful for any member of the organization "to engage in any employment in any defense facility." In *Communist Party of U. S.* v. *Subversive Activities Control Board*, 367 U.S. 1, 81 S.Ct. 1357,

1. The Act was passed over the veto of President Truman. In his veto message, President Truman told Congress, "The Department of Justice, the Department of Defense, the Central Intelligence Agency, and the Department of State have all advised me that the bill would seriously damage the security and the intelligence operations for which they are responsible. They have strongly expressed the hope that the bill would not become law." H.R.Doc. No. 708, 81st Cong., 2d Sess., 1 (1950).

President Truman also observed that "the language of the bill is so broad and vague that it might well result in penalizing the legitimate activities of people who are not Communists at all, but loyal citizens.". . .

2. Section 3(3) (a) of the Act, 50 U.S.C. § 782(3) (a), defines a "Communist-action organization" as:
"any organization in the United States (other than a diplomatic representative or mission of a foreign government accredited as such by the Department of State) which (i) is substantially directed, dominated, or controlled by the foreign government or foreign organization *controlling* the world Communist movement . . . and (ii) operated primarily to advance the objectives of such world Communist movement. . . ."

6 L.Ed.2d 625, this Court sustained an order of the SACB requiring the Communist Party of the United States to register as a Communist-action organization under the Act. The Board's order became final on October 20, 1961. At that time appellee, a member of the Communist Party, was employed as a machinist at the Seattle, Washington, shipyard of Todd Shipyards Corporation. On August 20, 1962, the Secretary of Defense, acting under authority delegated by § 5(b) of the Act, designated that shipyard a "defense facility." Appellee's continued employment at the shipyard after that date subjected him to prosecution under § 5(a) (1) (D), and on May 21, 1963, an indictment was filed charging him with a violation of that section. The indictment alleged in substance that appellee had "unlawfully and willfully engage[d] in employment" at the shipyard with knowledge of the outstanding order against the Party and with knowledge and notice of the shipyard's designation as a defense facility by the Secretary of Defense. The United States District Court for the Western District of Washington granted appellee's motion to dismiss the indictment on October 5, 1965. To overcome what it viewed as a "likely constitutional infirmity" in § 5(a) (1) (D), the District Court read into that section "the requirement of active membership and specific intent." Because the indictment failed to allege that appellee's Communist Party membership was of that quality, the indictment was dismissed. . . . On the Government's motion, the case was certified here as properly a direct appeal to this Court under 18 U.S.C. § 3731. We noted probable jurisdiction. 384 U.S. 937, 86 S.Ct. 1458, 16 L.Ed.2d 537. We affirm the judgment of the District Court, but on the ground that § 5(a) (1) (D) is an unconstitutional abridgment of the right of association protected by the First Amendment.

We cannot agree with the District Court that § 5(a) (1) (D) can be saved from constitutional infirmity by limiting its application to active members of Communist-action organizations who have the specific intent of furthering the unlawful goals of such organizations. The District Court relied on *Scales* v. *United States*, 367 U.S. 203, 81 S.Ct. 1469, 6 L.Ed.2d 782, in placing its limiting construction on § 5(a) (1) (D). It is true that in *Scales* we read the elements of active membership and specific intent into the membership clause of the Smith Act. However, in *Aptheker* v. *Secretary of State*, 378 U.S. 500, 84 S.Ct. 1659, 12 L.Ed.2d 992, we noted that the Smith Act's membership clause required a defendant to have knowledge of the organization's illegal advocacy, a requirement that "was intimately connected with the construction limiting membership to 'active' members." . . . *Aptheker* involved a challenge to § 6 of the Subversive Activities Control Act, which provides that, when a Communist organization is registered or under a final order to register, it shall be unlawful for any member thereof with knowledge or notice thereof to apply for a passport. We held that "[t]he clarity and preciseness of the provision in question make it impossible to narrow its indiscriminately cast and overly broad scope without substantial rewriting." . . . We take the same view of § 5(a) (1) (D). It is precisely because that statute sweeps indiscriminately across all types of associations with Communist-action groups, without regard to the quality and degree of membership, that it runs afoul of the First Amendment.

In *Aptheker*, we held § 6 unconstitutional because it too broadly and indiscriminately infringed upon constitutionally protected rights. The Government has argued that, despite the overbreadth which is obvious on the face of § 5(a) (1) (D), *Aptheker* is not controlling in this case because the right to travel is a more basic freedom than the right to be employed in a defense facility. We agree *Aptheker* is not controlling since it was decided under the Fifth Amendment. But we cannot agree with the Government's characterization of the essential issue in this case. It is true that the specific disability imposed by § 5(a) (1) (D) is to limit the employment opportunities of those who fall within its coverage, and such a limitation is not without serious constitutional implications. . . . But the operative fact upon which the job disability depends is the exercise of an individual's right of association, which is protected by the provisions of the First Amendment. Wherever one would place the right to travel on a scale of constitutional values, it is clear that those rights protected by the First Amendment are no less basic in our democratic scheme.

The Government seeks to defend the statute on the ground that it was passed pursuant to Congress' war power. The Government argues that this Court has given broad deference to the exercise of that constitutional power by the national legislature. That argument finds support in a number of decisions of this Court. However, the phrase "war power" cannot be invoked as a talismanic incantation to support any exercise of congressional power which can be brought within its ambit. "[E]ven the war power does not remove constitutional limitations safeguarding essential liberties." . . . More specifically in this case, the Government asserts that § 5(a) (1) (D) is an "expression of the growing concern shown by the executive and legislative branches of government over the risks of internal subversion in plants on which the national defense depend[s]." Yet, this concept of "national defense" cannot be deemed an end in itself, justifying any exercise of legislative power designed to promote such a goal. Implicit in the term "national defense" is the notion of defending those values and ideals which set this Nation apart. For almost two centuries, our country has taken singular pride in the democratic ideals enshrined in its Constitution, and the most cherished of those ideals have found expression in the First Amendment. It would indeed be ironic if, in the name of national defense, we would sanction the subversion of one of those liberties—the freedom of association—which makes the defense of the Nation worthwhile.

When Congress' exercise of one of its enumerated powers clashes with those individual liberties protected by the Bill of Rights, it is our "delicate and difficult task" to determine whether the resulting restriction on freedom can be tolerated. . . . The Government emphasizes that the purpose of § 5(a) (1) (D) is to reduce the threat of sabotage and espionage in the Nation's defense plants. The Government's interest in such a prophylactic measure is not insubstantial. But it cannot be doubted that the means chosen to implement that governmental purpose in this instance cuts deeply into the right of association. Section 5(a) (1) (D) put appellee to the choice of surrendering his organizational affiliation, regardless of whether his membership threatened the security of a defense facility,[10] or giving up his job.[11] When appellee refused to make that choice, he became subject to a possible criminal penalty of five years' imprisonment and a $10,000 fine. The statute quite literally establishes guilt by association alone, without any need to establish that an individual's association poses the threat feared by the Government in proscribing it.[13] The inhibiting effect on

the exercise of First Amendment rights is clear.

It has become axiomatic that "[p]recision of regulation must be the touchstone in an area so closely touching our most precious freedoms." . . . Such precision is notably lacking in § 5(a) (1) (D). That statute casts its net across a broad range of associational activities, indiscriminately trapping membership which can be constitutionally punished and membership which cannot be so proscribed. It is made irrelevant to the statute's operation that an individual may be a passive or inactive member of a designated organization, that he may be unaware of the organization's unlawful aims, or that he may disagree with those unlawful aims.[16] It is also made irrelevant that an individual who is subject to the penalties of § 5(a) (1) (D) may occupy a nonsensitive position in a defense facility.[17] Thus, § 5(a) (1) (D) contains the fatal defect of overbreadth because it seeks to bar employment both for association which

---

10. The appellee has worked at the shipyard, apparently without incident and apparently without concealing his Communist Party membership, for more than 10 years. And we are told that, following appellee's indictment and arrest, "he was released on his own recognizance and immediately returned to his job as a machinist at the Todd Shipyards, where he has worked ever since."
. . .

11. We recognized in *Greene* v. *McElroy*, 360 U.S., at 492, 79 S.Ct., at 1411, 3 L.Ed.2d 1377, that "the right to hold specific private employment and to follow a chosen profession free from unreasonable governmental interference comes within the 'liberty' and 'property' concepts of the Fifth Amendment."

13. The Government has insisted that Congress, in enacting § 5(a) (D), has not sought "to punish membership in 'Communist-action' . . . organizations." . . .

Rather, the Government asserts, Congress has simply sought to regulate access to employment in defense facilities. But it is clear the employment disability is imposed only because of such membership.

16. A number of complex motivations may impel an individual to align himself with a particular organization. . . . It is for that reason that the mere presence of an individual's name on an organization's membership rolls is insufficient to impute to him the organization's illegal goals.

17. See *Cole* v. *Young*, 351 U.S. 536, 546, 76 S.Ct. 861, 868, 100 L.Ed. 1396: "[I]t is difficult to justify summary suspensions and nonreviewable dismissals on loyalty grounds of employees who are not in 'sensitive' positions and who are thus not situated where they could bring about any discernible adverse effects on the Nation's security."

may be proscribed and for association which may not be proscribed consistently with First Amendment rights. . . . This the Constitution will not tolerate.

We are not unmindful of the congressional concern over the danger of sabotage and espionage in national defense industries, and nothing we hold today should be read to deny Congress the power under narrowly drawn legislation to keep from sensitive positions in defense facilities those who would use their positions to disrupt the Nation's production facilities. We have recognized that, while the Constitution protects against invasions of individual rights, it does not withdraw from the Government the power to safeguard its vital interests. . . . Spies and saboteurs do exist, and Congress can, of course, prescribe criminal penalties for those who engage in espionage and sabotage.[18] The government can deny access to its secrets to those who would use such information to harm the Nation.[19] And Congress can declare sensitive positions in national defense industries off limits to those who would use such positions to disrupt the production of defense mate-

rials. The Government has told us that Congress, in passing § 5(a) (1) (D), made a considered judgment that one possible alternative to that statute—an industrial security screening program—would be inadequate and ineffective to protect against sabotage in defense facilities. It is not our function to examine the validity of that congressional judgment. Neither is it our function to determine whether an industrial security screening program exhausts the possible alternatives to the statute under review. We are concerned solely with determining whether the statute before us has exceeded the bounds imposed by the Constitution when First Amendment rights are at stake. The task of writing legislation which will stay within those bounds has been committed to Congress. Our decision today simply recognizes that, when legitimate legislative concerns are expressed in a statute which imposes a substantial burden on protected First Amendment activities, Congress must achieve its goal by means which have a "less drastic" impact on the continued vitality of First Amendment freedoms.[20] . . . The Constitution and the basic position

---

18. Congress has already provided stiff penalties for those who conduct espionage and sabotage against the United States. 18 U.S.C. §§ 792–798 (espionage); §§ 2151–2156 (sabotage).

19. The Department of Defense, pursuant to Executive Order 10865, as amended by Executive Order 10909, has established detailed procedures for screening those working in private industry who, because of their jobs, must have access to classified defense information. 32 C.F.R. Part 155. The provisions of those regulations are not before the Court in this case.

20. It has been suggested that this case should be decided by "balancing" the

governmental interests expressed in § 5(a) (1) (D) against the First Amendment rights asserted by the appellee. This we decline to do. We recognize that both interests are substantial, but we deem it inappropriate for this Court to label one as being more important or more substantial than the other. Our inquiry is more circumscribed. Faced with a clear conflict between a federal statute enacted in the interests of national security and an individual's exercise of his First Amendment rights, we have confined our analysis to whether Congress has adopted a constitutional means in achieving its concededly legitimate legislative goal. In making this

of First Amendment rights in our democratic fabric demand nothing less.
Affirmed.

MR. JUSTICE MARSHALL *took no part in the consideration or decision of this case.*

MR. JUSTICE BRENNAN, *concurring in the result.*

I too agree that the judgment of the District Court should be affirmed but I reach that result for different reasons.

Like the Court, I disagree with the District Court that § 5(a) (1) (D) can be read to apply only to active members who have the specific intent to further the Party's unlawful objectives. In *Apetheker* v. *Secretary of State,* 378 U.S. 500, 84 S.Ct. 1659, 12 L.Ed.2d 992, we rejected that reading of § 6 of the Act which provides that, when a Communist organization is registered or under final order to register, it shall be unlawful for any member thereof with knowledge or notice of the order to apply for or use a passport. We held that "[t]he clarity and preciseness of the provision in question make it impossible to narrow its indiscrimi-

nately cast and overly broad scope without substantial rewriting." . . . I take the same view of § 5(a) (1) (D).

. . . Indeed, a member such as appellee, who has worked at the Todd Shipyards without complaint or known ground for suspicion for over 10 years, is afforded no opportunity to prove that the statute's presumption that he is a security risk is invalid as applied to him. And no importance whatever is attached to the sensitivity of the jobs held by Party members, a factor long considered relevant in security cases. . . .

It is true, however, as the Government points out, that Congress often regulates indiscriminately, through preventive or prophylactic measures, . . . and that such regulation has been upheld even where fundamental freedoms are potentially affected, . . . Each regulation must be examined in terms of its potential impact upon fundamental rights, the importance of the end sought and the necessity for the means adopted. The Government argues that § 5(a) (1) (D) may be distinguished from § 6 on the basis of those factors. Section 5(a) (1) (D) limits employment only in "any defense facility," while § 6 deprived every Party member of

---

determination we have found it necessary to measure the validity of the means adopted by Congress against both the goal it has sought to achieve and the specific prohibitions of the First Amendment. But we have in no way "balanced" those respective interests. We have ruled only that the Constitution requires that the conflict between congressional power and individual rights be accommodated by legislation drawn more narrowly to avoid the conflict. There is, of course, nothing novel in that analysis. Such a course of adjudication was enun-

ciated by Chief Justice Marshall when he declared: "Let the end be legitimate, let it be within the scope of the constitution, and all means which are appropriate, which are plainly adapted to that end, *which are not prohibited, but which consist with the letter and spirit of the constitution,* are constitutional." *M'Culloch* v. *State of Maryland,* 4 Wheat. 316, 421, 4 L.Ed. 579 (emphasis added). In this case, the means chosen by Congress are contrary to the "letter and spirit" of the First Amendment.

the right to apply for or to hold a passport. If § 5(a) (1) (D) were in fact narrowly applied, the restrictions it would place upon employment are not as great as those placed upon the right to travel by § 6.[2] The problems presented by the employment of Party members at defense facilities, moreover, may well involve greater hazards to national security than those created by allowing Party members to travel abroad. We may assume, too, that Congress may have been justified in its conclusion that alternatives to § 5(a) (1) (D) were inadequate. For these reasons, I am not persuaded to the Court's view that overbreadth is fatal to this statute, as I agreed it was in other contexts: ...

However, acceptance of the validity of these distinctions and recognition of congressional power to utilize a prophylactic device such as § 5(a) (1) (D) to safeguard against espionage and sabotage at essential defense facilities, would not end inquiry in this case. Even if the statute is not overbroad on its face—because there may be "defense facilities" so essential to our national security that Congress could constitutionally exclude all Party members from employment in them—the congressional delegation of authority to the Secre-

tary of Defense to designate "defense facilities" creates the danger of overbroad, unauthorized, and arbitrary application of criminal sanctions in an area of protected freedoms and therefore, in my view, renders this statute invalid. Because the statute contains no meaningful standard by which the Secretary is to govern his designations, and no procedures to contest or review his designations, the "defense facility" formulation is constitutionally insufficient to mark "the field within which the [Secretary] is to act so that it may be known whether he has kept within it in compliance with the legislative will." ...

The Secretary's role in designating "defense facilities" is fundamental to the potential breadth of the statute since the greater the number and types of facilities designated the greater is the indiscriminate denial of job opportunities, under threat of criminal punishment, to Party members because of their political associations. A clear, manageable standard might have been a significant limitation upon the Secretary's discretion. But the standard under which Congress delegated the designating power is so indefinite as to be meaningless. The statute defines "facility" broadly enough to include virtually

2. The Government also points out that § 5(a) (1) (D) applies only to members of "Communist-action" organizations, while § 6 applied also to members of "Communist-front" organizations, groups which the Government contends are less dangerous to the national security under Congress' definitions, and whose members are therefore presumably less dangerous. This distinction is, however, open to some doubt. Even if a "front" organization, which is defined as an organization either dominated by or primarily operated for the purpose of aiding and supporting "action" organizations, could in some fashion be regarded as less dangerous. *Aptheker* held § 6 invalid because it failed to discriminate among affected persons on the bases of their activity and commitment to unlawful purposes, and nothing in the opinion indicates the result would have been different if Congress had been indiscriminate in these respects with regard only to "Communist-action" group members.

every place of employment in the United States; the term includes "any plant, factory or other manufacturing, producing or servicing establishment, airport, airport facility, vessel, pier, waterfront-facility, mine, railroad, public utility, laboratory, station, or other establishment or facility, or any part, division or department of any of the foregoing." And § 5(b) grants the Secretary of Defense untrammelled discretion to designate as a "defense facility" any facility "with respect to the operation of which he finds and determines that the security of the United States requires . . ." that Party members should not be employed there. Congress could easily have been more specific. Instead, Congress left the Secretary completely at large in determining the relevance and weight to be accorded such factors as the importance and secrecy of the facility and of the work being done there, and the indispensability of the facility's service or product to the national security.

Congress ordinarily may delegate power under broad standards. . . . No other general rule would be feasible or desirable. Delegation of power under general directives is an inevitable consequence of our complex society, with its myriad, ever changing, highly technical problems. "The Constitution has never been regarded as denying to the Congress the necessary resources of flexibility and practicality . . . to perform its function. . . ." It is generally enough that, in conferring power upon an appropriate authority, Congress indicate its general policy, and act in terms or within a context which

limits the power conferred. . . .

The area of permissible indefiniteness narrows, however, when the regulation invokes criminal sanctions and potentially affects fundamental rights, as does § 5(a) (1) (D). . . .

First. The failure to provide adequate standards in § 5(a) (1) (D) reflects Congress' failure to have made a "legislative judgment." . . . Formulation of policy is a legislature's primary responsibility, entrusted to it by the electorate, and to the extent Congress delegates authority under indefinite standards, this policy-making function is passed on to other agencies, often not answerable or responsive in the same degree to the people. "[S]tandards of permissible statutory vagueness are strict . . ." in protected areas. . . . "Without explicit action by lawmakers, decisions of great constitutional import and effect would be relegated by default to administrators who, under our system of government are not endowed with authority to decide them." . . .

Congress has the resources and the power to inform itself, and is the appropriate forum where the conflicting pros and cons should have been presented and considered. But instead of a determination by Congress reflected in guiding standards of the types of facilities to which § 5(a) (1) (D) should be applied, the statute provides for a resolution by the Secretary of Defense acting on his own accord. . . . [T]he Secretary is in effect determining which facilities are so important to the national security that Party members, active or inactive, well-intentioned or ill, should be prohibited from working within them in any capacity, sensitive or innocuous, under threat of criminal prosecution. In resolving this conflict of interests, the Secretary's judgment, colored by his overriding obligation to protect the national defense, is not a constitutionally acceptable substitute for Congress' judgment, in the absence of further, limiting guidance.[5]

. . .

Second. We said in *Watkins* v. *United States*, 354 U.S. 178, 205, 77 S.Ct. 1173, 1188, 1 L.Ed.2d 1273, that Congress must take steps to assure "respect for constitutional liberties" by preventing the existence of "a wide gulf between the responsibility for the use of . . . power and the actual exercise of that power." Procedural protections to avoid that gulf have been recognized as essential when fundamental freedoms are regulated, . . .

. . . However, the text and history of this section compels the conclusion that Congress deliberately chose not to provide for protest either to the Secretary or the courts from any designation by the Secretary of a facility as a "defense facility." The absence of any provision in this regard contrasts strongly with the care that Congress took to provide for

the determination by the SACB that the Party is a Communist-action organization, and for judicial review of that determination. The Act "requires the registration only of organizations which . . . are found to be under the direction, domination, or control of certain foreign powers and to operate primarily to advance certain objectives. This finding must be made after full administrative hearing, subject to judicial review which opens the record for the reviewing court's determination whether the administrative findings as to fact are supported by the preponderance of the evidence." . . . In contrast, the Act nowhere provides for an administrative hearing on the Secretary's designation, either public or private, nor is his finding subject to review. A Party member charged with notice of the designation must quit the Party or his job; he cannot contest the Secretary's action on trial if he retains both and is prosecuted.[6]

This is persuasive evidence that the matter of the designation of "defense facilities" was purposely committed by Congress entirely to the discretionary judgment of the Secretary. Unlike the opportunities for hearing and judicial review afforded the Party itself, the Party member

---

5. The Secretary has published criteria which guide him in applying the statute:

"The list of 'defense facilities' is comprised of (1) facilities engaged in important classified military projects; (2) facilities producing important weapons systems, subassemblies and their components; (3) facilities producing essential common components, intermediates, basic materials and raw materials; (4) important utility and service facilities; and (5) research laboratories whose contributions are important to the national defense. The list, which will

be amended from time to time as necessary, has been classified for reasons of security." Department of Defense Release No. 1362–63, Aug. 20, 1962. These broad standards, which might easily justify applying the statute to most of our major industries, cannot be read into the statute to limit the Secretary's discretion, since they are subject to unreviewable amendment.

6. The statute contemplates only four significant findings before criminal liability attaches: (1) that the Communist Party is a "Communist-action organization"; (2)

was not to be heard by the Secretary to protest the designation of his place of employment as a "defense facility," nor was the member to have recourse to the courts. . . .

.   .   .

Third. The indefiniteness of the delegation in this case also results in inadequate notice to affected persons. Although the form of notice provided for in § 5(b) affords affected persons reasonable opportunity to conform their behavior to avoid punishment, it is not enough that persons engaged in arguably protected activity be reasonably well advised that their actions are subject to regulation. Persons so engaged must not be compelled to conform their behavior to commands, no matter how unambiguous, from delegated agents whose authority to issue the commands is unclear. . . . There is no way for persons affected by § 5(a) (1) (D) to know whether the Secretary is acting within his authority, and therefore no fair basis upon which they may determine whether or not to risk disobedience in the exercise of activities normally protected.

Section 5(a) (1) (D) denies significant employment rights under threat of criminal punishment to persons simply because of their political associations. The Government makes no claim that Robel is a security risk. He has worked as a

machinist at the shipyards for many years, and we are told is working there now. We are in effect invited by the Government to assume that Robel is a law abiding citizen, earning a living at his chosen trade. The justification urged for punishing him is that Congress may properly conclude that members of the Communist Party, even though nominal or inactive members and believing only in change through lawful means, are more likely than other citizens to engage in acts of espionage and sabotage harmful to our national security. This may be so. But in areas of protected freedoms, regulation based upon mere association and not upon proof of misconduct or even of intention to act unlawfully, must at least be accompanied by standards or procedural protections sufficient to safeguard against indiscriminate application. . . .

MR. JUSTICE WHITE, *with whom* MR. JUSTICE HARLAN *joins, dissenting.*

The Court holds that because of the First Amendment a member of the Communist Party who knows that the Party has been held to be a Communist-action organization may not be barred from employment in defense establishments important to the security of the Nation. It therefore refuses to enforce the con-

that defendant is a member of the Communist Party; (3) that defendant engaged in employment at a "defense facility"; and (4) that he had notice that his place of employment was a "defense facility." The first finding was made by the Subversive Activities Control Board. The third finding —that the shipyard is a "defense facility"—

was made by the Secretary of Defense. The fourth finding refers to the notice requirement which is no more than a presumption from the posting required of the employer by § 5(b). Thus the only issue which a defendant can effectively contest is whether he is a Communist Party member. . . .

trary judgments of the Legislative and Executive Branches of the Government. Respectfully disagreeing with this view, I dissent.

The constitutional right found to override the public interest in national security defined by Congress is the right of association, here the right of respondent Robel to remain a member of the Communist Party after being notified of its adjudication as a Communist-action organization. Nothing in the Constitution requires this result. The right of association is not mentioned in the Constitution. It is a judicial construct appended to the First Amendment rights to speak freely, to assemble, and to petition for redress of grievances.[1] While the right of association has deep roots in history and is supported by the inescapable necessity for group action in a republic as large and complex as ours, it has only recently blossomed as the controlling factor in constitutional litigation; its contours as yet lack delineation. Although official interference with First Amendment rights has drawn close scrutiny, it is now apparent that the right of association is not absolute and is subject to significant regulation by the State. The law of criminal conspiracy restricts the purposes for which men may associate and the means they may use to implement their plans. Labor unions, and membership in them, are intricately controlled by statutes, both federal and state, as are political parties and corporations.

The relevant cases uniformly reveal the necessity for accommodating the right of association and the public interest. *NAACP* v. *State of Alabama ex rel. Patterson*, 357 U.S. 449, 78 S.Ct. 1163, 2 L.Ed.2d 1488 (1958), which contained the first substantial discussion of the right in an opinion of this Court, exemplifies the judicial approach. There, after noting the impact of official action on the right to associate, the Court inquired "whether Alabama has demonstrated an interest in obtaining the disclosures it seeks from petitioner which is sufficient to justify the deterrent effect which we have concluded these disclosures may well have on the free exercise by petitioner's members of their constitutionally protected right of association." ... [T]he Court weighed the right to associate in an organization furnishing salaried legal services to its members against the State's interest in insuring adequate and personal legal representation, and found the State's interest insufficient to justify its restrictions.

Nor does the Court mandate a different course in this case. Apparently "active" members of the Communist Party who have demonstrated their commitment to the illegal aims of the Party may be barred from

---

1. If men may speak as individuals, they may speak in groups as well. If they may assemble and petition, they must have the right to associate to some extent. In this sense the right of association simply extends constitutional protection to First Amendment rights when exercised with others rather than by an individual alone. In *NAACP* v. *State of Alabama ex rel. Patter-* *son*, the Court said that the freedom to associate for the advancement of beliefs and ideas is constitutionally protected and that it is "immaterial whether the beliefs sought to be advanced by association pertain to political, economic, religious or cultural matters. . . ." 357 U.S. 449, 460, 78 S.Ct. 1163, 1171, 2 L.Ed.2d 1488 (1958). . . .

defense facilities. This exclusion would have the same deterrent effect upon associational rights as the statute before us, but the governmental interest in security would override that effect. *Also, the Court would seem to permit barring respondent, although not an "active" member of the Party, from employment in "sensitive" positions in the defense establishment.** Here, too, the interest in anticipating and preventing espionage or sabotage would outweigh the deterrent impact of job disqualification. If I read the Court correctly, associating with the Communist Party may at times be deterred by barring members from employment and non-membership may at times be imposed as a condition of engaging in defense work. In the case before us the Court simply disagrees with the Congress and the Defense Department, ruling that Robel does not present a sufficient danger to the national security to require him to choose between membership in the Communist Party and his employment in a defense facility. Having less confidence than the majority in the prescience of this remote body when dealing with threats to the security of the country, I much prefer the judgment of Congress and the Executive Branch that the interest of respondent in remaining a member of the Communist Party, knowing that it has been adjudicated a Communist-action organization, is less substantial than the public interest in excluding him from employment in critical defense industries.

The national interest asserted by the Congress is real and substantial.

After years of study, Congress prefaced the Subversive Activities Control Act of 1950, 64 Stat. 987, 50 U.S.C. §§ 781–798, with its findings that there exists an international Communist movement which by treachery, deceit, espionage, and sabotage seeks to overthrow existing governments; that the movement operates in this country through Communist-action organizations which are under foreign domination and control and which seek to overthrow the Government by any necessary means, including force and violence; that the Communist movement in the United States is made up of thousands of adherents, rigidly disciplined, operating in secrecy, and employing espionage and sabotage tactics in form and manner evasive of existing laws. Congress therefore, among other things, defined the characteristics of Communist-action organizations, provided for their adjudication by the SACB, and decided that the security of the United States required the exclusion of Communist-action organization members from employment in certain defense facilities. After long and complex litigation, the SACB found the Communist Party to be a Communist-action organization within the meaning of the Act. That conclusion was affirmed both by the Court of Appeals, *Communist Party of U. S. v. SACB*, 107 U.S.App.D.C. 279, 277 F.2d 78 (1959), and this Court, 367 U.S. 1, 81 S.Ct. 1357, 6 L.Ed.2d 625 (1961). Also affirmed were the underlying determinations, required by the Act, that the Party is directed or controlled by a foreign govern-

*[Editor's Note: Emphasis added.]

ment or organization, that it operates primarily to advance the aims of the world Communist movement, and that it sufficiently satisfies the criteria of Communist-action organizations specified by § 792(e), including the finding by the Board that many Party members are subject to or recognize the discipline of the controlling foreign government or organization. This Court accepted the congressional appraisal that the Party posed a threat "not only to existing government in the United States, but to the United States as a sovereign, independent nation. . . ."

Against this background protective measures were clearly appropriate. . . . Given the characteristics of the Party, its foreign domination, its primary goal of government overthrow, the discipline which it exercises over its members, and its propensity for espionage and sabotage, the exclusion of members of the Party who know the Party is a Communist-action organization from certain defense plants is well within the powers of Congress.

Congress should be entitled to take suitable precautionary measures. *Some Party members may be no threat at all, but many of them undoubtedly are, and it is exceedingly difficult to identify those in advance of the very events which Congress seeks to avoid.** If Party members such as Robel may be barred from "sensitive positions," it is because they are potential threats to security. For the same reason they should be excludable from employment in defense plants which Congress and the

Secretary of Defense consider of critical importance to the security of the country.

*The statute does not prohibit membership in the Communist Party. Nor are respondent and other Communists excluded from all employment in the United States, or even from all defense plants.** The touchstones for exclusion are the requirements of national security, and the facilities designated under this standard amount to only about one percent of all the industrial establishments in the United States.

It is this impact on associational rights, although specific and minimal, which the Court finds impermissible. But as the statute's dampening effect on associational rights is to be weighed against the asserted and obvious government interest in keeping members of Communist-action groups from defense facilities, it would seem important to identify what interest Robel has in joining and remaining a member of a group whose primary goals he may not share. We are unenlightened, however, by the opinion of the Court or by the record in this case, as to the purposes which Robel and others like him may have in associating with the Party. The legal aims and programs of the Party are not identified or appraised nor are Robel's activities as a member of the Party. The Court is left with a vague and formless concept of associational rights and its own notions of what constitutes an unreasonable risk to defense facilities.

The Court says that mere member-

*[Editor's Note: Emphasis added.]

ship in an association with knowledge that the association pursues unlawful aims cannot be the basis for criminal prosecution. *Scales* v. *United States*, 367 U.S. 203, 81 S.Ct. 1469, 6 L.Ed. 2d 782 (1961), or for denial of a passport, *Aptheker* v. *Secretary of State*, 378 U.S. 500, 84 S.Ct. 1659, 12 L.Ed.2d 992 (1964). But denying the opportunity to be employed in some defense plants is a much smaller deterrent to the exercise of associational rights than denial of a passport or a criminal penalty attached solely to membership, and the Government's interest in keeping potential spies and saboteurs from defense plants is much greater than its interest in keeping disloyal Americans from traveling abroad or in committing all Party members to prison. The "delicate and difficult judgment" to which the Court refers should thus result in a different conclusion from that reached in the *Scales* and *Aptheker* cases.[2]

The Court's motives are worthy.

It seeks the widest bounds for the exercise of individual liberty consistent with the security of the country. In so doing it arrogates to itself an independent judgment of the requirements of national security. These are matters about which judges should be wary. James Madison wrote:

"Security against foreign danger is one of the primitive objects of civil society....

". . . The means of security can only be regulated by the means and the danger of attack. They will in fact be ever determined by these rules, and by no others. It is in vain to oppose constitutional barriers to the impulse of self-preservation. It is worse than in vain; because it plants in the Constitution itself necessary usurpations of power, every precedent of which is a germ of unnecessary and multiplied repetitions."[3]

QUESTIONS

1. Does it make sense to have a Communist Party member working in a U.S. defense plant? How about a Ku Klux Klan member working for the N.A.A.C.P.? Isn't there some basic inconsistency here that the Supreme Court has overlooked? Justify whichever position you take.

2. Is there or should there be a *right* to work for any employer? Why yes? Why no?

2. I cannot agree with my Brother Brennan that Congress delegated improperly when it authorized the Secretary of Defense to determine "with respect to the operation of which [defense facilities] . . . the security of the United States requires the application of the provisions of subsection (a) of this section." Rather I think this

is precisely the sort of application of a legislative determination to specific facts within the administrator's expertise that today's complex governmental structure requires and that this Court has frequently upheld. . . .

3. The Federalist No. 41. . . .

3. Is there a constitutional right to work for the U.S. Government or corporations which contract with it? Should there be? Why yes? Why not?

4. Do you think the minority opinion is correct when it implies that the majority is employing a double standard for "sensitive" and "non-sensitive" jobs? Does this standard—if it is being used—make sense if Robel is harmless or has a *right* to work in a defense plant?

5. Do you believe that a person who joins or stays in the Communist Party must basically be disloyal to the United States? Why or why not?

BRANDENBURG v. OHIO

395 U.S. 444; 89 S. Ct. 1827; 23 L.Ed. 2d 430 (1969)

PER CURIAM.

The appellant, a leader of a Ku Klux Klan group, was convicted under the Ohio Criminal Syndicalism statute of "advocat[ing] . . . the duty, necessity, or propriety of crime, sabotage, violence, or unlawful methods of terrorism as a means of accomplishing industrial or political reform" and of "voluntarily assembl[ing] with any society, group or assemblage of persons formed to teach or advocate the doctrines of criminal syndicalism." Ohio Rev. Code § 2923.13. He was fined $1,000 and sentenced to one to 10 years' imprisonment. The appellant challenged the constitutionality of the criminal syndicalism statute under the First and Fourteenth Amendments to the United States Constitution, but the intermediate appellate court of Ohio affirmed his conviction without opinion. The Supreme Court of Ohio dismissed his appeal, *sua sponte,* "for the reason that no sub-stantial constitutional question exists herein." It did not file an opinion or explain its conclusions. Appeal was taken to this Court, and we noted probable jurisdiction. 393 U.S. 948, 89 S.Ct. 377, 21 L.Ed.2d 360 (1968). We reverse.

The record shows that a man, identified at trial as the appellant, telephoned an announcer-reporter on the staff of a Cincinnati television station and invited him to come to a Ku Klux Klan "rally" to be held at a farm in Hamilton County. With the cooperation of the organizers, the reporter and a cameraman attended the meeting and filmed the events. Portions of the films were later broadcast on the local station and on a national network.

The prosecution's case rested on the films and on testimony identifying the appellant as the person who communicated with the reporter and who spoke at the rally. The State also introduced into evidence several articles appearing in the film, including a pistol, a rifle, a shotgun, ammunition, a Bible, and a red hood worn by the speaker in the films.

One film showed 12 hooded figures, some of whom carried firearms. They were gathered around a large wooden cross, which they burned. No one was present other than the participants and the newsmen who made the film. Most of the words uttered during the scene were incomprehensible when the film was projected, but scattered phrases could be understood that were derogatory of Negroes and, in one instance, of Jews.[1] Another scene on the same film showed the appellant, in Klan regalia, making a speech. The speech, in full, was as follows:

"This is an organizers' meeting. We have had quite a few members here today which are—we have hundreds, hundreds of members throughout the State of Ohio. I can quote from a newspaper clipping from the *Columbus Ohio Dispatch*, five weeks ago Sunday morning. The Klan has more members in the State of Ohio than does any other organization. We're not a revengent organization, but if our President, our Congress, our Supreme Court, continues to suppress the white, Caucasian race, it's possible that there might have to be some revengence taken.

"We are marching on Congress

July the Fourth, four hundred thousand strong. From there we are dividing into two groups, one group to march on St. Augustine, Florida, the other group to march into Mississippi. Thank you."

The second film showed six hooded figures one of whom, later identified as the appellant, repeated a speech very similar to that recorded on the first film. The reference to the possibility of "revengence" was omitted, and one sentence was added: "Personally, I believe the nigger should be returned to Africa, the Jew returned to Israel." Though some of the figures in the films carried weapons, the speaker did not.

The Ohio Criminal Syndicalism Statute was enacted in 1919. From 1917 to 1920, identical or quite similar laws were adopted by 20 States and two territories. . . . In 1927, this Court sustained the constitutionality of California's Criminal Syndicalism Act, Cal. Penal Code §§ 11400–11402, the text of which is quite similar to that of the laws of Ohio. *Whitney* v. *California*, 274 U.S. 357, 47 S.Ct. 641, 71 L.Ed. 1095 (1927). The Court upheld the statute on the ground that, without more, "advocating" violent means to effect political and economic change involves such danger to the security of the State that the State may outlaw it. Cf. *Fiske* v. *Kansas*, 274 U.S.

---

1. The significant phrases that could be understood were:
"How far is the nigger going to—yeah"
"This is what we are going to do to the niggers"
"A dirty nigger"
"Send the Jews back to Israel"
"Let's give them back to the dark garden"
"Save America"
"Let's go back to constitutional betterment"
"Bury the niggers"
"We intend to do our part"
"Give us our state rights"
"Freedom for the whites"
"Nigger will have to fight for every inch he gets from now on."

380, 47 S.Ct. 655, 71 L.Ed. 1108 (1927). But *Whitney* has been thoroughly discredited by later decisions. See *Dennis* v. *United States,* 341 U.S. 494, at 507, 71 S.Ct. 857, at 866, 95 L.Ed. 1137 (1951). These later decisions have fashioned the principle that the constitutional guarantees of free speech and free press do not permit a State to forbid or proscribe advocacy of the use of force or of law violation except where such advocacy is directed to inciting or producing imminent lawless action and is likely to incite or produce such action.[2] As we said in *Noto* v. *United States,* 367 U.S. 290, 297–298, 81 S.Ct. 1517, 1520–1521, 6 L.Ed.2d 836 (1961), "the mere abstract teaching . . . of the moral propriety or even moral necessity for a resort to force and violence, is not the same as preparing a group for violent action and steeling it to such action." . . . A statute which fails to draw this distinction impermissibly intrudes upon the freedoms guaranteed by the First and Fourteenth Amendments. It sweeps within its condemnation speech which our Constitution has immunized from governmental control. . . .

Measured by this test, Ohio's Criminal Syndicalism Act cannot be sustained. The Act punishes persons who "advocate or teach the duty, necessity, or propriety" of violence "as a means of accomplishing industrial or political reform"; or who publish or circulate or display any book or paper containing such advocacy; or who "justify" the commission of violent acts "with intent to exemplify, spread or advocate the propriety of the doctrines of criminal syndicalism"; or who ". . . voluntarily assemble" with a group formed "to teach or advocate the doctrines of criminal syndicalism." Neither the indictment nor the trial judge's instructions to the jury in any way refined the statute's bald definition of the crime in terms of mere advocacy not distinguished from incitement to imminent lawless action.[3]

Accordingly, we are here confronted with a statute which, by its own words and as applied, purports to punish mere advocacy and to forbid, on pain of criminal punishment,

---

2. It was on the theory that the Smith Act, 54 Stat. 670, 18 U.S.C. § 2385, embodied such a principle and that it had been applied only in conformity with it that this Court sustained the Act's constitutionality. *Dennis* v. *United States,* 341 U.S. 494, 71 S.Ct. 857, 95 L.Ed. 1137 (1951). That this was the basis for *Dennis* was emphasized in *Yates* v. *United States,* 354 U.S. 298, 320–324, 77 S.Ct. 1064, 1077–1079, 1 L.Ed.2d 1356 (1957), in which the Court overturned convictions for advocacy of the forcible overthrow of the Government under the Smith Act, because the trial judge's instructions had allowed conviction for mere advocacy, unrelated to its tendency to produce forcible action.

3. The first count of the indictment charged that appellant "did unlawfully by word of mouth advocate the necessity, or propriety of crime, violence, or unlawful methods of terrorism as a means of accomplishing political reform. . . ." The second count charged that appellant "did unlawfully voluntarily assembly with a group or assemblage of persons formed to advocate the doctrines of criminal syndicalism . . . ." The trial judge's charge merely followed the language of the indictment. No construction of the statute by the Ohio courts has brought it within constitutionally permissible limits. . . .

assembly with others merely to advocate the described type of action. Such a statute falls within the condemnation of the First and Fourteenth Amendments. The contrary teaching of *Whitney* v. *California, supra,* cannot be supported, and that decision is therefore overruled.
Reversed.

MR. JUSTICE BLACK, *concurring.*

I agree with the views expressed by MR. JUSTICE DOUGLAS in his concurring opinion in this case that the "clear and present danger" doctrine should have no place in the interpretation of the First Amendment. I join the Court's opinion, which, as I understand it, simply cites *Dennis* v. *United States*, 341 U.S. 494, 71 S.Ct. 857, 95 L.Ed. 1137 (1951), but does not indicate any agreement on the Court's part with the "clear and present danger" doctrine on which *Dennis* purported to rely.

MR. JUSTICE DOUGLAS, *concurring.*

While I join the opinion of the Court, I desire to enter a *caveat.*

The "clear and present danger" test was adumbrated by Mr. Justice Holmes in a case arising during World War I—a war "declared" by the Congress not by the Chief Executive. The case was *Schenck* v. *United States*, 249 U.S. 47, 52, 39 S.Ct. 247, 249, 63 L.Ed. 470, where the defendant was charged with attempts to cause insubordination in the military and obstruction of enlistment. The pamphlets that were distributed

urged resistance to the draft, denounced conscription, and impugned the motives of those backing the war effort. The First Amendment was tendered as a defense. Mr. Justice Holmes in rejecting that defense said:

"The question in every case is whether the words used are used in such circumstances and are of such a nature as to create a clear and present danger that they will bring about the substantive evils that Congress has a right to prevent. It is a question of proximity and degree."

. . . Though I doubt if the "clear and present danger" test is congenial to the First Amendment in time of a declared war, I am certain it is not reconcilable with the First Amendment in days of peace.

The Court quite properly overrules *Whitney* v. *California*, 274 U.S. 357, 47 S.Ct. 641, 71 L.Ed. 1095, which involved advocacy for ideas which the majority of the Court deemed unsound and dangerous.

Mr. Justice Holmes, though never formally abandoning the "clear and present danger" test, moved closer to the First Amendment ideal when he said in dissent in *Gitlow* [*Gitlow* v. *People of State of New York*, 268 U.S. 652, 45 S.Ct. 626, 69 L.Ed. 1138]:

"Every idea is an incitement. It offers itself for belief and if believed it is acted on unless some other belief outweighs it or some failure of energy stifles the movement at its birth. The only difference between the expression of an opinion and an incitement in the narrower sense is the speaker's enthusiasm for the result. Eloquence may set fire to reason. But whatever may be thought of the redundant discourse before us it had no chance of starting a present conflagration. If in the long run the beliefs expressed in proletarian dictatorship are destined to be accepted by the dominant forces of the community, the only meaning of free speech is that they should be given their chance and have their way."

We have never been faithful to the philosophy of that dissent.

The Court in *Herndon* v. *Lowry*, 301 U.S. 242, 57 S.Ct. 732, 81 L.Ed. 1066, overturned a conviction for exercising First Amendment rights to incite insurrection because of lack of evidence of incitement. In *Bridges* v. *California* 314 U.S. 252 . . . we approved the "clear and present danger" test in an elaborate dictum that tightened it and confined it to a narrow category. But in *Dennis* v. *United States*, 341 U.S. 494, 71 S.Ct. 857, 95 L.Ed. 1137, we opened wide the door, distorting the "clear and present danger" test beyond recognition.

In that case the prosecution dubbed an agreement to teach the Marxist creed—a "conspiracy." The case was submitted to a jury on a charge that the jury could not convict unless they found the defendants "intended to overthrow the government 'as speedily as circumstances would permit.' " 341 U.S., at 509–

511, 71 S.Ct., at 867. The Court sustained convictions under that charge, construing it to mean a determination of "whether the gravity of the 'evil, discounted by its improbability, justifies such invasion of free speech as is necessary to avoid the danger.' "
. . .

Out of the "clear and present danger" test came other offspring. Advocacy and teaching of forcible overthrow of government as an abstract principle is immune from prosecution. *Yates* v. *United States*, 354 U.S. 298, 318, 77 S.Ct. 1064, 1076, 1 L.Ed.2d 1356. But an "active" member, who has a guilty knowledge and intent of the aim to overthrow the Government by violence, *Noto* v. *United States*, 367 U.S. 290, 81 S.Ct. 1517, 6 L.Ed.2d 836, may be prosecuted. *Scales* v. *United States*, 367 U.S. 203, 228, 81 S.Ct. 1469, 1485, 6 L.Ed.2d 782. And the power to investigate, backed by the powerful sanction of contempt, includes the power to determine which of the two categories fits the particular witness. *Barenblatt* v. *United States*, 360 U.S. 109, 130, 79 S.Ct. 1081, 1094, 3 L.Ed.2d 1115. And so the investigator roams at will through all of the beliefs of the witness, ransacking his conscience and his innermost thoughts.

Judge Learned Hand who wrote for the Court of Appeals in affirming the judgment in *Dennis*, coined the "not improbable" test, *United States* v. *Dennis*, 2 Cir., 183 F.2d 201, 214, which this Court adopted and which Judge Hand preferred over the "clear and present danger" test. Indeed, in his book, The Bill of Rights, p. 59

(1958), in referring to Holmes' creation of the "clear and present danger" test, he said, "I cannot help thinking that for once Homer nodded."

My own view is quite different. I see no place in the regime of the First Amendment for any "clear and present danger" test whether strict and tight as some would make it or free-wheeling as the Court in *Dennis* rephrased it.

When one reads the opinions closely and sees when and how the "clear and present danger" test has been applied, great misgivings are aroused. First, the threats were often loud but always puny and made serious only by judges so wedded to the *status quo* that critical analysis made them nervous. Second, the test was so twisted and perverted in *Dennis* as to make the trial of those teachers of Marxism an all-out political trial which was part and parcel of the Cold War that has eroded substantial parts of the First Amendment.

Action is often a method of expression and within the protection of the First Amendment.

Suppose one tears up his own copy of the Constitution in eloquent protest to a decision of this Court. May he be indicted?

Suppose one rips his own Bible to shreds to celebrate his departure from one "faith" and his embrace of atheism. May he be indicted?

Last Term the Court held in *United States* v. *O'Brien*, 391 U.S. 367, 377, 88 S.Ct. 1673, 1679, 20 L.Ed.2d 672, that a registrant under Selective Service who burned his draft card in protest to the war in Vietnam could be prosecuted. The First Amendment was tendered as a defense and rejected, the Court saying:

"The issuance of certificates indicating the registration and eligibility classification of individuals is a legitimate and substantial administrative aid in the functioning of this system. And legislation to insure the continuing availability of issued certificates serves a legitimate and substantial purpose in the system's administration." . . .

But O'Brien was not prosecuted for not having his draft card available when asked for by a federal agent. He was indicted, tried and convicted for burning the card. And this Court's affirmance of that conviction was not, with all respect, consistent with the First Amendment.

The act of praying often involves body posture and movement as well as utterances. It is nonetheless protected by the Free Exercise Clause. Picketing, as we have said on numerous occasions, is "free speech plus." . . . That means that it can be regulated when it comes to the "plus" or "action" side of the protest. It can be regulated as to the number of pickets and the place and hours . . . because traffic and other community problems would otherwise suffer.

But none of these considerations are implicated in the symbolic protest to the Vietnam war in the burning of a draft card.

One's beliefs have long been thought to be sanctuaries which government could not invade. . . . The lines drawn by the Court between the criminal act of being an "active" Communist and the innocent act of being a nominal or inactive Communist mark the difference only between deep and abiding belief and casual or uncertain belief. But I think that all matters of belief are beyond the reach of subpoenas or the probings of investigators. That is why the invasions of privacy made by investigating committees was notoriously unconstitutional. That is the deep-seated fault in the infamous loyalty-security hearings which, since 1947 when Truman launched them, have processed 20,000,000 men and women. Those hearings were primarily concerned with one's thoughts, ideas, beliefs, and convictions. They were the most blatant violations of the First Amendment we have ever known.

The line between what is permissible and not subject to control and what may be made impermissible and subject to regulation is the line between ideas and overt acts.

The example usually given by those who would punish speech is the case of one who falsely shouts fire in a crowded theatre.

This is, however, a classic case where speech is brigaded with action. . . . They are indeed inseparable and a prosecution can be launched for the overt acts actually caused. Apart from rare instances of that kind, speech is, I think, immune from prosecution. Certainly there is no constitutional line between advocacy of abstract ideas as in *Yates* and advocacy of political action as in *Scales*. The quality of advocacy turns on the depth of the conviction; and government has no power to invade that sanctuary of belief and conscience.

QUESTIONS

1. Do you think Brandenburg's remarks at the rally and on the two films were protected speech or advocacy of *criminal* action? How do you reach your conclusion?

2. If you do not think Brandenburg advocated criminal action, do you think his words and activities constituted a sufficient "clear and present danger" of violence to justify the state's conviction? Why yes? Why no?

3. What relationship, if any, do you see between the Douglas-Black position on the "clear and present danger" test and the concept of the "preferred position of the First Amendment?"

4. What social utility—if any—do you see society deriving from the rally and films described in this case? If none—why should the rally be allowed to take place?

5. Do you think the Black Justice (Marshall) and the Jewish Justice (Fortas) should have disqualified themselves from sitting on the case because of the content of Brandenburg's remarks? If yes, Why? If no, why not?

WHITEHILL v. ELKINS

389 U.S. 54; 88 S. Ct. 184; 19 L.Ed. 2d 228 (1967)

MR. JUSTICE DOUGLAS *delivered the opinion of the Court.*

This suit for declaratory relief that a Maryland teacher's oath required of appellant was unconstitutional was heard by a three-judge court and dismissed. D.C., 258 F.Supp. 589. We noted probable jurisdiction. 386 U.S. 906, 87 S.Ct. 852, 17 L.Ed.2d 781.

Appellant, who was offered a teaching position with the University of Maryland, refused to take the following oath:

"I, _____, do hereby (Print Name—including middle initial) certify that I am not engaged in one way or another in the attempt to overthrow the Government of the United States, or the State of Maryland, or any political subdivision of either of them, by force or violence.

"I further certify that I understand the aforegoing statement is made subject to the penalties of perjury prescribed in Article 27, Section 439 of the Annotated Code of Maryland (1957 edition)."

The question is whether the oath is to be read in isolation or in connection with the Ober Act (Art. 85A, Md.Ann. Code, 1957) which by §§ 1 and 13 defines a "subversive" as ". . . any person who commits, attempts to commit, or aids in the commission, or advocates, abets, ad-

vises or teaches by any means any person to commit, attempt to commit, or aid in the commission of any act intended to overthrow, destroy or *alter*, or to assist in the overthrow, destruction or *alteration* of, the constitutional form of the government of the United States, or of the State of Maryland, or any political subdivision of either of them, *by revolution, force, or violence*; or who is a *member of a subversive organization* or a foreign subversive organization, as more fully defined in this article." (Italics supplied.) Section 1 defines the latter terms: "subversive organization" meaning a group that would, *inter alia*, "alter" the form of government "by revolution, force, or violence"; "foreign subversive organization" is such a group directed, dominated, or controlled by a foreign government which engages in such activities.

The oath was prepared by the Attorney General and approved by the Board of Regents that has exclusive management of the university. It is conceded that the Board had authority to provide an oath, as § 11 of the Act directs every agency of the State which appoints, employs, or supervises officials or employees to establish procedures designed to ascertain before a person is appointed or employed that he or she "is not a subversive person." And that term is, as noted, defined by §§ 1 and 13. Our conclusion is that, since the authority to prescribe oaths is provided by § 11 of the Act and since it is in turn tied to §§ 1 and 13, we must consider the oath with reference to §§ 1 and 13, not in isolation. Nor can we assume that the Board of Regents meant to encompass less than the Ober Act, as construed, sought to cover.

If the Federal Constitution is our guide, a person who might wish to "alter" our form of government may not be cast into the outer darkness. For the Constitution prescribes the method of "alteration" by the amending process in Article V; and while the procedure for amending it is restricted, there is no restraint on the kind of amendment that may be offered. Moreover, the First Amendment, which protects a controversial as well as a conventional dialogue . . . is as applicable to the States as it is to the Federal Government; and it extends to petitions for redress of grievances . . . as well as to advocacy and debate. So if §§ 1 and 13 of the Ober Act are the frame of reference in which the challenged oath is to be adjudged, we have important questions to resolve.

We are asked to treat §§ 1 and 13 as if they barred only those who seek to overthrow or destroy the Government by force or violence. Reference is made to *Gerende* v. *Board of Supervisors of Elections of Baltimore City*, 341 U.S. 56, 71 S.Ct. 565, 95 L.Ed. 745, where, in considering the definition of "subversive" person applicable to § 15 of the Act, governing candidates for office, we accepted the representation of the Attorney General that he would advise the proper authorities in Maryland to take and adopt the narrower version of the term "subversive." The Court of Appeals of Maryland had indicated in *Shub* v. *Simpson*, 196 Md. 177, 76 A.2d 332, that the purpose of the Act was to reach that group, and that the words "revolution, force, or violence" in § 1 did not include a peaceful revolution but one accomplished by force or violence. . . . In that view the "alteration" defined would be an alteration by force and violence. That construction had not yet been fashioned into an oath or certificate when *Gerende* reached us. That case involved an attempt by a candidate for public office in Maryland to require the election officials to dispense with an oath that incorporated the statutory language. The Court of Appeals refused the relief asked. We referred to the narrow construction of §§ 1 and 15 given in the *Shub* case saying:

"We read this decision to hold that to obtain a place on a Maryland ballot a candidate need only make oath that he is not a person who is engaged 'in one way or another in the attempt to overthrow the government *by force or violence*,' and that he is not knowingly a member of an organization engaged in such an attempt. [196 Md. at 191] 76 A.2d at 338. At the bar of this Court the Attorney General of the State of Maryland declared that he would advise the proper authorities to accept an affidavit in these terms as satisfying in full the statutory requirement. Under these circumstances and with this understanding, the judgment of the Maryland Court of Appeals is affirmed." . . .

. . . [W]e did not pass upon or approve the statutory definition of a "subversive" person in the *Gerende* case. Rather we accepted the narrowing construction tendered by the Attorney General during oral argument so as to avoid the constitutional issue that was argued.

. . .

As we have seen, §§ 1 and 13 reach (1) those who would "alter" the form of government "by revolution, force, or violence" and (2) those who are members of a subversive organization or a foreign subversive organization.

The prescribed oath requires, under threat of perjury, a statement that the employee is not engaged "in one way or another" in an attempt to overthrow the Government by force or violence. Though we assume *arguendo* that the Attorney General and the Board of Regents were authorized so to construe the Act as to prescribe a narrow oath (1) that excluded "alteration" of the Government by peaceful "revolution" and (2) that excluded all specific reference to membership in subversive groups, we still are beset with difficulties. Would a member of a group that was out to overthrow the Government by force or violence be engaged in that attempt "in one way or another" within the meaning of the oath, *even though he was ignorant of the real aims of the group and wholly innocent of any illicit purpose?** We do not know; nor could a prospective employee know, save

as he risked a prosecution for perjury.

We are in the First Amendment field. The continuing surveillance[1] which this type of law places on teachers is hostile to academic freedom. As we said in *Sweezy* v. *State of New Hampshire*, 354 U.S. 234, 250, 77 S.Ct. 1203, 1211, 1 L.Ed.2d 1311:

"The essentiality of freedom in the community of American universities is almost self-evident. No one should underestimate the vital role in a democracy that is played by those who guide and train our youth. To impose any strait-jacket upon the intellectual leaders in our colleges and universities would imperil the future of our Nation. No field of education is so thoroughly comprehended by man that new discoveries cannot yet be made. *Particularly is that true in the social sciences, where few, if any, principles are accepted as absolutes. Scholarship cannot flourish in an atmosphere of suspicion and distrust.** Teachers and students must always remain free to inquire, to study and to evaluate, to gain new maturity and understanding; otherwise our civilization will stagnate and die."

The restraints on conscientious teachers are obvious. As we noted in the *Elfbrandt* case, even attendance at an international conference might

---

1. There is not only the provision for perjury prescribed in § 11, but § 14 which provides in part that "Reasonable grounds

on all the evidence to believe that any person is a subversive person, as defined in this article, shall be cause for discharge" of the employee.

be a trap for the innocent if that conference were predominantly composed of those who would overthrow the Government by force or violence. . . . "Juries might convict though the teacher did not subscribe to the wrongful aims of the organization."
. . .

In sum, we read the oath as an integral part of the Ober Act; and we undertake to read §§ 1 and 13 of that Act in light of the gloss that the Maryland courts have placed on it. We know that the *Shub* case says that "[a] person who *advocates* the overthrow of the Government of the United States . . . through force or violence could scarcely in good faith, take the constitutional oath of office . . . ." 196 Md., at 190, 76 A.2d, at 337. (Italics supplied.) Yet that case does little more than afford the basis for argument that membership in a subversive organization means that the member must advocate a violent overthrow. This, however, is speculation, not certainty. Another Maryland case bearing on the question is *Character Committee, etc.* v. *Mandras*, 233 Md. 285, 196 A.2d 630. There an applicant for admission to the Maryland bar answered "No" to the question "Are you now or have you ever been a subversive

person as defined by the [Ober Act]?" He had apparently at one time been a member of the Communist Party. At a hearing he testified he had joined the party because he was interested in the candidacy of Henry Wallace and in the cause of civil liberties; but he denied he had been a subversive person or that he had advocated violent overthrow of the Government. The Court of Appeals affirmed the Board of Law Examiners, finding that the applicant was not a subversive person. So it can be argued that passive membership as a matter of Maryland law does not make a person a subversive. Yet, as we read §§ 1 and 13 of the Ober Act, the alteration clause and membership clause are still befogged.[2] The lines between permissible and impermissible conduct are quite indistinct. Precision and clarity are not present. Rather we find an overbreadth that makes possible oppressive or capricious application as regimes change. That very threat, as we said in another context (*N.A.A.C.P.* v. *Button*, 371 U.S. 415, 432–433, 83 S.Ct. 328, 337–338, 9 L.Ed.2d 405) may deter the flowering of academic freedom as much as successive suits for perjury.

Like the other oath cases men-

---

2. Art. 15, § 11, of the Maryland Constitution reads:
"No person who is a member of an organization that advocates the overthrow of the Government of the United States or of the State of Maryland through force or violence shall be eligible to hold any office, be it elective or appointive, or any other position of profit or trust in the Government of or in the administration of the business of this State or of any county, municipality or other political subdivision of this State."

Shub tells us that the Ober Act was enacted pursuant to this state constitutional provision. 196 Md., at 192, 76 A. 2d 332. Our attention is not drawn to, nor have we found, any severability clause applicable to this constitutional provision. It is certainly dubious, then, whether the severability clause of the Ober Act can operate to "sever" the membership clause in the definition of subversive person so that it reads more narrowly than the constitutional provision upon which the Ober Act rests.

tioned, we have another classic example of the need for "narrowly drawn" legislation (*Cantwell* v. *State of Connecticut*, 310 U.S. 296, 311, 60 S.Ct. 900, 906, 84 L.Ed. 1213) in this sensitive and important First Amendment area.
Reversed.

MR. JUSTICE HARLAN, *whom* MR. JUSTICE STEWART *and* MR. JUSTICE WHITE *join, dissenting.*

Maryland will doubtless be surprised to learn that its meticulous efforts to conform the state "loyalty oath" to the requirements of *Gerende* v. *Board of Supervisors of Elections of Baltimore City*, 341 U.S. 56, 71 S.Ct. 565, 95 L.Ed. 745, have been to no avail. It will also be entitled to feel baffled by an opinion which, while recognizing the continuing authority of *Gerende*, undertakes to bypass that decision by a process of reasoning that defies analysis.

Petitioner Whitehill was denied employment in the state university as a temporary lecturer by reason of his refusal to sign an oath that more than meets the requirements of *Gerende*. He was asked only whether he is *now*, in one way or another *engaged in* an attempt to overthrow the Government *by force and violence*.[1] References to international conferences, controversial discussions, support of minority candidates, academic freedom and the like cannot disguise the fact that Whitehill was asked simply to disclaim actual, present activity, amounting in effect to treasonable conduct. Allusions to the constitutional amending process cannot obscure the fact that this oath

makes no reference to "alteration" of our form of government or to "believing in" or "being a member of" anything whatsoever. The oath itself, then, in no way violates, jeopardizes, or beclouds petitioner's freedom of speech or of association. So much, indeed, the Court's opinion appears to concede.

The Court concludes, however, that the oath must be read "in connection with" certain sections of the Ober Law because, as a state matter, the authority of the Board of Regents to require an oath derives from that law. The Court does not pause to tell us what the "connection" is or to explain how it serves to invalidate the unambiguous oath required of this petitioner. On the one hand, it is plain, as the Court artistically avoids conceding, that the only effect of the law on this petitioner is to deny him state employment if he refuses to sign an oath which, in itself, he can have no constitutional objection to signing. On the other hand, nowhere does the Court suggest that the character of the oath itself is altered by any language in the statute authorizing the Regents to impose it. The oath does not refer to the statute or otherwise incorporate it by reference. It contains no terms that are further defined in the statute. In short, the oath must be judged on its own bottom.

The only thing that does shine through the opinion of the majority is that its members do not like loyalty oaths. Believing that it is not within

1. The oath did not even include the limited sort of "membership" clause also approved in *Gerende*. . . .

the province of this Court to pass upon the wisdom or unwisdom of Maryland's policy in this regard, and finding nothing *unconstitutional* about the oath tendered to this petitioner, I would affirm the judgment of the court below.

QUESTIONS

1. What rationale or reasoning is there for the state to require its employees to take loyalty oaths?

2. If someone who was working for the state, was disloyal or engaged in "subversive" activities, do you suppose he would take a loyalty oath? If this is a reasonable assumption, what—if anything—do these oaths accomplish?

3. In all honesty, don't you think the oath in this case was reasonably clear and certainly was not vague?

4. Do you agree with the dissent of Justice Harlan that apparently it is simply a fact that the majority does not like loyalty oaths? If you don't—in what way was the oath vague? If you do agree with Harlan, why doesn't the Court majority just come out and say loyalty oaths are unconstitutional?

5. If a person is loyal to the United States, what reasonable objection could he have to taking a "loyalty oath?" If he isn't loyal to the U.S., doesn't the requirement of the oath make good sense?

PICKERING v. BOARD OF EDUCATION

391 U.S. 563; 88 S. Ct. 1731; 20 L.Ed. 2d 811 (1968)

MR. JUSTICE MARSHALL *delivered the opinion of the Court.*

Appellant Marvin L. Pickering, a teacher in Township High School District 205, Will County, Illinois, was dismissed from his position by the appellee Board of Education for sending a letter to a local newspaper in connection with a recently proposed tax increase that was critical of the way in which the Board and the district superintendent of schools had handled past proposals to raise new revenue for the schools. Appellant's dismissal resulted from a determination by the Board, after a full hearing, that the publication of the letter was "detrimental to the efficient operation and administration of the schools of the district" and hence, under the relevant Illinois statute, Ill.Rev.Stat. 1963, c. 122, § 10–22.4, that "interests of the schools require[d] [his dismissal]."

Appellant's claim that his writing of the letter was protected by the First and Fourteenth Amendments was rejected. Appellant then sought review of the Board's action in the Circuit Court of Will County, which affirmed his dismissal on the ground that the determination that appellant's letter was detrimental to the interests of the school system was supported by substantial evidence and that the interests of the schools overruled appellant's First Amendment rights. On appeal, the Supreme Court of Illinois, two Justices dissenting, affirmed the judgment of the Circuit Court. 36 Ill.2d 568, 225 N.E. 2d 1 (1966). We noted probable jurisdiction of appellant's claim that the Illinois statute permitting his dismissal on the facts of this case was unconstitutional as applied under the First and Fourteenth Amendments. 389 U.S. 925, 88 S.Ct. 291, 19 L.Ed. 2d 276 (1967). For the reasons detailed below we agree that appellant's rights to freedom of speech were violated and we reverse.

I.

In February of 1961 the appellee Board of Education asked the voters of the school district to approve a bond issue to raise $4,875,000 to erect two new schools. The proposal was defeated. Then, in December of 1961, the Board submitted another bond proposal to the voters which called for the raising of $5,500,000 to build two new schools. This second proposal passed and the schools were built with the money raised by the bond sales. In May of 1964 a proposed increase in the tax rate to be used for educational purposes was submitted to the voters by the Board and was defeated. Finally, on September 19, 1964, a second proposal to increase the tax rate was submitted by the Board and was likewise defeated. It was in connection with this last proposal of the School Board that appellant wrote the letter to the editor . . . that resulted in his dismissal.

Prior to the vote on the second tax increase proposal a variety of articles attributed to the District 205 Teachers' Organization appeared in the local paper. These articles urged passage of the tax increase and stated that failure to pass the increase would result in a decline in the quality of education afforded children in the district's schools. A letter from the superintendent of schools making the same point was published in the paper two days before the election and submitted to the voters in mimeographed form the following day. It was in response to the foregoing material, together with the failure of the tax increase to pass, that appellant submitted the letter in question to the editor of the local paper.

The letter constituted, basically, an attack on the school board's handling of the 1961 bond issue proposals and its subsequent allocation of financial resources between the schools' educational and athletic programs. It also charged the superintendent of schools with attempting to prevent teachers in the district from opposing or criticizing the proposed bond issue.

The Board dismissed Pickering for writing and publishing the letter. Pursuant to Illinois law, the Board was then required to hold a hearing on the dismissal. At the hearing the Board charged that numerous statements in the letter were false and that the publication of the statements unjustifiably impugned the "motives, honesty, integrity, truthfulness, responsibility and competence" of both the Board and the school administration. The Board also charged that the false statements damaged the professional reputations of its members and of the school administrators, would be disruptive of faculty discipline, and would tend to foment "controversy, conflict and dissension" among teachers, administrators, the Board of Education, and the residents of the district. Testimony was introduced from a variety of witnesses on the truth or falsity of the particular statements in the letter with which the Board took issue. The Board found the statements to be false as charged. No evidence was introduced at any point in the proceedings as to the effect of the publication of the letter on the community as a whole or on the administration of the school system in particular, and no specific findings along these lines were made.

The Illinois courts reviewed the proceedings solely to determine whether the Board's findings were supported by substantial evidence and whether, on the facts as found, the Board could reasonably conclude that appellant's publication of the letter was "detrimental to the best interests of the schools." Pickering's claim that his letter was protected by the First Amendment was rejected

on the ground *that his acceptance of a teaching position in the public schools obliged him to refrain from making statements about the operation of the schools* "which in the absence of such position he would have an undoubted right to engage in." It is not altogether clear whether the Illinois Supreme Court held that the First Amendment had no applicability to appellant's dismissal for writing the letter in question or whether it determined that the particular statements made in the letter were not entitled to First Amendment protection. In any event, it clearly rejected Pickering's claim that, on the facts of this case, he could not constitutionally be dismissed from his teaching position.

II.

To the extent that the Illinois Supreme Court's opinion may be read to suggest that teachers may constitutionally be compelled to relinquish the First Amendment rights they would otherwise enjoy as citizens to comment on matters of public interest in connection with the operation of the public schools in which they work, it proceeds on a premise that has been unequivocally rejected in numerous prior decisions of this Court. . . . "[T]he theory that public employment which may be denied altogether may be subjected to any conditions, regardless of how unreasonable, has been uniformly rejected." *Keyishian* v. *Board of Regents, supra,* 385 U.S. at 605–606, . . . At the same time it cannot be gainsaid that

*[Editor's Note: Emphasis added.]

the State has interests as an employer in regulating the speech of its employees that differ significantly from those it possesses in connection with regulation of the speech of the citizenry in general. The problem in any case is to arrive at a balance between the interests of the teacher, as a citizen, in commenting upon matters of public concern and the interest of the State, as an employer, in promoting the efficiency of the public services it performs through its employees.

III.

The Board contends that "the teacher by virtue of his public employment has a duty of loyalty to support his superiors in attaining the generally accepted goals of education and that, if he must speak out publicly, he should do so factually and accurately, commensurate with his education and experience." Appellant, on the other hand, argues that the test applicable to defamatory statements directed against public officials by persons having no occupational relationship with them, namely, that statements to be legally actionable must be made "with knowledge that [they were] . . . false or with reckless disregard of whether [they were] . . . false or not," *New York Times Co.* v. *Sullivan*, 376 U.S. 254, 280, 84 S.Ct. 710, 726, 11 L.Ed.2d 686 (1964), should also be applied to public statements made by teachers. . . .

An examination of the statements in appellant's letter objected to by the Board reveals that they, like the letter as a whole, consist essentially of criticism of the Board's allocation of school funds between educational and athletic programs, and of both the Board's and the superintendent's methods of informing, or preventing the informing of, the district's taxpayers of the real reasons why additional tax revenues were being sought for the schools. The statements are in no way directed towards any person with whom appellant would normally be in contact in the course of his daily work as a teacher. Thus no question of maintaining either discipline by immediate superiors or harmony among coworkers is presented here. . . .

We next consider the statements in appellant's letter which we agree to be false. The Board's original charges included allegations that the publication of the letter damaged the professional reputations of the Board and the superintendent and would foment controversy and conflict among the Board, teachers, administrators, and the residents of the district. However, no evidence to support these allegations was introduced at the hearing. So far as the record reveals, Pickering's letter was greeted by everyone but its main target, the Board, with massive apathy and total disbelief. . . .

However, the only way in which the Board could conclude, absent any evidence of the actual effect of the letter, that the statements contained therein were *per se* detrimental to the interest of the schools was to equate the Board members' own interests with that of the schools. Certainly an accusation that too much money is being spent on athletics by the administrators of the school system (which is precisely the import of that portion of appellant's letter containing the statements that we have found to be false) ... cannot reasonably be regarded as *per se* detrimental to the district's schools. Such an accusation reflects rather a difference of opinion between Pickering and the Board as to the preferable manner of operating the school system, a difference of opinion that clearly concerns an issue of general public interest.

In addition, the fact that particular illustrations of the Board's claimed undesirable emphasis on athletic programs are false would not normally have any necessary impact on the actual operation of the schools, beyond its tendency to anger the Board. For example, Pickering's letter was written after the defeat at the polls of the second proposed tax increase. It could, therefore, have had no effect on the ability of the school district to raise necessary revenue, since there was no showing that there was any proposal to increase taxes pending when the letter was written.

More importantly, the question whether a school system requires additional funds is a matter of legitimate public concern on which the judgment of the school administration, including the School Board, cannot, in a society that leaves such questions to popular vote, be taken as conclusive. On such a question free and open debate is vital to informed decision-making by the electorate. Teachers are, as a class, the members of a community most likely to have informed and definite opinions as to how funds allotted to the operation of the schools should

be spent. Accordingly, it is essential that they be able to speak out freely on such questions without fear of retaliatory dismissal.

In addition, the amounts expended on athletics which Pickering reported erroneously were matters of public record on which his position as a teacher in the district did not qualify him to speak with any greater authority than any other taxpayer. The Board could easily have rebutted appellant's errors by publishing the accurate figures itself, either via a letter to the same newspaper or otherwise. We are thus not presented with a situation in which a teacher has carelessly made false statements about matters so closely related to the day-to-day operations of the schools that any harmful impact on the public would be difficult to counter because of the teacher's presumed greater access to the real facts. Accordingly, we have no occasion to consider at this time whether under such circumstances a school board could reasonably require that a teacher make substantial efforts to verify the accuracy of his charges before publishing them.

What we do have before us is a case in which a teacher has made erroneous public statements upon issues then currently the subject of public attention, which are critical of his ultimate employer but which are neither shown nor can be presumed to have in any way either impeded the teacher's proper performance of his daily duties in the classroom or to have interfered with the regular operation of the schools generally. In these circumstances we conclude that the interest of the school administration in limiting teachers' opportunities to contribute to public debate is not significantly greater than its interest in limiting a similar contribution by any member of the general public.

IV.

The public interest in having free and unhindered debate on matters of public importance—the core value of the Free Speech Clause of the First Amendment—is so great that it has been held that a State cannot authorize the recovery of damages by a public official for defamatory statements directed at him except when such statements are shown to have been made cither with knowledge of their falsity or with reckless disregard for their truth or falsity. *New York Times Co.* v. *Sullivan*, 376 U.S. 254, 84 S.Ct. 710 (1964); . . . The same test has been applied to suits for invasion of privacy based on false statements where a "matter of public interest" is involved. *Time, Inc.* v. *Hill*, 385 U.S. 374, 87 S.Ct. 534, 17 L.Ed.2d 456 (1967). It is therefore perfectly clear that, were appellant a member of the general public, the State's power to afford the appellee Board of Education or its members any legal right to sue him for writing the letter at issue here would be limited by the requirement that the letter be judged by the standard laid down in *New York Times*.

.　　.　　.

In sum, we hold that, in a case such as this, absent proof of false statements knowingly or recklessly made by him, a teacher's exercise of

his right to speak on issues of public importance may not furnish the basis for his dismissal from public employment. Since no such showing has been made in this case . . . his dismissal for writing it cannot be upheld and the judgment of the Illinois Supreme Court must, accordingly, be reversed and the case remanded for further proceedings not inconsistent with this opinion. It is so ordered.

Judgment reversed and case remanded with directions. *

MR. JUSTICE WHITE, *concurring in part and dissenting in part.*

The Court holds that truthful statements by a school teacher critical of the school board are within the ambit of the First Amendment. So also are false statements innocently or negligently made. The State may not fire the teacher for making either unless, as I gather it, there are special circumstances, not present in this case, demonstrating an overriding state interest, such as the need for confidentiality or the special obligations which a teacher in a particular position may owe to his superiors. The core of today's decision is the holding that Pickering's discharge must be tested by the standard of *New York Times Co.* v. *Sullivan*, 376 U.S. 254, 84 S.Ct. 710 (1964). To this extent I am in agreement.

. . . The Court then gratuitously suggests that when statements are

---

* [*The concurring opinion of* MR. JUSTICE DOUGLAS, *which* MR. JUSTICE BLACK *joined, is omitted.*]

found to be knowingly or recklessly false, it is an open question whether the First Amendment still protects them unless they are shown or can be presumed to have caused harm. . . . Deliberate or reckless falsehoods serve no First Amendment ends and deserve no protection under that Amendment. The Court unequivocally recognized this in *Garrison*, where after reargument the Court said that "the knowingly false statement and the statement made with reckless disregard of the truth, do not enjoy constitutional protection." . . . As I see it, a teacher may be fired without violation of the First Amendment for knowingly or recklessly making false statements regardless of their harmful impact on the schools. As the Court holds, however, in the absence of special circumstances he may not be fired if his statements were true or only negligently false, even if there is some harm to the school system. I therefore see no basis or necessity for the Court's foray into factfinding with respect to whether the record supports a finding as to injury. If Pickering's false statements were either knowingly or recklessly made, injury to the school system becomes irrelevant, and the First Amendment would not prevent his discharge. . . .

QUESTIONS

1. When the two are in conflict, should a teacher's loyalty to the school Administration take precedence over an appeal to the voters as the letter in this case represented? Why?

2. If a teacher's freedom of expression is not to be diminished by the fact that he (she) is employed by the school system, would you approve of criticism about the Administration or budget being voiced to the students themselves in class? Out of class? Why? Or why not?

3. Do you recognize any limitations on the teacher's right to criticize— as opposed to an ordinary citizen—because the teacher is identified with and employed by the school district? If you see limitations—what are they? What standards would you use to establish them? If there are no unusual limitations—What loyalty, if any, does a teacher's professional responsibilities impose?

4. Since any Administrative decisions about allocations of funds and what constitutes good education are in the last analysis professional value-judgments, do you think it was Pickering's place to attempt to interfere with his superiors' decisions? Why?

5. If you were Pickering's superior *and you could get away with it*, would you fire him? Why yes? Why no?

STREET v. NEW YORK

394 U.S. 576; 89 S. Ct. 1354; 22 L.Ed. 2d 572 (1969)

MR. JUSTICE HARLAN *delivered the opinion of the Court.*

Appellant Street has been convicted in the New York courts of violating former § 1425 (16) (d) of the New York Penal Law, McKinney's Consol. Laws, c. 40, which makes it a misdemeanor "publicly [to] mutilate, deface, defile, or defy, trample upon, or cast contempt upon either by words or act [any flag of the United States]."[1] He was given a suspended sentence. We must decide whether, in light of all the circumstances, that conviction denied to him rights of free expression protected by the First Amendment and assured against state infringement by the Fourteenth Amendment. . . .

According to evidence given at trial, the events which led to the conviction were these. Appellant testified that during the afternoon of June 6, 1966, he was listening to the radio in his Brooklyn apartment. He heard a news report that civil rights leader James Meredith had been shot by a sniper in Mississippi. Saying to himself, "They didn't protect him," appellant, himself a Negro, took from his drawer a neatly folded, 48-star American flag which he formerly had displayed on national holidays. Appellant left his apartment and carried the still-folded flag

to the nearby intersection of St. James Place and Lafayette Avenue. Appellant stood on the northeast corner of the intersection, lit the flag with a match, and dropped the flag on the pavement when it began to burn.

Soon thereafter, a police officer halted his patrol car and found the burning flag. The officer testified that he then crossed to the northwest corner of the intersection, where he found appellant "talking out loud" to a small group of persons. The officer estimated that there were some 30 persons on the corner near the flag and five to 10 on the corner with appellant. The officer testified that as he approached within 10 or 15 feet of appellant, he heard appellant say "We don't need no damn flag," and that when he asked appellant whether he had burned the flag appellant replied: "Yes; that is my flag; I burned it. If they let that happen to Meredith, we don't need an American flag." Appellant admitted making the latter response, but he denied that he said anything else and asserted that he always had remained on the corner with the flag.

Later the same day, appellant was charged, by an information sworn to before a judge of the New York City Criminal Court, with having committed "the crime of Malicious Mis-

1. N.Y.Penal Law § 1425 (16) (d) (1909). In 1967 § 1425 (16) (d) was superseded by § 136 of the General Business Law, McKinney's Consol.Laws, c. 20, which defines the offense in identical language. See N.Y.Laws, c. 1031, § 52 (1965).

chief in that [he] did wilfully and unlawfully defile, cast contempt upon and burn an American Flag, in violation of 1425–16–D of the Penal Law, under the following circumstances: . . . [he] did wilfully and unlawfully set fire to an American Flag and shout, 'If they did that to Meredith, We don't need an American Flag.' "

Appellant was tried before another Criminal Court judge, sitting without a jury, and was convicted of malicious mischief in violation of § 1425 (16) (d).² He was subsequently given a suspended sentence. The Appellate Division, Second Department, affirmed without opinion. Leave was granted to appeal to the New York Court of Appeals, and after plenary consideration that court unanimously affirmed. 20 N.Y.2d 231, 282 N.Y.S.2d 491, 229 N.E.2d 187 (1967). We noted probable jurisdiction. 392 U.S. 923 (1968).

Street argues that his conviction was unconstitutional for three different reasons. *First*, he claims that § 1425 (16) (d) is overbroad, both on its face and as applied, because the section makes it a crime "publicly [to] defy . . . or cast contempt upon [an American flag] *by words* . . . ." (Emphasis added.) *Second*, he contends that § 1425 (16) (d) is vague and imprecise because it does not clearly define the conduct which it forbids. *Third*, he asserts that New York may not constitutionally punish one who publicly destroys or

damages an American flag as a means of protest, because such an act constitutes expression protected by the Fourteenth Amendment. We deem it unnecessary to consider the latter two arguments, for we hold that § 1425 (16) (d) was unconstitutionally applied in appellant's case because it permitted him to be punished merely for speaking defiant or contemptuous words about the American flag. In taking this course, we resist the pulls to decide the constitutional issues involved in this case on a broader basis than the record before us imperatively requires.

Though our conclusion is a narrow one, it requires pursuit of four lines of inquiry: (1) whether the constitutionality of the "words" part of the statute was passed upon by the New York Court of Appeals; (2) whether, if appellant's conviction may have rested in whole or in part on his utterances and if the statute as thus applied is unconstitutional, these factors in themselves require reversal; (3) whether Street's words may in fact have counted independently in his conviction; and (4) whether the "words" provision of the statute, as presented by this case, is unconstitutional.

I.

The New York Court of Appeals did not mention in its opinion the constitutionality of the "words" part of § 1425 (16) (d).⁴ Hence, in

2. Appellant was simultaneously tried for disorderly conduct in connection with the same events. He was acquitted of that offense.

4. Also, we are unable to read the opinion

of the Court of Appeals as reading the "words" clause out of the statute and authoritatively construing it to reach only the *act* of flag burning, whether as a protest or otherwise.

order to vindicate our jurisdiction to deal with this particular issue, we must inquire whether that question was presented to the New York courts in such a manner that it was necessarily decided by the New York Court of Appeals when it affirmed appellant's conviction. If the question was not so presented, then we have no power to consider it. . . .

In this case, any want of presentation by the appellant must have occurred at the trial level, for there appears to be no doubt that the issue of the constitutionality of the "words" part of the statute was raised in appellant's briefs in both the Appellate Division and the Court of Appeals, and the State does not suggest the contrary. In the trial court, appellant's counsel raised the constitutional issues by means of the following motion:

"Before we plead to this case, I would like to make a motion to dismiss the information upon the following grounds: The defendant was engaged in a constitutionally protected activity, to wit, freedom of speech. The allegation simply says that the defendant did wilfully and unlawfully set fire to an American flag and did say: 'If they did that to Meredith we don't need an American flag.' Under the first amendment of the Constitution of the United States and under the New York State Constitution they provide for protest in many forms, whether by burning a flag, demonstration or picketing. This is a form of demonstration and protest."

The motion was denied. It was re-newed at the end of the State's case and at the end of the trial, and on both occasions was again denied.

. . . [W]e think appellant has met the burden of showing that the issue of the constitutionality of the "words" part of § 1425 (16) (d) was adequately raised in the state trial court. The motion quoted above explicitly referred to appellant's words. Appellant's counsel termed appellant's overall activity a "demonstration" or "protest," terms which encompass words as well as conduct. Indeed, if appellant's intention was to protest alleged governmental inaction in connection with the shooting of James Meredith, his words were an essential element, for without them no one would have known the object of his protest.

. . .

II.

We next consider whether it is our duty to reverse if we find, as we do in Parts III and IV, *infra*, that Street's words could have been an independent cause of his conviction and that a conviction for uttering such words would violate the Constitution.

That such is our duty is made apparent by a number of decisions of this Court. In the leading case of *Stromberg* v. *California*, 283 U.S. 359, 51 S.Ct. 532, 75 L.Ed. 1117 (1931), the appellant was convicted by a jury under a California statute making it an offense publicly to display a red flag for any one of three purposes. Finding that it would be unconstitutional to punish one who displayed for the first-named reason, this Court rejected the state court's reasoning that the appellant's conviction could nevertheless be sustained because the other two statutory reasons were severable and constitutional. This Court said:

> "The verdict against the appellant was a general one. It did not specify the ground upon which it rested. . . . [I]t is impossible to say under which clause of the statute the conviction was obtained. If any one of these clauses . . . was invalid, it cannot be determined upon this record that the appellant was not convicted under that clause. . . . It follows that . . . the conviction cannot be upheld." . . .

The principle established in *Stromberg* has been consistently followed. In *Williams* v. *North Carolina*, 317 U.S. 287, 63 S.Ct. 207, 87 L.Ed. 279 (1942), this Court again held itself compelled to reverse a conviction based upon a general jury verdict when the record failed to prove that the conviction was not founded upon a theory which could not constitutionally support a verdict. . . .

.   .   .

As in *Thomas*, appellant here was charged with two acts violative of the statute: burning a flag and publicly speaking defiant or contemptuous words about the flag; and evidence was introduced to show the commission of both acts. Here too the verdict was general and the sentence a single penalty. Hence, unless the record negates the possibility that the conviction was based on both alleged violations, *Thomas* dictates that "[t]he judgment . . . must be affirmed as to both or as to neither."

We take the rationale of *Thomas* to be that when a single-count indictment or information charges the commission of a crime by virtue of having done both a constitutionally protected act and one which may be unprotected, and a guilty verdict ensues without elucidation, there is an unacceptable danger that the trier of fact will have regarded the two acts as "intertwined" and have rested the conviction on both together. . . .

III.

We turn to considering whether appellant's words could have been the sole cause of his conviction, or whether the conviction could have been based on both his words and his burning of the flag. As *Stromberg* teaches, we cannot take the opinion of the New York Court of Appeals as obviating our duty to examine the record for ourselves in order to ascertain whether the conviction may have rested upon such grounds. The sworn information which charged appellant with the crime of malicious mischief, and which is quoted more fully *supra*, at 2, recited not only that appellant had burned an American flag but also that he "[did] shout, 'If they did that to Meredith, We don't need an American flag.' " Section 1425 (16) (d), the statute which appellant was charged with violating, made it a crime not only publicly to mutilate a flag but also "publicly [to] defy . . . or cast contempt upon [any American flag] by words."

The State argues that appellant's words were at most used to establish his unlawful intent in burning the flag.[10] However, after a careful examination of the comparatively brief trial record, we find ourselves unable to say with certainty that appellant's words were not an independent cause of his conviction. While it is true that at trial greater emphasis was placed upon appellant's action in burning the flag than upon his words, a police officer did testify to the utterance of the words. The State never announced that it was relying exclusively upon the burning. The trial judge never indicated during the trial that he regarded appellant's words as relating solely to intent. The judge found appellant guilty immediately after the end of the trial, and he delivered no oral or written opinion.

In the face of an information explicitly setting forth appellant's words as an element of his alleged crime, and of appellant's subsequent conviction under a statute making it an offense to speak words of that sort, we find this record insufficient to eliminate the possibility either that appellant's words were the sole basis of his conviction or that appellant was convicted for both his words and his deed.

IV.

We come finally to the question whether, in the circumstances of this case, New York may constitutionally inflict criminal punishment upon one who ventures "publicly [to] defy . . . or cast contempt upon [any American flag] by words. . . ."

. . .

. . . [W]e can think of four governmental interests which might conceivably have been furthered by punishing appellant for his words: (1) an interest in deterring appellant from vocally inciting others to commit unlawful acts; (2) an interest in preventing appellant from uttering words so inflammatory that they would provoke others to retaliate physically against him, thereby causing a breach of the peace; (3) an interest in protecting the sensibilities of passers-by who might be shocked by appellant's words about the American flag; and (4) an interest in assuring that appellant, regardless of the impact of his words upon others, showed proper respect for our national emblem.

In the circumstances of this case, we do not believe that any of these interests may constitutionally justify appellant's conviction under § 1425

10. The State also contends that appellant's words could not have been a ground of conviction because they obviously were not spoken "publicly," as required by § 1425 (16) (d). However, although appellant testified that he spoke solely to a police officer, the officer himself gave evidence from which the trial judge might have concluded that appellant's remarks were made either to or within hearing of a small crowd. . . . Moreover, the sworn information recited that appellant "shout[ed]" his words on a city street, thereby apparently satisfying the statutory requirement that the words be said "publicly."

Nor do we think it impossible for the trial judge to have found that by his statements, "We don't need no damn flag" and "I they let that happen to Meredith, we don't need an American flag," appellant "def[ied] . . . or cast contempt upon [an American flag] by words" in violation of § 1425 (16) (d).

(16) (d) for speaking as he did. We begin with the interest in preventing incitement. Appellant's words, taken alone, did not urge anyone to do anything unlawful. They amounted only to somewhat excited public advocacy of the idea that the United States should abandon, at least temporarily, one of its national symbols. It is clear that the Fourteenth Amendment prohibits the States from imposing criminal punishment for public advocacy of peaceful change in our institutions. . . .

Nor could such a conviction be justified on the second ground mentioned above: the possible tendency of appellant's words to provoke violent retaliation. Though it is conceivable that some listeners might have been moved to retaliate upon hearing appellant's disrespectful words, we cannot say that appellant's remarks were so inherently inflammatory as to come within that small class of "fighting words" which are "likely to provoke the average person to retaliation, and thereby cause a breach of the peace." *Chaplinsky* v. *New Hampshire*, 315 U.S. 568, 574, 62 S.Ct. 766, 770, 86 L.Ed. 1031 (1942). . . .

Again, such a conviction could not be sustained on the ground that appellant's words were likely to shock passers-by. Except perhaps for appellant's incidental use of the word "damn," upon which no emphasis was placed at trial, any shock effect of appellant's speech must be attributed to the content of the ideas expressed. It is firmly settled that under our Constitution the public expression of ideas may not be prohibited merely because the ideas are themselves offensive to some of their hearers. . . .

Finally, such a conviction could not be supported on the theory that by making the above-quoted remarks about the flag appellant failed to show the respect for our national symbol which may properly be demanded of every citizen. In *West Virginia State Board of Educ.* v. *Barnette*, 319 U.S. 624, 63 S.Ct. 1178, 87 L.Ed. 1628 (1943), this Court held that to require unwilling schoolchildren to salute the flag would violate rights of free expression assured by the Fourteenth Amendment. In his opinion for the Court, Mr. Justice Jackson wrote words which are especially apposite here:

"The case is made difficult not because the principles of its decision are obscure but because the flag involved is our own. Nevertheless, we apply the limitations of the Constitution with no fear that freedom to be intellectually and spiritually diverse or even contrary will disintegrate the social organization. . . . [F]reedom to differ is not limited to things that do not matter much. That would be a mere shadow of freedom. The test of its substance is the right to differ as to things that touch the heart of the existing order.

"If there is any fixed star in our constitutional constellation, it is that no official, high or petty, can prescribe what shall be orthodox in politics, nationalism, religion, or other matters of opinion or force citizens to confess by word or act their faith therein. If there are any circumstances which permit an exception, they do not now occur to us." . . .

We have no doubt that the constitutionally guaranteed "freedom to be intellectually . . . diverse and even contrary," and the "right to differ as to things that touch the heart of the existing order," encompass the freedom to express publicly one's opinions about our flag, including those opinions which are defiant or contemptuous.

Since appellant could not constitutionally be punished under § 1425 (16) (d) for his speech, and since we have found that he may have been so punished, his conviction cannot be permitted to stand. In so holding, we reiterate that we have no occasion to pass upon the validity of this conviction insofar as it was sustained by the state courts on the basis that Street could be punished for his burning of the flag, even though the burning was an act of protest. . . .

We add that disrespect for our flag is to be deplored no less in these vexed times than in calmer periods of our history. . . . Nevertheless, we are unable to sustain a conviction that may have rested on a form of expression, however distasteful, which the Constitution tolerates and protects.

For the reasons previously set forth, we reverse the judgment of the New York Court of Appeals and remand the case for further proceedings not inconsistent with this opinion.

It is so ordered.
Reversed and remanded.

MR. CHIEF JUSTICE WARREN, *dissenting.*

I dissent from the reversal of this judgment, not only because the Court in my opinion has strained to bring this trial within *Stromberg* v. *California*, 283 U.S. 359, 51 S.Ct. 532, 75 L.Ed. 1117 (1931), but more particularly because it has declined to meet and resolve the basic question presented in the case. That question has been variously stated by the New York Court of Appeals and the parties. The court below employed the following statement of the question:

> "We are called upon to decide whether the deliberate act of burning an American flag in public as a 'protest' may be punished as a crime."

Appellant tells us that the issue presented is:

> "May New York State constitutionally impose penal sanctions upon an individual charged with destroying or damaging an American flag in an attempt to dramatize his concern with social conditions existing in the country?"

New York's statement of the issue is identical:

> "May the State of New York constitutionally impose penal sanctions upon one who is charged with

publicly and deliberately desecrating an American flag as a means of dramatizing his dissatisfaction with social conditions existing within our Country?"

Any distinctions between the above questions are without a significant difference. The parties obviously believe that the constitutionality of flag desecration statutes is before the Court. The question posed by the Court of Appeals is the most succinct. Chief Judge Fuld, writing for a unanimous Court of Appeals, answered the question squarely; we should do likewise if we are to meet our responsibility. But the Court specifically refuses to decide this issue. Instead, it searches microscopically for the opportunity to decide the case on the peripheral *Stromberg* ground, holding that it is impossible to determine the basis for appellant's conviction. In my opinion a reading of the short trial record leaves no doubt that appellant was convicted solely for burning the American flag.

I.

From the beginning to the end of the proceedings below the parties placed only two matters in issue: (1) is burning the flag protected symbolic speech and (2) did appellant burn the flag for the purpose of casting contempt upon it or did he burn it in a dignified manner? . . .

    .   .   .

The trial testimony confirms my belief that appellant's act was the sole basis for the verdict as it contains nothing to suggest that either the parties or the trial judge believed that appellant was on trial for his words. The arresting officer testified that, as he was investigating the source of a fire, he heard appellant say, "We don't need no damn flag." The officer then asked appellant whether he was responsible for the burning of the flag; appellant replied that he was and that "If they let that happen to Meredith, we don't need an American flag." The officer's testimony concluded with a description of the number of people in the vicinity and the extinguishing of the fire. During cross-examination of the officer, defense counsel asked not one question concerning what, if anything, appellant said.

Appellant did not dispute the prosecution's version of the facts. He testified that, hearing the news report of Meredith's shooting, he removed a flag from his dresser drawer, walked to the corner of St. James Place and Lafayette Avenue and burned the flag. According to appellant, he made no remarks to the crowd that had gathered and his reference to Meredith was made to the police officer. Cross-examination by the prosecution explored appellant's motivation for burning the flag; no mention was made of words appellant might have spoken.

We are told by the Court that at least in part appellant's conviction rests on his words. If it does, the trial record is strangely silent, for the State made no attempt to prove that appellant's words were heard by the crowd. Appellant insisted that he spoke only to the officer, yet the New York statute requires that the accused's flag desecration be public. The State argues, without contradiction by appellant, that words spoken to a policeman would not be spoken publicly for purposes of the statute. I think it evident that appellant's words were mentioned in the indictment and introduced at trial only to show that he burned the flag with an intent to desecrate it, a necessary element of the State's case. . . .

Neither the prosecution nor the defense nor the New York courts attached any independent significance to his words. To interpret this record in any other manner ignores the very basic fact that the trial judge and the parties thought that there was one issue in this trial— whether appellant could be criminally punished for burning the flag. This record is not sufficiently ambiguous to justify the Court's speculation that the verdict below might rest even in part upon a conviction for appellant's words.

II.

I do not believe that the *Stromberg* line of cases allows us to avoid deciding whether flag burning is protected by the First Amendment. This case does not fit the *Stromberg* mold.

. . .

The teaching of *Stromberg* is that, if there is any possibility the general verdict below rests on speech or conduct entitled to constitutional protection, then the conviction must be reversed. The *Stromberg* analysis cannot be applied to appellant's conviction as the factual patterns in

the two cases are distinct. The record leaves no doubt that appellant did burn the flag. Nor can appellant argue that his act was not an act of desecration. The trial judge emphatically stated that the issue was whether appellant burned the flag to destroy it in a dignified manner or to cast contempt upon it. Appellant's conviction therefore must be based upon a finding that he desecrated the flag by burning and neither he nor the Court suggests otherwise. We are not confronted with a jury trial and the consequent inability to determine the basis for the verdict below. The trial judge at the very outset of the trial made known his view that appellant's motivation for burning the flag was the probative issue. Combining this act of burning with a verbalization of the reasons for it does not allow the Court to avoid determining the constitutionality of appellant's conduct. Since there can be no claim that appellant was convicted for his speech, *Stromberg* simply does not apply.

. . .

Terminello v. *City of Chicago*, 337 U.S. 1, 69 S.Ct. 894, 93 L.Ed. 1131 (1949), reflects the same approach. Terminello was charged with disorderly conduct. The jury was allowed to convict if it found that Terminello's speech either stirred the public to anger or constituted "fighting words." Since only the latter may be constitutionally prohibited, the Court reversed. It was possible that the jury found that Terminello's speech merely stirred the public to anger yet convicted him. Terminello could have been convicted for constitutionally protected conduct; he was therefore entitled to a reversal. *Yates* v. *United States*, 354 U.S. 298, 77 S.Ct. 1064, 1 L.Ed.2d 1356 (1957), also conforms to this pattern. Charged with a violation of the Smith Act, Yates was convicted under instructions which made either "advocacy" or "organizing" a statutory violation. The Court decided that the jury instruction with regard to the organizing charge was erroneous; since the jury could have convicted Yates for organizing even if it found that he was not guilty of advocacy, the conviction was reversed.

The Court does not, however, base its reversal only upon a misapplication of *Stromberg*. Relying also on *Thomas* v. *Collins*, 323 U.S. 516, 65 S.Ct. 315, 89 L.Ed. 430 (1945), the Court holds that even if "the record precludes the inference that appellant's conviction might have been based *solely* on his words, we are still bound to reverse if the conviction could have been based upon *both* his words and his act." . . . My reading of *Thomas* v. *Collins* indicates, however, that *Thomas* does not serve as justification for the Court's disposition of this case. In *Thomas* a union organizer was held in contempt, fined and imprisoned for disobeying a state court order enjoining him from violating a Texas statute. The statute required that labor organizers register with and procure an organizer's card from a designated Texas official before soliciting memberships in labor unions. Without either registering or procuring a card,

the organizer made a speech before a group of workers. He extolled the virtues of union membership in general terms and also asked a specific individual to become a union member. As I read the case, *Thomas*, holds that both the general solicitation and the solicitation of a named individual were within the protection of the First Amendment:

"The occasion was clearly protected. The speech was an essential part of the occasion, unless all meaning and purpose were to be taken from it. And the invitations, both general and particular, were parts of the speech, inseparable incidents of the occasion and all of that was said or done. . . . How one might 'laud unionism,' as the State and the State Supreme Court concede Thomas was free to do, yet in these circumstances not imply an invitation, is hard to conceive. This is the nub of the case, which the State fails to meet because it cannot do so." *Id.*, at 534–535, 65 S.Ct., at 324.

Having so held, it was unnecessary for the Court to determine if an individual solicitation could have been enjoined. The union organizer therefore was entitled to relief without regard to whether his conviction was based upon the general or the individual solicitation.

I reiterate my belief that appellant was convicted for his act not his words. *Stromberg* and the cases based upon it do not allow us the luxury of refusing to treat appellant's claim that the burning of the flag as a protest is worthy of constitutional protection.

III.

I am in complete agreement with the general rule that this Court should not treat broad constitutional questions when narrow ones will suffice to dispose of the litigation. However, where only the broad question is presented, it is our task and our responsibility to confront that question squarely and resolve it. In a time when the American flag has increasingly become an integral part of public protests, the constitutionality of the flag desecration statutes enacted by all of the States and Congress is a matter of the most widespread concern. Both those who seek constitutional shelter for acts of flag desecration perpetrated in the course of a political protest and those who must enforce the law are entitled to know the scope of constitutional protection. The Court's explicit reservation of the constitutionality of flag burning prohibitions encourages others to test in the streets the power of our States and national government to impose criminal sanctions upon those who would desecrate the flag.

I believe that the States and the Federal Government do have the power to protect the flag from acts of desecration and disgrace. But because the Court has not met the issue, it would serve no purpose to delineate my reasons for this view. However, it is difficult for me to imagine that, had the Court faced this issue, it would have concluded

otherwise. Since I am satisfied that the constitutionality of appellant's conduct should be resolved in this case and am convinced that this conduct can be criminally punished, I dissent.

MR. JUSTICE BLACK, *dissenting.*

I agree with the excellent opinion written by Chief Judge Fuld for a unanimous Court of Appeals, upholding the New York statute which this Court now holds unconstitutional as applied. The entire state court construed the statute as applied to this appellant as making it an offense publicly to burn an American flag in order to protest something that had occurred. In other words the offense which that court sustained was the burning of the flag and not the making of any statements about it. The Court seems to console itself for holding this New York flag-burning law unconstitutional as applied by saying that, as it reads the record, the conviction could have been based on the words spoken by the appellant as he was burning the flag. Those words indicated a desire on appellant's part to degrade and defame the flag. If I could agree with the Court's interpretation of the record as to the possibility of the conviction's resting on these spoken words, I would firmly and automatically agree that the law is unconstitutional. I would not feel constrained, as the Court seems to be, to search my imagination to see if I could think of interests the State may have in suppressing this freedom of speech. I would not balance away the First Amendment right that speech not be abridged in any fashion whatsoever. But I accept the unanimous opinion of the New York Court of Appeals that the conviction does not and could not have rested merely on the spoken words but that it rested entirely on the fact that the defendants had publicly burned the American flag—against the law of the State of New York.

It passes my belief that anything in the Federal Constitution bars a State from making the deliberate burning of the American flag an offense. It is immaterial to me that words are spoken in connection with the *burning*. It is the *burning* of the flag that the State has set its face against. "It rarely has been suggested that the constitutional freedom for speech and press extends its immunity to speech or writing used as an integral part of conduct in violation of a valid criminal statute." *Giboney* v. *Empire Storage Co.*, 336 U.S. 490, 498, 69 S.Ct. 684, 688, 93 L.Ed. 834 (1949). In my view this quotation from the *Giboney* case precisely applies here. The talking that was done took place "as an integral part of conduct in violation of a valid criminal statute" against burning the American flag in public. I would therefore affirm this conviction.

MR. JUSTICE WHITE, *dissenting.*

The Court has spun an intricate, technical web but I fear it has ensnared itself in its own remorseless logic and arrived at a result having no support in the facts of the case or the governing law.

The Court's schema is this: the statute forbids insults to the flag either by act or words; the charge alleged both flag burning and speech; the Court rendered a general judgment; since the conviction might logically have been for speech alone or for both words and deeds and since in either event the conviction is invalid, the judgment of the New York courts must be set aside without passing upon the validity of a conviction for burning the flag. I reach precisely the opposite conclusion; before Street's conviction can either be reversed or affirmed, the Court *must* reach and decide the validity of a conviction for flag burning.

I reject first the Court's suggestion that we must assume from the trial court's judgment—which was that "on the charge of Malicious Mischief the defendant is convicted"—that Street might have been convicted for speech alone. True, the complaint referred to both burning and speaking and the statute permits conviction for either insulting words or physical desecration. But surely the Court has its tongue in its cheek when it infers from this record the possibility that Street was not convicted for burning the flag but only for the words he uttered. It is a distortion of the record to read it in this manner, as THE CHIEF JUSTICE convincingly demonstrates. But even if it were fair to infer that he was convicted for speaking as well as burning, it is sheer fancy to conclude that the trial court convicted him for speech alone and acquitted him of flag burning. The appellant does not seriously argue such a claim; his major point is that he *was* convicted for burning as a protest and that such a conviction cannot stand. The Court of Appeals of New York characterized the issue before it as whether the defendant could be validly convicted for burning the flag as a protest. Moreover, without clear indication from the state courts, I would not assume that the particular words which Street spoke in this case would be deemed within the coverage of the statute. In any event, if Street was convicted for speaking, he most certainly was also convicted for flag burning. Hence, *Stromberg v. California*, 283 U.S. 359, 51 S.Ct. 532, 75 L.Ed. 1117 (1931), and like cases to which I adhere, have no application by their own terms.

I reject also the proposition that if Street was convicted for both burning and talking, his conviction must be reversed if the speech conviction is unconstitutional. . . .

.   .   .

Even accepting the notion that where there is a conviction on each of several counts and a general sentence is imposed, affirmance requires upholding the conviction on each and every count, the rule would have no application to the facts of this case. Such a rule would be based on the notion that the trial judge might have given a lesser sentence if he had known that some of the counts were infirm. Reversal of the judgment on less than all the counts would call only for resentencing, not for reversal of the convictions on the other counts.

Viewed in this light, the judgment of the New York courts, insofar as it convicted Street for flag burning, cannot be reversed simply because Street was also convicted for speaking and a general sentence was given. Neither can the case be remanded for resentencing since no sentence was imposed. Sentence was suspended under the then applicable New York law and the time for imposing a sentence had expired even before the judgment was reviewed in the New York Court of Appeals.

.   .   .

The Court is obviously wrong in reversing the judgment below because it believes that Street was unconstitutionally convicted for speaking. Reversal can follow only if the Court reaches the conviction for flag burning and finds that conviction, as well as the assumed conviction for speech, to be violative of the First Amendment. For myself, without the benefit of the majority's thinking if it were to find flag burning protected by the First Amendment, I would sustain such a conviction. I must dissent.

MR. JUSTICE FORTAS, *dissenting.*

I agree with the dissenting opinion filed by THE CHIEF JUSTICE, but I believe that it is necessary briefly to set forth the reasons why the States and the Federal Government have the power to protect the flag from acts of desecration committed in public.

If the national flag were nothing more than a chattel, subject only to the rules governing the use of private personalty, its use would nevertheless be subject to certain types of state regulation. For example, regulations concerning the use of chattels which are reasonably designed to avoid danger to life or property, or impingement upon the rights of others to the quiet use of their property and of public facilities, would unquestionably be a valid exercise of police power. They would not necessarily be defeated by a claim that they conflicted with the rights of the owner of the regulated property. . . .

If a state statute provided that it is a misdemeanor to burn one's shirt or trousers or shoes on the public thoroughfare, it could hardly be asserted that the citizen's constitutional right is violated. If the arsonist asserted that he was burning his shirt or trousers or shoes as a protest against the Government's fiscal policies, for example, it is hardly possible that his claim to First Amendment shelter would prevail against the State's claim of a right to avert danger to the public and to avoid obstruction to traffic as a result of the fire. This is because action, even if clearly for serious protest purposes, is not entitled to the pervasive protection that is given to speech alone. . . . It may be subjected to reasonable regulation that appropriately takes into account the competing interests involved.

The test that is applicable in every case where conduct is restricted or prohibited is whether the regulation or prohibition is reasonable, due account being taken of the paramountcy of First Amendment values. *If, as I submit, it is permissible to prohibit the burning of personal property on the public sidewalk, there is no basis for applying a different rule to flag burning. And the* *fact that the law is violated for purposes of protest does not immunize the violator.* . . .*

Beyond this, however, the flag is a special kind of personalty. *Its use is traditionally and universally subject to special rules and regulation.** As early as 1907, this Court affirmed the constitutionality of a state statute making it a crime to use a representation of the United States flag for purposes of advertising. *Halter* v. *Nebraska*, 205 U.S. 34, 27 S.Ct. 419, 51 L.Ed 696 (1907). Statutes prescribe how the flag may be displayed; how it may lawfully be disposed of; when, how, and for what purposes it may and may not be used. See, *e. g.*, 4 U.S.C. § 3; 36 U.S.C. §§ 172–177. A person may "own" a flag, but ownership is subject to special burdens and responsibilities. *A flag may be property, in a sense; but it is property burdened with peculiar obligations and restrictions.** Certainly, as *Halter* v. *Nebraska, supra,* held, these special conditions are not *per se* arbitrary or beyond governmental power under our Constitution.

One may not justify the burning of a house, even if it is his own, on the ground, however sincere, that he does so as a protest. One may not justify breaking the windows of a government building on that basis. Protest does not exonerate lawlessness. And the prohibition against flag burning on the public thoroughfare being valid, the misdemeanor is not excused merely because it is an act of flamboyant protest.*

**[Editor's Note: Emphasis added.]*

QUESTIONS

1. Is a flag a special piece of property which the state has the right to protect against desecration? Why would you argue "yes"? Why "no"?

2. *Precisely* what is the state's interest in preventing the desecration of the national flag?

3. Would the dissenting Justices in this case (*i.e.*, Chief Justice Warren, Justices Black, White, and Fortas) be likely to find Mr. Street guilty and constitutionally punishable for this type of "protest" if he were a farmer in upstate New York and burned the flag on his own property with other people watching? Why do you think the answer is "yes" or "no"?

4. Do you agree with Chief Justice Warren that the Court's opinion (by Justice Harlan) *strains* to avoid the constitutionality question of a statute forbidding contemptuous flag burning? If you do—why do you suppose Harlan wants to avoid the issue of constitutionality of such a statute? If you do not agree with Warren's interpretation of Harlan's opinion what is your understanding of Harlan's motivation?

5. In your opinion, should the guaranteed constitutional freedom of political protest protect the burning of one's own property anywhere and at any time? If not—why not? If so—would you argue that the state (or community) by law can make no constitutional exceptions to this right? How would you justify your position?

3. the courtroom and political expression

1. Introductory Essay

2. Courtroom Order And Procedural Rights Case:

   Illinois v. *Allen*, 397 U.S. 337 (1970): "The Courtroom Decorum Case."

3. The Contempt Power And Free Expression Outside The Courtroom Case:

   Garrison v. *Louisiana*, 379 U.S. 64 (1964): "The Defaming Of The Judges Case."

3. the courtroom and political expression

Unlike any other section of this book, the two cases herein raise entirely separate questions. The cases are related, however, in that both involve the judicial process itself and are concerned with protestation in the courtroom and/or the conduct of judges. They also raise the question of the use of the "contempt of court" power to silence criticism—whether justified or not—of judicial behavior.

Politicization of Trials and Decorum in the Courtroom

" 'The American Courtroom' said one Washington legal authority . . . 'is no place either for a political trial or a propaganda demonstration.' The case of the United States v. The Chicago Seven was both—and its consequences would reverberate in American law for years to come," wrote *Newsweek Magazine* on March 2, 1970. The trial of the "Chicago Seven," Dr. Benjamin Spock *et al.* in Boston, and the Black Panthers in New York raise serious questions for the American legal system, the right of American society to defend itself, and the individual's right of political dissent. What is a "political trial?" Is the shooting of a President a political act if you believe he is a Communist leading the nation toward disaster? What constitutes a conspiracy against society? When does dissent and protest become—if ever—conspiracy? How do you try people who have been accused of committing crimes which have political overtones if they are intent on disrupting the courtroom? How do you secure for dissenters a fair trial if their political cause is so distasteful to the public that it is hard to get an impartial judge and jury?

To illustrate just one of the problems, in the New York trial of thirteen

Black Panthers indicted for conspiracy to bomb public places and commit acts of arson, it took approximately six weeks just to select a jury, at a time when court calendars are overly congested with criminal cases waiting to be tried. [*New York Times*, October 16, 1970, 37:8.] There are no easy answers to these questions or the many more that could be asked about trials such as those that took place in Boston in 1969 and Chicago in 1970.

We have mentioned in our discussion of the due process clause of the Fourteenth Amendment that the Supreme Court in recent years has been concerned that constitutionally guaranteed procedural rights in state criminal cases be carefully followed. It is easy to understand that a defendant cannot get a fair trial if he doesn't have an effective attorney who knows the law to prepare his defense and present his case. Equally understandable is the right of the defendant to confront his accusers so that his attorney may have an opportunity to discredit their testimony, which the prosecution will try to use to convict the accused. These procedural guarantees and the other procedural rights applied to the states through the Fourteenth Amendment due process clause do *in fact* make it more difficult for the accused to be convicted.

The Framers of the Bill of Rights, when they included the guarantees against unreasonable searches and seizures, counsel, confrontation, the right against compulsory self-incrimination, etc. knew that convictions of defendants would be made more difficult by these constitutional guarantees. They knew also that these rights would make it more difficult to convict those innocent and accused as well as those who are guilty and accused. Their experience with British colonial justice immediately before the Revolution dictated their choice—they preferred that a guilty man go free rather than that an innocent man be convicted. They knew that no human judicial system could guarantee the "right" verdict all of the time. A system with careful procedural safeguards, honestly followed, would increase the probability of the desired goal—that "justice" be done. This was their commitment and the Constitution enshrined it and made it the "supreme Law of the Land."

Throughout the 1940's, 1950's and 1960's, the Supreme Court has increased its vigilance in supervising state criminal cases to insure that defendants have been accorded due process and a fair trial as guaranteed by the Fourteenth Amendment. As Chapter Two details, the Court has even increased the procedural guarantees inherent in the concept of a fair trial. Nevertheless, despite this concern, the "politicization" of trials has caused the High Court to indicate clearly that procedural rights are no more absolutely guaranteed in all situations than are the substantive constitutional rights of speech, press, religion, assembly and petition. These rights too (procedural rights) may be reasonably conditioned if circumstances demand it.

Illinois v. *Allen*, 397 U.S. 337 (1970), spoke to this point. In this case, the Supreme Court established rules to guide the lower courts—federal and state—as to when procedural rights may be constitutionally curtailed. The case has great implications for future trials if defendants—or their attorneys—attempt to turn the courtroom into a political forum with disruptive tactics.

Unfortunately *Illinois v. Allen, supra,* may be the right case, at the right time, with the wrong defendant. As Justice Douglas pointed out in his separate opinion, the Court went far to establish rules of decorum in a case in which the original trial was thirteen years old and involved outbursts by a man who may have been mentally ill. Despite this, the opinion of the Court by Mr. Justice Black established that systematic disruption of a trial by the defendant or his attorney may have lead to a constitutional suspension of certain procedural rights (e.g., the defendant's right to confront his accusers or to be physically present at his trial). And the suspension of these rights could not in the future have been used as valid grounds in a plea for reversal of a conviction.

The Freedom to Criticize Judges—and Other Public Officials

Can you call a judge incompetent and get away with it? Are you subject to his contempt powers which may imprison you for as long as six months without trial? Can he privately sue you for libel or slander if he chooses not to cite you for contemptuous accusations? Can both actions be invoked against you? In short, how free is a man to criticize a public official in the performance of his public duties without fear of official retribution?

These questions are raised and, to a great degree, settled in *Garrison* v. *Louisiana,* 379 U.S. 64 (1964), and the precedent cases upon which it relied. Before Jim Garrison, the controversial district attorney of New Orleans was investigating the assassination of President John F. Kennedy, he was aggressively closing down "clip joints." In the process he had some "most unkind" things to say about eight criminal district court judges at a press conference which he had called. He was subsequently indicted, tried, and convicted for "criminal libel," a conviction which the U.S. Supreme Court reversed.

Garrison v. *Louisiana, supra,* was an especially interesting case because it brought together in one case two trends on criticism of public officials: one concerning the medium of criticism—the press; the other the nature of the officials criticized—judges. A brief look at the history of Supreme Court rulings in libel cases may lend an understanding of the precedents of the *Garrison* case.

For the first time, in *Near* v. *Minnesota,* 283 U.S. 697 (1931), the Supreme Court invalidated a state statute as a violation of one of the "fundamental liberties" guaranteed by the First Amendment. A narrowly divided court (5-4) speaking through Mr. Chief Justice Hughes held that a Minnesota law which allowed for the permanent quashing of "malicious, scandalous, and defamatory" newspapers or other periodicals because of their public nuisance by court injunction was a "prior restraint" on publication and as such was an unconstitutional invasion of freedom of the press.

The majority opinion did not condone malicious periodicals but ruled that permanent injunctions against a man's right to print constituted an unnecessary prejudgment of what it was he intended to say and, as such, was equal to the suppression of the right to print itself. The majority indicated that freedom of the press was not absolute and, if abused, the guilty party could be called to account in a civil action for damages. But the majority opinion went on to underscore the fact that the object of the Minnesota statute was not to redress a right which had been abused, but rather to suppress that right in the future. Hughes held that a man may be called to account for what he had published but his right to publish again could not be the penalty he had to pay without his liberty to print being effectively withdrawn. That penalty, the Court held, was incompatible with the liberty to print guaranteed by the Fourteenth Amendment.

In *Near*, the Court made some other important observations about criticism of governmental officials. Near's magazine, *The Saturday Press*, had criticized the Mayor and Chief of Police of Minneapolis and charged them with "corruption," "malfeasance in office" and "serious neglect of duty." The majority of the High Court said such charges, "by their very nature create a public scandal." The Court held that the charges were certainly "scandalous and defamatory within the meaning of the Statute" and therefore newspaper criticism proceeded against government at a most perilous risk if the Minnesota statute were upheld. To the majority it seemed clear that discouragement of criticism of government would not serve democracy well.

New York Times v. *Sullivan* 376 U.S. 254 (1964) followed in this tradition of *Near* v. *Minnesota* although this case was one for civil damages brought by the Commissioner of Public Affairs of Montgomery, Alabama against the *New York Times* for libeling him by printing an "ad" which contained falsehoods, *admitted* to by the *New York Times*, but which did not contain Sullivan's name as such. The extent of the guilt of the *Times* was in printing an "ad" signed by nationally prominent people which Sullivan claimed ascribed to the police acts of "intimidation and violence." Since he was head of the police establishment he claimed he had been libeled by the "ad." The *Times* lost in the Alabama Courts and an initial jury finding against it for damages of $500,000 was finally appealed to the Supreme Court.

The justices unanimously defended the media against civil damages for statements made about public officials acting in their public capacity. The disagreement on the High Court centered solely on the issue of whether the media were absolutely immune from libel actions by public officials or whether they could be held accountable for printing "reckless falsehoods." This would be printing what was known to be untrue for malicious purposes. [That disagreement among the justices can be read in the *Garrison* case itself.]

The *New York Times* case is most significant because it in effect held that when a man voluntarily entered public life he could no longer claim the privacy of an ordinary member of the community. His life became part of the public domain. This principle was extended to all people whose lives became "newsworthy" whether by their actions or not in *Time, Inc.* v. *Hill,* 385 U.S. 374 (1967).

The *New York Times* case was significant for another reason. It unequivocally endorsed the principle that freedom of the press extended to the printing of what was *untrue* unless the falsehood were knowingly printed for malicious purposes. The Court considered this protection vital if big newspapers and magazines were to be printed.

As if already aware of the issue in *Garrison* v. *Louisiana, supra,* the majority in *New York Times* v. *Sullivan, supra,* citing the precedent cases of *Bridges* v. *California,* 314 U.S. 252 (1941), and *Craig* v. *Harney,* 331 U.S. 367 (1947) invoked the "clear and present danger" doctrine to indicate that only a "clear and present" danger to the effective running of the judicial system would justify silencing constitutionally protected criticism of public officials even if they were members of the judiciary. Justice Brennan wrote for the Court:

> Just as factual error affords no warrant for repressing speech that would otherwise be free, the same is true of injury to official reputation. Where judicial officers are involved, this Court has held that concern for the dignity and reputation of the courts does not justify the punishment as criminal contempt of criticism of the judge or his decision. *Bridges* v. *California,* 314 U.S. 252. This is true even though the utterance contains "half-truths" and "misinformation." *Pennekamp* v. *Florida,* 328 U.S. 331, 342, 343, n.5, 345. Such repression can be justified, if at all, only by a clear and present danger of the obstruction of justice. See also *Craig* v. *Harney,* 331 U.S. 367; *Wood* v. *Georgia,* 370 U.S. 375. If judges are to be treated as "men of fortitude, able to thrive in a hardy climate," *Craig* v. *Harney, supra,* 331 U.S., at 376, surely the same must be true of other government officials, such as elected city commissioners. Criticism of their official conduct does not lose its constitutional protection merely because it is effective criticism and hence diminishes their official reputations.

ILLINOIS v. ALLEN

397 U.S. 337; 90 S. Ct. 1057; 25 L.Ed. 2d 353 (1970)

MR. JUSTICE BLACK *delivered the opinion of the Court.*

The Confrontation Clause of the Sixth Amendment to the United States Constitution provides that "In all criminal prosecutions, the accused shall enjoy the right . . . to be confronted with the witnesses against him. . . ." We have held that the Fourteenth Amendment makes the guarantees of this clause obligatory upon the States. *Pointer* v. *Texas,* 380 U.S. 400, 85 S.Ct. 1065, 13 L.Ed.2d 923 (1965). One of the most basic of the rights guaranteed by the Confrontation Clause is the accused's right to be present in the courtroom at every stage of his trial. . . . The question presented in this case is whether an accused can claim the benefit of this constitutional right to remain in the courtroom while at the same time he engages in speech and conduct which is so noisy, disorderly, and disruptive that it is exceedingly difficult or wholly impossible to carry on the trial.

The issue arose in the following way. The respondent, Allen, was convicted by an Illinois jury of armed robbery and was sentenced to serve 10 to 30 years in the Illinois State Penitentiary. The evidence against him showed that on August 12, 1956, he entered a tavern in Illinois and, after ordering a drink, took $200 from the bartender at gunpoint. The Supreme Court of Illinois affirmed his conviction, . . . and this Court denied *certiorari.* 389 U.S. 907, 88 S.Ct. 226, 19 L.Ed.2d 225 (1967). Later Allen filed a petition for a writ of *habeas corpus* in federal court alleging that he had been wrongfully deprived by the Illinois trial judge of his constitutional right to remain present throughout his trial. Finding no constitutional violation, the District Court declined to issue the writ. The Court of Appeals reversed, 413 F.2d 232 (1969), Judge Hastings dissenting. The facts surrounding Allen's expulsion from the courtroom are set out in the Court of Appeals' opinion sustaining Allen's contention:

"After his indictment and during the pretrial stage, the petitioner [Allen] refused court-appointed counsel and indicated to the trial court on several occasions that he wished to conduct his own defense. After considerable argument by the petitioner, the trial judge told him, 'I'll let you be your own lawyer, but I'll ask Mr. Kelly [court-appointed counsel] [to] sit in and protect the record for you, insofar as possible.'

"The trial began on September 9, 1956. After the State's Attorney had accepted the first four jurors following their *voir dire* examination, the petitioner began examining the first juror and continued at great length. Finally, the trial judge interrupted the petitioner, requesting him to confine his questions solely to matters relating to the prospective juror's qualifications. At that point, the petitioner started to argue with the judge in a most abusive and disrespectful manner. At last, and seemingly in desperation, the judge asked appointed counsel to proceed with the examination of the jurors. The petitioner continued to talk, proclaiming that the appointed attorney was not going to act as his lawyer. He terminated his remarks by saying, 'When I go out for lunchtime, you're [the judge] going to be a corpse here.' At that point he tore the file which his attorney had and threw the papers on the floor. The trial judge thereupon stated to the petitioner, 'One more outbreak of that sort and I'll remove you from the courtroom.' This warning had no effect on the petitioner. He continued to talk back to the judge, saying, 'There's not going to be no trial, either. I'm going to sit here and you're going to talk and you can bring your shackles out and straight jacket and put them on me and tape my mouth, but it will do no good because there's not going to be no trial.' After more abusive remarks by the petitioner, the trial judge ordered the trial to proceed in the petitioner's absence. The petitioner was removed from the courtroom. The *voir dire* examination then continued and the jury was selected in the absence of the petitioner.

"After a noon recess and before the jury was brought into the courtroom, the petitioner, appearing before the judge, complained about the fairness of the trial and his appointed attorney. He also said he wanted to be present in the court during his trial. In reply, the judge said that the petitioner would be permitted to remain in the courtroom if he 'behaved [himself] and [did] not interfere with the introduction of the case.' The jury was brought in and seated. Counsel for the petitioner then moved to exclude the witnesses from the courtroom. The defendant protested this effort on the part of his attorney, saying: 'There is going to be no proceeding. I'm going to start talking and I'm going to keep on talking all through the trial. There's not going to be no trial like this. I want my sister and my friends here in court to testify for me.' The trial judge thereupon ordered the petitioner removed from the courtroom." . . .

After this second removal, Allen remained out of the courtroom during the presentation of the State's case-in-chief, except that he was brought in on several occasions for purposes of identification. During one of these latter appearances, Allen responded to one of the judge's questions with vile and abusive language. After the prosecution's case had been presented, the trial judge reiterated his promise to Allen that he could return to the courtroom whenever he agreed to conduct himself properly. Allen gave some assurances of proper conduct and was permitted to be present through the remainder of the trial, principally his defense, which was conducted by his appointed counsel.

.   .   .

The Court of Appeals felt that the defendant's Sixth Amendment right to be present at his own trial was so "absolute" that, no matter how unruly or disruptive the defendant's conduct might be, he could never be held to have lost that right so long as he continued to insist upon it, as Allen clearly did. Therefore the Court of Appeals concluded that a trial judge could never expel a defendant from his own trial and that the judge's ultimate remedy when faced with an obstreperous defendant like Allen who determines to make his trial impossible is to bind and gag him. We cannot agree that the Sixth Amendment, the cases upon which the Court of Appeals relied, or any other cases of this Court so handicap a trial judge in conducting a criminal trial. . . . We accept instead the statement of Mr. Justice Cardozo who, speaking for the Court in *Snyder* v. *Massachusetts*, 291 U.S. 97, 106, 54 S.Ct. 330, 332, 78 L.Ed. 674 (1938), said: "No doubt the privilege [of personally confronting witnesses] may be lost by consent or at times even by misconduct."[2] Although mindful that courts must indulge every reasonable presumption against the loss of constitutional rights, *Johnson* v. *Zerbst*, 304 U.S. 458, 464, 58 S.Ct. 1019, 1023, 82 L.Ed. 1461 (1938), we explicitly hold today that a defendant can lose his right to be present at trial if, after he has been warned by the judge that he will be removed if he continues his disruptive behavior, he

nevertheless insists on conducting himself in a manner so disorderly, disruptive, and disrespectful of the court that his trial cannot be carried on with him in the courtroom. Once lost, the right to be present can, of course, be reclaimed as soon as the defendant is willing to conduct himself consistently with the decorum and respect inherent in the concept of courts and judicial proceedings.

It is essential to the proper administration of criminal justice that dignity, order, and decorum be the hallmarks of all court proceedings in our country. The flagrant disregard in the courtroom of elementary standards of proper conduct should not and cannot be tolerated. We believe trial judges confronted with disruptive, contumacious, stubbornly defiant defendants must be given sufficient discretion to meet the circumstances of each case. No one formula for maintaining the appropriate courtroom atmosphere will be best in all situations. We think there are at least three constitutionally permissible ways for a trial judge to handle an obstreperous defendant like Allen: (1) bind and gag him, thereby keeping him present; (2) cite him for contempt; (3) take him out of the courtroom until he promises to conduct himself properly.

I.

Trying a defendant for a crime while he sits bound and gagged be-

---

2. Rule 43 of the Federal Rules of Criminal Procedure provides that "[i]n prosecutions for offenses not punishable by death, the defendant's voluntary absence after the trial has been commenced in his presence shall not prevent continuing the trial to and including the return of the verdict."

fore the judge and jury would to an extent comply with that part of the Sixth Amendment's purposes that accords the defendant an opportunity to confront the witnesses at the trial. But even to contemplate such a technique, much less see it, arouses a feeling that no person should be tried while shackled and gagged except as a last resort. Not only is it possible that the sight of shackles and gags might have a significant effect on the jury's feelings about the defendant, but the use of this technique is itself something of an affront to the very dignity and decorum of judicial proceedings that the judge is seeking to uphold. Moreover, one of the defendant's primary advantages of being present at the trial, his ability to communicate with his counsel, is greatly reduced when the defendant is in a condition of total physical restraint. It is in part because of these inherent disadvantages and limitations in this method of dealing with disorderly defendants that we decline to hold with the Court of Appeals that a defendant cannot under any possible circumstances be deprived of his right to be present at trial. However, in some situations which we need not attempt to foresee, binding and gagging might possibly be the fairest and most reasonable way to handle a defendant who acts as Allen did here.

II.

In a footnote the Court of Appeals suggested the possible availability of contempt of court as a remedy to make Allen behave in his robbery trial, and it is true that citing or threatening to cite a con-

tumacious defendant for criminal contempt might in itself be sufficient to make a defendant stop interrupting a trial. If so, the problem would be solved easily, and the defendant could remain in the courtroom. Of course, if the defendant is determined to prevent *any* trial, then a court in attempting to try the defendant for contempt is still confronted with the identical dilemma that the Illinois court faced in this case. And criminal contempt has obvious limitations as a sanction when the defendant is charged with a crime so serious that a very severe sentence such as death or life imprisonment is likely to be imposed. . . .

Another aspect of the contempt remedy is the judge's power, when exercised consistently with state and federal law, to imprison an unruly defendant such as Allen for civil contempt and discontinue the trial until such time as the defendant promises to behave himself. This procedure is consistent with the defendant's right to be present at trial, and yet it avoids the serious shortcomings of the use of shackles and gags. It must be recognized, however, that a defendant might conceivably, as a matter of calculated strategy, elect to spend a prolonged period in confinement for contempt in the hope that adverse witnesses might be unavailable after a lapse of time. A court must guard against allowing a defendant to profit from his own wrong in this way.

III.

The trial court in this case decided under the circumstances to remove the defendant from the courtroom and to continue his trial in his absence until and unless he promised to conduct himself in a manner befitting an American courtroom. As we said earlier, we find nothing unconstitutional about this procedure. Allen's behavior was clearly of such an extreme and aggravated nature as to justify either his removal from the courtroom or his total physical restraint. Prior to his removal he was repeatedly warned by the trial judge that he would be removed from the courtroom if he persisted in his unruly conduct, and, as Judge Hastings observed in his dissenting opinion, the record demonstrates that Allen would not have been at all dissuaded by the trial judge's use of his criminal contempt powers. Allen was constantly informed that he could return to the trial when he would agree to conduct himself in an orderly manner. Under these circumstances we hold that Allen lost his right guaranteed by the Sixth and Fourteenth Amendments to be present throughout his trial.

IV.

It is not pleasant to hold that the respondent Allen was properly banished from the court for a part of his own trial. But our courts, palladiums of liberty as they are, cannot be treated disrespectfully with impunity. Nor can the accused be permitted by his disruptive conduct indefinitely to avoid being tried on the charges brought against him. It would degrade our country and our judicial system to permit our courts to be bullied, insulted, and humil-

iated and their orderly progress thwarted and obstructed by defendants brought before them charged with crimes. As guardians of the public welfare, our state and federal judicial systems strive to administer equal justice to the rich and the poor, the good and the bad, the native and foreign born of every race, nationality and religion. Being manned by humans, the courts are not perfect and are bound to make some errors. But, if our courts are to remain what the Founders intended, the citadels of justice, their proceedings cannot and must not be infected with the sort of scurrilous, abusive language and conduct paraded before the Illinois trial judge in this case. The record shows that the Illinois judge at all times conducted himself with that dignity, decorum, and patience that befits a judge. Even in holding that the trial judge had erred, the Court of Appeals praised his "commendable patience under severe provocation."

We do not hold that removing this defendant from his own trial was the only way the Illinois judge could have constitutionally solved the problem he had. We do hold, however, that there is nothing whatever in this record to show that the judge did not act completely within his discretion. Deplorable as it is to remove a man from his own trial, even for a short time, we hold that the judge did not commit legal error in doing what he did.

The judgment of the Court of Appeals is reversed.

Reversed.

MR. JUSTICE BRENNAN, *concurring.*

The safeguards that the Constitution accords to criminal defendants presuppose that government has a sovereign prerogative to put on trial those accused in good faith of violating valid laws. Constitutional power to bring an accused to trial is fundamental to a scheme of "ordered liberty" and prerequisite to social justice and peace. History has known the breakdown of lawful penal authority—the feud, the vendetta, and the terror of penalties meted out by mobs or roving bands of vigilantes. It has known, too, the perversion of that authority. In some societies the penal arm of the state has reached individual men through secret denunciation followed by summary punishment. In others the solemn power of condemnation has been confided to the caprice of tyrants. Down the corridors of history have echoed the cries of innocent men convicted by other irrational or arbitrary procedures. These are some of the alternatives history offers to the procedure adopted by our Constitution. The right of a defendant to trial—to trial by jury—has long been cherished by our people as a vital restraint on the penal authority of government. And it has never been doubted that under our constitutional traditions trial in accordance with the Constitution is the proper mode by which government exercises that authority.

Lincoln said this Nation was "conceived in liberty and dedicated to the proposition that all men are created equal." The Founders' dream of a society where all men are free and equal has not been easy to realize. The degree of liberty and equality that exists today has been the product of unceasing struggle and sacrifice. Much remains to be done—so much that the very institutions of our society have come under challenge. Hence, today, as in Lincoln's time, a man may ask "whether [this] nation or any nation so conceived and so dedicated can long endure." It cannot endure if the Nation falls short on the guarantees of liberty, justice, and equality embodied in our founding documents. But it also cannot endure if we allow our precious heritage of ordered liberty to be ripped apart amid the sound and fury of our time. It cannot endure if in individual cases the claims of social peace and order on the one side and of personal liberty on the other cannot be mutually resolved in the forum designated by the Constitution. If that resolution cannot be reached by judicial trial in a court of law, it will be reached elsewhere and by other means, and there will be grave danger that liberty, equality, and the order essential to both will be lost.

The constitutional right of an accused to be present at his trial must be considered in this context. Thus there can be no doubt whatever that the governmental prerogative to proceed with a trial may not be defeated by conduct of the accused that prevents the trial from going forward. . . .

To allow the disruptive activities of a defendant like respondent to prevent his trial is to allow him to profit from his own wrong. The Constitution would protect none of us if it prevented the courts from acting to preserve the very processes which the Constitution itself prescribes.

Of course, no action against an unruly defendant is permissible except after he has been fully and fairly informed that his conduct is wrong and intolerable, and warned of the possible consequences of continued misbehavior. The record makes clear that respondent was so informed and warned in this case. Thus there can be no doubt that respondent, by persisting in his reprehensible conduct, surrendered his right to be present at the trial.

As the Court points out, several remedies are available to the judge faced with a defendant bent on disrupting his trial. He can have him bound, shackled, and gagged; he can hold him in civil or criminal contempt; he can exclude him from the trial and carry on in his absence. No doubt other methods can be devised. I join the Court's opinion and agree that the Constitution does not require or prohibit the adoption of any of these courses. The constitutional right to be present can be surrendered if it is abused for the purpose of frustrating the trial. Due process does not require the presence of the defendant if his presence means that there will be no orderly process at all. However, I also agree with the Court that these three methods are not equally acceptable. In particular, shackling and gagging a defendant is surely the least of them. It offends not only judicial dignity and decorum, but also that respect for the individual which is the lifeblood of the law.

I would add only that when a defendant is excluded from his trial, the court should make reasonable efforts to enable him to communicate with his attorney and, if possible, to keep apprised of the progress of his trial. Once the court has removed the contumacious defendant, it is not weakness to mitigate the disadvantages of his expulsion as far as technologically possible in the circumstances.

MR. JUSTICE DOUGLAS.

I agree with the Court that a criminal trial, in the constitutional sense, cannot take place where the courtroom is a bedlam and either the accused or the judge is hurling epithets at the other. A courtroom is a hallowed place where trials must proceed with dignity and not become occasions for entertainment by the participants, by extraneous persons, by modern mass media or otherwise.

My difficulty is not with the basic hypothesis of this decision, but with the use of this case to establish the appropriate guidelines for judicial control.

This is a state case, the trial having taken place nearly 13 years ago. That elapse of time is not necessarily a barrier to a challenge of the constitutionality of a criminal conviction. But in this case it should be.

There is more than an intimation in the present record that the defendant was a mental case. The passage of time since 1957, the date of the trial, makes it, however, impossible to determine what the mental condition of the defendant was at that time. The fact that a defendant has been found to understand "the nature and object of the proceedings against him" and thus competent to stand trial does not answer the difficult questions as to what a trial judge should do with an otherwise mentally ill defendant who creates a courtroom disturbance. What a judge should do with a defendant whose courtroom antics may not be volitional is a perplexing problem which we should not reach except on a clear record. This defendant had no lawyer and refused one, though the trial judge properly insisted that a member of the bar be present to represent him. He tried to be his own lawyer and what transpired was pathetic, as well as disgusting and disgraceful.

We should not reach the merits but should reverse the case for staleness of the record and affirm the denial of relief by the District Court. . . .

Our real problems of this type lie not with this case but with other kinds of trials. *First* are the political trials. They frequently recur in our history and insofar as they take place in federal courts we have broad supervisory powers over them. That is one setting where the question arises whether the accused has rights of confrontation that the law invades at its peril.

In Anglo-American law, great injustices have at times been done to unpopular minorities by judges, as well as by prosecutors. . . .

. . .

Problems of political indictments and of political judges raise profound questions going to the heart of the social compact. For that compact is two-sided: majorities undertake to press their grievances within limits of the Constitution and in accord with its procedures; minorities agree to abide by constitutional procedures in resisting those claims.

Does the answer to that problem involve defining the procedure for conducting political trials or does it involve the designing of constitutional methods for putting an end to them? This record is singularly inadequate to answer those questions. It will be time enough to resolve those weighty problems when a political trial reaches this Court for review.

Second are trials used by minorities to destroy the existing constitutional system and bring on repressive measures. Radicals on the left historically have used those tactics to incite the extreme right with the calculated design of fostering a regime of repression from which the radicals on the left hope to emerge as the ultimate victor. The left in that role is the provocateur. The Constitution was not designed as an instrument for that form of rough-and-tumble contest. The social compact has room for tolerance, patience, and restraint, but not for sabotage and violence. Trials involving that spectacle strike at the very heart of constitutional government.

I would not try to provide in this case the guidelines for those two strikingly different types of cases. The case presented here is the classical criminal case without any political or subversive overtones. It involves a defendant who was a sick person and who may or may not have been insane in the classical sense[5] but who apparently had a diseased mind. And, as I have said,

the record is so stale that it is now much too late to find out what the true facts really were.

5. In a 1956 pretrial sanity hearing, Allen was found to be incompetent to stand trial. Approximately a year later, however, on October 19, 1957, in a second competency hearing, he was declared sane and competent to stand trial.

Allen's sister and brother testified in Allen's behalf at the trial. They recited instances of Allen's unusual past behavior and stated that he was confined to a mental institution in 1953, although no reason for this latter confinement was given. A doctor called by the prosecution testified that he had examined Allen shortly after the commission of the crime which took place on August 12, 1956, and on other subsequent occasions, and that, in his opinion, Allen was sane at the time of each examination. This evidence was admitted on the question of Allen's sanity at the time of the offense. The jury found him sane at that time and the Illinois Supreme Court affirmed that finding. See *People* v. *Allen*, 37 Ill.2d 167, 226 N.E.2d 1.

QUESTIONS

1. Why should the Court guarantee the accused the right to confront the witnesses against him?

2. In your opinion, is disruption of a courtroom ever justified? If so, when? If not, not under any circumstances?

3. If you were a judge, what criteria would you use to determine whether the defendant was trying to disrupt the proceedings to "sabotage" the trial or whether he was sincere in raising a valid objection? If he *were sincere* but persisted what would you do if he would not keep quiet? Would you bind and gag him?

4. What standards do you use to judge whether or not a trial is a "political" trial as opposed to a "common criminal" trial? Was the trial of Robert Kennedy's murderer a "political trial?" Why yes? Why no? How about the trial of Martin Luther King's assassin?

5. Do you think it serves the "cause of justice" to turn the courtroom into a political arena? Under what circumstances—if any—would you say "yes?" Can you give a specific instance? Under what circumstances would you say "no?" Can you give an instance?

GARRISON v. LOUISIANA

379 U.S. 64; 85 S. Ct. 209; 13 L.Ed. 2d 125 (1964)

MR. JUSTICE BRENNAN *delivered the opinion of the Court.*

Appellant is the District Attorney of Orleans Parish, Louisiana. During a dispute with the eight judges of the Criminal District Court of the Parish, he held a press conference at which he issued a statement disparaging their judicial conduct. As a result, he was tried without a jury before a judge from another Parish and convicted of criminal defamation under the Louisiana Defamation Statute.[1] The principal charges alleged to be defamatory were his attribution of a large backlog of pending criminal cases to the ineffi-ciency, laziness, and excessive vacations of the judges, and his accusation that, by refusing to authorize disbursements to cover the expenses of undercover investigations of vice in New Orleans, the judges had hampered his efforts to enforce the vice laws. In impugning their motives, he said:

> "The judges have now made it eloquently clear where their sympathies lie in regard to aggressive vice investigations by refusing to authorize use of the DA's funds to pay for the cost of closing down the Canal Street clip joints. . . .

1. La.Rev.Stat.1950, Tit. 14:

"§ 47. Defamation

"Defamation is the malicious publication or expression in any manner, to anyone other than the party defamed, of anything which tends:

"(1) To expose any person to hatred, contempt, or ridicule, or to deprive him of the benefit of public confidence or social intercourse; or

"(2) To expose the memory of one deceased to hatred, contempt, or ridicule; or

"(3) To injure any person, corporation, or association of persons in his or their business or occupation.

"Whoever commits the crime of defamation shall be fined not more than three thousand dollars, or imprisoned for not more than one year, or both.

"§ 48. Presumption of malice

"Where a non-privileged defamatory publication or expression is false it is presumed to be malicious unless a justifiable motive for making it is shown.

"Where such a publication or expression is true, actual malice must be proved in order to convict the offender.

"§ 49. Qualified privilege

"A qualified privilege exists and actual malice must be proved, regardless of whether the publication is true or false, in the following situations:

"(1) Where the publication or expression is a fair and true report of any judicial, legislative, or other public or official proceeding, or of any statement, speech, argument, or debate in the course of the same.

"(2) Where the publication or expression is a comment made in the reasonable belief of its truth, upon,

"(a) The conduct of a person in respect to public affairs; or

"(b) A thing which the proprietor thereof offers or explains to the public.

"(3) Where the publication or expression is made to a person interested in the communication, by one who is also interested or who stands in such a relation to the former as to afford a reasonable ground for supposing his motive innocent.

"(4) Where the publication or expression is made by an attorney or party in a judicial proceeding."

La.Rev.Stat.1962 Cum.Supp., Tit. 14:

"§ 50. Absolute privilege. . . ."

. . .

"This raises interesting questions about the racketeer influences on our eight vacation-minded judges."[2]

The Supreme Court of Louisiana affirmed the conviction, 244 La. 787, 154 So.2d 400. The trial court and the State Supreme Court both rejected appellant's contention that the statute unconstitutionally abridged his freedom of expression. We noted probable jurisdiction of the appeal. 375 U.S. 900, 84 S.Ct. 195, 11 L.Ed.2d 142. Argument was first heard in the 1963 Term, and the case was ordered restored to the calendar for reargument, 377 U.S. 986, 84 S.Ct. 1906, 12 L.Ed.2d 1042. We reverse.

I.

In *New York Times Co.* v. *Sullivan*, 376 U.S. 254, 84 S.Ct. 710, 11 L.Ed. 2d 686, we held that the Constitution limits state power, in a civil action brought by a public official for criticism of his official conduct, to an award of damages for a false statement "made with 'actual malice' —that is, with knowledge that it was false or with reckless disregard of whether it was false or not." . . . At the outset, we must decide whether, in view of the differing history and purposes of criminal libel, the *New York Times* rule also limits state power to impose criminal sanctions for criticism of the official conduct of public officials. We hold that it does.

Where criticism of public officials is concerned, we see no merit in the argument that criminal libel statutes serve interests distinct from those secured by civil libel laws, and therefore should not be subject to the same limitations. At common law, truth was no defense to criminal libel. Although the victim of a true but defamatory publication might not have been unjustly damaged in reputation by the libel, the speaker was still punishable since the remedy was designed to avert the possibility that the utterance would provoke an enraged victim to a breach of peace. . . .

. . .

2. The dispute between appellant and the judges arose over disbursements from a Fines and Fees Fund, which was to be used to defray expenses of the District Attorney's office; disbursements could be made only on motion of the District Attorney and approval by a judge of the Criminal District Court. After appellant took office, one of the incumbent judges refused to approve a disbursement from the Fund for furnishings for appellant's office. When the judge went on vacation prior to his retirement in September 1962, appellant obtained the approval of another judge, allegedly by misrepresenting that the first judge had withdrawn his objection. Thereupon, the eight judges, on October 5, 1962, adopted a rule that no further disbursements of the District Attorney from the Fund would be approved except with the concurrence of five of the eight judges. On October 26, 1962, the judges ruled that disbursements to pay appellant's undercover agents to conduct investigations of commercial vice in the Bourbon and Canal Street districts of New Orleans would not be approved, and expressed doubt as to the legality of such a use of the Fund under the State Constitution. A few days later, on November 1, 1962, the judge, now retired, who had turned down the original motion issued a public statement criticizing appellant's conduct of the office of District Attorney. The next day, appellant held the press conference at which he made the statement for which he was prosecuted.

Moreover, even where the utterance is false, the great principles of the Constitution which secure freedom of expression in this area preclude attaching adverse consequences to any except the knowing or reckless falsehood. Debate on public issues will not be uninhibited if the speaker must run the risk that it will be proved in court that he spoke out of hatred; even if he did speak out of hatred, utterances honestly believed contribute to the free interchange of ideas and the ascertainment of truth. Under a rule like the Louisiana rule, permitting a finding of malice based on an intent merely to inflict harm, rather than an intent to inflict harm through falsehood, "it becomes a hazardous matter to speak out against a popular politician, with the result that the dishonest and incompetent will be shielded."...

We held in *New York Times* that a public official might be allowed the civil remedy only if he establishes that the utterance was false and that it was made with knowledge of its falsity or in reckless disregard of whether it was false or true. The reasons which led us to hold in *New York Times*, 376 U.S., at 278–279, . . . that the unqualified defense of truth was insufficient apply with no less force merely because the remedy is criminal. The constitutional guarantees of freedom of expression compel application of the same standard to the criminal remedy. Truth may not be the subject of either civil or criminal sanctions where discussion of public affairs is concerned. And since ". . . erroneous statement is inevitable in free debate, and . . . it must be protected if the freedoms of expression are to have the 'breathing space' that they 'need . . . to survive' . . . ," 376 U.S., at 271–272, . . . only those false statements made with the high degree of awareness of their probable falsity demanded by *New York Times* may be the subject of either civil or criminal sanctions. For speech concerning public affairs is more than self-expression; it is the essence of self-government. The First and Fourteenth Amendments embody our "profound national commitment to the principle that debate on public issues should be uninhibited, robust, and wide-open, and that it may well include vehement, caustic, and sometimes unpleasantly sharp attacks on government and public officials."...

The use of calculated falsehood, however, would put a different cast on the constitutional question. Although honest utterance, even if inaccurate, may further the fruitful exercise of the right of free speech, it does not follow that the lie, knowingly and deliberately published about a public official, should enjoy a like immunity. At the time the First Amendment was adopted, as today, there were those unscrupulous enough and skillful enough to use the deliberate or reckless falsehood as an effective political tool to unseat the public servant or even topple an administration. . . . That speech is used as a tool for political ends does not automatically bring it under the protective mantle of the Constitution. For the use of the known lie as a tool is at once at odds with the premises of democratic government and with the orderly manner in which economic, social, or political change is to be effected. Calculated falsehood falls into that class of utterances which "are no essential part of any exposition of ideas, and are of such slight social value as a step to truth that any benefit that may be derived from them is clearly outweighed by the social interest in order and morality. . . . " *Chaplinsky v. New Hampshire*, 315 U.S. 568, 572, 62 S.Ct. 766, 769, 86 L.Ed. 1031. Hence the knowingly false statement and the false statement made with reckless disregard of the truth, do not enjoy constitutional protection.

II.

We find no difficulty in bringing the appellant's statement within the purview of criticism of the official conduct of public officials, entitled to the benefit of the *New York Times* rule. As the Louisiana Supreme Court viewed the statement, it constituted an attack upon the personal integrity of the judges, rather than on official conduct. In sustaining the finding of the trial court that the appellant's statement was defamatory, the Louisiana Supreme Court held that ". . . the use of the words 'racketeering influences' when applied to anyone suggests and imputes that he has been influenced to practice fraud, deceit, trickery, cheating, and dishonesty"; that "The expression that the judges have enjoyed 300 days vacation out of 19 months suggests and connotes a violation of the 'Deadhead' statute, LSA—R.S. 14:138, Public Payroll Fraud"; that "Other expressions set

out in the Bill of Information connote malfeasance in office. LSA–R.S. 14:134; Art. IX, Sec. 1, La.Const. of 1921." The court concluded that "Defendant's expressions . . . are not criticisms of a court trial or of the manner in which any one of the eight judges conducted his court when in session. The expressions charged contain personal attacks upon the integrity and honesty of the eight judges. . . ." 244 La., at 834–835, 154 So.2d, at 417–418.

We do not think, however, that appellant's statement may be considered as one constituting only a purely private defamation. The accusation concerned the judges' conduct of the business of the Criminal District Court. Of course, any criticism of the manner in which a public official performs his duties will tend to affect his private, as well as his public, reputation. The *New York Times* rule is not rendered inapplicable merely because an official's private reputation, as well as his public reputation, is harmed. The public official rule protects the paramount public interest in a free flow of information to the people concerning public officials, their servants. To this end, anything which might touch on an official's fitness for office is relevant. Few personal attributes are more germane to fitness for office than dishonesty, malfeasance, or improper motivation, even though these characteristics may also affect the official's private character. . . .

III.

Applying the principles of the *New York Times* case, we hold that the Louisiana statute, as authoritatively interpreted by the Supreme Court of Louisiana, incorporates constitutionally invalid standards in the context of criticism of the official conduct of public officials. For, contrary to the *New York Times* rule, which absolutely prohibits punishment of truthful criticism, the statute directs punishment for true statements made with "actual malice,". . . And "actual malice" is defined in the decisions below to mean "hatred, ill will or enmity or a wanton desire to injure. . . ." 244 La., at 851, 154 So.2d at 423. The statute is also unconstitutional as interpreted to cover false statements against public officials. The *New York Times* standard forbids the punishment of false statements, unless made with knowledge of their falsity or in reckless disregard of whether they are true or false. But the Louisiana statute punishes false statements without regard to that test if made with ill-will; even if ill-will is not established, a false statement concerning public officials can be punished if not made in the reasonable belief of its truth. The Louisiana Supreme Court affirmed the conviction solely on the ground that the evidence sufficed to support the trial court's finding of ill-will, enmity, or a wanton desire to injure. But the trial court also rested the conviction on additional findings that the state-

ment was false and not made in the reasonable belief of its truth. . . .

This is not a holding applying the *New York Times* test. The reasonable-belief standard applied by the trial judge is not the same as the reckless disregard of truth standard. According to the trial court's opinion, a reasonable belief is one which "an ordinarily prudent man might be able to assign a just and fair reason for"; the suggestion is that under this test the immunity from criminal responsibility in the absence of ill-will disappears on proof that the exercise of ordinary care would have revealed that the statement was false. The test which we laid down in *New York Times* is not keyed to ordinary care; defeasance of the privilege is conditioned, not on mere negligence, but on reckless disregard for the truth. *Reversed.*

MR. JUSTICE DOUGLAS, *whom* MR. JUSTICE BLACK *joins, concurring.*

I am in hearty agreement with the conclusion of the Court that this prosecution for a seditious libel was unconstitutional. Yet I feel that the gloss which the Court has put on "the freedom of speech" in the First Amendment to reach that result (and like results in other cases) makes that basic guarantee almost unrecognizable.[1]

---

1. The Constitution says in the First Amendment that "Congress shall make no law . . . abridging the freedom of speech"; and the Due Process Clause of the Fourteenth Amendment puts the States under the same restraint. There is one school of thought, so far in the minority, which holds that the due process freedom of speech honored by the Fourteenth Amendment is a watered-down version of the First Amendment freedom of speech. See my Brother HARLAN in *Roth v. United States*, . . . While that view has never obtained, the construction which the majority has given the First Amendment has been burdened with somewhat the same kind of qualifications and conditions.

Recently in *New York Times Co. v. Sullivan*, . . . a majority of the Court held that criticism of an official for official conduct was protected from state civil libel laws by the First and Fourteenth Amendments, unless there was proof of actual malice. . . . We now hold that proof of actual malice is relevant to seditious libel—that seditious libel will lie for a knowingly false statement or one made with reckless disregard of the truth.

If malice is all that is needed, inferences from facts as found by the jury will easily oblige. How can we sit in review on a cold record and find no evidence of malice . . . when it is the commonplace of life that heat and passion subtly turn to malice in actual fact? If "reckless disregard of the truth" is the basis of seditious libel, that nebulous standard could be easily met. The presence of "actual malice" is made critical in seditious libel, as well as in civil actions involving charges against public officials, when in truth there is nothing in the Constitution about it, any more than there is about "clear and present danger."

While the First Amendment remains the same, the gloss which the Court has written on it in this field of the discussion of public issues robs it of much vitality.

Why does "the freedom of speech" that the Court is willing to protect turn out to be so pale and tame?

It is because, as my Brother BLACK has said,[2] the Bill of Rights is constantly watered-down through judicial "balancing" of what the Constitution says and what judges think is needed for a well-ordered society.

.   .   .

MR. JUSTICE BLACK, *with whom* MR. JUSTICE DOUGLAS *joins, concurring.*

For reasons stated at greater length in my opinions concurring in *New York Times Co.* v. *Sullivan*, 376 U.S. 254, 293, 84 S.Ct. 710, 733, 11 L.Ed.2d 686, and dissenting in *Beauharnais* v. *Illinois*, 343 U.S. 250, 267, 72 S.Ct. 725, 736, 96 L.Ed. 919, as well as in the opinion of MR. JUSTICE DOUGLAS in this case, . . . I concur in reversing the conviction of appellant Garrison, based as it is purely on his public discussion and criticism of public officials. I believe that the First Amendment, made applicable to the States by the Fourteenth, protects every person from having a state or

---

2. The Bill of Rights and the Federal Government, in The Great Rights (Cahn ed. 1963), p. 60:

"In reality this [balancing] approach returns us to the state of legislative supremacy which existed in England and which the Framers were so determined to change once and for all. On the one hand, it denies the judiciary its constitutional power to measure acts of Congress by the standards set down in the Bill of Rights. On the other hand, though apparently reducing judicial powers by saying that acts of Congress may be held unconstitutional only when they are found to have no rational legislative basis, this approach really gives the Court, along with Congress, a greater power, that of overriding the plain commands of the Bill of Rights on a finding of weighty public interest. In effect, it changes the direction of our form of government from a government of limited powers to a government in which Congress may do anything that courts believe to be 'reasonable.'"

the federal government fine, imprison, or assess damages against him when he has been guilty of no conduct . . . other than expressing an opinion, even though others may believe that his views are unwholesome, unpatriotic, stupid or dangerous. I believe that the Court is mistaken if it thinks that requiring proof that statements were "malicious" or "defamatory" will really create any substantial hurdle to block public officials from punishing those who criticize the way they conduct their office. Indeed, "malicious," "seditious," and other such evilsounding words often have been invoked to punish people for expressing their views on public affairs. Fining men or sending them to jail for criticizing public officials not only jeopardizes the free, open public discussion which our Constitution guarantees, but can wholly stifle it. I would hold now . . . that under our Constitution there is absolutely no place in this country for the old, discredited English Star Chamber law of seditious criminal libel.

MR. JUSTICE GOLDBERG, *concurring.*

I agree with the Court that there is "no difficulty in bringing the appellant's statement within the purview of criticism of the official conduct of public officials. . . ." In *New York Times Co.* v. *Sullivan,* 376 U.S. 254, 297, 84 S.Ct. 710, 735, 11 L.Ed.2d 686, I expressed my conviction "that the Constitution accords citizens and press an unconditional freedom to criticize official conduct." . . . *New York Times* was a civil libel case; this is a criminal libel prosecution. In my view, "[i]f the rule that libel on government has no place in our Constitution is to have real meaning, then libel [criminal or civil] on the official conduct of the governors likewise can have no place in our Constitution.". . .

QUESTIONS

1. What is meant by the term "seditious libel?" How would you differentiate it from plain "libel?"

2. What interests does the state have in passing a law which makes illegal the "defaming" of public officials? Do you think these interests are valid— *i.e.*, in the interests of the community? Why yes? Why no?

3. Should that which is later discovered to be untrue, but which is thought to be true when printed about a public official, be protected from a civil or criminal libel action? Why yes? Why no?

4. How would you respond to the argument that decisions like *N.Y. Times* v. *Sullivan* and *Garrison* v. *Louisiana* drive capable people out of politics because they do not want to expose themselves or their families to public, and often incompetent, ridicule or scrutiny?

5. How would you establish standards to separate a public official's private life from his public responsibility? Is the possibility that he drinks too much in private—a matter of his private life or is it also important to his public life? What about his financial investments; who he owes money to; the possibility of drug addiction; sexual maladjustment; his gambling habits; his religious convictions—are these factors of his private life or are they part of his public life? Can he have a private life that isn't important to his public life?

4. protest and public property

4. protest and public property

The "People" and Public Property

Do "the streets belong to the people?" Who are "the people?" Which "people?" At what time and for what purpose do the streets belong to them? Can the "people" with their many diverse interests and purposes not lay irreconcilable claims to the same streets and other publicly owned property? How should a pluralistic society reconcile these conflicting claims should they arise?

The Supreme Court has dealt with many of these questions in cases concerning the struggle of Black Americans to claim their constitutional rights and to end their *de facto* status as second-class citizens. As the case of *Gregory* v. *Chicago*, 394 U.S. 111 (1969) illustrates, this discrimination against Black Americans is not just a Southern phenomenon—it is part of the whole American condition.

Perhaps it is timely to ask why has "direct action" in the form of demonstrations in the streets and at the seats of government been necessary in order for Blacks to achieve equality before the law? Perhaps, as background to these cases, a review of the struggle to change the legal status of Blacks in the United States would not be an inappropriate point of departure.

The "Separate but Equal" Doctrine

The "separate but equal" doctrine was first inaugurated in the landmark case of *Plessy* v. *Ferguson*, 163 U.S. 537 (1896). In that controversy, a Louisiana Statute, requiring segregation in intrastate railroad carriers, was attacked as a violation of the "equal protection" clause of the Fourteenth

Amendment which prohibits all states from depriving "any persons within its jurisdiction the equal protection of the laws." The case provided an opportunity for the Supreme Court to speak to the larger issue—the constitutionality of all state acts establishing intrastate racial segregation. Sustaining the Louisiana enactment, Mr. Justice Brown held, in the opinion of the Court, that the legislative authority to segregate the races *was* within the police power of the state. Separate facilities *did not* violate the Fourteenth Amendment as long as the civil and political rights of both races were equal:

> . . . We consider the underlying fallacy of the plaintiff's argument to consist in the assumption that the enforced separation of the two races stamps the colored race with a badge of inferiority. If this be so, it is not by reason of anything found in the act but solely because the colored race chooses to put that construction upon it. . . . If the civil and political rights of both races be equal one cannot be inferior to the other civilly or politically. If one race be inferior to the other socially, the Constitution of the United States cannot put them upon the same plane. . . .

The lone dissenter, the first Mr. Justice John Marshall Harlan, in vain attempted to arouse the conscience of the nation:

> . . .There is no cast here. Our Constitution is color blind, and neither knows nor tolerates classes among citizens. In respect of civil rights, all citizens are equal before the law. . . . The arbitrary separation of citizens, on the basis of race, while they are on a public highway, is a badge of servitude wholly inconsistent with the civil freedom and the equality before the law established by the Constitution. It cannot be justified upon any legal grounds. . . . The thin disguise of "equal" accommodation for passengers in railroad coaches will not mislead anyone, nor atone for the wrong this day done. . . .

Once established, the *Plessy* doctrine was soon employed to defend state schemes for segregated public schools in *Cummings* v. *County Board of Education*, 175 U.S. 528 (1899), and institutions of higher education in *Berea College* v. *Kentucky*, 211 U.S. 45, (1908).

Within a short time, state laws were enacted in the South which virtually separated the races in all spheres of publicly and privately financed social activity. State laws prohibited the use of the same private eating establishments, bathrooms, hotel rooms, barber shops, public drinking fountains, public recreational facilities, as well as public educational institutions. Where state law did not restrict the intermixing of the races, strict social practices enforced segregation. The legal pattern of requiring segregation by use of state authority was mainly confined to the states of the Old

South. The more subtle patterns of *de facto* segregation, namely separating the races by covert social convention and varied economic techniques—which proved equally effective—were employed in the northern states.

The attack on legally required segregation began in earnest during the days of the New Deal. The "separate but equal" doctrine was never an effective guarantee of the rights of Blacks or other minorities. Any brief look at the expenditures by the states—northern as well as southern—for educating Black and other minority children, servicing their neighborhoods, providing minority groups with parks and other recreational facilities from the period of the *Plessy* case to the early 1950's, would show a great disparity in the funds provided for similar state services to the white population. In short, since *Plessy* the facilities were separate but they were not equal. As a practical formula for guaranteeing the "equal protection of the laws" the *Plessy* doctrine was bankrupt from its inception. *In fact* it proved to be little more than a legal rationalization for perpetuating unequal state treatment for minority groups without seeming to flaunt the command of the Fourteenth Amendment.

Proof of the ineffectiveness of the *Plessy* doctrine is provided by almost every Supreme Court decision that examined how the doctrine actually worked. For instance, in *Missouri ex rel. Gaines* v. *Canada*, 305 U.S. 337 (1938), the University of Missouri was ordered by the Supreme Court to admit a Negro student to its all-white law school because there was no separate—let alone equal—law school for Blacks in the state. A similar situation arose ten years later in *Sipuel* v. *Bd. of Regents of Oklahoma*, 332 U.S. 631 (1948), when the Supreme Court ordered that the state university law school be opened to a prospective Negro law student.

Again, the *Plessy* requirement of equal facilities was lacking in *Mitchell* v. *United States*, 313 U.S. 80 (1941). In this case, a Negro passenger, who was traveling by train first-class across state lines had to board a second-class segregated coach because of Arkansas law. He sued for equal treatment with whites traveling first-class. The Supreme Court ruled that because Mitchell had been denied accommodations, equal in comforts and conveniences to those enjoyed by white first-class passengers because of his race, this violated both the Interstate Commerce Act and a "fundamental individual right which is guaranteed against state action by the Fourteenth Amendment."

In the field of public recreational facilities, the "separate but equal" doctrine proved equally ineffective. Kansas City Negroes, suing for admission to all-white public swimming pools in the summer of 1953, were awarded relief because of the municipality's failure to provide members of the Black race with facilities equal to those of whites. The federal court holding was narrow in scope and afforded no class relief, (i.e., admission of all Blacks who would otherwise be eligible for entrance to the swimming pools had they been white.) It simply gained admission to the Negroes who challenged their exclusion. [See *Kansas City* v. *Williams*, 205 F. 2d 47 (1953)].

In all of these cases, the Supreme Court applied the *Plessy* doctrine and afforded the affected Negroes remedies where the state had failed to supply equal separate facilities. The greater question as to whether separate facilities could ever be equal due to the lack of intangible factors, rather than by failure of a state to meet its economic responsibilities, was first raised by implication in *Sweatt* v. *Painter*, 339 U.S. 629 (1950), involving the admission of a Black student to the University of Texas Law School.

In the *Sweatt* case the Supreme Court implied that similar physical facilities, for both races, *did not necessarily* satisfy the call for equality before the law demanded by the Fourteenth Amendment. A unanimous Court ruled that a Texas law school established solely for Blacks would not, and in effect could not, be equal to the long-established University of Texas, due to the lack of equal library and building facilities, equal faculty, and equal prestige. The demand for an equal faculty and prestige could hardly be provided without admission to the University of Texas Law School of which they were both an inextricable part. This proved to be the Court's legal remedy. This case, because of its reasoning, proved to be the precursor of the historic *Brown* decision of 1954.

The Demise of Legal Segregation

The *Plessy* doctrine was first set aside in the field of public education. The charge, that segregated schools could not meet the constitutional command of the equal protection clause, was initially sustained by the Supreme Court in *Brown* v. *Topeka*, 347 U.S. 483 (1954). In a unanimous opinion, the High Tribunal, speaking through Mr. Chief Justice Warren, overruled the decision of 1896, as it applied to public educational institutions, and concluded "that in the field of public education the doctrine of 'separate but equal' has no place." Employing the latest "modern psychological authority," the Court evolved a new rule which might appropriately be called the theory of "inherent inequality."

The *Brown* doctrine was written in language more scientific than juridical. The Court accepted the views of psychologists and sociologists that "segregation of white and colored children in public schools has a detrimental effect upon the colored children." Sanctioned by law it tended to stamp them with a "badge of inferiority." They concluded:

> . . . Segregation with the sanction of law, therefore, has a tendency to retard the educational and mental development of Negro children and to deprive them of some of the benefits they would receive in a racially integrated school system.

. . . *Separate educational facilities are inherently unequal.* [Editor's emphasis.]

The Federal concept of dual sovereignty necessitated the companion case of *Bolling* v. *Sharpe*, 347 U.S. 497 (1954), since the Fourteenth Amendment was not a restriction on the Federal Government. The segregated school system in the Federal District of Columbia was found to be a violation of the Fifth Amendment:

> . . . Segregation in public education is not reasonably related to any proper governmental objective, and thus it imposes on Negro children of the District of Columbia a burden that constitutes an arbitrary deprivation of their liberty in violation of the Due Process Clause.

In May, 1955, in the second *Brown* case, 349 U.S. 294, the Supreme Court announced a general order for implementation of integration in the segregated school systems. The Federal District Courts were commanded to require defendant school districts to make a *"prompt and reasonable start toward full compliance"* [Editor's emphasis.] with the ruling of May 17, 1954. Further, the cases pending before the Supreme Court in this classification, were sent back "to the District Courts to take such proceedings and enter such orders and decrees . . . as [were] necessary and proper to admit" defendants "on a racially non-discriminatory basis with all deliberate speed."

The Extension of the Brown Doctrine

Shortly after the *Brown* holding (May 17, 1954), the intent of the Supreme Court to eventually overrule the *Plessy* case in many other fields of public activity became clear. Having declared unequivocally the unconstitutionality of racially segregated public primary and secondary schools, the Supreme Court, for the next three years, proceeded without comment to deny writs of *certiorari* to school districts appealing from desegregation decisions applying the *Brown* doctrine announced in the various Federal Circuit Courts of Appeal.

Turning next to the field of higher education the Supreme Court quickly replaced the *Plessy* doctrine with the *Brown* doctrine. One week after the original Brown decision, in *Hawkins* v. *Bd. of Control*, 347 U.S. 471 (1954), Virgil Hawkins' legal battle to gain admission to the University of Florida was sent by the United States Supreme Court to the Supreme Court of Florida with instructions to reconsider the Negro student's bid in light of the *Brown* finding. Subsequently, the Florida High Court contended that Hawkins had no legal right to demand *immediate* admission under any court decision on the segregation issue. Hawkins reappealed to the Federal Supreme Court.

After hearing this case for the second time, in *Hawkins* v. *Bd. of Control*, 350 U.S. 413 (1956), the nation's High Tribunal vacated its previous mandate of May 24, 1954; held that the second *Brown* decision was not applicable in the present controversy; and entered a new order:

> As this case involves the *admission of a Negro to a graduate profes-sional school, there is no reason for delay*. He is entitled to prompt admission under the rules and regulations applicable to other qualified candidates. [Editor's emphasis.]

The *Brown* doctrine was fully applied to public higher education in *University of North Carolina* v. *Frasier*, 350 U.S. 979 (1956). The Supreme Court, in a *Per Curiam* decision, affirmed without opinion, the expansion of the doctrine by a Federal District Court.

The original action was brought by three Negroes, who sought to enter the undergraduate school of the University of North Carolina. Rejecting the University's contention that segregation in higher education, unlike segregation in public primary and secondary schools, was not a violation of the equal protection clause, the District Court in *Frasier* v. *North Carolina* 134 F. Supp. 589, broadened the holding in *Brown* v. *Topeka, supra*:

> The only answer to this far reaching decision, and the only defense on the merits of the cases offered by the defendants in this suit is that the Supreme Court in *Brown* v. *Topeka, Kansas*, decided that segrega-tion of the races was prohibited by the Fourteenth Amendment only in respect to the lower public schools and did not decide that the separation of the races in schools on the college and university level is unlawful. We think that the contention is without merit. That the decision of the Supreme Court was limited to the facts before it is true, but the reasoning on which the decision was based is as applicable to schools for higher education as to schools on the lower level.

Within a year, the decision in the Girard College case, *Pennsylvania* v. *Bd. of Directors of City Trusts of Philadelphia*, 353 U.S. 230 (1957), extended the requirement of integrated facilities to private institutions of higher education which operated as agents of the state. Girard College had been established and operated by a fund in trust which limited admission to qualified persons of the white race. The City of Philadelphia was named as a trustee and the board administering the institution was created by an act of the State Legislature. A *Per Curiam* opinion of the Supreme Court held that the college could no longer continue as a segregated institution due to the fact that the governing board was an agency of the state and consequently its actions were subject to the restraints of the Fourteenth Amendment.

The *Brown* decision was soon used to challenge racial segregation in public common carriers. In the first action under the doctrine a Black woman brought suit in *Flemming* v. *South Carolina Elec. & Gas Co.*, 224 F. 2d 752 (1955), because a bus driver required her to change seats in accordance with the motor vehicle carrier segregation law of South Carolina. The *Per Curiam* opinion of the Federal Fourth Circuit Court of Appeals found the *Plessy* case outdated and applied the *Brown* doctrine:

> We do not think that the separate but equal doctrine of *Plessy* v. *Ferguson* can any longer be regarded as a correct statement of the law. That case recognizes segregation of the races by common carriers as being governed by the same principles as segregation in the public schools; and the recent decisions in *Brown* v. *Board of Education* and *Bolling* v. *Sharpe* which relate to public schools, leave no doubt that the separate but equal doctrine approved in *Plessy* v. *Ferguson* has been repudiated. . . .

The Supreme Court dismissed the case on procedural grounds [351 U.S. 901 (1956)] without endorsing the Circuit Court's abandonment of the *Plessy* doctrine. However, the constitutional issue was decided with finality in a matter of months in *Browder* v. *Gayle*, 352 U.S. 903 (1956).

The *Browder* case brought the issue of segregation in common carriers before the Supreme Court for the second time. In the court of first instance, [at 142 F. Supp. 707] enactments requiring segregation of the races on a public carrier in the State of Alabama and the City of Montgomery were declared invalid exercises of the state police power in conflict with two provisions of the Fourteenth Amendment:

> We cannot in good conscience perform our duty as judges by blindly following the precedent of *Plessy* v. *Ferguson* (when our study leaves us in complete agreement with *Flemming* v. *South Carolina*) that the separate but equal doctrine can no longer be safely followed as a correct statement of the law. In fact, we think that *Plessy* v. *Ferguson* has been impliedly, though not explicitly, overruled, and that under the later decisions, there is now no rational basis upon which the separate but equal doctrine can be validly applied to public carrier transportation within the City of Montgomery and its police jurisdiction. The application of that doctrine cannot be justified as a proper execution of the state police power. . . .
>
> We hold that the statutes and ordinances . . . violate the due process and equal protection of the law clauses of the Fourteenth Amendment to the Constitution of the United States.

The Supreme Court affirmed this judgment in a *Per Curiam* decision without opinion [*Browder* v. *Gayle, supra*] thereby establishing the *Brown* doctrine as the governing principle of law for future litigation challenging segregation on public common carriers. *Plessy* v. *Ferguson, supra*, was now obsolete in the field of public transportation.

The recreational facilities provided by state funds were also quickly affected by the *Brown* decision. In 1953, a Federal District Court in *Muir* v. *Louisville*, 202 F. 2d 275, had held that although Negroes were entitled to participate in the enjoyment of golf courses and fishing facilities maintained by public funds, they did not have a legal right to gain admission to operatic performances staged by a private company which had leased, from the city, an amphitheater located in a public park. Months later on appeal to the Supreme Court, the holding was reversed and the case sent to the District Court to be reconsidered in light of the decision in *Brown* v. *Topeka, supra*.

The *Brown* doctrine was officially applied by a federal court in March of 1955 in *Dawson* v. *Baltimore*, 220 F. 2d 386. A Court of Appeals decision ordering desegregation of public bathhouses and beaches in Baltimore, Maryland, held that the *Plessy* doctrine, as governing public recreational facilities, had been swept away by subsequent decisions of the Supreme Court in *McLauren* v. *Oklahoma*, 339 U.S. 637 (1950); *Henderson* v. *United States, supra*; *Brown* v. *Topeka, supra*, and *Bolling v. Sharpe, supra*. The "inherent inequality" of segregated facilities and the impotence of the police power to enforce segregation highlighted the opinion:

> . . . It is now obvious, however, that segregation cannot be justified as a means to preserve the public peace merely because the tangible facilities furnished to one race are equal to those furnished to the other, . . . it is obvious that racial segregation can no longer be sustained as a proper exercise of the police power of the State; for if that power cannot be invoked to sustain racial segregation in the schools, where attendance is compulsory and racial friction may be apprehended from the enforced commingling of the races, it cannot be sustained with respect to public beach and bathhouse facilities, the use of which is entirely optional.

The Supreme Court concurred in a *Per Curiam* decision without opinion at 350 U.S. 877 (1955).

If any doubt remained as to the position of the High Court on public recreational facilities, it was removed in *Holmes* v. *Atlanta*, 223 F. 2d 93 (1955). Holmes, a Black resident of Atlanta, Georgia, sued the city for denying him equal protection of the laws by refusing him the same golfing privileges provided for whites. The Federal District Court's ruling held that *Plessy* v. *Ferguson, supra*, was not overruled by *Brown* v. *Topeka*, *supra*, in any field but public education. Atlanta was allowed "a reasonable opportunity to prepare and put into effect regulations for the use of municipal golf facilities," which, while preserving segregation, would be in fair accord with the principle of equality of privileges provided by law to the separated groups within the state.

Holmes appealed from the decision because the trial court failed to order Negroes promptly admitted to public golf facilities under the same rules, regulations, and conditions applicable to all other persons. The Court of Appeals rejected his claim contending that the lower court had granted Holmes all the relief for which he had asked. In early November, 1955, the Supreme Court, after having granted *certiorari*, reversed both lower courts and sent the case to the Federal District Court with instructions to find for Holmes in accordance with *Baltimore City* v. *Dawson, supra*. Thus, the High Court unmistakably applied the *Brown* doctrine to public recreational facilities.

Even the claim that recreational facilities, where operated under state proprietary rather than state governmental capacity, did not prevent invalidation of racially discriminatory regulations. Using the *Dawson* case as precedent, the Fifth Circuit Court of Appeals in *St. Petersburg* v. *Alsup*, 238 F. 2d 830 (1957), warned that "a state cannot, by judicial decision or otherwise, remove any of its activities from the inhibitions of the Fourteenth Amendment." Further, the Circuit Court held that financial loss, anticipated or actual, arising from the integration of recreational facilities would not justify their continued operation on a segregated basis in violation of the Constitution. In sum, in the area of public expenditures and state provided facilities, racial segregation, long justified by the Fourteenth Amendment, was at last *legally* dead.

The Public Trespass Cases

As we have seen in Chapter Two, the end of constitutionally defended segregation in the 1950's did not produce an integrated society, end racial discrimination, nor appreciably improve the economic, social or psychological condition of Blacks. The legal barriers were removed but the residual elements which remained intact still made for second-class citizenship, *in fact*, if not *in law*.

Having used the courts successfully to strike discriminatory state action, Black Americans still found themselves frustrated and excluded from the social mainstream and economic benefits of American life. This was true in the North as well as the South. Despairing that the judicial system could do no more, the struggle for equality in the 1960's moved from litigation in the courts to demonstrations in the streets. Using the constitutional guarantees of speech, assembly, and petition, Blacks took their grievances to the seats of local government and, through publicity and mass media, into the homes of the rest of the American people. The cases in this section document, in small part, that story and the new frustrations the Blacks had to face.

In *Edwards* v. *South Carolina*, 372 U.S. 229 (1963), a group of Negroes, protesting the general discriminatory conditions of Blacks in the state, were convicted for breach of the peace. The demonstration took place outside the State Legislature and involved peaceful picketing, chanting, and the singing of the "Star Spangled Banner." Reversing the convictions in the lower courts, Mr. Justice Stewart in the opinion of the Supreme Court held that the Fourteenth Amendment prohibited a state from restricting the peaceful expression of unpopular views simply because a crowd gathered and there was the possibility of trouble. On the face of the record there appeared to be no violation of the law on the part of the demonstrators.

In a lone dissent, Mr. Justice Clark read the facts differently. Seeing no evidence that officials tried to disperse this attempt to "redress grievances" because of their inherent unpopularity, Clark stressed that the value-judgments of public officials about the probable explosiveness of a situation which they were witnessing, had to be given more respect if violence and disorder were to be successfully anticipated and avoided before those evils were upon us.

In *Cox* v. *Louisiana*, 379 U.S. 536 (1965), the Court, this time through Mr. Justice Goldberg, reversed a lower court's convictions for "disturbing the peace," "obstructing public passages," and "courthouse picketing." The reversal for "disturbing the peace" followed the rationale of the *Edwards* case while the overturning of the "obstruction" charge flowed from the uneven administrative application of the local law prohibiting all parades or marches in the City of Baton Rouge.

Recognizing the right of a state to ban all demonstrations which interfered with the constitutional right of a fair trial free from "mob," or otherwise outside interference near a courthouse, the majority nevertheless reversed the convictions in this case because an unwritten agreement had been reached prior to the picketing to allow the demonstration near the courthouse. After initially adhering to the agreement, police officials suddenly reversed their position and summarily ordered dispersal of the demonstrators. For the majority this seemed too much like arbitrary, *ad hoc* administrative discretion to be constitutional under the Fourteenth Amendment.

In *Cox*, Mr. Justice Black dissented in part over the conviction reversal for picketing near the courthouse. Black stressed the importance of keeping the judicial process as distinct from political involvement and pressures as possible. Black believed that if justice was to be truly served it would most likely be in the calm of the courthouse. [Note that this theme has already been mentioned in the introductory essay to Section III.]

Justice Black developed a similar theme in his opinion for a narrowly divided Court (5-4) in *Adderley* v. *Florida*, 385 U.S. 39 (1966). Upholding the lower court convictions for Black college students found guilty of "trespass with malicious and mischievous intent," Black stressed that the state had no less property rights over public property than did a private owner over his property. The trespass on the grounds of the county jail was specifically prohibited by a narrowly drawn state statute. The statutory vagueness and unbridled administrative discretion encountered in the *Edwards* and *Cox* cases—which might have infringed free speech, assembly, and petition—were lacking in this case, Black held, because of the clarity of the trespass statute and the warnings clearly given by the sheriff to the students.

A strong dissent by Mr. Justice Douglas, with whom Chief Justice Warren and Justices Brennan and Fortas joined, indicated that, unlike private property, certain state-owned property such as the seats of government may not be closed to public petition for the redress of grievances if the First and Fourteenth Amendments were to have any substantive meaning. Unlike the majority, the minority opinion saw the *Adderley* case at odds with the *Edwards* case. Justice Douglas also warned the Court that not all segments of society had effective ways of protesting acts of government which they deemed oppressive through the political system. He feared that the use of such trespass laws as in the present case only served to frustrate further the politically disenchanted.

Walker v. *Birmingham*, 388 U.S. 307 (1967), found another narrowly divided Court (5-4) sustaining the contempt convictions of eight ministers among whom was the late Dr. Martin Luther King, Jr. The case turned on whether the defendant ministers should have disobeyed a court injunction against marching into Birmingham without a parade permit or should have first taken legal action to show that a permit was being unconstitutionally and arbitrarily denied them by the Commissioner of Public Safety. The majority opinion by Mr. Justice Stewart refused to consider the substantive constitutional questions arising out of the general wording of the parade ordinance or the vagueness of the temporary injunction because these were not raised in a proper legal challenge before the march, but instead were invoked as a defense for violating the court's injunction. The theme, that acts of government suspected of unconstitutionality ought to be first challenged in court before a court order was flagrantly disregarded ran through the majority opinion.

The two dissenting opinions cited the unwillingness of city officials to grant a parade permit and the summary dismissal of their attempt to follow the law. The minority opinions also stressed the "symbolic" quality of the days for which the march was scheduled (Good Friday and Easter Sunday). In addition the *ex parte* process by which the temporary injunction was obtained in the first instance was questioned. For the dissenters, the whole fabric of official frustration of the legitimate expression of freedom of assembly and peaceful protest of the Black condition in the South did more to call into contempt and derision the judicial and legal process than did the march of the defendants. The dissenting opinions seemed to reflect Justice Holmes' admonition that "in order for the law to be respected it has to be respectable."

Gregory v. *Chicago*, 394 U.S. 111 (1969), raised similar issues to the cases discussed above with the significant exception being that the *Gregory* case took place in a major northern city. The circumstances, which can be read in the case itself, inescapably bear witness to the fact that racism and its attendant words, (i.e., "nigger") were not the special province of any section of this nation.

Carroll v. *Princess Anne County, Maryland*, 393 U.S. 175 (1968) was somewhat dissimilar from the preceding cases in that the defendants were members of the "white supremacist" National States Rights Party. Displaying its consistent concern with the protection of First Amendment rights for all individuals and groups, the Supreme Court, with no dissenters, disposed of the case on the grounds that the *ex parte* proceeding, which secured the court injunction against a public Party rally was held without sufficient prior notice to the Party. To the Supreme Court, this tactic of securing injunctions against rallies in "secret" *ex parte* actions seemed to constitute the newest technique to silence unpopular and unorthodox opinions. The freedom of people to reasonably and peacefully express their opinions in public places was forcefully defended against this newly invoked procedure which the Court implied amounted to an unconstitutional "prior restraint" on First Amendment freedoms.

In the light of these cases, is it unreasonable to conclude—at least in part—that there has been much "lawlessness" on the part of men in positions of power, authority and responsibility (i.e., governmental officials ignoring established constitutional rights)? Is there an inconsistency in the call of minority groups to help reestablish "law and order" when many in high places may, by unfair application of the law, do violence to that civilized concept?

EDWARDS v. SOUTH CAROLINA

372 U.S. 229; 83 S. Ct. 680; 9 L.Ed. 2d 697 (1963)

MR. JUSTICE STEWART *delivered the opinion of the Court.*

The petitioners, 187 in number, were convicted in a magistrate's court in Columbia, South Carolina, of the common-law crime of breach of the peace. Their convictions were ultimately affirmed by the South Carolina Supreme Court, 239 S.C. 339, 123 S.E.2d 247. We granted *certiorari*, 369 U.S. 870, 82 S.Ct. 1141, 8 L.Ed.2d 274, to consider the claim that these convictions cannot be squared with the Fourteenth Amendment of the United States Constitution.

There was no substantial conflict in the trial evidence. Late in the morning of March 2, 1961, the petitioners, high school and college students of the Negro race, met at the Zion Baptist Church in Columbia. From there, at about noon, they walked in separate groups of about 15 to the South Carolina State House grounds, an area of two city blocks open to the general public. Their purpose was "to submit a protest to the citizens of South Carolina, along with the Legislative Bodies of South Carolina, our feelings and our dissatisfaction with the present condition of discriminatory actions against Negroes, in general, and to let them know that we were dissatisfied and that we would like for the laws which prohibited Negro privileges in this State to be removed."

Already on the State House grounds when the petitioners arrived were 30 or more law enforcement officers, who had advance knowledge that the petitioners were coming.[2] Each group of petitioners entered the grounds through a driveway and parking area known in the record as the "horseshoe." As they entered, they were told by the law enforcement officials that "they had a right, as a citizen, to go through the State House grounds, as any other citizen has, as long as they were peaceful." During the next half hour or 45 minutes, the petitioners, in the same small groups, walked single file or two abreast in an orderly way through the grounds, each group carrying placards bearing such messages as "I am proud to be a Negro," and "Down with segregation."

During this time a crowd of some 200 to 300 onlookers had collected in the horseshoe area and on the adjacent sidewalks. There was no evidence to suggest that these onlookers were anything but curious, and no evidence at all of any threat-

2. The Police Chief of Columbia testified that about 15 of his men were present, and that there were, in addition, "some State Highway Patrolmen; there were some South Carolina Law Enforcement officers present and I believe, I'm not positive, I believe there were about three Deputy Sheriffs."

ening remarks, hostile gestures, or offensive language on the part of any member of the crowd. The City Manager testified that he recognized some of the onlookers, whom he did not identify, as "possible trouble makers," but his subsequent testimony made clear that nobody among the crowd actually caused or threatened any trouble.[4] There was no obstruction of pedestrian or vehicular traffic within the State House grounds. No vehicle was prevented from entering or leaving the horseshoe area. Although vehicular traffic at a nearby street intersection was slowed down somewhat, an officer was dispatched to keep traffic moving. There were a number of by-

standers on the public sidewalks adjacent to the State House grounds, but they all moved on when asked to do so, and there was no impediment of pedestrian traffic.[6] Police protection at the scene was at all times sufficient to meet any foreseeable possibility of disorder.[7]

In the situation and under the circumstances thus described, the police authorities advised the petitioners that they would be arrested if they did not disperse within 15 minutes.[8] Instead of dispersing, the petitioners engaged in what the City Manager described as "boisterous," "loud," and "flamboyant" conduct, which, as his later testimony made clear, consisted of listening to a "re-

4. "Q. Who were those persons?
"A. I can't tell you who they were. I can tell you they were present in the group. They were recognized as possible trouble makers.
"Q. Did you and your police chief do anything about placing those people under arrest?
"A. No, we had no occasion to place them under arrest.
"Q. Now, sir, you have stated that there were possible trouble makers and your whole testimony has been that, as City Manager, as supervisor of the City Police, your object is to preserve the peace and law and order?
"A. That's right.
"Q. Yet you took no official action against people who were present and possibly might have done some harm to these people?
"A. We took no official action because there was none to be taken. They were not creating a disturbance, those particular people were not at that time doing anything to make trouble but they could have been."
6. The Police Chief of Columbia testified:
"A. At times they blocked the sidewalk and we asked them to move over and they did.
"Q. They obeyed your commands on that?

"A. Yes.
"Q. So that nobody complained that he wanted to use the sidewalk and he could not do it?
"A. I didn't have any complaints on that."
7. The City Manager testified:
"Q. You had ample time, didn't you, to get ample police protection, if you thought such was needed on the State House grounds, didn't you?
"A. Yes, we did.
"Q. So, if there were not ample police protection there, it was the fault of those persons in charge of the Police Department, wasn't it?
"A. There was ample police protection there."
8. The City Manager testified:
"Q. Mr. McNayr, what action did you take?
"A. I instructed Dave Carter to tell each of these groups, to call them up and tell each of the groups and the group leaders that they must disperse, they must disperse in the manner which I have already described, that I would give them fifteen minutes from the time of my conversation with him to have them dispersed and, if they were not dispersed, I would direct my Chief of Police to place them under arrest."

ligious harangue" by one of their leaders, and loudly singing "The Star Spangled Banner" and other patriotic and religious songs, while stamping their feet and clapping their hands. After 15 minutes had passed, the police arrested the petitioners and marched them off to jail.

Upon this evidence the state trial court convicted the petitioners of breach of the peace, and imposed sentences ranging from a $10 fine or five days in jail, to a $100 fine or 30 days in jail. In affirming the judgments, the Supreme Court of South Carolina said that under the law of that State the offense of breach of the peace "is not susceptible of exact definition," but that the "general definition of the offense" is as follows:

"In general terms, a breach of the peace is a violation of public order, a disturbance of the public tranquility, by any act or conduct inciting to violence . . . , it includes any violation of any law enacted to preserve peace and good order. It may consist of an act of violence or an act likely to produce violence. It is not necessary that the peace be actually broken to lay the foundation for a prosecution for this offense. If what is done is unjustifiable and unlawful, tending with sufficient directness to break the peace, no more is required. Nor is actual personal violence an essential element in the offense. . . .

"By 'peace,' as used in the law in this connection, is meant the tranquility enjoyed by citizens of a municipality or community where good order reigns among its members, which is the natural right of all persons in political society." 239 S.C. 339, 123 S.E.2d, at 249.

The petitioners contend that there was a complete absence of any evidence of the commission of this offense, and that they were thus denied one of the most basic elements of due process of law. . . . Whatever the merits of this contention, we need not pass upon it in the present case. The state courts have held that petitioners' conduct constituted breach of the peace under state law, and we may accept their decision as binding upon us to that extent. But it nevertheless remains our duty in a case such as this to make an independent examination of the whole record. . . . And it is clear to us that in arresting, convicting, and punishing the petitioners under the circumstances disclosed by this record, South Carolina infringed the petitioners' constitutionally protected rights of free speech, free assembly, and freedom to petition for redress of their grievances.

It has long been established that these First Amendment freedoms are protected by the Fourteenth Amendment from invasion by the States. . . . The circumstances in this case reflect an exercise of these basic constitutional rights in their most pristine and classic form. The petitioners felt aggrieved by laws of South Carolina which allegedly "prohibited Negro privileges in this State." They peaceably assembled at the site of the State Government[10] and there peaceably expressed their grievances "to the citizens of South Carolina, along with the Legislative Bodies of South Carolina." Not until they were told by police officials that they must disperse on pain of arrest did they do more. Even then, they but sang patriotic and religious songs after one of their leaders had delivered a "religious harangue." There was no violence or threat of violence on their part, or on the part of any member of the crowd watching them. Police protection was "ample."

This, therefore, was a far cry from the situation in *Feiner* v. *New York,* 340 U.S. 315, 71 S.Ct. 303, 95 L.Ed. 267, where two policemen were faced with a crowd which was "pushing, shoving, and milling around," . . . where at least one member of the crowd "threatened violence if the police did not act," . . . where "the crowd was pressing closer around petitioner and the officer," . . . and where "the speaker passes the bounds of argument or persuasion and undertakes incitement to riot." . . . And the record is barren of any evidence of "fighting words." See *Chaplinsky* v. *New Hampshire,* 315 U.S. 568, . . .

We do not review in this case criminal convictions resulting from the even-handed application of a precise and narrowly drawn regulatory statute evincing a legislative judgment that certain specific conduct be limited or proscribed. *If, for example, the petitioners had been convicted upon evidence that they had violated a law regulating traffic, or had disobeyed a law reasonably limiting the periods during which the State House grounds were open to the public, this would be a different case.*[11]*. . . . These petitioners were convicted of an offense so generalized as to be, in the words of the South Carolina Supreme Court, "not susceptible of exact definition." *And they were convicted upon evidence which showed no more than that the opinions which they were peaceably expressing were sufficiently opposed*

---

10. It was stipulated at trial "that the State House grounds are occupied by the Executive Branch of the South Carolina government, the Legislative Branch and the Judicial Branch, and that, during the period covered in the warrant in this matter, to wit: March the 2nd, the Legislature of South Carolina was in session."

[Editor's Note: Emphasis added.]

11. Section 1–417 of the 1952 Code of Laws of South Carolina (Cum.Supp.1960) provides as follows:

"It shall be unlawful for any person:

"(1) Except State officers and employees and persons having lawful business in the buildings, to use any of the driveways, alleys or parking spaces upon any of the property of the State, bounded by Assembly, Gervais, Bull and Pendleton Streets in Columbia upon any regular weekday, Saturdays and holidays excepted, between the hours of 8:30 a. m. and 5:30 p. m., whenever the buildings are open for business; or

"(2) To park any vehicle except in the spaces and manner marked and designated by the State Budget and Control Board, in cooperation with the Highway Department, or to block or impede traffic through the alleys and driveways."

The petitioners were not charged with violating this statute, and the record contains no evidence whatever that any police official had this statute in mind when ordering the petitioners to disperse on pain of arrest, or indeed that a charge under this statute could have been sustained by what occurred.

*to the views of the majority of the community to attract a crowd and necessitate police protection.**

*The Fourteenth Amendment does not permit a State to make criminal the peaceful expression of unpopular views. "[A] function of free speech under our system of government is to invite dispute. It may indeed best serve its high purpose when it induces a condition of unrest, creates dissatisfaction with conditions as they are, or even stirs people to anger.** Speech is often provocative and challenging. It may strike at prejudices and preconceptions and have profound unsettling effects as it presses for acceptance of an idea. That is why freedom of speech, . . . is . . . protected against censorship or punishment, unless shown likely to produce a clear and present danger of a serious substantive evil that rises far above public inconvenience, annoyance, or unrest. . . . There is no room under our Constitution for a more restrictive view. *For the alternative would lead to standardization of ideas either by legislatures, courts, or dominant political or community groups."**. . .*

As Chief Justice Hughes wrote in *Stromberg* v. *California, "The maintenance of the opportunity for free political discussion to the end that government may be responsive to the will of the people and that changes may be obtained by lawful means, an opportunity essential to the security of the Republic, is a fundamental principle of our constitutional system.** A statute which upon its face, and as authoritatively construed, is so vague and indefinite

as to permit the punishment of the fair use of this opportunity is repugnant to the guaranty of liberty contained in the Fourteenth Amendment. . . ."*

For these reasons we conclude that these criminal convictions cannot stand.

Reversed.

MR. JUSTICE CLARK, *dissenting.*

The convictions of the petitioners, Negro high school and college students, for breach of the peace under South Carolina law are accepted by the Court "as binding upon us to that extent" but are held violative of "petitioners' constitutionally protected rights of free speech, free assembly, and freedom to petition for redress of grievances." Petitioners, of course, had a right to peaceable assembly, to espouse their cause and to petition, but in my view the manner in which they exercised those rights was by no means the passive demonstration which this Court relates; rather, as the City Manager of Columbia testified, "a dangerous situation was building up" which South Carolina's courts expressly found had created "an actual interference with traffic and an imminently threatened disturbance of the peace of the community." Since the Court does not attack the state courts' findings and accepts the convictions as "binding" to the extent that the petitioners' conduct constituted a breach of the peace, it is difficult for me to understand its

*[Editor's Note: Emphasis added.]

understatement of the facts and reversal of the convictions.

The priceless character of First Amendment freedoms cannot be gainsaid, but it does not follow that they are absolutes immune from necessary state action reasonably designed for the protection of society. . . . For that reason it is our duty to consider the context in which the arrests here were made. Certainly the city officials would be constitutionally prohibited from refusing petitioners access to the State House grounds merely because they disagreed with their views. . . . But here South Carolina's courts have found: "There is no indication whatever in this case that the acts of the police officers were taken as a subterfuge or excuse for the suppression of appellants' views and opinions." It is undisputed that the city officials specifically granted petitioners permission to assemble, imposing only the requirement that they be "peaceful." Petitioners then gathered on the State House grounds, during a General Assembly session, in a large number of almost 200, marching and carrying placards with slogans such as "Down with segregation"

and "You may jail our bodies but not our souls." Some of them were singing.

The activity continued for approximately 45 minutes, during the busy noon-hour period, while a crowd of some 300 persons congregated in front of the State House and around the area directly in front of its entrance, known as the "horseshoe," which was used for vehicular as well as pedestrian ingress and egress. During this time there were no efforts made by the city officials to hinder the petitioners in their rights of free speech and assembly; rather, the police directed their efforts to the traffic problems resulting from petitioners' activities. It was only after the large crowd had gathered, among which the City Manager and Chief of Police recognized potential troublemakers, and which together with the students had become massed on and around the "horseshoe" so closely that vehicular and pedestrian traffic was materially impeded,[3] that any action against the petitioners was taken. Then the City Manager, in what both the state intermediate and Supreme Court found to be the utmost good faith, decided that

---

3. The City Manager testified as follows:
"Q. Now, with relation, Mr. McNayr, to the sidewalks around the horseshoe and the lane for vehicular traffic, how was the crowd distributed, with regard to those sidewalks and roadways?
"A. Well, the conditions varied from time to time, but at numerous times they were blocked almost completely with probably as many as thirty or forty persons, both on the sidewalks and in the street area. . . .
"Q. Did you observe the pedestrian traffic on the walkway?
"A. Yes, I did.

"Q. What was the condition there?
"A. The condition there was that it was extremely difficult for a pedestrian wanting to get through, to get through. Many of them took to the street area, even to get through the street area or the sidewalk."
The Chief of Police testified as follows:
"Q. Was the street blocked?
"A. We had to place a traffic man at the intersection of Gervais and Main to handle traffic and pedestrians.
"Q. Was a vehicular traffic lane blocked?
"A. It was, that was in the horseshoe."

danger to peace and safety was imminent. Even at this juncture no orders were issued by the City Manager for the police to break up the crowd, now about 500 persons, and no arrests were made. Instead, he approached the recognized leader of the petitioners and requested him to tell the various groups of petitioners to disperse within 15 minutes, failing which they would be arrested. Even though the City Manager might have been honestly mistaken as to the imminence of danger this was certainly a reasonable request by the city's top executive officer in an effort to avoid a public brawl. But the response of petitioners and their leader was defiance rather than co-operation. The leader immediately moved from group to group among the students, delivering a "harangue" which, according to testimony in the record, "aroused [them] to a fever pitch causing this boisterousness, this singing and stomping."

For the next 15 minutes the petitioners sang "I shall not be moved" and various religious songs, stamped their feet, clapped their hands, and conducted what the South Carolina Supreme Court found to be "a noisy demonstration in defiance of [the dispersal] orders." 239 S.C. 339, 123 S E.2d 247, 250. Ultimately, the petitioners were arrested, as they apparently planned from the beginning, and convicted on evidence the sufficiency of which the Court does not challenge. *The question thus seems to me whether a State is constitutionally prohibited from enforcing laws to prevent breach of the peace in a situation where city offi-*

*cials in good faith believe, and the record shows, that disorder and violence are imminent, merely because the activities constituting that breach contain claimed elements of constitutionally protected speech and assembly.** To me the answer under our cases is clearly in the negative.

Beginning, as did the South Carolina courts, with the premise that the petitioners were entitled to assemble and voice their dissatisfaction with segregation, the enlargement of constitutional protection for the conduct here is as fallacious as would be the conclusion that free speech necessarily includes the right to broadcast from a sound truck in the public streets. . . . This Court said in *Thornhill* v. *Alabama,* 310 U.S. 88, 105, 60 S.Ct. 736, 745, 84 L.Ed. 1093 (1940), that "[t]he power and the duty of the State to take adequate steps to preserve the peace and to protect the privacy, the lives, and the property of its residents cannot be doubted." Significantly, in holding that the petitioner's picketing was constitutionally protected in that case the Court took pains to differentiate it from "picketing *en masse* or otherwise conducted which might occasion . . . imminent and aggravated danger. . . ." Here the petitioners were permitted without hindrance to exercise their rights of free speech and assembly. Their arrests occurred only after a situation arose in which the law-enforcement officials on the scene considered that a dangerous disturbance was imminent.[4] The County Court found that "the evi-

---

*[Editor's Note: Emphasis added.]

dence is clear that the officers were motivated solely by a proper concern for the preservation of order and the protection of the general welfare in the face of an actual interference with traffic and an imminently threatened disturbance of the peace of the community." In affirming, the South Carolina Supreme Court said the action of the police was "reasonable and motivated solely by a proper concern for the preservation of order and prevention of further interference with traffic upon the public streets and sidewalks.". . .

In *Cantwell* v. *Connecticut*, . . . this Court recognized that "[w]hen clear and present danger of riot, disorder, interference with traffic upon the public streets, or other immediate threat to public safety, peace, or order, appears, the power of the state to prevent or punish is obvious." And in *Feiner* v. *New York*, . . . we upheld a conviction for breach of the peace in a situation no more dangerous than that found here. There the demonstration was conducted by only one person and the crowd was limited to approximately 80, as compared with the present lineup of some 200 demonstrators and 300 onlookers. There the petitioner was "endeavoring to arouse the Negro people against the whites, urging that they rise up in arms and fight for equal rights." . . . Only one person—in a city having an entirely different historical background—was exhorting adults. Here 200 youthful Negro demonstrators were being aroused to a "fever pitch" before a crowd of some 300 people who undoubtedly were hostile. Perhaps their speech was not so animated but in this setting their actions, their placards reading "You may jail our bodies but not our souls" and their chanting of "I shall not be moved," accompanied by stamping feet and clapping hands, created a much greater danger of riot and disorder. It is my belief that anyone conversant with the almost spontaneous combustion in some Southern communities in such a situation will agree that the City Manager's action may well have averted a major catastrophe.

The gravity of the danger here surely needs no further explication. The imminence of that danger has been emphasized at every stage of this proceeding, from the complaints

4. The City Manager testified as follows:
"Q. Did you hear any singing, chanting or anything of that nature from the student group?
"A. Yes.
"Q. Describe that as best you can.
"A. With the harangues, which I have just described, witnessed frankly by everyone present and in this area, the students began answering back with shouts. They became boisterous. They stomped their feet. They sang in loud voices to the point where, again, in my judgment, a dangerous situation was really building up."

The Police Chief testified as follows:
"Q. Chief, you were questioned on cross examination at length about the appearance and orderliness of the student group. Were they orderly at all times?
"A. Not at the last.
"Q. Would you describe the activities at the last?
"A. As I have stated, they were singing and, also, when they were getting certain instructions, they were very loud and boisterous."

charging that the demonstrations "tended directly to immediate violence" to the State Supreme Court's affirmance on the authority of *Feiner, supra*. This record, then, shows no steps backward from a standard of "clear and present danger." But to say that the police may not intervene until the riot has occurred is like keeping out the doctor until the patient dies. . . .

I would affirm the convictions.

QUESTIONS

1. On your reading of the facts, do you think the conditions were such at the statehouse to justify the police order that the demonstrators ought to disperse in 15 minutes? Why yes? Why no?

2. Can there be a meaningful right of assembly to petition government in the halls of the legislature if a peaceful—but loud—protest can be disbanded by police order? If yes, what do you think the "right of assembly for a redress of grievances" means? If no, aren't the legislators entitled to conduct their business without chanting, singing, and perhaps fear of intimidation being brought to their statehouse offices?

3. If you agree that the facts of this case constituted an "illegal disturbance" under the South Carolina law, what do you think a legitimate protest would be?

4. Why—if for any reason—should a "mob" protest like this be constitutionally protected?

5. In the first place, who decides at the event, whether or not there is a *real* and *imminent* danger of disorder? On what basis should that decision be made? Can you advance some *specific* criteria or conditions you would use to make that judgment if it was yours to make on the spot? Were those elements present in this case?

COX v. LOUISIANA

379 U.S. 536; 85 S. Ct. 453; 13 L.Ed. 2d 471 (1965)

MR. JUSTICE GOLDBERG *delivered the opinion of the Court.*

Appellant, the Reverend Mr. B. Elton Cox, the leader of a civil rights demonstration, was arrested and charged with four offenses under Louisiana law—criminal conspiracy, disturbing the peace, obstructing public passages and picketing before a courthouse. In a consolidated trial before a judge without a jury, and on the same set of facts, he was acquitted of criminal conspiracy but convicted of the other three offenses. He was sentenced to serve four months in jail and pay a $200 fine for disturbing the peace, to serve five months in jail and pay a $500 fine for obstructing public passages, and to serve one year in jail and pay a $5,000 fine for picketing before a courthouse. The sentences were cumulative.

In accordance with Louisiana procedure the Louisiana Supreme Court reviewed the "disturbing the peace" and "obstructing public passages" convictions on *certiorari* and the "courthouse picketing" conviction on appeal. The Louisiana court, in two judgments, affirmed all three convictions. 244 La. 1087, 156 So. 2d 448; 245 La. 303, 158 So.2d 172. Appellant filed two separate appeals to this Court from these judgments contending that the three statutes under which he was convicted were unconstitutional on their face and as applied. We noted probable jurisdiction of both appeals, 377 U.S. 921, 84 S.Ct. 1219, 1222, 12 L.Ed.2d 214. This case, No. 24, involves the convictions for disturbing the peace and obstructing public passages, and No. 49 concerns the conviction for picketing before a courthouse.

I.

The Facts.

On December 14, 1961, 23 students from Southern University, a Negro college, were arrested in downtown Baton Rouge, Louisiana, for picketing stores that maintained segregated lunch counters. This picketing, urging a boycott of those stores, was part of a general protest movement against racial segregation, directed by the local chapter of the Congress of Racial Equality, a civil rights organization. The appellant, an ordained Congregational minister, the Reverend Mr. B. Elton Cox, a Field Secretary of CORE, was an advisor to this movement. On the evening of December 14, appellant and Ronnie Moore, student president of the local CORE chapter, spoke at a mass meeting at the college. The students resolved to demonstrate the next day in front of the courthouse in protest of segregation and the arrest and imprisonment of the picketers who were being held in the parish jail located on the upper floor of the courthouse building.

The next morning about 2,000 students left the campus, which was located approximately five miles from downtown Baton Rouge. Most of them had to walk into the city since the drivers of their busses were arrested. Moore was also arrested at the entrance to the campus while parked in a car equipped with a loudspeaker, and charged with violation of an antinoise statute. Because Moore was immediately taken off to jail and the vice president of the CORE chapter was already in jail for picketing, Cox felt it his duty to take over the demonstration and see that it was carried out as planned. He quickly drove to the city "to pick up this leadership and keep things orderly."

When Cox arrived, 1,500 of the 2,000 students were assembling at the site of the Old State Capitol building, two and one-half blocks from the courthouse. Cox walked up and down cautioning the students to keep to one side of the sidewalk while getting ready for their march to the courthouse. The students circled the block in a file two or three abreast occupying about half of the sidewalk. The police had learned of the proposed demonstration the night before from news media and other sources. Captain Font of the City Police Department and Chief Kling of the Sheriff's office, two high-ranking subordinate officials, approached the group and spoke to Cox at the northeast corner of the capitol grounds. Cox identified himself as the group's leader, and, according to Font and Kling, he explained that the students were demonstrating to protest "the illegal arrest of some of their people who were being held in jail." The version of Cox and his witnesses throughout was that they came not "to protest just the arrest but . . . [also] to protest the evil of discrimination." Kling asked Cox to disband the group and "take them back from whence they came." Cox did not acquiesce in this request but told the officers that they would march by the courthouse, say prayers, sing hymns, and conduct a peaceful program of protest. The officer repeated his request to disband, and Cox again refused. Kling and Font then returned to their car in order to report by radio to the Sheriff and Chief of Police who were in the immediate vicinity; while this was going on, the students, led by Cox,

began their walk toward the courthouse.

They walked in an orderly and peaceful file, two or three abreast, one block east, stopping on the way for a red traffic light. In the center of this block they were joined by another group of students. The augmented group now totaling about 2,000[1] turned the corner and proceeded south, coming to a halt in the next block opposite the courthouse.

As Cox, still at the head of the group, approached the vicinity of the courthouse, he was stopped by Captain Font and Inspector Trigg and brought to Police Chief Wingate White, who was standing in the middle of St. Louis street. The Chief then inquired as to the purpose of the demonstration. Cox, reading from a prepared paper, outlined his program to White, stating that it would include a singing of the Star Spangled Banner and a "freedom song," recitation of the Lord's Prayer and the Pledge of Allegiance, and a short speech. White testified that he told Cox that "he must confine" the demonstration "to the west side of the street." White added, "This, of course, was not—I didn't mean it in the import that I was giving him any permission to do it, but I was presented with a situation that was accomplished, and I had to make a decision." Cox testified that the officials agreed to permit the meeting. James Erwin, news director of radio station WIBR, a witness for the State, was present and overheard the

---

1. Estimates of the crowd's size varied from 1,500 to 3,800. Two thousand seems to have been the general consensus and was the figure accepted by the Louisiana Supreme Court, 244 La., at 1095, 156 So.2d, at 451.

conversation. He testified that "My understanding was that they would be allowed to demonstrate if they stayed on the west side of the street and stayed within the recognized time," and that this was "agreed to" by White.

The students were then directed by Cox to the west sidewalk, across the street from the courthouse, 101 feet from its steps. They were lined up on this sidewalk about five deep and spread almost the entire length of the block. The group did not obstruct the street. It was close to noon and, being lunch time, a small crowd of 100 to 300 curious white people, mostly courthouse personnel, gathered on the east sidewalk and courthouse steps, about 100 feet from the demonstrators. Seventy-five to eighty policemen, including city and state patrolmen and members of the Sheriff's staff, as well as members of the fire department and a fire truck were stationed in the street between the two groups. Rain fell throughout the demonstration.

Several of the students took from beneath their coats picket signs similar to those which had been used the day before. These signs bore legends such as "Don't buy discrimination for Christmas," "Sacrifice for Christ, don't buy," and named stores which were proclaimed "unfair." They then sang "God Bless America," pledged allegiance to the flag, prayed briefly, and sang one or two hymns, including "We Shall Overcome." The 23 students, who were locked in jail cells in the courthouse building out of the sight of the demonstrators, responded by themselves singing; this in turn was greeted with cheers and applause by the demonstrators. Appellant gave a speech, described by a State's witness as follows:

"He said that in effect that it was a protest against the illegal arrest of some of their members and that other people were allowed to picket and he said that they were not going to commit any violence, that if anyone spit on them, they would not spit back on the person that did it."

Cox then said:

"All right. It's lunch time. Let's go eat. There are twelve stores we are protesting. A number of these stores have twenty counters; they accept your money from nineteen. They won't accept it from the twentieth counter. This is an act of racial discrimination. These stores are open to the public. You are members of the public. We pay taxes to the Federal Government and you who live here pay taxes to the state."[6]

In apparent reaction to these last remarks, there was what state witnesses described as "muttering" and "grumbling" by the white onlookers.

---

6. Sheriff Clemens objected strongly to these words. He testified on cross-examination as follows:

"Q. Now, what part of his speech became objectionable to him being assembled there?

"A. The inflammatory manner in which he addressed that crowd and told them to go on up town, go to four places on the protest list, sit down and if they don't feed you, sit there for one hour.

The Sheriff, deeming, as he testified, Cox's appeal to the students to sit in at the lunch counters to be "inflammatory," then took a power microphone and said, "Now, you have been allowed to demonstrate. Up until now your demonstration has been more or less peaceful, but what you are doing now is a direct violation of the law, a disturbance of the peace, and it has to be broken up immediately." The testimony as to what then happened is disputed. Some of the State's witnesses testified that Cox said, "don't move"; others stated that he made a "gesture of defiance." It is clear from the record, however, that Cox and the demonstrators did not then and there break up the demonstration. Two of the Sheriff's deputies immediately started across the street and told the group, "You have heard what the Sheriff said, now, do what he said." A state witness testified that they put their hands on the shoulders of some of the students "as though to shove them away."

Almost immediately thereafter— within a time estimated variously at two to five minutes—one of the policemen exploded a tear gas shell at the crowd. This was followed by several other shells. The demonstrators quickly dispersed, running back towards the State Capitol and the downtown area; Cox tried to calm them as they ran and was himself one of the last to leave.

No Negroes participating in the demonstration were arrested on that day. The only person then arrested was a young white man, not a part of the demonstration, who was arrested "because he was causing a disturbance." The next day appellant was arrested and charged with the four offenses above described.

II.

The Breach of the Peace Conviction.

Appellant was convicted of violating a Louisiana "disturbing the peace" statute, which provides:

"Whoever with intent to provoke a breach of the peace, or under circumstances such that a breach of the peace may be occasioned thereby . . . crowds or congregates with others . . . in or upon . . . a public street or public highway, or upon a public sidewalk, or any other public place or building . . . and who fails or refuses to disperse and move on, . . . when ordered so to do by any law enforcement officer of any municipality, or parish, in which such act or acts are committed, or by any law enforcement officer of the state of Louisiana, or any other authorized person . . . shall be guilty of disturbing the peace." LSA—Rev.Stat. 14:103.1 (Cum.Supp.1962).

It is clear to us that on the facts of this case, which are strikingly similar to those present in *Edwards* v. *South Carolina*, 372 U.S. 229, 83 S.Ct. 680, 9 L.Ed.2d 697, and *Fields* v. *South Carolina*, 375 U.S. 44, 84 S.Ct. 149, 11 L.Ed.2d 107, Louisiana infringed appellant's rights of free speech and free assembly by convicting him under this statute. As in *Edwards*, we do not find it necessary to pass upon appellant's contention that there was a complete absence of evidence so that his conviction deprived him of liberty without due process of law. . . . We hold that Louisiana may not constitutionally punish appellant under this statute for engaging in the type of conduct which this record reveals, and also that the statute as authoritatively interpreted by the Louisiana Supreme Court is unconstitutionally broad in scope.

The Louisiana courts have held that appellant's conduct constituted a breach of the peace under state law, and as in *Edwards*, "we may accept their decision as binding upon us to that extent," . . . but our independent examination of the record, which we are required to make,[8] shows no conduct which the State had a right to prohibit as a breach of the peace.

. . . The Sheriff testified that the sole aspect of the program to which he objected was "the inflammatory manner in which he [Cox] addressed the crowd and told them to go on uptown, go to four places on the protest list, sit down and if they don't feed you, sit there for one hour." Yet this part of Cox's speech obviously did not deprive the demonstration of its protected character under the Constitution as free speech and assembly. . . .

The State argues, however, that while the demonstrators started out to be orderly, the loud cheering and clapping by the students in response to the singing from the jail converted the peaceful assembly into a riotous one.[9] The record, however, does not support this assertion. It is true that the students, in response to the singing of their fellows who were in custody, cheered and applauded. However, the meeting was an outdoor meeting and a key state witness testified that while the singing was loud, it was not disorderly. There is, moreover, no indication that the mood of the students was ever hostile, aggressive, or unfriendly. Our conclusion that the entire meeting from the beginning until its dispersal by tear gas was orderly and not riotous is confirmed by a film of the events taken by a television news photographer, which was offered in evidence as a state

---

8. Because a claim of constitutionally protected right is involved, it "remains our duty in a case such as this to make an independent examination of the whole record." *Edwards* v. *South Carolina, supra*; . . . In the area of First Amendment freedoms as well as areas involving other constitutionally protected rights, "we cannot avoid our responsibilities by permitting ourselves to be 'completely bound by state court determination of any issue essential to decision of a claim of federal right, else federal law could be frustrated by distorted fact finding.'" *Haynes* v. *State of Washington*, 373 U.S. 503, 515–516. . . .

9. This cheer and shout was described differently by different witnesses, but the most extravagant descriptions were the following: "a jumbled roar like people cheering at a football game," "loud cheering and spontaneous clapping and screaming and a great hullabaloo," "a great outburst," a cheer of "conquest . . . much wilder than a football game," "a loud reaction, not disorderly, loud," "a shout, a roar," and an emotional response "in jubilation and exhortation." Appellant agreed that some of the group "became emotional" and "tears flowed from young ladies' eyes."

exhibit. We have viewed the film, and it reveals that the students, though they undoubtedly cheered and clapped, were well-behaved throughout. . . .

Our conclusion that the record does not support the contention that the students' cheering, clapping and singing constituted a breach of the peace is confirmed by the fact that these were not relied on as a basis for conviction by the trial judge, who, rather, stated as his reason for convicting Cox of disturbing the peace that "[i]t must be recognized to be inherently dangerous and a breach of the peace to bring 1,500 people, colored people, down in the predominantly white business district in the City of Baton Rouge and congregate across the street from the courthouse and sing songs as described to me by the defendant as the CORE national anthem carrying lines such as 'black and white together,' and to urge those 1,500 people to descend upon our lunch counters and sit there until they are served. That has to be an inherent breach of the peace, and our statute 14:103.1 has made it so."

Finally, the State contends that the conviction should be sustained because of fear expressed by some of the state witnesses that "violence was about to erupt" because of the demonstration. It is virtually undisputed, however, that the students themselves were not violent and threatened no violence. The fear of violence seems to have been based upon the reaction of the group of white citizens looking on from across the street. One state witness testified that "he felt the situation was get-

ting out of hand" as on the courthouse side of St. Louis street "were small knots or groups of white citizens who were muttering words, who seemed a little bit agitated." . . .

. . . Here again, as in *Edwards*, this evidence, "showed no more than that the opinions which [the students] were peaceably expressing were sufficiently opposed to the views of the majority of the community to attract a crowd and necessitate police protection." . . . Conceding this was so, the "compelling answer . . . is that constitutional rights may not be denied simply because of hostility to their assertion or exercise." *Watson* v. *City of Memphis*, 373 U.S. 526, 535, . . .

There is an additional reason why this conviction cannot be sustained. The statute at issue in this case, as authoritatively interpreted by the Louisiana Supreme Court, is unconstitutionally vague in its overly broad scope. The statutory crime consists of two elements: (1) congregating with others "with intent to provoke a breach of the peace, or under circumstances such that a breach of the peace may be occasioned," and (2) a refusal to move on after having been ordered to do so by a law enforcement officer. While the second part of this offense is narrow and specific, the first element is not. The Louisiana Supreme Court in this case defined the term "breach of the peace" as "to agitate, to arouse from a state of repose, to molest, to interrupt, to hinder, to disquiet." 244 La., at 1105, 156 So.2d, at 455. In *Edwards*, defendants had been convicted of a common-law crime similarly defined by the South Carolina

Supreme Court. Both definitions would allow persons to be punished merely for peacefully expressing unpopular views. . . . In *Terminiello* convictions were not allowed to stand because the trial judge charged that speech of the defendants could be punished as a breach of the peace " 'if it stirs the public to anger, invites dispute, brings about a condition of unrest, or creates a disturbance, or if it molests the inhabitants in the enjoyment of peace and quiet by arousing alarm.' " *Id.*, 337 U.S., at 3, 69 S.Ct., at 895. The Louisiana statute, as interpreted by the Louisiana court, is at least as likely to allow conviction for innocent speech as was the charge of the trial judge in *Terminiello*. Therefore, as in *Terminiello* and *Edwards* the conviction under this statute must be reversed as the statute is unconstitutional in that it sweeps within its broad scope activities that are constitutionally protected free speech and assembly. . . .

For all these reasons we hold that appellant's freedom of speech and assembly, secured to him by the First Amendment as applied to the States, by the Fourteenth Amendment, were denied by his conviction for disturbing the peace. The conviction on this charge cannot stand.

III.

The Obstructing Public Passages Conviction.

We now turn to the issue of the validity of appellant's conviction for violating the Louisiana statute, LSA–

Rev.Stat. 14:100.1 (Cum.Supp. 1962), which provides:

"Obstructing Public Passages"

"No person shall wilfully obstruct the free, convenient and normal use of any public sidewalk, street, highway, bridge, alley, road, or other passageway, or the entrance, corridor or passage of any public building, structure, water craft or ferry, by impeding, hindering, stifling, retarding or restraining traffic or passage thereon or therein.

"Providing however nothing herein contained shall apply to a bona fide legitimate labor organization or to any of its legal activities such as picketing, lawful assembly or concerted activity in the interest of its members for the purpose of accomplishing or securing more favorable wage standards, hours of employment and working conditions."

Appellant was convicted under this statute, not for leading the march to the vicinity of the courthouse, which the Louisiana Supreme Court stated to have been "orderly," 244 La., at 1096, 156 So. 2d, at 451, but for leading the meeting on the sidewalk across the street from the courthouse. *Id.*, at 1094, 1106–1107, 156 So.2d, at 451, 455. In upholding appellant's conviction under this statute, the Louisiana Supreme Court thus construed the statute so as to apply to public assemblies which do not have as their specific purpose the obstruction of traffic. There is no doubt from the record in this case that this far sidewalk was obstructed, and thus, as so construed, appellant violated the statute.

Appellant, however, contends that as so construed and applied in this case, the statute is an unconstitutional infringement on freedom of speech and assembly. This contention on the facts here presented raises an issue with which this Court has dealt in many decisions. That is, the right of a State or municipality to regulate the use of city streets and other facilities to assure the safety and convenience of the people in their use and the concomitant right of the people of free speech and assembly. . . .

From these decisions certain clear principles emerge. The rights of free speech and assembly, while fundamental in our democratic society, still do not mean that everyone with opinions or beliefs to express may address a group at any public place and at any time. The constitutional guarantee of liberty implies the existence of an organized society maintaining public order, without which liberty itself would be lost in the excesses of anarchy. The control of travel on the streets is a clear example of governmental responsibility to insure this necessary order. A restriction in that relation, designed to promote the public convenience in the interest of all, and not susceptible to abuses of discriminatory application, cannot be disregarded by the attempted exercise of some civil right which, in other circumstances,

would be entitled to protection. One would not be justified in ignoring the familiar red light because this was thought to be a means of social protest. Nor could one, contrary to traffic regulations, insist upon a street meeting in the middle of Times Square at the rush hour as a form of freedom of speech or assembly. Governmental authorities have the duty and responsibility to keep their streets open and available for movement. A group of demonstrators could not insist upon the right to cordon off a street, or entrance to a public or private building, and allow no one to pass who did not agree to listen to their exhortations. . . .

We emphatically reject the notion urged by appellant that the First and Fourteenth Amendments afford the same kind of freedom to those who would communicate ideas by conduct such as patrolling, marching, and picketing on streets and highways, as these amendments afford to those who communicate ideas by pure speech. . . .

We have no occasion in this case to consider the constitutionality of the uniform, consistent, and nondiscriminatory application of a statute forbidding all access to streets and other public facilities for parades and meetings. Although the statute here involved on its face precludes all street assemblies and parades,[14] it has not been so applied and enforced by the Baton Rouge authori-

14. With the express exception, of course, of labor picketing. This exception points up the fact that the statute reaches beyond mere traffic regulation to restrictions on expression.

ties. City officials who testified for the State clearly indicated that certain meetings and parades are permitted in Baton Rouge, even though they have the effect of obstructing traffic, provided prior approval is obtained. This was confirmed in oral argument before this Court by counsel for the State. He stated that parades and meetings are permitted, based on "arrangements . . . made with officials." The statute itself provides no standards for the determination of local officials as to which assemblies to permit or which to prohibit. Nor are there any administrative regulations on this subject which have been called to our attention. From all the evidence before us it appears that the authorities in Baton Rouge permit or prohibit parades or street meetings in their completely uncontrolled discretion.

The situation is thus the same as if the statute itself expressly provided that there could only be peaceful parades or demonstrations in the unbridled discretion of the local officials. The pervasive restraint on freedom of discussion by the practice of the authorities under the statute is not any less effective than a statute expressly permitting such selective enforcement. A long line of cases in this Court make it clear that a State or municipality cannot "require all who wish to disseminate ideas to present them first to police authorities for their consideration and approval, with a discretion in the police to say some ideas may, while others may not, be . . . disseminate[d]. . . ."

This Court has recognized that the lodging of such broad discretion in a public official allows him to determine which expressions of view will be permitted and which will not. This thus sanctions a device for the suppression of the communication of ideas and permits the official to act as a censor. . . .

It is, of course, undisputed that appropriate, limited discretion, under properly drawn statutes or ordinances, concerning the time, place, duration, or manner of use of the streets for public assemblies may be vested in administrative officials, provided that such limited discretion is "exercised with 'uniformity of method of treatment upon the facts of each application, free from improper or inappropriate considerations and from unfair discrimination' . . . [and with] a 'systematic, consistent and just order of treatment, with reference to the convenience of public use of the highways. . . .'" *Cox* v. *State of New Hampshire, supra,* 312 U.S., at 576, 61 S.Ct., at 766. . . .

But here it is clear that the practice in Baton Rouge allowing unfettered discretion in local officials in the regulation of the use of the streets for peaceful parades and meetings is an unwarranted abridgment of appellant's freedom of speech and assembly secured to him by the First Amendment, as applied to the States by the Fourteenth Amendment. It follows, therefore, that appellant's conviction for violating the statute as so applied and enforced must be reversed.

For the reasons discussed above the judgment of the Supreme Court of Louisiana is reversed.

No. 49*

MR. JUSTICE GOLDBERG *delivered the opinion of the Court.*

Appellant was convicted of violating a Louisiana statute which provides:

"Whoever, with the intent of interfering with, obstructing, or impeding the administration of justice, or with the intent of influencing any judge, juror, witness, or court officer, in the discharge of his duty pickets or parades in or near a building housing a court of the State of Louisiana . . . shall be fined not more than five thousand dollars or imprisoned not more than one year, or both." LSA—Rev. Stat. § 14:401 (Cum.Supp.1962).

This charge was based upon the same set of facts as the "disturbing the peace" and "obstructing a public passage" charges. . . .

I.

We shall first consider appellant's contention that this statute must be declared invalid on its face as an unjustified restriction upon freedoms guaranteed by the First and Fourteenth Amendments to the United States Constitution.

This statute was passed by Louisiana in 1950 and was modeled after an identical statute pertaining to the federal judiciary, which Congress passed in 1949, 64 Stat. 1018, 18 U.S.C. § 1507 (1958 ed.). . . .

.   .   .

There can be no question that a State has a legitimate interest in protecting its judicial system from the pressures which picketing near a courthouse might create. Since we are committed to a government of laws and not of men, it is of the utmost importance that the administration of justice be absolutely fair and orderly. This Court has recognized that the unhindered and untrammeled functioning of our courts is part of the very foundation of our constitutional democracy. . . . The constitutional safeguards relating to the integrity of the criminal process attend every stage of a criminal proceeding, starting with arrest and culminating with a trial "in a courtroom presided over by a judge." *Rideau* v. *Louisiana*, 373 U.S. 723, 727, . . . There can be no doubt that they embrace the fundamental conception of a fair trial, and that they exclude influence or domination by either a hostile or friendly mob. There is no room at any stage of judicial proceedings for such intervention; mob law is the very antithesis of due process. . . . A State may adopt safeguards necessary and appropriate to assure that the administration of justice at all stages is free from outside control and influence. A narrowly drawn statute such as the one under review is obviously a

---

*[*The opinion of the Court in No. 49, delivered by* MR. JUSTICE GOLDBERG *is at* 379 *U.S. 560; 85 S. Ct. 478; 13 L.Ed. 2d 489.*]

safeguard both necessary and appropriate to vindicate the State's interest in assuring justice under law.

Nor does such a statute infringe upon the constitutionally protected rights of free speech and free assembly. The conduct which is the subject of this statute—picketing and parading—is subject to regulation even though intertwined with expression and association. The examples are many of the application by this Court of the principle that certain forms of conduct mixed with speech may be regulated or prohibited. . . .

.   .   .

We hold that this statute on its face is a valid law dealing with conduct subject to regulation so as to vindicate important interests of society and that the fact that free speech is intermingled with such conduct does not bring with it constitutional protection.

II.

We now deal with the Louisiana statute as applied to the conduct in this case. The group of 2,000, led by appellant, paraded and demonstrated before the courthouse. Judges and court officers were in attendance to discharge their respective functions. It is undisputed that a major purpose of the demonstration was to protect what the demonstrators considered an "illegal" arrest of 23 students the previous day. While the arraignment or trial of the students had not been set for any day certain, they were charged with violation of the law, and the judges responsible for trying them and passing upon the legality

of their arrest were then in the building.

It is, of course, true that most judges will be influenced only by what they see and hear in court. However, judges are human; and the legislature has the right to recognize the danger that some judges, jurors, and other court officials, will be consciously or unconsciously influenced by demonstrations in or near their courtrooms both prior to as well as at the time of the trial. A State may also properly protest the judicial process from being misjudged in the minds of the public. Suppose demonstrators paraded and picketed for weeks with signs asking that indictments be dismissed, and that a judge, completely uninfluenced by these demonstrations, dismissed the indictments. A State may protect against the possibility of a conclusion by the public under these circumstances, that the judge's action was in part a product of intimidation and did not flow only from the fair and orderly working of the judicial process. . . .

.   .   .

III.

Appellant additionally argues that his conviction violated due process as there was no evidence of intent to obstruct justice or influence any judicial official as required by the statute. *Thompson* v. *Louisville*, 362 U.S. 199, 80 S.Ct. 624, 4 L.Ed.2d 654. We cannot agree that there was no evidence within the "due process" rule enunciated in *Thompson* v. *Louisville*. We have already noted that various witnesses and Cox himself stated that a major purpose of the demonstration was to protest what was considered to be an illegal arrest of 23 students. Thus, the very subject matter of the demonstration was an arrest which is normally the first step in a series of legal proceedings. The demonstration was held in the vicinity of the courthouse where the students' trials would take place. The courthouse contained the judges who in normal course would be called upon to try the students' cases just as they tried appellant. Ronnie Moore, the student leader of the demonstration, a defense witness, stated, as we understand his testimony, that the demonstration was in part to protest injustice; he felt it was a form of "moral persuasion" and hoped it would have its effects. . . .

While this case contains direct evidence taking it out of the *Thompson* v. *Louisville* doctrine, even without this evidence, we would be compelled to reject the contention that there was no proof of intent. Louisiana surely has the right to infer the appropriate intent from circumstantial evidence. At the very least, a group of demonstrators parading and picketing before a courthouse where a criminal charge is pending, in protest against the arrest of those charged, may be presumed to intend to influence judges, jurors, witnesses or court officials. . . .

Absent an appropriately drawn and applicable statute, entirely different considerations would apply if, for example, the demonstrators were picketing to protest the actions of a mayor or other official of a city completely unrelated to any judicial proceedings, who just happened to have an office located in the courthouse building. . . .

IV.

There are, however, more substantial constitutional objections arising from appellant's conviction on the particular facts of this case. Appellant was convicted for demonstrating not "in," but "near" the courthouse. It is undisputed that the demonstration took place on the west sidewalk, the far side of the street, exactly 101 feet from the courthouse steps and, judging from the pictures in the record, approximately 125 feet from the courthouse itself. The question is raised as to whether the failure of the statute to define the word "near" renders it unconstitutionally vague. . . . It is clear that there is some lack of specificity in a word such as "near." While this lack of specificity may not render the statute unconstitutionally vague, at least as applied to a demonstration within the sight and hearing of those in the courthouse, it is clear that the statute, with respect to the determination of how near the courthouse a particular demonstration can be, foresees a degree of on-the-spot administrative interpretation by officials charged with responsibility for administering and enforcing it. It is apparent that demonstrators, such as those involved here, would justifiably tend to rely on this administrative interpretation of how "near" the courthouse a particular demonstration might take place. Louisiana's statutory policy of preserving order around the courthouse would counsel encouragement of just such reliance. This administrative discretion to construe the term "near" concerns a limited control of the streets and other areas in the immediate vicinity of the courthouse and is the type of narrow discretion which this Court has recognized as the proper role of responsible officials in making determinations concerning the time, place, duration, and manner of demonstrations. . . .

The record here clearly shows that the officials present gave permission for the demonstration to take place across the street from the courthouse. Cox testified that they gave him permission to conduct the demonstration on the far side of the street. This testimony is not only uncontradicted but is corroborated by the State's witnesses who were present. Police Chief White testified that he told Cox "he must confine" the demonstration "to the west side of the street." . . .

The record shows that at no time did the police recommend, or even suggest, that the demonstration be held further from the courthouse than it actually was. The police admittedly had prior notice that the demonstration was planned to be held in the vicinity of the courthouse. They were prepared for it at that point and so stationed themselves and their equipment as to keep the demonstrators on the far side of the street. As Cox approached the vicinity of the courthouse, he was met by the Chief of Police and other officials. At this point not only was it not suggested that they hold their assembly elsewhere, or disband, but they were affirmatively told that they

could hold the demonstration on the sidewalk of the far side of the street, 101 feet from the courthouse steps. This area was effectively blocked off by the police and traffic rerouted.

Thus, the highest police officials of the city, in the presence of the Sheriff and Mayor, in effect told the demonstrators that they could meet where they did, 101 feet from the courthouse steps, but could not meet closer to the courthouse. In effect, appellant was advised that a demonstration at the place it was held would not be one "near" the courthouse within the terms of the statute.

     •   •   •

There remains just one final point: the effect of the Sheriff's order to disperse. The State in effect argues that this order somehow removed the prior grant of permission and reliance on the officials' construction that the demonstration on the far side of the street was not illegal as being "near" the courthouse. This, however, we cannot accept. Appellant was led to believe that his demonstration on the far side of the street violated no statute. He was expressly ordered to leave, not because he was peacefully demonstrating too near the courthouse, nor because a time limit originally set had expired, but because officials erroneously concluded that what he said threatened a breach of the peace. This is apparent from the face of the Sheriff's statement when he ordered the meeting dispersed: "Now you have been allowed to demonstrate. Up until now your demonstration has been more or less peaceful, but what you are doing now is a direct violation of the law, a disturbance of the peace, and it has got to be broken up immediately." . . . Appellant correctly conceived, . . . that this was not a valid reason for the dispersal order. He therefore was still justified in his continued belief that because of the original official grant of permission he had a right to stay where he was for the few additional minutes required to conclude the meeting. In addition, even if we were to accept the state's version that the sole reason for terminating the demonstration was that appellant exceeded the narrow time limits set by the police, his conviction could not be sustained. Assuming the place of the meeting was appropriate—as appellant justifiably concluded from the official grant of permission— nothing in this courthouse statute, nor in the breach of the peace or obstruction of public passages statutes with their broad sweep and application that we have condemned . . . authorizes the police to draw the narrow time line, unrelated to any policy of these statutes, that would be approved if we were to sustain appellant's conviction on this ground. . . . In any event, as we have stated, it is our conclusion from the record that the dispersal order had nothing to do with any time or place limitation, and thus, on this ground alone, it is clear that the dispersal order did not remove the protection accorded appellant by the original grant of permission.

Of course this does not mean that the police cannot call a halt to a meeting which though originally peaceful, becomes violent. Nor does it mean that, under properly drafted and administered statutes and ordinances, the authorities cannot set reasonable time limits for assemblies related to the policies of such laws and then order them dispersed when these time limits are exceeded. . . . We merely hold that, under circumstances such as those present in this case, appellant's conviction cannot be sustained on the basis of the dispersal order.

Nothing we have said here . . . is to be interpreted as sanctioning riotous conduct in any form or demonstrations, however peaceful their conduct or commendable their motives, which conflict with properly drawn statutes and ordinances designed to promote law and order, protect the community against disorder, regulate traffic, safeguard legitimate interests in private and public property, or protect the administration of justice and other essential governmental functions.

Liberty can only be exercised in a system of law which safeguards order. We reaffirm the repeated holdings of this Court that our constitutional command of free speech and assembly is basic and fundamental and encompasses peaceful social protest, so important to the preservation of the freedoms treasured in a democratic society. We also reaffirm the repeated decisions of this Court that there is no place for violence in a democratic society dedicated to liberty under law, and that the right of peaceful protest does not mean that everyone with opinions or beliefs to express may do so at any time and at any place. There is a proper time and place for even the most peaceful protest and a plain duty and responsibility on the part of all citizens to obey all valid laws and regulations. There is an equally plain requirement for laws and regulations to be drawn so as to give citizens fair warning as to what is illegal; for regulation of conduct that involves freedom of speech and assembly not to be so broad in scope so as to stifle First Amendment freedoms, which "need breathing space to survive," . . . for appropriate limitations on the discretion of public officials where speech and assembly are intertwined with regulated conduct; and for all such laws and regulations to be applied with an equal hand. We believe that all of these requirements can be met in an ordered society dedicated to liberty. We reaffirm our conviction that "[f]reedom and viable government are . . . indivisible concepts." . . .

The application of these principles requires us to reverse the judgment of the Supreme Court of Louisiana.

Reversed.

MR. JUSTICE BLACK, *concurring in No. 24 and dissenting in No. 49.* . . .

I concur in the Court's judgment reversing appellant Cox's conviction for violation of the Louisiana statutes prohibiting breach of the peace and obstructing public passages, but I do so for reasons which differ somewhat from those stated in the

Court's opinion. I therefore deem it appropriate to state separately my reasons for voting to hold both these statutes unconstitutional and to reverse the convictions under them. On the other hand, I have no doubt that the State has power to protect judges, jurors, witnesses, and court officers from intimidation by crowds which seek to influence them by picketing, patrolling, or parading in or near the courthouses in which they do their business or the homes in which they live, and I therefore believe that the Louisiana statute which protects the administration of justice by forbidding such interferences is constitutional, both as written and as applied. Since I believe that the evidence showed practically without dispute that appellant violated this statute, I think this conviction should be affirmed.

. . .

I.

The Breach-of-Peace Conviction.

I agree with that part of the Court's opinion holding that the Louisiana breach-of-the-peace statute on its face and as construed by the State Supreme Court is so broad as to be unconstitutionally vague under the First and Fourteenth Amendments. . . . The statute does not itself define the conditions upon which people who want to express views may be allowed to use the public

*[MR. JUSTICE BLACK'S *opinion begins at* 379 *U.S.* 575; 85 *S. Ct.* 466; 13 *L.Ed.* 2d 498.]

streets and highways, but leaves this to be defined by law enforcement officers. The statute therefore neither forbids all crowds to congregate and picket on streets, nor is it narrowly drawn to prohibit congregating or patrolling under certain clearly defined conditions while preserving the freedom to speak of those who are using the streets as streets in the ordinary way that the State permits. A state statute of either of the two types just mentioned, regulating *conduct*—patrolling and marching—as distinguished from *speech*, would in my judgment be constitutional, subject only to the condition that if such a law had the effect of indirectly impinging on freedom of speech, press, or religion, it would be unconstitutional if under the circumstances it appeared that the State's interest in suppressing the conduct was not sufficient to outweigh the individual's interest in engaging in conduct closely involving his First Amendment freedoms. . . .

The First and Fourteenth Amendments, I think, take away from government, state and federal, all power to restrict freedom of speech, press, and assembly *where people have a right to be for such purposes.* This does not mean however, that these amendments also grant a constitutional right to engage in the conduct of picketing or patrolling, whether on publicly owned streets or on privately owned property. . . . Were the law otherwise, people on the streets, in their homes and anywhere else could be compelled to listen against their will to speakers they did not want to hear. Picketing, though it may be utilized to communicate ideas, is not speech, and therefore is not of itself protected by the First Amendment. . . .

However, because Louisiana's breach-of-peace statute is not narrowly drawn to assure nondiscriminatory application, I think it is constitutionally invalid under our holding in *Edwards* v. *South Carolina*, 372 U.S. 229, . . . In the case before us Louisiana has by a broad, vague statute given policemen an unlimited power to order people off the streets, not to enforce a specific, nondiscriminatory state statute forbidding patrolling and picketing, but rather whenever a policeman makes a decision on his own personal judgment that views being expressed on the street are provoking or might provoke a breach of the peace. Such a statute does not provide for government by clearly defined laws, but rather for government by the moment-to-moment opinions of a policeman on his beat. . . . This kind of statute provides a perfect device to arrest people whose views do not suit the policeman or his superiors, while leaving free to talk anyone with whose views the police agree. . . . Moreover, because the statute makes an exception for labor organizations and therefore tries to limit access to the streets to some views but not others, I believe it is unconstitutional for the reasons discussed in Part II of this opinion, dealing with the street-obstruction statute, infra. For all the reasons stated I concur in reversing the conviction based on the breach-of-peace statute.

II.

The Obstructing-Public-Passages Conviction.

The Louisiana law against obstructing the streets and sidewalks,[2] while applied here so as to convict Negroes for assembling and picketing on streets and sidewalks for the purpose of publicly protesting racial discrimination, expressly provides that the statute shall not bar picketing and assembly by labor unions protesting unfair treatment of union members. I believe that the First and Fourteenth Amendments require that if the streets of a town are open to some views, they must be open to all. It is worth noting in passing that the objections of labor unions and of the group led by Cox here may have much in common. Both frequently protest discrimination against their members in the matter of employment. . . . This Louisiana law opens the streets for union assembly, picketing, and public advocacy, while denying that opportunity to groups protesting against racial discrimination. As I said above, I have no doubt about the general power of Louisiana to bar all picketing on its streets and highways. Standing, pa-

trolling, or marching back and forth on streets is conduct, not speech, and as conduct can be regulated or prohibited. But by specifically permitting picketing for the publication of labor union views, Louisiana is attempting to pick and choose among the views it is willing to have discussed on its streets. It thus is trying to prescribe by law what matters of public interest people it allows to assemble on its streets may and may not discuss. This seems to me to be censorship in a most odious form, unconstitutional under the First and Fourteenth Amendments. And to deny this appellant and his group use of the streets because of their views against racial discrimination, while allowing other groups to use the streets to voice opinions on other subjects, also amounts, I think, to an invidious discrimination forbidden by the Equal Protection Clause of the Fourteenth Amendment. . . .

III.

The Conviction for Picketing Near a Courthouse.

I would sustain the conviction of appellant for violation of LSA–R.S. § 14:401 (Cum.Supp.1962), which makes it an offense for anyone, under

---

2. LSA–Rev.Stat. § 14:100.1 (Cum. Supp. 1962) provides in relevant part:
"No person shall wilfully obstruct the free, convenient and normal use of any public sidewalk, street, highway, bridge, alley, road, or other passageway, or the entrance, corridor or passage of any public building, structure, watercraft or ferry, by impeding, hindering, stifling, retarding or restraining traffic or passage thereon or therein.

"Providing however nothing herein contained shall apply to a bona fide legitimate labor organization or to any of its legal activities such as picketing, lawful assembly or concerted activity in the interest of its members for the purpose of accomplishing or securing more, favorable wage standards, hours of employment and working conditions. . . ."

any conditions, to picket or parade near a courthouse, residence or other building used by a judge, juror, witness, or court officer, "with the intent of influencing" any of them.[4] Certainly the record shows beyond all doubt that the purpose of the 2,000 or more people who stood right across the street from the courthouse and jail was to protest the arrest of members of their group who were then in jail. As the Court's opinion states, appellant Cox so testified. Certainly the most obvious reason for their protest at the courthouse was to influence the judge and other court officials who used the courthouse and performed their official duties there. The Court attempts to support its holding by its inference that the Chief of Police gave his consent to picketing the courthouse. But quite apart from the fact that a police chief cannot authorize violations of his State's criminal laws, there was strong, emphatic testimony that if any consent was given it was limited to telling Cox and his groups to come no closer to the courthouse than they had already come without the consent of any official, city, state, or federal. And there was also testimony that when told to leave appellant Cox defied the order by telling the crowd not to move. I fail to understand how the Court can justify the reversal of these convictions because of a permission which testimony in the record denies was given, which could not have been authoritatively given anyway, and which even if given was soon afterwards revoked. While I agree that the record does not show boisterous or violent conduct or indecent language on the part of the "demonstrators," the ample evidence that this group planned the march on the courthouse and carried it out for the express purpose of influencing the courthouse officials in the performance of their official duties brings this case squarely within the prohibitions of the Louisiana statute and I think leaves us with no alternative but to sustain the conviction unless the statute itself is unconstitutional, and I do not believe that this statute is unconstitutional, either on its face or as applied.

This statute, like the federal one which it closely resembles was enacted to protect courts and court officials from the intimidation and dangers that inhere in huge gatherings at courthouse doors and jail doors to protest arrests and to influence court officials in performing their duties. The very purpose of a court system is to adjudicate controversies, both criminal and civil, in the calmness and solemnity of the courtroom according to legal procedures. Justice cannot be rightly ad-

---

4. LSA–Rev.Stat. § 14:401 (Cum.Supp. 1962) provides in relevant part:

"Whoever, with the intent of interfering with, obstructing, or impeding the administration of justice, or with the intent of influencing any judge, juror, witness, or court officer, in the discharge of his duty pickets or parades in or near a building housing a court of the State of Louisiana, or in or near a building or residence occupied or used by such judge, juror, witness, or court officer, or with such intent uses any sound-truck or similar device or resorts to any other demonstration in or near any such building or residence, shall be fined not more that five thousand dollars or imprisoned not more than one year, or both. . . ."

ministered, nor are the lives and safety of prisoners secure, where throngs of people clamor against the processes of justice right outside the courthouse or jailhouse doors. The streets are not now and never have been the proper place to administer justice. Use of the streets for such purposes has always proved disastrous to individual liberty in the long run, whatever fleeting benefits may have appeared to have been achieved. And minority groups, I venture to suggest, are the ones who always have suffered and always will suffer most when street multitudes are allowed to substitute their pressures for the less glamorous but more dependable and temperate processes of the law. Experience demonstrates that it is not a far step from what to many seems the earnest, honest, patriotic, kind-spirited multitude of today, to the fanatical, threatening, lawless mob of tomorrow. And the crowds that press in the streets for noble goals today can be supplanted tomorrow by street mobs pressuring the courts for precisely opposite ends.

Minority groups in particular need always to bear in mind that the Constitution, while it requires States to treat all citizens equally and protect them in the exercise of rights granted by the Federal Constitution and laws, does not take away the State's power, indeed its duty, to keep order and to do justice according to law. Those who encourage minority groups to believe that the United States Constitution and federal laws give them

a right to patrol and picket in the streets whenever they choose, in order to advance what they think to be a just and noble end, do no service to those minority groups, their cause, or their country. I am confident from this record that this appellant violated the Louisiana statute because of a mistaken belief that he and his followers had a constitutional right to do so, because of what they believed were just grievances. But the history of the past 25 years if it shows nothing else shows that his group's constitutional and statutory rights have to be protected by the courts, which must be kept free from intimidation and coercive pressures of any kind. Government under law as ordained by our Constitution is too precious, too sacred, to be jeopardized by subjecting the courts to intimidatory practices that have been fatal to individual liberty and minority rights wherever and whenever such practices have been allowed to poison the streams of justice. I would be wholly unwilling to join in moving this country a single step in that direction.

MR. JUSTICE CLARK, *concurring in No. 24 and dissenting in No. 49.**

. . .

MR. JUSTICE WHITE, *with whom* MR. JUSTICE HARLAN *joins, concurring in part and dissenting in part.*

*[The opinions of MR. JUSTICE CLARK and MR. JUSTICE WHITE, with whom MR. JUSTICE HARLAN concurs, are omitted.]

QUESTIONS

1. Exactly what constituted the "breach of the peace" in this case? What words did Cox utter which were considered inflammatory? Do you consider them inflammatory? Why?

2. Does the possibility of bringing 1,500 Blacks into a white area, as the trial judge said, constitute for you an inherent breach of the peace? Why yes? Why no? If you do believe 1,500 Black students in downtown Baton Rouge inherently constitutes a breach of the peace, how do you reconcile this with the constitutional right of peaceful assembly?

3. Should any group acting peacefully within their constitutional rights be penalized because of crowd reaction to their protest? Why yes? Why no?

4. To what extent has the way the law has been enforced against obstructing public passages contributed to the infringement of constitutional rights?

5. Justice Black would sustain the conviction for picketing near the courthouse on the grounds that the police chief cannot authorize violations of the law. Do you agree or disagree with Black? Why or why not? If a policeman waved you through a red light would you wait for it to turn green?

ADDERLEY v. FLORIDA

385 U.S. 39; 87 S. Ct. 242; 17 L.Ed. 2d 149 (1966)

MR. JUSTICE BLACK *delivered the opinion of the Court.*

Petitioners, Harriett Louise Adderley and 31 other persons, were convicted by a jury in a joint trial in the County Judge's Court of Leon County, Florida, on a charge of "trespass with a malicious and mischievous intent" upon the premises of the county jail contrary to § 821.18 of the Florida statutes set out below.[1] Petitioners, apparently all students of the Florida A. & M. University in Tallahassee, had gone from the school to the jail about a mile away, along with many other students, to "demonstrate" at the jail their protests because of arrests of other protesting students the day before, and perhaps to protest more generally against state and local pol-

---

1. "Every trespass upon the property of another, committed with a malicious and mischievous intent, the punishment of which is not specially provided for, shall be punished by imprisonment not exceeding three months, or by fine not exceeding one hundred dollars." Fla.Stat. § 821.18, F.S.A. (1965).

icies and practices of racial segregation, including segregation of the jail. The county sheriff, legal custodian of the jail and jail grounds, tried to persuade the students to leave the jail grounds. When this did not work, he notified them that they must leave, notified them that they must leave or he would arrest them for trespassing, and notified them further that if they resisted arrest he would arrest them for resisting arrest as well. Some of the students left but others, including petitioners, remained and they were arrested. On appeal the convictions were affirmed by the Florida Circuit Court and then by the Florida District Court of Appeals, 175 So.2d 249. That being the highest state court to which they could appeal, petitioners applied to us for *certiorari* contending that, in view of petitioners' purpose to protest against jail and other segregation policies, their conviction denied them "rights of free speech, assembly, petition, due process of law and equal protection of the laws as guaranteed by the Fourteenth Amendment to the Constitution of the United States." On this "Question Presented" we granted *certiorari*. 382 U.S. 1023, 86 S.Ct. 643, 15 L.Ed.2d 538. Petitioners present their argument on this question in four separate points, and for convenience we deal with each of their points in the order in which they present them.

I.

Petitioners have insisted from the beginning of these cases that they are controlled and must be reversed because of our prior cases of *Edwards* v. *South Carolina*, 372 U.S. 229, 83 S.Ct. 680, 9 L.Ed.2d 697, and *Cox* v. *State of Louisiana*, 379 U.S. 536, 559, 85 S.Ct. 453, 476, 13 L.Ed.2d 471, 487. We cannot agree.

The *Edwards* case, like this one, did come up when a number of persons demonstrated on public property against their State's segregation policies. They also sang hymns and danced, as did the demonstrators in this case. But here the analogies to this case end. In *Edwards*, the demonstrators went to the South Carolina State Capitol grounds to protest. In this case they went to the jail. Traditionally, state capitol grounds are open to the public. Jails, built for security purposes, are not. The demonstrators at the South Carolina Capitol went in through a public driveway and as they entered they were told by state officials there that they had a right as citizens to go through the State House grounds as long as they were peaceful. Here the demonstrators entered the jail grounds through a driveway used only for jail purposes and without warning to or permission from the sheriff. More importantly, South Carolina sought to prosecute its State Capitol demonstrators by charging them with the common-law crime of breach of the peace. This Court in *Edwards* took pains to point out at length the indefinite, loose, and broad nature of this charge; indeed, this Court pointed out, . . . that the South Carolina Supreme Court had itself declared that the "breach of the peace charge" is "not susceptible of exact definition." South Carolina's power to prosecute, it was emphasized, . . .

would have been different had it proceeded under a "precise and narrowly drawn regulatory statute evincing a legislative judgment that certain specific conduct be limited or proscribed" such as, for example, "limiting the periods during which the State House grounds were open to the public. . . ." The South Carolina breach-of-the-peace statute was thus struck down as being so broad and all-embracing as to jeopardize speech, press, assembly and petition. . . . And it was on this same ground of vagueness that in *Cox* v. *State of Louisiana,* the Louisiana breach-of-the-peace law used to prosecute Cox was invalidated.

The Florida trespass statute under which these petitioners were charged cannot be challenged on this ground. It is aimed at conduct of one limited kind, that is for one person or persons to trespass upon the property of another with a malicious and mischievous intent. There is no lack of notice in this law, nothing to entrap or fool the unwary.

Petitioners seem to argue that the Florida trespass law is void for vagueness because it requires a trespass to be "with a malicious and mischievous intent. . . ." But these words do not broaden the scope of trespass so as to make it cover a multitude of types of conduct as does

the common-law breach-of-the-peace charge. On the contrary, these words narrow the scope of the offense. The trial court charged the jury as to their meaning and petitioners have not argued that this definition, set out below,[2] is not a reasonable and clear definition of the terms. The use of these terms in the statute, instead of contributing to uncertainty and misunderstanding, actually makes its meaning more understandable and clear.

II.

Petitioners in this Court invoke the doctrine of abatement announced by this Court in *Hamm* v. *City of Rock Hill,* 379 U.S. 306, 85 S.Ct. 384, 13 L.Ed.2d 300. But that holding was that the Civil Rights Act of 1964, 78 Stat. 241, which made it unlawful for places of public accommodation to deny service to any person because of race, effected an abatement of prosecutions of persons for seeking such services that arose prior to the passage of the Act. But this case in no way involves prosecution of petitioners for seeking service in establishments covered by the Act. It involves only an alleged trespass on jail grounds—a trespass which can be prosecuted regardless of the fact that it is the means of

2. " 'Malicious' means wrongful, you remember back in the original charge, the State has to prove beyond a reasonable doubt there was a malicious and mischievous intent. The word 'malicious' means that the wrongful act shall be done voluntarily, unlawfully, and without excuse or justification. The word 'malicious' that is used in these affidavits does not necessarily allege nor require the State to prove that the defendant had actual malice in his mind at

the time of the alleged trespass. Another way of stating the definition of 'malicious' is by 'malicious' is meant the act was done knowingly and willfully and without any legal justification.

" 'Mischievous,' which is also required, means that the alleged trespass shall be inclined to cause petty and trivial trouble, annoyance and vexation to others in order for you to find that the alleged trespass was committed with mischievous intent.". . .

protesting segregation of establishments covered by the Act.

III.

Petitioners next argue that "petty criminal statutes may not be used to violate minorities' constitutional rights." This of course is true but this abstract proposition gets us nowhere in deciding this case.

IV.

Petitioners here contend that "Petitioners' convictions are based on a total lack of relevant evidence." If true, this would be a denial of due process. . . . Both in the petition for *certiorari* and in the brief on the merits petitioners state that their summary of the evidence "does not conflict with the facts contained in the Circuit Court's opinion" which was in effect affirmed by the District Court of Appeals. 175 So.2d 249. That statement is correct and petitioners' summary of facts as well as that of the Circuit Court show an abundance of facts to support the jury's verdict of guilty in these cases.

In summary both these statements show testimony ample to prove this: Disturbed and upset by the arrest of

their schoolmates the day before, a large number of Florida A. & M. students assembled on the school grounds and decided to march down to the county jail. Some apparently wanted to get themselves put in jail too, along with the students already there.[3] A group of around 200 marched from the school and arrived at the jail singing and clapping.[4] They went directly to the jail door entrance where they were met by a deputy sheriff, evidently surprised by their arrival. He asked them to move back, claiming they were blocking the entrance to the jail and fearing that they might attempt to enter the jail. They moved back part of the way, where they stood or sat, singing, clapping and dancing on the jail driveway and on an adjacent grassy area upon the jail premises. This particular jail entrance and driveway were not normally used by the public, but by the sheriff's department for transporting prisoners to and from the courts several blocks away and by commercial concerns for servicing the jail. Even after their partial retreat, the demonstrators continued to block vehicular passage over this driveway up to the entrance of the jail.[5] Someone called the sheriff who was at the moment ap-

3. The three petitioners who testified insisted that they had not come to the jail for the purpose of being arrested. But both the sheriff and a deputy testified that they heard several of the demonstrators present at the jail loudly proclaim their desire to be arrested. Indeed, this latter version is borne out by the fact that, though assertedly protesting the prior arrests of their fellow students and the city's segregation policies, none of the demonstrators carried any signs and upon arriving at the jail, no speeches or other verbal protests were made.

4. There is no evidence that any attempt was made by law enforcement officers to interfere with this march, or for that matter, that such officers even knew of the march or its ultimate destination.

5. Although some of the petitioners testified that they had no intention of interfering with vehicular traffic to and from the jail entrance and that they noticed no vehicle trying to enter or leave the driveway, the deputy sheriff testified that it would have been impossible for automobiles to drive up to the jail entrance

parently conferring with one of the state court judges about incidents connected with prior arrests for demonstrations. When the sheriff returned to the jail, he immediately inquired if all was safe inside the jail and was told it was. He then engaged in a conversation with two of the leaders. He told them that they were trespassing upon jail property and that he would give them 10 minutes to leave or he would arrest them. Neither of the leaders did anything to disperse the crowd, and one of them told the sheriff that they wanted to get arrested. A local minister talked with some of the demonstrators and told them not to enter the jail, because they could not arrest themselves, but just to remain where they were. After about 10 minutes, the sheriff, in a voice loud enough to be heard by all, told the demonstrators that he was the legal custodian of the jail and its premises, that they were trespassing on county property in violation of the law, that they should all leave forthwith or he would arrest them, and that if they attempted to resist arrest, he would charge them with that as a separate offense. Some of the group then left. Others, including all petitioners, did not leave. Some of them sat down. In a few minutes, realizing that the remaining demonstrators had no intention of leaving, the sheriff ordered his deputies to surround those remaining on jail premises and placed

them, 107 demonstrators, under arrest. The sheriff unequivocally testified that he did not arrest any person other than those who were on the jail premises. Of the three petitioners testifying, two insisted that they were arrested before they had a chance to leave, had they wanted to, and one testified that she did not intend to leave. The sheriff again explicitly testified that he did not arrest any person who was attempting to leave.

Under the foregoing testimony the jury was authorized to find that the State had proven every essential element of the crime, as it was defined by the state court. That interpretation is, of course, binding on us, leaving only the question of whether conviction of the state offense, thus defined, unconstitutionally deprives petitioners of their rights to freedom of speech, press, assembly or petition. We hold it does not. The sheriff, as jail custodian, had power, as the state courts have here held, to direct that this large crowd of people get off the grounds. There is not a shred of evidence in this record that this power was exercised, or that its exercise was sanctioned by the lower courts, because the sheriff objected to what was being sung or said by the demonstrators or because he disagreed with the objectives of their protest. The record reveals that he objected only to their presence on that part of the

and that one serviceman, finished with his business in the jail, waited inside because the demonstrators were sitting around and leaning against his truck parked outside. The sheriff testified that the time the demonstrators were there, between 9:30 and

10 a. m. Monday morning, was generally a very busy time for using the jail entrance to transport week-end inmates to the courts and for tradesmen to make service calls on the jail.

jail grounds reserved for jail uses. There is no evidence at all that on any other occasion had similarly large groups of the public been permitted to gather on this portion of the jail grounds for any purpose.[6] Nothing in the Constitution of the United States prevents Florida from even-handed enforcement of its general trespass statute against those refusing to obey the sheriff's order to remove themselves from what amounted to the curtilage of the jailhouse. *The State, no less than a private owner of property, has power to preserve the property under its control for the use to which it is lawfully dedicated.** For this reason there is no merit to the petitioners' argument that they had a constitutional right to stay on the property, over the jail custodian's objections, because this "area chosen for the peaceful civil rights demonstration was not only 'reasonable' but also particularly appropriate. . . ." *Such an argument has as its major unarticulated premise the assumption that*

*people who want to propagandize protests or views have a constitutional right to do so whenever and however and wherever they please.** That concept of constitutional law was vigorously and forthrightfully rejected in two of the cases petitioners rely on, *Cox v. State of Louisiana, supra,*[7] . . . We reject it again. *The United States Constitution does not forbid a State to control the use of its own property for its own lawful nondiscriminatory purpose.**

These judgments are affirmed. *Affirmed.*

MR. JUSTICE DOUGLAS, *with whom* THE CHIEF JUSTICE, MR. JUSTICE BRENNAN, *and* MR. JUSTICE FORTAS *concur, dissenting.*

The First Amendment, applicable to the States by reason of the Fourteenth . . . provides that "Congress shall make no law respecting . . . the right of the people peaceably to assemble, and to petition the Government for a redress of grievances."

6. In *Cox v. State of Louisiana, supra,* 379 U.S. at 558, 85 S.Ct. at 466, the Court emphasized: "It is, of course, undisputed that appropriate, limited discretion, under properly drawn statutes or ordinances, concerning the time, place, duration, or manner of use of the streets for public assemblies may be vested in administrative officials, provided that such limited discretion is 'exercised with "uniformity of method of treatment upon the facts of each application, free from improper or inappropriate considerations and from unfair discrimination" . . . [and with] a "systematic, consistent and just order of treatment, with reference to the convenience of public use of the highways. . . ." ' "

7. "The rights of free speech and assembly, while fundamental in our democratic society, still do not mean that everyone with opinions or beliefs to express may

address a group at any public place and at any time. The constitutional guarantee of liberty implies the existence of an organized society maintaining public order, without which liberty itself would be lost in the excesses of anarchy. . . . A group of demonstrators could not insist upon the right to cordon off a street, or entrance to a public or private building, and allow no one to pass who did not agree to listen to their exhortations." . . .

"The conduct which is the subject of this statute—picketing and parading—is subject to regulation even though intertwined with expression and association. The examples are many of the application by this Court of the principle that certain forms of conduct mixed with speech may be regulated or prohibited." . . .

*[Editor's Note: Emphasis added.]

These rights, along with religion, speech, and press, are preferred rights of the Constitution, made so by reason of that explicit guarantee and what Edmond Cahn in *Confronting Injustice* (1966) referred to as "The Firstness of the First Amendment."[1] With all respect, therefore, the Court errs in treating the case as if it were an ordinary trespass case or an ordinary picketing case.

The jailhouse, like an executive mansion, a legislative chamber, a courthouse or the statehouse itself . . . is one of the seats of government whether it be the Tower of London, the Bastille, or a small county jail. And when it houses political prisoners or those whom many think are unjustly held, it is an obvious center for protest. The right to petition for the redress of grievances has an ancient history and is not limited to writing a letter or sending a telegram to a congressman; it is not confined to appearing before the local city council, or writing letters to the President or Governor or Mayor. . . . Conventional methods of petitioning may be, and often have been, shut off to large groups of our citizens. Legislators may turn deaf ears; formal complaints may be

routed endlessly through a bureaucratic maze; courts may let the wheels of justice grind very slowly. Those who do not control television and radio, those who cannot afford to advertise in newspapers or circulate elaborate pamphlets may have only a more limited type of access to public officials. Their methods should not be condemned as tactics of obstruction and harassment as long as the assembly and petition are peaceable, as these were.

There is no question that petitioners had as their purpose a protest against the arrest of Florida A. & M. students for trying to integrate public theatres. The sheriff's testimony indicates that he well understood the purpose of the rally. The petitioners who testified unequivocally stated that the group was protesting the arrests, and state and local policies of segregation, including segregation of the jail. This testimony was not contradicted or even questioned. The fact that no one gave a formal speech, that no elaborate handbills were distributed, and that the group was not laden with signs would seem to be immaterial. . . . There was no violence; no threats of violence; no attempted jail break; no storming

---

1. "Where would we really find the principal danger to civil liberty in a republic? Not in the governors as governors, not in the governed as governed, but in the governed unequipped to function as governors. The chief enemies of republican freedom are mental sloth, conformity, bigotry, superstition, credulity, monopoly in the market of ideas, and utter, benighted ignorance. Relying as it does on the consent of the governed, representative government cannot succeed unless the community receives enough information to grasp public issues and make sensible decisions. As lights which may have been enough for the past do not meet the needs of the present, so present lights will not suffice for the more extensive and complex problems of the future. Heretofore public enlightenment may have been only a manifest desideratum; today it constitutes an imperative necessity. The First Amendment, says Justice Black, 'reflects the faith that a good society is not static but advancing, and that the fullest possible interchange of ideas and beliefs is essential to attainment of this goal.'" (From *Feldman* v. *United States,* 322 U.S. 487, 501, 64 S.Ct. 1082, 1088, 88 L.Ed. 1408, dissenting opinion.) *Cahn, supra,* p. 102.

of a prison; no plan or plot to do anything but protest. The evidence is uncontradicted that the petitioners' conduct did not upset the jailhouse routine; things went on as they normally would. None of the group entered the jail. Indeed, they moved back from the entrance as they were instructed. There was no shoving, no pushing, no disorder or threat of riot. It is said that some of the group blocked part of the driveway leading to the jail entrance. The chief jailer to be sure testified that vehicles would not have been able to use the driveway. Never did the students locate themselves so as to cause interference with persons or vehicles going to or coming from the jail. Indeed, it is undisputed that the sheriff and deputy sheriff, in separate cars, were able to drive up the driveway to the parking places near the entrance and that no one obstructed their path. Further, it is undisputed that the entrance to the jail was not blocked. And wherever the students were requested to move they did so. If there was congestion, the solution was a further request to move to lawns or parking areas, not complete ejection and arrest. The claim is made that a tradesman waited inside the jail because some of the protestants were sitting around and leaning on his truck. The only evidence supporting such a conclusion is the testimony of a deputy sheriff that the tradesman "came to the door and then did not leave." His remaining is just as consistent with a desire to satisfy his curiosity as it is with a restraint. Finally the fact that some of the protestants may have felt their cause so just that they

were willing to be arrested for making their protest outside the jail seems wholly irrelevant. A petition is nonetheless a petition, though its futility may make martyrdom attractive.

We do violence to the First Amendment when we permit this "petition for redress of grievances" to be turned into a trespass action. It does not help to analogize this problem to the problem of picketing. Picketing is a form of protest usually directed against private interests. I do not see how rules governing picketing in general are relevant to this express constitutional right to assemble and to petition for redress of grievances. In the first place the jailhouse grounds were not marked with "NO TRESPASSING!" signs, nor does respondent claim that the public was generally excluded from the grounds. Only the sheriff's fiat transformed lawful conduct into an unlawful trespass. To say that a private owner could have done the same if the rally had taken place on private property is to speak of a different case, as an assembly and a petition for redress of grievances run to government not to private proprietors.

The Court forgets that prior to this day our decisions have drastically limited the application of state statutes inhibiting the right to go peacefully on public property to exercise First Amendment rights. As Mr. Justice Roberts wrote . . .

". . . Wherever the title of streets and parks may rest, they have immemorially been held in trust for the use of the public and, time out of mind, have been used for purposes of assembly, communicating thoughts between citizens, and discussing public questions. Such use of the streets and public places has, from ancient times, been a part of the privileges, immunities, rights, and liberties of citizens. The privilege of a citizen of the United States to use the streets and parks for communication of views on national questions may be regulated in the interest of all; it is not absolute, but relative, and must be exercised in subordination to the general comfort and convenience, and in consonance with peace and good order; but it must not, in the guise of regulation, be abridged or denied."

. . . When we allow Florida to construe her "malicious trespass" statute to bar a person from going on property knowing it is not his own and to apply that prohibition to public property, we discard *Cox* and *Edwards*. Would the case be any different if, as is common, the demonstration took place outside a building which housed both the jail and the legislative body? I think not.

There may be some public places which are so clearly committed to other purposes that their use for the airing of grievances is anomalous. There may be some instances in which assemblies and petitions for redress of grievances are not consistent with other necessary purposes of public property. A noisy meeting may be out of keeping with the serenity of the statehouse or the quiet of the courthouse. No one, for example, would suggest that the Senate gallery is the proper place

*for a vociferous protest rally.** And, in other cases it may be necessary to adjust the right to petition for redress of grievances to the other interests inhering in the uses to which the public property is normally put. . . . But this is quite different than saying that all public places are off-limits to people with grievances. . . . And it is farther yet from saying that the "custodian" of the public property in his discretion can decide when public places shall be used for the communication of ideas, especially the constitutional right to assemble and petition for redress of grievances. . . . For to place such discretion in any public official, be he the "custodian" of the public property, or the local police commissioner . . . is to place those who assert their First Amendment rights at his mercy. It gives him the awesome power to decide whose ideas may be expressed and who shall be denied a place to air their claims and petition their government. Such power is out of step with all our decisions prior to today where we have insisted that before a First Amendment right may be curtailed under the guise of a criminal law, any evil that may be collateral to the exercise of the right, must be isolated and defined in a "narrowly drawn" statute . . . lest the power to control excesses of conduct be used to suppress the constitutional right itself. . . .

That tragic consequence happens today when a trespass law is used to bludgeon those who peacefully exercise a First Amendment right to

[Editor's Note: Emphasis added.]

protest a government against one of the most grievous of all modern oppressions which some of our States are inflicting on our citizens.

. . .

Today a trespass law is used to penalize people for exercising a constitutional right. Tomorrow a disorderly conduct statute, a breach of the peace statute, a vagrancy statute will be put to the same end.[3] It is said that the sheriff did not make the arrests because of the views which petitioners espoused. That excuse is usually given, as we know from the many cases involving arrests of minority groups for breaches of the peace, unlawful assemblies, and parading without a permit. . . . such arrests are usually sought to be justified by some legitimate function of government.[4] Yet by allowing these orderly and civilized protests against injustice to be suppressed, we only increase the forces of frustration which the conditions of second-class citizenship are generating amongst us.

QUESTIONS

1. Under what, if any, conditions could a demonstration be held at either a prison or military base?

2. If the exercise of freedom of speech and/or assembly disrupts a legitimate state service, or in any other way hampers its function, should these rights still be protected? Why yes? Why no? Does this apply here according to Justice Douglas?

3. How is a prison different from a courthouse, statehouse or public park? If the prison is normally open to the public, what were the grounds for the arrests of peaceful demonstrators? Would such action have been taken at a park, or on a public street?

4. Consider Justice Douglas' statement that trespass laws are used today to penalize people for exercising a constitutional right; in terms of public properties such as prisons and vital public industries (such as pumping stations for a city's water), which should have priority? Why?

5. If you were a member of the Supreme Court in this case, how would you vote and why?

3. In 1932 over 28,000 veterans marched on Washington, D.C., demanding a bonus, paraded the streets, and camped mostly in parks and other public lands in the District, Virginia, and Maryland only to be routed by the Army. See *Waters*, B.E.F. (1933).

4. . . . If the invalidity of regulations and official conduct curtailing First Amendment rights turned on an unequivocal showing that the measure was intended to inhibit the rights, protection would be sorely lacking. It is not the intent or purpose of the measure but its effect on First Amendment rights which is crucial.

CARROLL v. PRESIDENT AND COMMISSIONERS OF PRINCESS ANNE COUNTY, MARYLAND

393 U.S. 175; 89 S. Ct. 347; 21 L.Ed. 2d 325 (1968)

MR. JUSTICE FORTAS *delivered the opinion of the Court.*

Petitioners are identified with a "white supremacist" organization called the National States Rights Party. They held a public assembly or rally near the courthouse steps in the town of Princess Anne, the county seat of Somerset County, Maryland, in the evening of August 6, 1966. The authorities did not attempt to interfere with the rally. Because of the tense atmosphere which developed as the meeting progressed, about 60 state policemen were brought in, including some from a nearby county. They were held in readiness, but for tactical reasons only a few were in evidence at the scene of the rally.

Petitioners' speeches, amplified by a public address system so that they could be heard for several blocks, were aggressively and militantly racist. Their target was primarily Negroes, and secondarily, Jews. It is sufficient to observe with the court below, that the speakers engaged in deliberately derogatory, insulting, and threatening language, scarcely disguised by disclaimers of peaceful purposes; and that listeners might well have construed their words as both a provocation to the Negroes in the crowd and an incitement to the whites. The rally continued for something more than an hour, concluding at about 8:25 p.m. The crowd listening to the speeches increased from about 50 at the beginning to about 150 of whom 25% were Negroes.

In the course of the proceedings it was announced that the rally would be resumed the following night, August 7.[1]

On that day, the respondents, officials of Princess Anne and of Somerset County, applied for and obtained a restraining order from the Circuit Court for Somerset County. The proceedings were *ex parte*, no notice being given to petitioners and, so far as appears, no effort being made informally to communicate with them, although this is expressly contemplated under Maryland procedure. The order restrained petitioners for 10 days from holding rallies or meetings in the county "which will tend to disturb and endanger the citizens of the County."[3] As a result, the rally scheduled for

---

1. Petitioner Norton said, "I want you to . . . be back here at the same place tomorrow night, bring every friend you have. . . . We're going to take it easy tonight . . ." and "You white folks bring your friends, come back tomorrow night. . . . Come on back tomorrow night, let's raise a little bit of hell for the white race."

3. The text of the Writ of Injunction is as follows:

"We command and strictly enjoin and prohibit you the said Joseph Carroll,

August 7 was not held. Ten days later, after trial, an injunction was issued by the Circuit Court, in effect extending the earlier injunction for 10 months. The court had before it, in addition to the testimony of witnesses, tape recordings made by the police of the August 6 rally.

On appeal, the Maryland Court of Appeals affirmed the 10-day order, but reversed the 10-month order on the ground that "the period of time was unreasonable and that it was arbitrary to assume that a clear and present danger of civil disturbance and riot would persist for ten months."

Petitioners sought review by this Court. . . . We granted *certiorari.*

•　　•　　•

Since the Maryland Court of Appeals reversed the 10-month injunction of August 30, 1966, we do not consider that order. We turn to the constitutional problems raised by the 10-day injunctive order.

The petitioners urge that the injunction constituted a prior restraint on speech and that it therefore violated the principles of the First Amendment which are applicable to the States by virtue of the Fourteenth Amendment. In any event, they assert, it was not constitutionally permissible to restrain petition-

ers' meetings because no "clear and present danger" existed.

Respondents, however, argue that the injunctive order in this case should not be considered as a "prior restraint" because it was based upon the events of the preceding evening and was directed to preventing a continuation of those events, and that, even if considered a "prior restraint," issuance of the order was justified by the clear and present danger of riot and disorder deliberately generated by petitioners.

We need not decide the thorny problem of whether, on the facts of this case, an injunction against the announced rally could be justified. The 10-day order here must be set aside because of a basic infirmity in the procedure by which it was obtained. It was issued *ex parte*, without notice to petitioners and without any effort, however informal, to invite or permit their participation in the proceedings. There is a place in our jurisprudence for *ex parte* issuance, without notice, of temporary restraining orders of short duration; but there is no place within the area of basic freedoms guaranteed by the First Amendment for such orders where no showing is made that it is impossible to serve or to notify the opposing parties and to

---

Richard Norton, J. B. Stoner, Connie Lynch, Robert Lyons, William Brailsford and National States Rights Party from holding rallies or meetings in Somerset County which will tend to disturb and endanger the citizens of the County and to enjoin you, the said defendants, from using and operating or causing to be operated within the County any devices or apparatus for the application of the

human voice or records from any radio, phonograph or other sound making or producing device thereby disturbing the tranquility of the populace of the County, until the matter can be heard and determined in equity, or for a period of ten days from the date hereof.

"Hereof, fail not, as you will act to the contrary at your peril."

give them an opportunity to participate.

We do not here challenge the principle that there are special, limited circumstances in which speech is so interlaced with burgeoning violence that it is not protected by the broad guaranty of the First Amendment. In *Cantwell* v. *State of Connecticut*, 310 U.S. 296, at 308, 60 S.Ct. 900, at 905, 84 L.Ed. 1213 (1940), this Court said that "No one would have the hardihood to suggest that the principle of freedom of speech sanctions incitement to riot." . . . Ordinarily, the State's constitutionally permissible interests are adequately served by criminal penalties imposed after freedom to speak has been so grossly abused that its immunity is breached. The impact and consequences of subsequent punishment for such abuse are materially different from those of prior restraint. Prior restraint upon speech suppresses the precise freedom which the First Amendment sought to protect against abridgment.

The Court has emphasized that "[a] system of prior restraints comes to this Court bearing a heavy presumption against its constitutional validity." *Bantam Books, Inc.* v. *Sullivan*, 372 U.S. 58, 70, 83 S.Ct. 631, 639, 9 L.Ed.2d 584 (1963); *Freedman* v. *State of Maryland*, 380 U.S. 51, 57, 85 S.Ct. 734, 738, 13 L.Ed.2d 649 (1965). And even where this presumption might otherwise be overcome, the Court has insisted upon careful procedural provisions, designed to assure the fullest presentation and consideration of the matter which the circumstances permit. As the Court said . . . a noncriminal process of prior restraints upon expression "avoids constitutional infirmity only if it takes place under procedural safe-guards designed to obviate the dangers of a censorship system."

Measured against these standards, it is clear that the 10-day restraining order in the present case, issued *ex parte*, without formal or informal notice to the petitioners or any effort to advise them of the proceeding, cannot be sustained. . . .

In the present case, the record discloses no reason why respondents were not notified of the application for injunction. They were apparently present in Princess Anne. They had held a rally there on the night preceding the application for and issuance of the injunction. They were scheduled to have another rally on the very evening of the day when the injunction was issued.[8] And some of them were actually served with the writ of injunction at 6:10 on that evening. In these circumstances, there is no justification for the *ex parte* character of the proceedings in the sensitive area of First Amendment rights.

The value of a judicial proceeding, as against self-help by the police, is substantially diluted where the process is *ex parte*, because the Court does not have available the fundamental instrument for judicial judgment: an adversary proceeding in which both parties may partici-

8. The petition for the temporary injunction recited that Carroll and the others against whom the injunction was sought "are presently in Somerset or Wicomico Counties of the State of Maryland."

pate. The facts in any case involving a public demonstration are difficult to ascertain and even more difficult to evaluate. Judgment as to whether the facts justify the use of the drastic power of injunction necessarily turns on subtle and controversial considerations and upon a delicate assessment of the particular situation in light of legal standards which are inescapably imprecise. In the absence of evidence and argument offered by both sides and of their participation in the formulation of value judgments, there is insufficient assurance of the balanced analysis and careful conclusions which are essential in the area of First Amendment adjudication.[10]

The same is true of the fashioning of the order. An order issued in the area of First Amendment rights must be couched in the narrowest terms that will accomplish the pinpointed objective permitted by constitutional mandate and the essential needs of the public order. In this sensitive field, the State may not employ "means that broadly stifle fundamental personal liberties when the end can be more narrowly achieved." . . . In other words, the order must be tailored as precisely as possible to the exact needs of the case. The participation of both sides is necessary for this purpose. Certainly, the failure to invite participation of the party seeking to exercise First Amendment rights reduces the possibility of a narrowly drawn order, and substantially imperils the protection which the Amendment seeks to assure.

Finally, respondents urge that the failure to give notice and an opportunity for hearing should not be considered to invalidate the order because, under Maryland procedure, petitioners might have obtained a hearing on not more than two days' notice. Maryland Rules of Procedure BB72. But this procedural right does not overcome the infirmity in the absence of a showing of justification for the *ex parte* nature of the proceedings. The issuance of an injunction which aborts a scheduled rally or public meeting, even if the restraint is of short duration, is a matter of importance and consequence in view of the First Amendment's imperative. The denial of a basic procedural right in these circumstances is not excused by the availability of post-issuance procedure which could not possibly serve to rescue the August 7 meeting, but at best, could have shortened the period in which petitioners were prevented from holding a rally.

We need not here decide that it is impossible for circumstances to arise in which the issuance of an *ex parte* restraining order for a minimum period could be justified because of the unavailability of the adverse parties or their counsel, or perhaps other reasons. In the present case, it is clear that the failure to give notice, formal or informal, and to provide an opportunity for an adversary proceeding before the holding of the rally was restrained, is incompatible with the First Amendment. Because we reverse the judgment below on this basis, we

---

10. There is a danger in relying exclusively on the version of events and dangers presented by prosecuting officials, because of their special interest. . . .

need not and do not decide whether the facts in this case provided a constitutionally permissible basis for temporarily enjoining the holding of the August 7 rally. *Reversed.*

MR. JUSTICE BLACK *concurs in the result.*

MR. JUSTICE DOUGLAS, *while joining the opinion of the Court, adheres to his dissent in Kingsley Books Inc.* v. *Brown,* 354 U.S. 436, *and to his concurring opinion in Freedman* v. *State of Maryland,* 380 U.S. 51. . .

QUESTIONS

1. What, if any, is the difference between the National States Rights Party rally and a rally held by militant Black Panthers or SDS urging revolution and sharply criticizing groups for their actions? Should any of these activities be constitutionally protected? Why or why not?
2. On what grounds did the Court set aside the 10 day order? What difference does it make whether or not the petitioners were present at the Circuit Court?
3. Justice Fortas recognizes that the Court reversed the decision on the grounds of the *ex parte* restraining order and not on grounds of constitutionality. Do you feel that the restraining order itself, disregarding the *ex parte* proceedings, is constitutional? How do you justify your decision?
4. Shouldn't all "hate groups" be banned from holding meetings because they serve no social utility and merely divide the nation? Why yes? Why no?
5. Does a democratic society have a right to defend itself from such groups as the Ku Klux Klan, the Minutemen, and the Communist Party? How should it defend itself *specifically*?

WALKER v. BIRMINGHAM

388 U.S. 307; 87 S. Ct. 1824; 18 L.Ed. 2d 1210 (1967)

MR. JUSTICE STEWART *delivered the opinion of the Court.*

On Wednesday, April 10, 1963, officials of Birmingham, Alabama, filed a bill in a state circuit court asking for injunctive relief against 139 individuals and two organizations. The bill and accompanying affidavits stated that during the preceding seven days:

"[R]espondents [had] sponsored and/or participated in and/or conspired to commit and/or to encourage and/or to participate in certain movements, plans or projects commonly called 'sit-in' demonstrations, 'kneel-in' demonstrations, mass street parades, trespasses on private property after being warned to leave the premises by the owners of said property, congregating in mobs upon the public streets and other public places, unlawfully picketing private places of business in the City of Birmingham, Alabama; violation of numerous ordinances and statutes of the City of Birmingham and State of Alabama. . . ."

It was alleged that this conduct was "calculated to provoke breaches of the peace," "threatens the safety, peace and tranquility of the City," and places "an undue burden and strain upon the manpower of the Police Department."

The bill stated that these infractions of the law were expected to continue and would "lead to further imminent danger to the lives, safety, peace, tranquility and general welfare of the people of the City of Birmingham," and that the "remedy by law is inadequate." The circuit judge granted a temporary injunction as prayed in the bill, enjoining the petitioners from, among other things, participating in or encouraging mass street parades or mass processions without a permit as required by a Birmingham ordinance.[1]

Five of the eight petitioners were served with copies of the writ early the next morning. Several hours later four of them held a press conference. There a statement was distributed, declaring their intention to disobey the injunction because it was "raw tyranny under the guise of maintaining law and order." At this press conference one of the petitioners stated: "That they had respect for the Federal Courts, or Federal Injunctions, but in the past the State Courts had favored local law enforcement, and if the police couldn't handle it, the mob would."

That night a meeting took place at which one of the petitioners announced that "[i]njunction or no injunction we are going to march

1. The Birmingham parade ordinance, § 1159 of the Birmingham City Code, provides that:

"It shall be unlawful to organize or hold, or to assist in organizing or holding, or to take part or participate in, any parade or procession or other public demonstration on the streets or other public ways of the city, unless a permit therefor has been secured from the commission.

"To secure such permit, written application shall be made to the commission, setting forth the probable number of persons, vehicles and animals which will be engaged in such parade, procession or other public demonstration, the purpose for which it is to be held or had, and the streets or other public ways over, along or in which it is desired to have or hold such parade, procession or other public demonstration. The commission shall grant a written permit for such parade, procession or other public demonstration, prescribing the streets or other public ways which may be used therefor, unless in its judgment the public welfare, peace, safety, health, decency, good order, morals or convenience require that it be refused. It shall be unlawful to use for such purposes any other streets or public ways than those set out in said permit.

"The two preceding paragraphs, however, shall not apply to funeral processions."

tomorrow." The next afternoon, Good Friday, a large crowd gathered in the vicinity of Sixteenth Street and Sixth Avenue North in Birmingham. A group of about 50 or 60 proceeded to parade along the sidewalk while a crowd of 1,000 to 1,500 onlookers stood by, "clapping, and hollering, and hooping." Some of the crowd followed the marchers and spilled out into the street. At least three of the petitioners participated in this march.

Meetings sponsored by some of the petitioners were held that night and the following night, where calls for volunteers to "walk" and go to jail were made. On Easter Sunday, April 14, a crowd of between 1,500 and 2,000 people congregated in the midafternoon in the vicinity of Seventh Avenue and Eleventh Street North in Birmingham. One of the petitioners was seen organizing members of the crowd in formation. A group of about 50, headed by three other petitioners, started down the sidewalk two abreast. At least one other petitioner was among the marchers. Some 300 or 400 people from among the onlookers followed in a crowd that occupied the entire width of the street and overflowed onto the sidewalks. Violence occurred. Members of the crowd threw rocks that injured a newspaperman and damaged a police motorcycle.

The next day the city officials who had requested the injunction applied to the state circuit court for an order to show cause why the petitioners

should not be held in contempt for violating it. At the ensuing hearing the petitioners sought to attack the constitutionality of the injunction on the ground that it was vague and overbroad, and restrained free speech. They also sought to attack the Birmingham parade ordinance upon similar grounds, and upon the further ground that the ordinance had previously been administered in an arbitrary and discriminatory manner.

The circuit judge refused to consider any of these contentions, pointing out that there had been neither a motion to dissolve the injunction, nor an effort to comply with it by applying for a permit from the city commission before engaging in the Good Friday and Easter Sunday parades. Consequently, the court held that the only issues before it were whether it had jurisdiction to issue the temporary injunction, and whether thereafter the petitioners had knowingly violated it. Upon these issues the court found against the petitioners, and imposed upon each of them a sentence of five days in jail and a $50 fine, in accord with an Alabama statute.

The Supreme Court of Alabama affirmed.[4] That court, too, declined to consider the petitioners' constitutional attacks upon the injunction and the underlying Birmingham parade ordinance:

"It is to be remembered that petitioners are charged with violating a temporary injunction. We are not

4. The Alabama Supreme Court quashed the conviction of one defendant because of insufficient proof that he knew of the injunction before violating it, and the convictions of two others because there was no showing that they had disobeyed the order. 279 Ala. 53, 64, 181 So.2d 493, 504.

reviewing a denial of a motion to dissolve or discharge a temporary injunction. Petitioners did not file any motion to vacate the temporary injunction until after the Friday and Sunday parades. Instead, petitioners deliberately defied the order of the court and did engage in and incite others to engage in mass street parades without a permit.

. . .

"We hold that the circuit court had the duty and authority, in the first instance, to determine the validity of the ordinance, and, until the decision of the circuit court is reversed for error by orderly review, either by the circuit court or a higher court, the orders of the circuit court based on its decision are to be respected and disobedience of them is contempt of its lawful authority, to be punished. *Howat* v. *State of Kansas,* 258 U.S. 181, 42 S.Ct. 277, 66 L.Ed. 550." 279 Ala. 53, 60, 62–63, 181 So.2d 493, 500, 502.

Howat v. *State of Kansas, supra,* was decided by this Court almost 50 years ago. That was a case in which people had been punished by a Kansas trial court for refusing to obey an antistrike injunction issued under the state industrial relations act. They had claimed a right to disobey the court's order upon the ground that the state statute and the injunction based upon it were invalid under the Federal Constitution. The Supreme Court of Kansas had affirmed the judgment, holding that the trial court "had general power to issue injunctions in equity, and that even if its exercise of the power

was erroneous, the injunction was not void, and the defendants were precluded from attacking it in this collateral proceeding . . . that, if the injunction was erroneous, jurisdiction was not thereby forfeited, that the error was subject to correction only by the ordinary method of appeal, and disobedience to the order constituted contempt." . . .

This Court, in dismissing the writ of error, not only unanimously accepted but fully approved the validity of the rule of state law upon which the judgment of the Kansas court was grounded:

"An injunction duly issuing out of a court of general jurisdiction with equity powers, upon pleadings properly invoking its action, and served upon persons made parties therein and within the jurisdiction, must be obeyed by them, however erroneous the action of the court may be, even if the error be in the assumption of the validity of a seeming, but void law going to the merits of the case. It is for the court of first instance to determine the question of the validity of the law, and until its decision is reversed for error by orderly review, either by itself or by a higher court, its orders based on its decision are to be respected, and disobedience of them is contempt of its lawful authority, to be punished." . . .

The rule of state law accepted and approved in *Howat* v. *State of Kansas* is consistent with the rule of law followed by the federal courts.

In the present case, however, we are asked to hold that this rule of law, upon which the Alabama courts relied, was constitutionally impermissible. We are asked to say that the Constitution compelled Alabama to allow the petitioners to violate this injunction, to organize and engage in these mass street parades and demonstrations, without any previous effort on their part to have the injunction dissolved or modified, or any attempt to secure a parade permit in accordance with its terms. Whatever the limits of *Howat* v. *State of Kansas*, we cannot accept the petitioners' contentions in the circumstances of this case.

Without question the state court that issued the injunction had, as a court of equity, jurisdiction over the petitioners and over the subject matter of the controversy. And this is not a case where the injunction was transparently invalid or had only a frivolous pretense to validity. We have consistently recognized the strong interest of state and local governments in regulating the use of their streets and other public places. . . .

. . . When protest takes the form of mass demonstrations, parades, or picketing on public streets and sidewalks, the free passage of traffic and the prevention of public disorder and violence become important objects of legitimate state concern. As the Court stated, in *Cox* v. *State of Louisiana*, "We emphatically reject the notion . . . that the First and Fourteenth Amendments afford the same kind of freedom to those who would communicate ideas by conduct such as patrolling, marching, and picketing on streets and highways, as these

amendments afford to those who communicate ideas by pure speech." 379 U.S. 536, 555, 85 S.Ct. 453, 464, 13 L.Ed.2d 471. . . .

The generality of the language contained in the Birmingham parade ordinance upon which the injunction was based would unquestionably raise substantial constitutional issues concerning some of its provisions. . . . The petitioners, however, did not even attempt to apply to the Alabama courts for an authoritative construction of the ordinance. Had they done so, those courts might have given the licensing authority granted in the ordinance a narrow and precise scope, as did the New Hampshire courts in *Cox* v. *State of New Hampshire* and *Poulos* v. *State of New Hampshire*, both *supra*. Cf. *Shuttlesworth* v. *City of Birmingham*, 382 U.S. 87, 91, 86 S.Ct. 211, 213, 15 L.Ed.2d 176; *City of Darlington* v. *Stanley*, 239 S.C. 139, 122 S.E.2d 207. Here, just as in *Cox* and *Poulos*, it could not be assumed that this ordinance was void on its face.

The breadth and vagueness of the injunction itself would also unquestionably be subject to substantial constitutional question. But the way to raise that question was to apply to the Alabama courts to have the injunction modified or dissolved. The injunction in all events clearly prohibited mass parading without a permit, and the evidence shows that the petitioners fully understood that prohibition when they violated it.

The petitioners also claim that they were free to disobey the injunction because the parade ordinance on which it was based had been administered in the past in an arbitrary and discriminatory fashion. In support of this claim they sought to introduce evidence that, a few days before the injunction issued, requests for permits to picket had been made to a member of the city commission. One request had been rudely rebuffed,[9] and this same official had later made clear that he was without power to grant the permit alone, since the issuance of such permits was the responsibility of the entire city commission.[10] Assuming the truth of this proffered evidence, it does not follow that the parade ordinance was void on its face. The petitioners, moreover, did not apply for a permit either to the commission itself or to any commissioner after the injunction issued. Had they done so, and had the permit been refused, it is clear that their claim of arbitrary or discriminatory administra-

tion of the ordinance would have been considered by the state circuit court upon a motion to dissolve the injunction.[11]

This case would arise in quite a different constitutional posture if the petitioners, before disobeying the injunction, had challenged it in the Alabama courts, and had been met with the delay or frustration of their constitutional claims. But there is no showing that such would have been the fate of a timely motion to modify or dissolve the injunction. There was an interim of two days between the issuance of the injunction and the Good Friday march. The petitioners give absolutely no explanation of why they did not make some applications to the state court during that period. The injunction had issued *ex parte*; if the court had been presented with the petitioners' contentions, it might well

---

9. Mrs. Lola Hendricks, *not* a petitioner in this case, testified that on April 3:

"I went to Mr. Connor's office, the Commissioner's office at the City Hall Building. We went up and Commissioner Connor met us at the door. He asked, 'May I help you?' I told him, 'Yes, sir, we came up to apply or see about getting a permit for picketing, parading, demonstrating.'

. . .

"I asked Commissioner Connor for the permit, and asked if he could issue the permit, or other persons who would refer me to, persons who would issue a permit. He said, 'No, you will not get a permit in Birmingham, Alabama to picket. I will picket you over to the City Jail,' and he repeated that twice."

10. Commissioner Connor sent the following telegram to one of the petitioners on April 5:

"Under the provisions of the city code of the City of Birmingham, a permit to picket as requested by you cannot be

granted by me individually but is the responsiboity [*sic*] of the entire commission. I insist that you and your people do not start any picketing on the streets in Birmingham, Alabama.

"Eugene 'Bull' Connor, Commissioner of Public Safety."

11. In its opinion, that court stated: "The legal and orderly processes of the Court would require the defendants to attack the unreasonable denial of such permit by the Commission of the City of Birmingham through means of a motion to dissolve the injunction at which time this Court would have the opportunity to pass upon the question of whether or not a compliance with the ordinance was attempted and whether or not an arbitrary and capricious denial of such request was made by the Commission of the City of Birmingham. Since this course of conduct was not sought by the defendants, the Court is of the opinion that the validity of its injunction order stands upon its *prima facie* authority to execute the same."

have dissolved or at least modified its order in some respects. If it had not done so, Alabama procedure would have provided for an expedited process of appellate review. It cannot be presumed that the Alabama courts would have ignored the petitioners' constitutional claims. Indeed, these contentions were accepted in another case by an Alabama appellate court that struck down on direct review the conviction under this very ordinance of one of these same petitioners.[13]

The rule of law upon which the Alabama courts relied in this case was one firmly established by previous precedents. We do not deal here, therefore, with a situation where a state court has followed a regular past practice of entertaining claims in a given procedural mode, and without notice has abandoned that practice to the detriment of a litigant who finds his claim foreclosed by a novel procedural bar. . . . This is not a case where a procedural requirement has been sprung upon an unwary litigant when prior practice did not give him fair notice of its existence. . . .

The Alabama Supreme Court has apparently never in any criminal contempt case entertained a claim of nonjurisdictional error. In *Fields v. City of Fairfield*, 273 Ala. 588, 143 So.2d 177, decided just three years before the present case, the defendants, members of a "White Supremacy" organization who had disobeyed an injunction, sought to challenge the constitutional validity

of a permit ordinance upon which the injunction was based. The Supreme Court of Alabama, finding that the trial court had jurisdiction, applied the same rule of law which was followed here:

"As a general rule, an unconstitutional statute is an absolute nullity and may not form the basis of any legal right or legal proceedings, yet until its unconstitutionality has been judicially declared in appropriate proceedings, no person charged with its observance under an order or decree may disregard or violate the order or the decree with immunity from a charge of contempt of court; and he may not raise the question of its unconstitutionality in collateral proceedings on appeal from a judgment of conviction for contempt of the order or decree. . . ." 273 Ala., at 590, 143 So. 2d, at 180.

These precedents clearly put the petitioners on notice that they could not bypass orderly judicial review of the injunction before disobeying it. Any claim that they were entrapped or misled is wholly unfounded, a conclusion confirmed by evidence in the record showing that when the petitioners deliberately violated the injunction they expected to go to jail.

The rule of law that Alabama followed in this case reflects a belief that in the fair administration of justice no man can be judge in his own case, however exalted his station, however righteous his motives,

---

13. *Shuttlesworth* v. *City of Birmingham*, 43 Ala.App. 68, 180 So.2d 114. The case is presently pending on *certiorari* review in the Alabama Supreme Court.

and irrespective of his race, color, politics, or religion.[16]* This Court cannot hold that the petitioners were constitutionally free to ignore all the procedures of the law and carry their battle to the streets. *One may sympathize with the petitioners' impatient commitment to their cause. But respect for judicial process is a small price to pay for the civilizing hand of law, which alone can give abiding meaning to constitutional freedom.**

Affirmed.

MR. CHIEF JUSTICE WARREN, *whom* MR. JUSTICE BRENNAN *and* MR. JUSTICE FORTAS *join, dissenting.*

Petitioners in this case contend that they were convicted under an ordinance that is unconstitutional on its face because it submits their First and Fourteenth Amendment rights to free speech and peaceful assembly to the unfettered discretion of local officials. They further contend that the ordinance was unconstitutionally applied to them because the local officials used their discretion to prohibit peaceful demonstrations by a group whose political viewpoint the officials opposed. The Court does not dispute these contentions, but holds that petitioners may nonetheless be convicted and sent to jail because the patently unconstitutional ordinance was copied into an injunction —issued *ex parte* without prior notice or hearing on the request of the Police Commissioner—forbidding all persons having notice of the injunction to violate the ordinance without any limitation of time. I dissent because I do not believe that the fundamental protections of the Constitution were meant to be so easily evaded, or that "the civilizing hand of judicial process" would be hampered in the slightest by enforcing the First Amendment in this case.

The salient facts can be stated very briefly. Petitioners are Negro ministers who sought to express their concern about racial discrimination in Birmingham, Alabama, by holding peaceful protest demonstrations in that city on Good Friday and Easter Sunday, 1963. For obvious reasons, it was important for the significance of the demonstrations that they be held on those particular dates. A representative of petitioners' organization went to the City Hall and asked "to see the person or persons in charge to issue permits, permits for parading, picketing and demonstrating." She was directed to Public Safety Commissioner Connor, who denied her request for a permit

16. The same rule of law was followed in *Kasper v. Brittain*, 6 Cir., 245 F.2d 92. There, a federal court had ordered the public high school in Clinton, Tennessee, to desegregate. Kasper "arrived from somewhere in the East," and organized a campaign "to run the Negroes out of the school." The federal court issued an *ex parte* restraining order enjoining Kasper from interfering with desegregation. Relying upon the First Amendment, Kasper harangued a crowd "to the effect that although he had been served with the restraining order, it did not mean anything . . . ." His conviction for criminal contempt was affirmed by the Court of Appeals for the Sixth Circuit. That court concluded that "an injunctional order issued by a court must be obeyed," whatever its seeming invalidity, citing *Howat v. State of Kansas*, 258 U.S. 181, 42 S.Ct. 277, 66 L.Ed. 550. This Court denied *certiorari*, 355 U.S. 834, 78 S.Ct. 54, 2 L.Ed.2d 46.

*[Editor's Note: Emphasis added.]

in terms that left no doubt that petitioners were not going to be issued a permit under any circumstances. "He said, 'No you will not get a permit in Birmingham, Alabama to picket. I will picket you over to the City Jail,' and he repeated that twice." A second, telegraphic request was also summarily denied, in a telegram signed by "Eugene 'Bull' Connor," with the added information that permits could be issued only by the full City Commission, a three-man body consisting of Commissioner Connor and two others.[1] According to petitioners' offer of proof, the truth of which is assumed for purposes of this case, parade permits had uniformly been issued for all other groups by the city clerk on the request of the traffic bureau of the police department, which was under Commissioner Connor's direction. The requirement that the approval of the full Commission be obtained was applied only to this one group.

Understandably convinced that the City of Birmingham was not going to authorize their demonstrations under any circumstances, petitioners proceeded with their plans despite Commissioner Connor's orders. On Wednesday, April 10, at 9:00 in the evening, the city filed in a state circuit court a bill of complaint seeking an *ex parte* injunction. The complaint recited that petitioners were engaging in a series of demonstrations as "part of a massive effort . . . to forcibly integrate all business establishments, churches and other institutions" in the city, with the result that the police department was strained in its resources and the safety, peace, and tranquility were threatened. It was alleged as particularly menacing that petitioners were planning to conduct "kneel-in" demonstrations at churches where their presence was not wanted. The city's police dogs were said to be in danger of their lives. Faced with

1. The uncontradicted testimony relating to the rebuffs of petitioners' attempts to obtain a permit is set out in footnotes 9 and 10 of the majority opinion. Petitioners were prevented by a ruling of the trial court from introducing further proof of the intransigence of Commissioner Connor and the other city officials towards any effort by Negroes to protest segregation and racial injustice. The attitude of the city administration in general and of its Police Commissioner in particular are a matter of public record, of course, and are familiar to this Court from previous litigation. See *Shuttlesworth* v. *City of Birmingham*, 382 U.S. 87, 86 S.Ct. 211, 15 L.Ed.2d 176 (1965); *Shuttlesworth* v. *City of Birmingham*, 376 U.S. 339, 84 S.Ct. 795, 11 L.Ed.2d 766 (1964); *Shuttlesworth* v. *City of Birmingham,*, 373 U.S. 262, 83 S.Ct. 1130, 10 L.Ed.2d 335 (1963); *Gober* v. *City of Birmingham*, 373 U.S. 374, 83 S.Ct. 1311, 10 L.Ed.2d 419 (1963); *In re Shuttlesworth*, 369 U.S. 35, 82 S.Ct. 551, 7 L.Ed.2d 548 (1962). The United States Commission on Civil Rights found continuing abuse of civil rights protesters by the Birmingham police, including use of dogs, clubs, and firehoses. 1963 Report of the United States Commission on Civil Rights (Government Printing Office, 1963), p. 114. Commissioner Eugene "Bull" Connor, a self-proclaimed white supremacist (see Congress and the Nation 1945–1964: A Review of Government and Politics in the Postwar Years (Congressional Quarterly Service, 1965), p. 1604) made no secret of his personal attitude toward the rights of Negroes and the decisions of this Court. He vowed that racial integration would never come to Birmingham, and wore a button inscribed "Never" to advertise that vow. Yet the Court indulges in speculation that these civil rights protesters might have obtained a permit from this city and this man had they made enough repeated applications.

these recitals, the Circuit Court issued the injunction in the form requested, and in effect ordered petitioners and all other persons having notice of the order to refrain for an unlimited time from carrying on any demonstrations without a permit. A permit, of course, was clearly unobtainable; the city would not have sought this injunction if it had any intention of issuing one.

Petitioners were served with copies of the injunction at various times on Thursday and on Good Friday. Unable to believe that such a blatant and broadly-drawn prior restraint on their First Amendment rights could be valid, they announced their intention to defy it and went ahead with the planned peaceful demonstrations on Easter weekend. On the following Monday, when they promptly filed a motion to dissolve the injunction, the court found them in contempt, holding that they had waived all their First Amendment rights by disobeying the court order.

These facts lend no support to the court's charges that petitioners were presuming to act as judges in their own case, or that they had a disregard for the judicial process. They did not flee the jurisdiction or refuse to appear in the Alabama courts. Having violated the injunction, they promptly submitted themselves to the courts to test the constitutionality of the injunction and the ordinance it parroted. They were in essentially the same position as persons who challenge the constitutionality of a statute by violating it, and then defend the ensuing criminal prosecution on constitutional grounds. It has never been thought that viola-tion of a statute indicated such a disrespect for the legislature that the violator always must be punished even if the statute was unconstitutional. On the contrary, some cases have required that persons seeking to challenge the constitutionality of a statute, first violate it to establish their standing to sue. Indeed, it shows no disrespect for law to violate a statute on the ground that it is unconstitutional and then to submit one's case to the courts with the willingness to accept the penalty if the statute is held to be valid.

The Court concedes that "[t]he generality of the language contained in the Birmingham parade ordinance upon which the injunction was based would unquestionably raise substantial constitutional issues concerning some of its provisions." That concession is well-founded but minimal. I believe it is patently unconstitutional on its face. Our decisions have consistently held that picketing and parading are means of expression protected by the First Amendment, and that the right to picket or parade may not be subjected to the unfettered discretion of local officials. . . . *Although a city may regulate the manner of use of its streets and sidewalks in the interest of keeping them open for the movement of traffic, it may not allow local officials unbridled discretion to decide who shall be allowed to parade or picket and who shall not.** "Wherever the title of streets and parks may rest, they have immemorially been held in trust for the use of the public and, time out of mind,

*[Editor's Note: Emphasis added.]

have been used for purposes of assembly, communicating thoughts between citizens, and discussing public questions. Such use of the streets and public places has, from ancient times, been a part of the privileges, immunities, rights, and liberties of citizens. The privilege of a citizen of the United States to use the street and parks for communication of views on national questions may be regulated in the interest of all; it is not absolute, but relative, and must be exercised in subordination to the general comfort and convenience, and in consonance with peace and good order; *but it must not, in the guise of regulation, be abridged or denied."** Hague* v. *C. I. O.*, 307, U.S. 496, 515–516, 59 S.Ct. 954, 964, 83 L.Ed. 1423 (1939) (opinion of Mr. Justice Roberts). When local officials are given totally unfettered discretion to decide whether a proposed demonstration is consistent with "public welfare, peace, safety, health, decency, good order, morals or convenience," as they were in this case, they are invited to act as censors over the views that may be presented to the public. The unconstitutionality of the ordinance is compounded, of course, when there is convincing evidence that the officials have in fact used their power to deny permits to organizations whose views they dislike. The record in this case hardly suggests that Commissioner Connor and the other city officials were motivated in prohibiting civil rights picketing only by their overwhelming concern for particular traffic prob-

[Editor's Note: Emphasis added.]

lems. Petitioners were given to understand that under no circumstances would they be permitted to demonstrate in Birmingham, not that a demonstration would be approved if a time and place were selected that would minimize the traffic difficulties. The only circumstance that the court can find to justify anything other than a *per curiam* reversal is that Commissioner Connor had the foresight to have the unconstitutional ordinance included in an *ex parte* injunction issued without notice or hearing or any showing that it was impossible to have notice or a hearing, forbidding the world at large (insofar as it knew of the order) to conduct demonstrations in Birmingham without the consent of the city officials. This injunction was such potent magic that it transformed the command of an unconstitutional statute into an impregnable barrier, challengeable only in what likely would have been protracted legal proceedings and entirely superior in the meantime even to the United States Constitution.

I do not believe that giving this Court's seal of approval to such a gross misuse of the judicial process is likely to lead to greater respect for the law any more than it is likely to lead to greater protection for First Amendment freedoms. The *ex parte* temporary injunction has a long and odious history in this country, and its susceptibility to misuse is all too apparent from the facts of the case. As a weapon against strikes, it proved so effective in the hands of judges friendly to employers that Congress was forced to take the drastic step of removing from federal district courts the jurisdiction to issue injunctions in labor disputes. The labor injunction fell into disrepute largely because it was abused in precisely the same way that the injunctive power was abused in this case. Judges who were not sympathetic to the union cause commonly issued, without notice or hearing, broad restraining orders addressed to large numbers of persons and forbidding them to engage in acts that were either legally permissible or, if illegal, that could better have been left to the regular course of criminal prosecution. The injunctions might later be dissolved, but in the meantime strikes would be crippled because the occasion on which concerted activity might have been effective had passed. Such injunctions so long discredited as weapons against concerted labor activities, have now been given new life by this Court as weapons against the exercise of First Amendment freedoms. Respect for the courts and for judicial process was not increased by the history of the labor injunction.[8]

Nothing in our prior decisions, or in the doctrine that a party subject to a temporary injunction issued by a court of competent jurisdiction to retain its power to decide a dispute properly before it must normally

challenge the injunction in the courts rather than by violating it, requires that we affirm the convictions in this case. The majority opinion in this case rests essentially on a single precedent, and that a case the authority of which has clearly been undermined by subsequent decisions. *Howat* v. *State of Kansas*, 258 U.S. 181, 42 S.Ct. 277, 66 L.Ed. 550 (1922), was decided in the days when the labor injunction was in fashion....

Insofar as *Howat* v. *State of Kansas* might be interpreted to approve an absolute rule that any violation of a void court order is punishable as contempt, it has been greatly modified by later decisions. In *In re Green*, 369 U.S. 689, 82 S.Ct. 1114, 8 L.Ed.2d 198 (1962), we reversed a conviction for contempt of a state injunction forbidding labor picketing because the petitioner was not allowed to present evidence that the labor dispute was arguably subject to the jurisdiction of the National Labor Relations Board and hence not subject to state regulation. If an injunction can be challenged on the ground that it deals with a matter arguably subject to the jurisdiction of the National Labor Relations Board, then *a fortiori* it can be challenged on First Amendment grounds.

---

8. "The history of the labor injunction in action puts some matters beyond question. In large part, dissatisfaction and resentment are caused, first, by the refusal of courts to recognize that breaches of the peace may be redressed through criminal prosecution and civil action for damages, and, second, by the expansion of a simple, judicial device to an enveloping code of prohibited conduct, absorbing, *en masse*, executive and police functions and affecting the livelihood, and even lives, of multitudes. Especially those

zealous for the unimpaired prestige of our courts have observed how the administration of law by decrees which through vast and vague phrases surmount law, undermines the esteem of courts upon which our reign of law depends. Not government, but 'government by injunction,' characterized by the consequences of a criminal prosecution without its safeguards, has been challenged." *Frankfurter and Greene, supra*, at 200.

It is not necessary to question the continuing validity of the holding in *Howat* v. *State of Kansas*, however, to demonstrate that neither it nor the *Mine Workers*[10] case supports the holding of the majority in this case. In *Howat* the subpoena and injunction were issued to enable the Kansas Court of Industrial Relations to determine an underlying labor dispute. In the *Mine Workers* case, the District Court issued a temporary antistrike injunction to preserve existing conditions during the time it took to decide whether it had authority to grant the Government relief in a complex and difficult action of enormous importance to the national economy. In both cases the orders were of questionable legality, but in both cases they were reasonably necessary to enable the court or administrative tribunal to decide an underlying controversy of considerable importance before it at the time. This case involves an entirely different situation. The Alabama Circuit Court did not issue this temporary injunction to preserve existing conditions while it proceeded to decide some underlying dispute. There was no underlying dispute before it, and the court in practical effect merely added a judicial signature to a preexisting criminal ordinance. Just as the court had no need to issue the injunction to preserve its ability to decide some underlying dispute, *the city had no need of an injunction to impose a criminal penalty for demonstrating on the streets without a permit. The ordinance already ac-*

complished that.* In point of fact, there is only one apparent reason why the city sought this injunction and why the court issued it: *to make it possible to punish petitioners for contempt rather than for violating the ordinance, and thus to immunize the unconstitutional statute and its unconstitutional application from any attack.** I regret that this strategy has been so successful.

It is not necessary in this case to decide precisely what limits should be set to the *Mine Workers* doctrine in cases involving violations of the First Amendment. Whatever the scope of that doctrine, it plainly was not intended to give a State the power to nullify the United States Constitution by the simple process of incorporating its unconstitutional criminal statutes into judicial decrees. I respectfully dissent.

MR. JUSTICE DOUGLAS, *with whom* THE CHIEF JUSTICE, MR. JUSTICE BRENNAN, *and* MR. JUSTICE FORTAS *concur, dissenting.*

We sit as a court of law functioning primarily as a referee in the federal system. Our function in cases coming to us from state courts is to make sure that state tribunals and agencies work within the limits of the Constitution. Since the Alabama courts have flouted the First Amendment, I would reverse these judgments.

Picketing and parading are methods of expression protected by the First Amendment against both state

---

10. *United States* v. *United Mine Workers,* 330 U.S. 258, 67 S.Ct. 677, 91 L.Ed. 884 (1947).

*[*Editor's Note: Emphasis added.*]

and federal abridgment. . . . Since they involve more than speech itself and implicate street traffic, the accommodation of the public and the like, they may be regulated as to the times and places of the demonstrations. . . . But a State cannot deny the right to use streets or parks or other public grounds for the purpose of petitioning for the redress of grievances. . . .

The rich can buy advertisements in newspapers, purchase radio or television time, and rent billboard space. Those less affluent are restricted to the use of handbills (*Murdock* v. *Commonwealth of Pennsylvania*, 319 U.S. 105, 108, 63 S.Ct. 870, 872, 87 L.Ed. 1292) or petitions, or parades, or mass meetings. This "right of the people peaceably to assemble, and to petition the Government for a redress of grievances," guaranteed by the First Amendment, applicable to the States by reason of the Fourteenth . . . was flouted here.

The evidence shows that a permit was applied for. Mrs. Lola Hendricks, a member of the Alabama Christian Movement for Human Rights, authorized by its president, Reverend Shuttlesworth, on April 3, went to the police department and asked to see the person in charge of issuing permits. . . . *Petitioners' efforts to show that the City Commission did not grant permits, but that they were granted by the city clerk at the request of the traffic division were cut off.**

The record shows that petitioners did not deliberately attempt to circumvent the permit requirement. Rather they diligently attempted to obtain a permit and were rudely

rebuffed and then reasonably concluded that any further attempts would be fruitless.

*The right to defy an unconstitutional statute is basic in our scheme. Even when an ordinance requires a permit to make a speech, to deliver a sermon, to picket, to parade, or to assemble, it need not be honored when it is invalid on its face.** . . .

*By like reason, where a permit has been arbitrarily denied one need not pursue the long and expensive route to this Court to obtain a remedy. The reason is the same in both cases. For if a person must pursue his judicial remedy before he may speak, parade, or assemble, the occasion when protest is desired or needed will have become history and any later speech, parade, or assembly will be futile or pointless.**

Howat v. *State of Kansas*, 258 U.S. 181, 42 S.Ct. 277, 66 L.Ed. 550, states the general rule that court injunctions are to be obeyed until error is found by normal and orderly review procedures. . . . But there is an exception where "the question of jurisdiction" is "frivolous and not substantial." . . .

As already related, petitioners made two applications to Commissioner "Bull" Connor for a permit and were turned down. *At the trial, counsel for petitioners offered to prove through the city clerk that the Commission never has granted a permit, the issuing authority being the city clerk who acts at the request of the traffic division. But he was not allowed to answer the question. And when asked to describe the practice*

*[Editor's Note: Emphasis added.]

*for granting permits an objection was raised and sustained.**

It is clear that there are no published rules or regulations governing the manner of applying for permits, and it is clear from the record that some permits are issued. One who reads this record will have, I think, the abiding conviction that these people were denied a permit solely because their skin was not of the right color and their cause was not popular.

A court does not have *jurisdiction* to do what a city or other agency of a State lacks *jurisdiction* to do. The command of the Fourteenth Amendment, through which the First Amendment is made applicable to the States, is that no "state" shall deprive any person of "liberty" without due process of law. The decree of a state court is "state" action in the constitutional sense . . . as much as the action of the state police, the state prosecutor, the state legislature, or the Governor himself. An ordinance—unconstitutional on its face or patently unconstitutional as applied—is not made sacred by an unconstitutional injunction that enforces it. It can and should be flouted in the manner of the ordinance itself. *Courts as well as citizens are not free "to ignore the procedure of the law," to use the Court's language. The "constitutional freedom" of which the Court speaks can be won only if judges honor the Constitution.**

MR. JUSTICE BRENNAN, *with whom* THE CHIEF JUSTICE, MR. JUSTICE DOUGLAS, *and* MR. JUSTICE FORTAS *join, dissenting.*

Under cover of exhortation that the Negro exercise "respect for judicial process," the Court empties the Supremacy Clause of its primacy by elevating a state rule of judicial administration above the right of free expression guaranteed by the Federal Constitution. And the Court does so by letting loose a devastatingly destructive weapon for suppression of cherished freedoms heretofore believed indispensable to maintenance of our free society. I cannot believe that this distortion in the hierarchy of values upon which our society has been and must be ordered can have any significance beyond its function as a vehicle to affirm these contempt convictions.

I.

Petitioners are eight Negro ministers. They were convicted of criminal contempt for violation of an *ex parte* injunction issued by the Circuit Court of Jefferson County, Alabama, by engaging in street parades without a municipal permit on Good Friday and Easter Sunday 1963. These were the days when Birmingham was a world symbol of implacable official hostility to Negro efforts to gain civil rights, however peacefully sought. The purpose of these demonstrations was peaceably to publicize and dramatize the civil rights grievances of the Negro people. The underlying permit ordinance made it unlawful "to organize

*[Editor's Note: Emphasis added.]

or hold . . . or to take part or participate in, any parade or procession or other public demonstration on the streets . . ." without a permit. A permit was issuable by the City Commission "unless in its judgment the public welfare, peace, safety, health, decency, good order, morals or convenience require that it be refused."

Attempts by petitioners at the contempt hearing to show that they tried to obtain a permit but were rudely rebuffed by city officials were aborted when the trial court sustained objections to the testimony. It did appear, however, that on April 3, a member of the Alabama Christian Movement for Human Rights (ACMHR) was sent by one of the petitioners, Reverend Shuttlesworth, to Birmingham city hall to inquire about permits for future demonstrations. The member stated at trial:

"I asked [Police] Commissioner Connor for the permit, and asked if he could issue the permit, or other persons who would refer me to, persons who would issue a permit. He said, 'No, you will not get a permit in Birmingham, Alabama to picket. I will picket you over to the City Jail,' and he repeated that twice."

Two days later Reverend Shuttlesworth sent a telegram to Police Commissioner Connor requesting a permit on behalf of ACMHR to picket on given dates "against the injustices of segregation and discrimination." Connor replied that the permit could be granted only by the full Commission and stated, "I insist that you and your people do not start any picketing on the streets in Birmingham, Alabama." Petitioners were also frustrated in their attempts at the contempt hearing to show that permits were granted not by the Commission, but by the city clerk at the request of the traffic department, and that they were issued in a discriminatory manner.

On April 6–7 and April 9–10, Negroes were arrested for parading without a permit. Late in the night of April 10, the city requested and immediately obtained an *ex parte* injunction without prior notice to petitioners. Notice of the issuance was given to five of petitioners on April 11.[1] The decree tracked the wording of the permit ordinance, except that it was still more broad and pervasive. It enjoined:

". . . engaging in, sponsoring, inciting or encouraging mass street parades or mass processions or like demonstrations without a permit, trespass on private property after being warned to leave the premises by the owner or person in possession of said private property, congregating on the street or public places into mobs, and unlawfully picketing business establishments or public buildings in the City of

1. Two of petitioners received no personal notice of the injunction at all. The trial court found that they were aware of the injunction, a conclusion here challenged. Because of the disposition I would make of this case, I would not reach this issue.

Birmingham, Jefferson County, State of Alabama or performing acts calculated to cause breaches of the peace in the City of Birmingham, Jefferson County, in the State of Alabama or from conspiring to engage in unlawful street parades, unlawful processions, unlawful demonstrations, unlawful boycotts, unlawful trespasses, and unlawful picketing or other like unlawful conduct or from violating the ordinances of the City of Birmingham and the Statutes of the State of Alabama or from doing any acts designed to consummate conspiracies to engage in said unlawful acts of parading, demonstrating, boycotting, trespassing and picketing or other unlawful acts, or from engaging in acts and conduct customarily known as 'kneel-ins' in churches in violation of the wishes and desires of said churches. . . ."

Several of the Negro ministers issued statements that they would refuse to comply with what they believed to be, and is indeed, a blatantly unconstitutional restraining order.

On April 12, Good Friday, a planned march took place, beginning at a church in the Negro section of the city and continuing to city hall. The police, who were notified in advance by one of petitioners of the time and route of the march, blocked the streets to traffic in the area of the church and excluded white persons from the Negro area. Approximately 50 persons marched, led by three petitioners, Martin Luther King, Ralph Abernathy, and Shuttlesworth. A large crowd of Negro onlookers which had gath-

ered outside the church remained separate from the procession. A few blocks from the church the police stopped the procession and arrested, and jailed, most of the marchers, including the three leaders.

On Easter Sunday another planned demonstration was conducted. The police again were given advance notice, and again blocked the streets to traffic and white persons in the vicinity of the church. Several hundred persons were assembled at the church. Approximately 50 persons who emerged from the church began walking peaceably. Several blocks from the church the procession was stopped, as on Good Friday, and about 20 persons, including five petitioners, were arrested. The participants in both parades were in every way orderly; the only episode of violence, according to a police inspector, was rock throwing by three onlookers on Easter Sunday, after petitioners were arrested; the three rock throwers were immediately taken into custody by the police.

On Monday, April 15, petitioners moved to dissolve the injunction, and the city initiated criminal contempt proceedings against petitioners. At the hearing, held a week later, the Jefferson County Court considered the contempt charge first. Petitioners urged that the injunction and underlying permit ordinance were impermissibly vague prior restraints on exercise of First Amendment rights and that the ordinance had been discriminatorily applied. The court, however, limited evidence primarily to two questions: notice of and violation of the injunction. The court stated that "the validity of its injunctive order stands upon the prima facie authority to execute the same." Petitioners were found guilty of criminal contempt and sentenced to five days in jail and a $50 fine. The Alabama Supreme Court, adopting the reasoning of *United States v. United Mine Workers*, 330 U.S. 258, 67 S.Ct. 677, 91 L.Ed. 884, applicable to federal court orders, affirmed, holding that the validity of the injunction and underlying permit ordinance could not be challenged in a contempt proceeding. 279 Ala. 53, 181 So.2d 493.

II.

The holding of the Alabama Supreme Court, and the affirmance of its decision by this Court, rest on the assumption that petitioners may be criminally punished although the parade ordinance and the injunction be unconstitutional on their faces as in violation of the First Amendment, and even if the permit ordinance was discriminatorily applied. It must therefore be assumed, for purposes of review of the Alabama Supreme Court's decision, and in assessing the Court's affirmance, that petitioners could successfully sustain the contentions (into which the Alabama courts refused to inquire) that the ordinance and injunction are in fact facially unconstitutional as excessively vague prior restraints on First Amendment rights and that the ordinance had been discriminatorily applied. It should be noted, without elaboration, that there is clearly sound basis in fact for this assumption: the Alabama Court of Appeals, in a case involving one of these peti-

tioners, has held that the ordinance is "void for vagueness because of overbroad, and consequently meaningless standards for the issuance of permits for processions," and that the ordinance has been enforced discriminatorily. *Shuttlesworth* v. *City of Birmingham*, 43 Ala.App. 68, 180 So. 2d 114 (1965). But it is not the merits of such claims, but the refusal of the Alabama courts to consider them, that is here involved.

Like the Court, I start with the premise that States are free to adopt rules of judicial administration designed to require respect for their courts' orders. See *Howat* v. *State of Kansas*, 258 U.S. 181, 42 S.Ct. 277, 66 L.Ed. 550. But this does not mean that this valid state interest does not admit of collision with other and more vital interests. Surely the proposition requires no citation that a valid state interest must give way when it infringes on rights guaranteed by the Federal Constitution. The plain meaning of the Supremacy Clause requires no less.

In the present case we are confronted with a collision between Alabama's interest in requiring adherence to orders of its courts and the constitutional prohibition against abridgment of freedom of speech, more particularly "the right of the people peaceably to assemble," and the right "to petition the Government for a redress of grievances." . . . Special considerations have time and again been deemed by us to attend protection of these freedoms in the face of state interests the vindication of which result in prior restraints upon their exercise, or their regulation in a vague or overbroad manner, or in a way which gives unbridled discretion to limit their exercise to an individual or group of individuals. To give these freedoms the necessary breathing space to survive, . . .

    .   .   .

Yet by some inscrutable legerdermain these constitutionally secured rights to challenge prior restraints invalid on their face are lost if the State takes the precaution to have some judge append his signature to an *ex parte* order which recites the words of the invalid statute. The State neatly insulates its legislation from challenge by mere incorporation of the identical stifling, overbroad, and vague restraints on exercise of the First Amendment freedoms into an even more vague and pervasive injunction obtained invisibly and upon a stage darkened lest it be open to scrutiny by those affected. The *ex parte* order of the judicial officer exercising broad equitable powers is glorified above the presumably carefully considered, even if hopelessly invalid, mandates of the legislative branch. I would expect this tribunal, charged as it is with the ultimate responsibility to safeguard our constitutional freedoms, to regard the *ex parte* injunctive tool to be far more dangerous than statutes to First Amendment freedoms. One would expect this Court particularly to remember the stern lesson history taught courts, in the context of the labor injunction, that the *ex parte* injunction represents the most devastating of restraints on constitutionally protected activities. Today, however, the weapon is given complete invulner-

ability in the one context in which the danger from broad prior restraints has been thought to be the most acute. Were it not for the *ex parte* injunction, petitioners could have paraded first and challenged the permit ordinance later. But because of the *ex parte* stamp of a judicial officer on a copy of the invalid ordinance they barred not only from challenging the permit ordinance, but also the potentially more stifling yet unconsidered restraints embodied in the injunction itself.

    .   .   .

It is said that petitioners should have sought to dissolve the injunction before conducting their processions. That argument is plainly repugnant to the principle that First Amendment freedoms may be exercised in the face of legislative prior restraints, and *a fortiori*, of *ex parte* restraints broader than such legislative restraints, which may be challenged in any subsequent proceeding for their violation. But at all events, prior resort to a motion to dissolve this injunction could not be required because of the complete absence of any time limits on the duration of the *ex parte* order. See *Freedman* v. *State of Maryland*, 380 U.S. 51, 85 S.Ct. 734, 13 L.Ed.2d 649. Even the Alabama Supreme Court's Rule 47 leaves the timing of full judicial consideration of the validity of the restraint to that court's untrammeled discretion.

    .   .   .

The suggestion that petitioners be muffled pending outcome of dissolution proceedings without any measurable time limits is particularly inappropriate in the setting of this case. Critical to the plain exercise of the right of protest was the timing of that exercise. First, the marches were part of a program to arouse community support for petitioners' assault on segregation there. A cessation of these activities, even for a short period, might deal a crippling blow to petitioners' efforts. Second, in dramatization of their cause, petitioners, all ministers, chose April 12, Good Friday, and April 14, Easter Sunday, for their protests hoping to gain the attention to their cause which such timing might attract. Petitioners received notice of the order April 11. The ability to exercise protected protest at a time when such exercise would be effective must be as protected as the beliefs themselves. . . . It is a flagrant denial of constitutional guarantees to balance away this principle in the name of "respect for the judicial process." To preach "respect" in this context is to deny the right to speak at all.

The Court today lets loose a devastatingly destructive weapon for infringement of freedoms jealously safeguarded not so much for the benefit of any given group of any given persuasion as for the benefit of all of us. *We cannot permit fears of "riots" and "civil disobedience" generated by slogans like "Black Power" to divert our attention from what is here at stake—not violence or the right of the State to control its streets and sidewalks, but the insulation from attack of* ex parte *orders and legislation upon which they are based even when patently impermissible prior restraints on the exercise of First Amendment rights, thus arming the state courts with the power to punish as a "contempt" what they otherwise could not punish at all.** Constitutional restrictions against abridgments of First Amendment freedoms limit judicial equally with legislative and executive power. Convictions for contempt of court orders which invalidly abridge First Amendment freedoms must be condemned equally with convictions for violation of statutes which do the same thing. I respectfully dissent.

*[Editor's Note: Emphasis added.]

QUESTIONS

1. Even though it would seem from the record that Commissioner Connor had no intention of granting a permit for the parade, don't you think the ministers were wrong to break the law when they had the further legal remedy to challenge his "arbitrary denial" in the courts? Why yes? Why no?

2. Do you think the ministers and the police chief were equally guilty in the disrespect for the law, or do you think one of the parties had a greater responsibility to act in accordance with it? Justify your position.

3. If you were asking for a permit to exercise your constitutional right of assembly and it was denied you as the testimony indicates in this case—

do you think you would have acted in disregard of the temporary court injunction? Why or why not?

4. What are the long-range implications for our society—if any—if public officials and citizens believe in the manner referred to in question 3 in regard to the law? Are either of the parties justified? Is one more guilty of law violation than the other? Which? Why?

5. Do you see a distinction between "law" and "justice" in this case? If so, what is it? If not, do you think the ministers got what they deserved in light of *all* the facts?

GREGORY v. CHICAGO

394 U.S. 111; 89 S.Ct. 946; 22 L.Ed. 2d 134 (1969)

MR. CHIEF JUSTICE WARREN *delivered the opinion of the Court.*

This is a simple case. Petitioners, accompanied by Chicago police and an assistant city attorney, marched in a peaceful and orderly procession from city hall to the mayor's residence to press their claims for desegregation of the public schools. Having promised to cease singing at 8:30 p. m., the marchers did so. Although petitioners and the other demonstrators continued to march in a completely lawful fashion, the onlookers became unruly as the number of bystanders increased. Chicago police, to prevent what they regarded as an impending civil disorder, demanded that the demonstrators, upon pain of arrest, disperse. When this command was not obeyed, petitioners were arrested for disorderly conduct.

Petitioners' march, if peaceful and orderly, falls well within the sphere of conduct protected by the First Amendment. . . . There is no evidence in this record that petitioners' conduct was disorderly. Therefore, under the principle first established in *Thompson* v. *City of Louisville,* 362 U.S. 199, 80 S.Ct. 624, 4 L.Ed.2d 654 (1960), convictions so totally devoid of evidentiary support violate due process.

The opinion of the Supreme Court of Illinois suggests that petitioners were convicted not for the manner in which they conducted their march but rather for their refusal to disperse when requested to do so by Chicago police. See 39 Ill.2d 47, 60, 233 N.E.2d 422, 429 (1968). However reasonable the police request may have been and however laudable the police motives, petitioners were charged and convicted for holding a demonstration not for a refusal to obey a police officer.* As we said

---

*The trial judge charged solely in terms of the Chicago ordinance. Neither the ordinance nor the charge defined disorderly

conduct as the refusal to obey a police order.

in *Garner* v. *Louisiana*, 368 U.S. 157, 164, 82 S.Ct. 248, 251, 7 L.Ed.2d 207 (1961): "[I]t is as much a denial of due process to send an accused to prison following conviction for a charge that was never made as it is to convict him upon a charge for which there is no evidence to support that conviction." ...

Finally, since the trial judge's charge permitted the jury to convict for acts clearly entitled to First Amendment protection, *Stromberg* v. *California*, 283 U.S. 359, 51 S.Ct. 532, 75 L.Ed. 1117 (1931), independently requires reversal of these convictions.

The judgments are reversed.
Reversed.

MR. JUSTICE DOUGLAS, *while joining the separate opinion of* MR. JUSTICE BLACK, *also joins this opinion.*

MR. JUSTICE STEWART *and* MR. JUSTICE WHITE *concur in the judgment of the Court and join its opinion insofar as it holds that under the principle established by Stromberg v. California, 283 U.S. 359, 51 S.Ct. 532, the petitioners' convictions cannot stand.*

MR. JUSTICE BLACK, *with whom* MR. JUSTICE DOUGLAS *joins, concurring.*

This we think is a highly important case which requires more detailed consideration than the Court's opinion gives it. It in a way tests the ability of the United States to keep the promises its Constitution makes to the people of the Nation. Among those promises appearing in the Preamble to the Constitution are the statements that the people of the United States ordained this basic charter "in Order to form a more perfect Union, establish Justice, insure domestic Tranquility . . . and secure the Blessings of Liberty to ourselves and our Posterity. . . ." Shortly after the original Constitution was adopted, again undoubtedly in an attempt to "secure the Blessings of Liberty," the Bill of Rights was added to the Constitution, in which the First Amendment, later made applicable to the States by the Fourteenth Amendment, provides that: "Congress shall make no law . . . abridging the freedom of speech, or of the press; or the right of the people peaceably to assemble, and to petition the Government for a redress of grievances."

In 1954 our Court held that laws segregating people on the basis of race or color in the public schools unconstitutionally denied Negroes equal protection of the laws. Negroes, and many others who sympathized with them, cooperatively undertook to speed up desegregation. These groups adopted plans under which they marched on the streets carrying placards, chanting, and singing songs, all designed to publicize their grievances and to petition the various units of government, state and national, for a redress of these grievances. Their activities along these lines quite obviously aroused highly emotional feelings both on their part and on the part of others who opposed the changes in local laws and customs which the "picketers" and "demonstrators" advocated. Agitation between groups brought about sharp conflicts and clashes, threats, fights, riots, and near riots. This

Court has, to be sure, had its difficulties and sharp differences of opinion in deciding the precise boundaries dividing the constitutionally permissible and impermissible in this field. There have also been sharp disputes over whether the Court can hold laws unconstitutional because the Court deems them to be "unreasonable," "arbitrary," or contrary to fundamental standards of ethics, morals, or conscience. Fortunately, however, these differences need not concern us here. For while we have pointed out in many cases that the States and their subordinate units do have constitutional power to regulate picketing, demonstrating, and parading by statutes and ordinances narrowly drawn so as not to abridge the rights of speech, press, assembly, or petition, neither Chicago, nor Illinois, at the time these petitioners were demonstrating had passed any such narrowly drawn laws.[4]

The facts upon which these arrests and convictions for disorderly conduct occurred were these.

Petitioner Gregory and his group had become dissatisfied because Benjamin Willis, Superintendent of Chicago's public school system, was not moving speedily enough to desegregate the public schools. While Mayor Daley did not appear to have legal authority to remove Dr. Willis, the group evidently believed the Mayor could cause him to be removed if he wanted to do so, and their prodding was therefore directed at the Mayor as well as against Willis. The group march began near the Chicago Loop District at 4:30 p. m. and ended five miles away in the neighborhood of Daley's home. A lieutenant of police, four police sergeants and about forty policemen met Gregory at the gathering place in Grant Park. There Gregory addressed the marchers saying:

"First we will go over to the snake pit [city hall]. When we leave there, we will go out to the snake's house [the mayor's home]. Then, we will continue to go out to Mayor Daley's home until he fires Ben Willis [Superintendent of Schools]."

The demonstrators marched to the city hall, and then they marched to the Mayor's home about five miles away, arriving at about 8 p. m. The demonstrators were accompanied by the police and by the Assistant City Attorney from the park to the Mayor's home. When they reached this neighborhood, the demonstrators began marching around and around near the Mayor's home. Meanwhile the crowd of spectators from the neighborhood kept increasing, and its language and conduct became rougher and tougher. The events leading up to the arrest of the demonstrators are set out in detail in the

---

4. The nearest thing to such a law in existence at that time was § 36–31 of the Municipal Code of Chicago, which required written permits for parades on "any public way" or for "any open air public meeting . . . in or upon any public way." Petitioners were neither charged with nor convicted for the offense of failing to obtain a written permit. Indeed, the city clearly gave its effective permission to the marchers by sending a city attorney and a detail of specially trained officers to protect them along every foot of their march. . . .

opinion of the Illinois Supreme Court, and we agree fully with that court's description of these events, which we have reprinted as an appendix to this opinion. This episode finally came to a conclusion at about 9:30 p. m. Fearful that the threatening crowd of on-lookers could no longer be contained, the police asked Gregory and his marchers to leave the area. When they refused, they were arrested and charged with violation of Chicago's disorderly conduct ordinance, which provides as follows:

"All persons who shall make, aid, countenance, or assist in making any improper noise, riot, disturbance, breach of the peace, or diversion tending to a breach of the peace, within the limits of the city; all persons who shall collect in bodies or crowds for unlawful purposes, or for any purpose, to the annoyance or disturbance of other persons; . . . shall be deemed guilty of disorderly conduct, and upon conviction thereof, shall be severally fined not less than one dollar nor more than two hundred dollars for each offense." Municipal Code of Chicago, § 193–1.

We agree with the Illinois Supreme Court that the "record shows a determined effort by the police to allow the marchers to peacefully demonstrate and at the same time maintain order." We also think the record shows that outside of the marching and propagandizing of their views and protests, Gregory and his group while marching did all in their power to maintain order.

Indeed, in the face of jeers, insults and assaults with rocks and eggs, Gregory and his group maintained a decorum that speaks well for their determination simply to tell their side of their grievances and complaints. Even the "snake" and "snake pit" invectives used by Gregory and his demonstrators, unlike some used by their hecklers, remained within the general give and take of heated political argument. Thus both police and demonstrators made their best efforts faithfully to discharge their responsibilities as officers and citizens, but they were nevertheless unable to restrain these hostile hecklers within decent and orderly bounds. These facts disclosed by the record point unerringly to one conclusion, namely, that when groups with diametrically opposed, deep-seated views are permitted to air their emotional grievances, side by side, on city streets, tranquility and order cannot be maintained even by the joint efforts of the finest and best officers and of those who desire to be the most law-abiding protestors of their grievances.

It is because of this truth, and a desire both to promote order and to safeguard First Amendment freedoms, that this Court has repeatedly warned States and governmental units that they cannot regulate conduct connected with these freedoms through use of sweeping, dragnet statutes that may, because of vagueness, jeopardize these freedoms. In those cases, however, we have been careful to point out that the Constitution does not bar enactment of laws regulating conduct, even though connected with speech, press, assembly, and petition, if such laws specifically bar only the conduct deemed obnoxious and are carefully and narrowly aimed at that forbidden conduct. The dilemma revealed by this record is a crying example of a need for some such narrowly drawn law. It is not our duty and indeed not within our power to set out and define with precision just what statutes can be lawfully enacted to deal with situations like the one confronted here by police and protestors, both of whom appear to us to have been conscientiously trying to do their duties as they understood them. Plainly, however, no mandate in our Constitution leaves States and governmental units powerless to pass laws to protect the public from the kind of boisterous and threatening conduct that disturbs the tranquility of spots selected by the people either for homes, wherein they can escape the hurly-burly of the outside business and political world, or for public and other buildings that require peace and quiet to carry out their functions, such as courts, libraries, schools and hospitals.

The disorderly conduct ordinance under which these petitioners were charged and convicted is not, however, a narrowly drawn law, particularly designed to regulate certain kinds of conduct such as marching or picketing or demonstrating along the streets or highways. Nor does it regulate the times or places or manner of carrying on such activities. To the contrary, it might better be described as a meat ax ordinance, gathering in one comprehensive definition of an offense a number of words which have a multiplicity of meanings, some of which would cover activity specifically protected by the First Amendment. The average person charged with its violation is necessarily left uncertain as to what conduct and attitudes of mind would be enough to convict under it. Who, for example, could possibly foresee what kind of noise or protected speech would be held to be "improper"? That, of course, would depend on sensibilities, nerves, tensions, and on countless other things. . . . Moreover, the ordinance goes on to state that it shall be a crime for persons to "collect in bodies or crowds for unlawful purposes, or for any purpose, to the annoyance or disturbance of other persons. . . ." Such language could authorize conviction simply because the form of the protest displeased some of the on-lookers, and of course a conviction on that ground would encroach on First Amendment rights. . . . And it must be remembered that only the tiniest bit of petitioners' conduct could possibly be thought illegal here—that is, what they did after the policeman's order to leave the area. The right "peaceably to assemble, and to petition the Government for a redress of grievances" is specifically protected by the First Amendment. For the entire five-mile march, the walking by petitioners in a group, the language, and the chants and songs were all treated by the city's assistant attorney and its specially detailed policemen as lawful, not lawless, conduct.

The so-called "diversion tending to a breach of the peace" here was limited entirely and exclusively to the fact that when the policeman in charge of the special police detail concluded that the hecklers observing the march were dangerously close to rioting and that the demonstrators and others were likely to be engulfed in that riot, he ordered Gregory and his demonstrators to leave, and Gregory—standing on what he deemed to be his constitutional rights—refused to do so. The "diversion" complained of on the part of Gregory and the other marchers was not any noise they made or annoyance or disturbance of "other persons" they had inflicted. Their guilt of "disorderly conduct" therefore turns out to be their refusal to obey instanter a policeman's individual command to leave the area of the Mayor's home. Since neither the city council nor the state legislature had enacted a narrowly drawn statute forbidding disruptive picketing or demonstrating in a residential neighborhood, the conduct involved here could become "disorderly" only if the policeman's command was a law which the petitioners were bound to obey at their peril. But under our democratic system of government, law making is not entrusted to the moment-to-moment judgment of the policeman on his beat. Laws, that is valid laws, are to be made by representatives chosen to make laws for the future, not by police officers whose duty is to enforce laws already enacted and to make arrests only for conduct already made criminal. One of our proudest boasts is that no man can be convicted of crime for conduct, innocent when engaged in, that is later made criminal. . . . To let a policeman's command become equivalent to a criminal statute comes

dangerously near making our government one of men rather than of law. . . . There are ample ways to protect the domestic tranquility without subjecting First Amendment freedoms to such a clumsy and unwieldy weapon.

The City of Chicago, recognizing the serious First Amendment problems raised by the disorderly conduct ordinance as it is written, argues that these convictions should nevertheless be affirmed in light of the narrowing construction placed on the ordinance by the Illinois Supreme Court in this case. That court held that the ordinance

"does not authorize the police to stop a peaceful demonstration merely because a hostile crowd may not agree with the views of the demonstrators. It is only where there is an imminent threat of violence, the police have made all reasonable efforts to protect the demonstrators, the police have requested that the demonstration be stopped and explained the request, if there be time, and there is a refusal of the police request, that an arrest for an otherwise lawful demonstration may be made."

This interpretation of the ordinance is, of course, binding on this Court, and the construction of the Illinois Supreme Court is as authoritative as if this limitation were written into the ordinance itself. But this cannot be the end of our problem. The infringement on First Amendment rights will not be cured if the narrowing construction is so unforeseeable that men of common intelligence could not have realized the law's limited scope at the only relevant time, when their acts were committed, . . . or if the law remains excessively sweeping even as narrowed, . . . Petitioners particularly press the Court to dispose of the case on this latter ground. They raise troublesome questions concerning the extent to which, even under the narrowed construction, guilt still depends on the mere refusal to obey a policeman's order. And they suggest that the scope of the police obligation to attempt first to deal with the hostile audience is still not made sufficiently clear.

It is not necessary for the Court to resolve such issues in the present case, however, because the Chicago ordinance, as applied here, infringed on First Amendment rights for an even more fundamental reason. Whatever the validity of the Illinois Supreme Court's construction, this was simply not the theory on which these petitioners were convicted. In explaining the elements of the offense to the jury, the trial judge merely read the language of the ordinance. The jury was not asked to find whether, as the Illinois Supreme Court's construction apparently requires, there was "an imminent threat of violence," or whether the police had "made all reasonable efforts to protect the demonstrators."

Rather, it was sufficient for the jury to decide that petitioners had made "an improper noise" or a "diversion tending to a breach of the peace," or had "collect[ed] in bodies for unlawful purposes, or for any purpose, to the annoyance or disturbance of other persons."

In fact, far from taking account of the limiting factors stressed by the Illinois Supreme Court, the judge's charge was based on precisely the opposite theory. The jury was instructed, over petitioners' objection, that "the fact that persons other than these defendants may or may not have violated any laws or may or may not have been arrested should not be considered by you in determining the guilt or innocence of these defendants." The significance of this instruction in the context of the evidence at trial is of course apparent— the jury was simply told to ignore questions concerning the acts of violence committed by the crowd of on-lookers and attempts made by the police to arrest those directly responsible for them.[7] Under these circumstances, the principle established by *Stromberg* v. *California*, 283 U.S. 359, 51 S.Ct. 532, 75 L.Ed. 1117 (1931), compels us to set aside these convictions. As we explained in *Williams* v. *North Carolina*, 317 U.S. 287, 292, 63 S.Ct. 207, 210, 87 L.Ed. 279 (1942):

7. The trial judge explained the need for this instruction to counsel, in chambers, as follows:
"[T]he record is replete with evidence that a Jury may well consider to establish the violation of the law on the part of the so-called spectators and neighbors, and the record is silent as to whether any of them were arrested or not.

. . .

"As far as why didn't they arrest these other people, why didn't they arrest the spectators and so on and so on, it seems to me that by virtue of the way the evidence went in, this will be a question that will bother these Jurors unless it is taken care of."

"That is to say, the verdict of the jury for all we know may have been rendered on [an unconstitutional] ground alone, since it did not specify the basis on which it rested. It therefore follows here as in *Stromberg* . . . that if one of the grounds for conviction is invalid under the Federal Constitution, the judgment cannot be sustained."

At the time the petitioner was tried, the Illinois Supreme Court had not yet announced its narrowing construction of the Chicago disorderly conduct ordinance. The trial judge's instructions supplied the jury only with the unadorned language of the statute. Thus it is entirely possible that the jury convicted the petitioner on the ground that he and the others who demonstrated with him had, in the language of the ordinance, "collect[ed] in bodies or crowds . . . to the annoyance or disturbance of other persons," simply because the form of their protest had displeased some of the onlookers. Since the petitioner could not constitutionally be convicted on this ground, *Stromberg* compels the reversal of these convictions.

In agreeing to the reversal of these convictions, however, we wish once more to say that we think our Federal Constitution does not render the States powerless to regulate the conduct of demonstrators and picketers, conduct which is more than "speech," more than "press," more than "assembly," and more than "petition" as those terms are used in the First Amendment. Narrowly drawn statutes regulating the conduct of demonstrators and picketers are not impossible to draft. And narrowly drawn statutes regulating these activities are not impossible to pass if the people who elect their legislators want them passed. Passage of such laws, however, like the passage of all other laws, constitutes in the final analysis a choice of policies by the elected representatives of the people.

We, of course, do not mean to say or even to intimate that freedom of speech, press, assembly, or petition can be abridged so long as the First Amendment remains unchanged in our Constitution. But to say that the First Amendment grants those broad rights free from any exercise of governmental power to regulate conduct, as distinguished from speech, press, assembly or petition, would subject all the people of the Nation to the uncontrollable whim and arrogance of speakers, and writers, and protesters, and grievance bearers. . . .

Were the authority of government so trifling as to permit anyone with a complaint to have the vast power to do anything he pleased, wherever he pleased, and whenever he pleased, our customs and our habits of conduct, social, political, economic, ethical and religious, would all be wiped out, and become no more than relics of a gone but not forgotten past. Churches would be compelled to welcome into their buildings invaders who came but to scoff and jeer; streets and highways and public buildings would cease to be available for the purposes for which they were constructed and dedicated whenever demonstrators and picketers wanted

*[Editor's Note: Emphasis added.]

to use them for their own purposes. And perhaps worse than all other changes, homes, the sacred retreat to which families repair for their privacy and their daily way of living, would have to throw their doors open to all who desired to convert the occupants to new views, new morals, and a new way of life. Men and women who hold public office would be compelled, simply because they did hold public office, to lose the comforts and privacy of an un-picketed home. We believe that our Constitution, written for the ages, to endure except as changed in the manner it provides, did not create a government with such monumental weaknesses. *Speech and press are, of course, to be free, so that public matters can be discussed with impunity. But picketing and demonstrating can be regulated like other conduct of men.* * We believe that the homes of men, sometimes the last citadel of the tired, the weary and the sick, can be protected by government from noisy, marching, tramping, threatening picketers and demonstrators bent on filling the minds of men, women, and children with fears of the unknown.

For these reasons we concur in the reversal.

Appendix
Opinion of the Supreme Court of Illinois.

"About 4:30 P.M. the marchers, two abreast, walked out of the park and went to the city hall in the loop. The marchers then walked south on State Street to 35th Street and then proceeded west to Lowe Avenue, a distance of about 5 miles from the city hall. The mayor's home is at 3536 South Lowe Avenue. The demonstrators had increased in number to about 85 and they arrived at the mayor's home about 8:00 o'clock P.M. In addition to the police, the marchers were accompanied by their attorney and an assistant city counsel. At the suggestion of an assistant city counsel, Gregory had agreed that the group would quit singing at 8:30 P.M. Commander Pierson, district commander of the 9th police district which encompasses this area, met Lieutenant Hougeson at the corner of 35th and Lowe and assumed command of the police operations.

"There were about 35 people on the corner and a group of about 6 or 8 youngsters carrying a sign 'We Love Mayor Daley' tried to join the marchers but the police stopped them. As the demonstrators started south into the 3500 block of Lowe Avenue, Gregory testified he went back through the line to tell everyone just to keep singing and to keep marching. 'Don't stop and don't answer anyone back. Don't worry about anything that is going to be said to you. Just keep marching. If anyone hits you or anything, try to remember what he looks like, but above all means, do not hit them back. Keep the line straight and keep it tight.' The demonstrators chanted 'Ben Willis must go, Snake Daley, also;' 'Ben Willis must go—When?—Now;' 'We are going to the home of the snake, the snake pit is down the street;' 'Hey, Hey, what do you know, Ben Willis must go' and

[Editor's Note: Emphasis added.]

'Hey, Hey, what do you know, Mayor Daley must go also.' They carried signs which read: 'Daley fire Willis;' 'Defacto, Desmacto, it is still segregation;' 'Ben Willis must go—now;' and 'Mayor Daley, fire Ben Willis.' They also sang the civil rights songs, 'We Shall Overcome' and 'We Shall Not Be Moved.'

"The police ordered the taverns closed during the march. Police from the task force, the 9th district and other districts surrounded the block in which the mayor's home is located. There were about 10 officers at each of the four intersections and about 10 officers spread along each of the four blocks. The rest of the 100 police officers assigned to the march accompanied the demonstrators as they marched around the block. The police tried to keep all spectators across the street from the marchers. They were equipped with walkie-talkie radios to relay reports of conditions to each other and they had a bullhorn with which they addressed the spectators and the demonstrators.

"As the marchers started around the block the first time the neighbors began coming out of their homes. On the second time around the block some of the residents had moved their lawn sprinklers onto the sidewalk and the demonstrators went into the street just long enough to get around the water. On the third trip around the block the water sprinklers had been removed, presumably by order of the police. Gregory himself testified to several instances when the police kept the crowd that was accumulating from interfering with the march. 'One of

the neighborhood people stood in front of the line, and we just stopped. This individual didn't move and we didn't move. After a few minutes, the officer standing on the corner asked him to move and he moved.' He said that on their fourth trip around the block (about 8:30 P.M.) people were yelling out the windows and the police made spectators in doorways close the doors. About 8:30 P.M. the demonstrators quit their singing and chanting and marched quietly. Shortly before 9:00 P.M. 100 to 150 spectators formed a line of march ahead of the demonstrators. Gregory said 'the lieutenant [Hougheson] asked me if I would hold up the line until they got those people out of the way. I said, I will hold up the line, but they have just as much right to march peacefully as we have.' The spectators were ordered to move. In order to avoid the appearance that the marchers were following the 100 to 150 spectators who had been ordered to move, Gregory said his group marched straight south crossing 36th Street thus taking them one block south of the block which they had been marching. They had to stop when they crossed 36th Street while the police opened a pathway through about 300 spectators they had confined on the corner across the street.

"Sergeant Golden testified that between 8:00 o'clock and 9:00 o'clock the crowd increased steadily to a few hundred, but that from 9:00 o'clock until about 9:20 o'clock the people just seemed to come from everywhere until it reached between 1,000 and 1,200. During this time the crowd became unruly. There was shouting and threats. 'God damned nigger, get the hell out of here;' 'Get out of here niggers—go back where you belong or we will get you out of here' and 'Get the hell out of here or we will break your blankety-blank head open.' Cars were stopped in the streets with their horns blowing. There were Ku Klux Klan signs and there was singing of the Alabama Trooper song. Children in the crowd were playing various musical instruments such as a cymbal, trumpet and drum.

"Rocks and eggs were also being thrown at the marchers from the crowd. The police were dodging the rocks and eggs and attempted to catch the persons who threw them. Sergeant Golden explained the problem. 'You could see these teen-agers behind the crowd. You could see a boil of activity and something would come over our heads and I or my partner would go down to try to apprehend who was doing it. You couldn't see who was doing it. They would vanish into the crowd.' He further testified that about 9:25 P.M., 'They were saying, "Let's get them," ' and with this they would step off the curb to try to cross 35th Street and we would push them back with force. Once in a while somebody would run out, and we would grab ahold of them and throw them back into the crowd.'

"About 9:30 P.M. Commander Pierson told Gregory the situation was dangerous and becoming riotous. He asked Gregory if he would cooperate and lead the marchers out of the area. The request to leave the area was made about five times.

Pierson then told the marchers that any of them who wished to leave the area would be given a police escort. Three of the marchers accepted the proposal and were escorted out of the area. The remaining demonstrators were arrested and taken away in two police vans.

"While we have gone into considerable detail in describing the events leading to the arrest of defendants, only a complete reading of the record can give one a true picture of the dilemma confronting the police. During the entire march from 4:30 P.M. until 9:30 P.M. the marchers were accompanied by their attorney who advised them, and the police were accompanied by an assistant city attorney who advised them. In short the record shows a determined effort by the police to allow the marchers to peacefully demonstrate and at the same time maintain order."

MR. JUSTICE HARLAN, *concurring in the result.*

Two factors in this case run afoul of well-established constitutional principles, and clearly call for reversal. These are the ambulatory sweep of the Chicago disorderly conduct ordinance, ... and the possibility that as the case went to the jury the convictions may have rested on a constitutionally impermissible ground. See *Stromberg* v. *California*, 283 U.S. 359, 51 S.Ct. 532, 75 L.Ed. 1117 (1931).

I agree with the opinion of my Brother BLACK on both of these scores, and to that extent join in it.

QUESTIONS

1. What if you were a motorist trying to get home. Would you think that your rights to drive in the public streets had been violated? Would you be annoyed? Why should your right to travel the public streets yield to the protestors' rights to use the public streets? Justify your answer!

2. If you were the mayor, or any other public official, or even a neighbor of the mayor, would you be of the opinion that you had a right to some peace and quiet in your own home? Should the right to protest be allowed to destroy the right of privacy? Isn't a man's home his "castle" under the Constitution? Doesn't the mayor have a right to be let alone *at home*? Shouldn't protests of this sort be confined to his *public office*—the mayor's office—or City Hall? Why yes? Why no?

3. Where was the greatest possibility of a disturbance, on the side of the marchers or the crowd? Justify your answer!

4. If you think the marchers caused the disturbance, aren't you in effect saying that their constitutional rights can only be exercised if no one threatens them or gets excited? Is that a valid position? Justify your answer!

5. If you think the on-lookers caused the disturbance, shouldn't they have been arrested? Why not? Weren't they uttering "fighting-words?"

5. protest and private property

5. protest and private property

Protest, Segregation and Private Trespass

How "private" can private property be in a mass society? To what extent does private property, when used to serve the public, take on a "non-private" or "public" character? To what extent may the state "reasonably" regulate "private" property which is used to serve the public? And who should determine the "reasonableness" of a regulation? For what goals or purposes should the state be able to regulate private property? How is it that racial segregation, declared unconstitutional in the 1950s, continued to exist throughout the nation in the 1960s and into the 1970s? All of these questions are related—some directly, some remotely—to the cases in this section.

The "sit-in" cases represent an entirely different manifestation of the segregation issue than did *Plessy* and *Brown* and the cases which followed them. Unlike the cases in the preceding section, the "sit-in" cases—*Peterson, Shuttlesworth* and *Lombard*—all involve segregationist practices maintained by *private* parties on *private* property used to service the public. None of the facilities are state-controlled, operated or owned, as such, and therefore do not *directly* come under the constitutional prohibition of the Fourteenth Amendment that "No *state* shall . . . deny to any persons within its jurisdiction the equal protection of the law."

Unless in some way, the owners of private restaurants, hotels, motels, barber shops and other entrepreneurs, who serve the public could be considered as agents acting for the state or in some way related to supportive state power, the Fourteenth Amendment and its prohibitions were not addressed to them and consequently did not circumscribe their decision-making power over the use of their "private" property. Perhaps a look at the historical precedents of private property would be helpful in understanding the cases in this section.

The Civil Rights Controversy of 1883

One of the last Reconstruction Acts to be passed was The Civil Rights Act of 1875. Its intent, in part, was to secure equal treatment for the newly freed slaves in privately owned facilities which served the public.

The crucial section of the act was its first which declared:

> . . . That all persons within the jurisdiction of the United States shall be entitled to the full and equal enjoyment of the accommodations, advantages, facilities, and privileges of inns, public conveyances on land and water, theaters, and other places of public amusement; subject only to the conditions and limitations established by law, and applicable alike to citizens of every race and color, regardless of any previous condition of servitude.

Within eight years after the act's passage, five cases challenging the validity of the law were simultaneously decided by the Supreme Court in the *Civil Rights Cases*, 109 U.S. 3 (1883). Two of the cases arose from denials of inn accommodations and privileges to Blacks. Two others involved the denial of theater and opera seats; and one involved racial discrimination against a Black woman on a railroad train.

Mr. Justice Bradley, delivering the opinion of the Court, held that the law of 1875 was unconstitutional. Essentially, the Court reasoned that the prohibitive sections of the Fourteenth Amendment were limitations on state authority and, under Section 5 of the Amendment, Congress could pass laws implementing those prohibitions. But the Congressional enactment in question in these cases sought to regulate the activities of private businessmen as well. The Fourteenth Amendment, said the Court, conferred no such legislative power on the Congress:

> The 1st section of the 14th Amendment, which is the one relied on, after declaring who shall be citizens of the United States, and of the several States, is prohibitory in its character, and prohibitory upon the States. It declares that "No State shall make or enforce any law which shall abridge the privileges or immunities of citizens of the United States; nor shall any State deprive any person of life, liberty or property without due process of law; nor deny to any person within its jurisdiction the equal protection of the laws." It is state action of a particular

character that is prohibited. *Individual invasion of individual rights is not the subject-matter of the Amendment.* It has a deeper and broader scope. It nullifies and makes void all state legislation, and state action of every kind, which impairs the privileges and immunities of citizens of the United States, or which injures them in life, liberty or property without due process of law, or which denies to any of them the equal protection of the laws. It not only does this, but, in order that the national will, thus declared, may not be a mere *brutum fulmen*, the last section of the Amendment invests Congress with power to enforce it by appropriate legislation. To enforce what? To enforce the prohibition. To adopt appropriate legislation for correcting the effects of such prohibited *state laws* and *state Acts*, and thus to render them effectually null, void and innocuous. This is the legislative power conferred upon Congress, and this is the whole of it. It does not invest Congress with power to legislate upon subjects which are within the domain of state legislation; but to provide modes of relief against state legislation or state action, of the kind referred to . . . [Editor's emphasis.]

Thus even before the *Plessy* case (1896), segregation of the races was accomplished in some states by private action which excluded Blacks from business establishments. These management policies were enforced by trespass laws which existed in every state.

With the advent of the *Brown* doctrine and the end of state-required segregation, segregationist practices remained unaffected in privately owned facilities which served the public. Hotels, motels, restaurants, theaters, all types of businesses which dealt in services could maintain racial segregation as a policy and be totally unaffected by the landmark decisions of the 1950's which overturned the "separate but equal" doctrine.

The Civil Rights Bill of 1964

After racial upheavals in some of the large cities of the nation during the summer of 1962 and the dispatching of federal marshals and troops to desegregate the Universities of Mississippi and Alabama, John F. Kennedy spoke to the nation about racism in the United States with a candor that had not been heard before from an incumbent President:

This is not a sectional issue. Difficulties over segregation and discrimination exist in every city, in every State of the Union, producing in many cities a rising tide of discontent that threatens the public safety. Nor is this a partisan issue. In a time of domestic crisis men of good will and generosity should be able to unite regardless of party or politics. This is not even a legal or legislative issue alone. It is better to settle these matters in the courts than on the streets, and new laws are needed at every level, but law alone cannot make men see right.

We are confronted primarily with a moral issue. It is as old as the scriptures and is as clear as the American Constitution.

The heart of the question is whether all Americans are to be afforded equal rights and equal opportunities, whether we are going to treat our fellow Americans as we want to be treated. If an American, because his skin is dark, cannot eat lunch in a restaurant open to the public, if he cannot send his children to the best public school available, if he cannot vote for the public officials who represent him, if, in short, he cannot enjoy the full and free life which all of us want, then who among us would be content to have the color of his skin changed and stand in his place? Who among us would be content with the counsels of patience and delay?

One hundred years of delay have passed since President Lincoln freed the slaves, yet their heirs, their grandsons, are not fully free. They are not yet freed from the bonds of injustice. They are not yet freed from social and economic oppression. And this Nation, for all its hopes and all its boasts, will not be fully free until all its citizens are free.

We preach freedom around the world, and we mean it, and we cherish our freedom here at home, but are we to say to the world, and much more importantly, to each other that this is a land of the free except for the Negroes; that we have no second-class citizens except Negroes; that we have no class or caste system, no ghettoes, no master race except with respect to Negroes?

Now the time has come for this Nation to fulfill its promise. The events in Birmingham and elsewhere have so increased the cries for equality that no city or State or legislative body can prudently choose to ignore them.

The fires of frustration and discord are burning in every city, North and South, where legal remedies are not at hand. Redress is sought in the streets, in demonstrations, parades, and protests which create tensions and threaten violence and threaten lives.

We face, therefore, a moral crisis as a country and as a people. It cannot be met by repressive police action. It cannot be left to increased demonstrations in the streets. It cannot be quieted by token moves or talk. It is a time to act in the Congress, in your State and local legislative body and, above all, in all of our daily lives.

It is not enough to pin the blame on others, to say this is a problem of one section of the country or another, or deplore the fact that we face. A great change is at hand, and our task, our obligation, is to make that revolution, that change, peaceful and constructive for all.

Those who do nothing are inviting shame as well as violence. Those who act boldly are recognizing right as well as reality.[1] [Editor's emphasis.]

Within days after the speech, Kennedy sent to the Congress the most comprehensive civil rights bill since Reconstruction days. The Civil Rights Act became the law of the land in 1964.

To those private persons who wanted to maintain their individual "right" to racially discriminate against persons in privately owned business establishments, Title II of the 1964 Civil Rights Act was the most restricting. Among other things it provided that:

> All persons shall be entitled to the full and equal enjoyment of the
> goods, services, facilities, privileges, advantages, and accommodations
> of any place of public accommodation as defined in this section, without discrimination or segregation on the ground of race, color, religion,
> or national origin.

Section 201 (b) of Title II included four classes of business establishments which "serve the public": inns, hotels, motels, and private homes which rent more than five rooms to transient guests; all restaurants and cafeterias, etc.; and motion picture houses and other places of amusement; and any establishment which is physically located within the premises of any establishment covered above (i.e., a barber shop located in a hotel).

The constitutionality of Title II was quickly challenged and sustained in *Heart of Atlanta Motel, Inc.* v. *United States*, 379 U.S. 241 (1964). The motel, which had 216 rooms, was located in downtown Atlanta close to Interstate Highways 75 and 85, and Highways 23 and 41. The motel owners advertised outside the state, solicited interstate patronage and accepted national convention business. It was estimated that approximately 75 per cent of its registered guests came from outside of Georgia.

Mr. Justice Clark's opinion for the Court rested primarily on the broad plenary power of the Congress to regulate "commerce among the states." Racial discrimination within the boundaries of a single state burdened interstate commerce and interstate travelers and as such was subject to the regulatory power of Congress. Justice Clark wrote in 1964:

> That Congress was legislating against moral wrongs in many of these
> areas rendered its enactments no less valid. In framing Title II of this
> Act, Congress was also dealing with what it considered a moral problem. But that fact does not detract from the overwhelming evidence
> of the disruptive effect that racial discrimination has had on commer-

1. From President John F. Kennedy's Radio and Television Report to the American People on Civil Rights; delivered June 11, 1963. *Public Papers of the Presidents of the United States* (Washington: U.S. Gov't. Printing Office; 1964).

cial intercourse. It was this burden which empowered Congress to enact appropriate legislation, and, given this basis for the exercise of its power, Congress was not restricted by the fact that the particular obstruction to interstate commerce with which it was dealing was also deemed a moral and social wrong.

It is said that the operation of the motel here is of a purely local character. But, assuming this to be true, "[i]f it is interstate commerce that feels the pinch, it does not matter how local the operation which applies the squeeze." . . . As Chief Justice Stone put it in *United States* v. *Darby*, [312 U.S. 100 (1941)]:

"The power of Congress over interstate commerce is not confined to the regulation of commerce among the states. It extends to those activities intrastate which so affect interstate commerce or the exercise of the power of Congress over it as to make regulation of them appropriate means to the attainment of a legitimate end, the exercise of the granted power of Congress to regulate interstate commerce. See *McCulloch* v. *Maryland*, 4 Wheat. 316, 421, 4 L.Ed. 579." [312 U.S. at 118, 61 S. Ct. at 459.]

Thus the power of Congress to promote interstate commerce also includes the power to regulate the local incidents thereof, including local activities in both the States of origin and destination, which might have a substantial and harmful effect upon that commerce. One need only examine the evidence which we have discussed above to see that Congress may—as it has—prohibit racial discrimination by motels serving travelers, however "local" their operations may appear.

The Private Trespass Cases

The passage of the Civil Rights Act of 1964 outlawed the discriminatory practices protested in *Peterson* v. *Greenville*, 373 U.S. 244 (1963), *Shuttlesworth* v. *Birmingham*, 373 U.S. 262 (1963), and *Lombard* v. *Louisiana*, 373 U.S. 267 (1963) and thus made future cases of this kind unnecessary. In each of these three cases, Blacks "sat-in" at restaurants which refused to serve them and whose owners eventually had them arrested for trespassing on private property. The majority opinion in all of these trespass suits equated the failure to serve the Blacks, by the private restaurant owner, with some manifestation of state action. By so doing the Court brought into play the Fourteenth Amendment and reversed all of the convictions because the restaurant owner—executor of state law and/or "custom"— failed to accord the Black defendants equal protection of the law (i.e., serve them as he would whites).

After the passage of the 1964 law, the Supreme Court did not have to labor any further to equate somehow the actions of private entrepreneurs with those of the states. Inasmuch as most businesses, which served the public, were in some way related to interstate commerce, the direct regulatory power of the Congress reached most, if not all, of these situations.

The concurring opinion of Mr. Justice Douglas and the dissent of Mr. Justice Harlan in the *Lombard* case discussed the important questions as to when "private" action and "private" parties ought to be equated with "state" actions and "state" agents. Obviously, the broader the equation the greater the scope of the restrictive nature of the Fourteenth Amendment on what might "appear" to be private behavior.

In the *Amalgamated Food Employees* v. *Logan Valley Plaza,* 391 U.S. 308 (1968), the Supreme Court, through Mr. Justice Marshall, held that peaceful picketing (as it is in this case) *could* be an expression of First and Fourteenth Amendment rights and as such could not be excluded from private property which had been opened to free public access. The dissents by Mr. Justice Black and White did not equate a shopping center opened for public use with the public streets. For them a facility could be opened for "public use" and still retain its character as "private" property. In addition, Mr. Justice Black indicated that all liberties are somewhat limited and that the "peaceful" picketing in this case is conducted so as to make inoperative the functioning of the shopping center. This he condemned as an unacceptable manifestation of even a constitutionally protected right. As Justice Frankfurter once put it: "The right to swing your arm ends where the other fellow's nose begins."

PETERSON v. GREENVILLE, S.C.

373 U.S. 244; 83 S. Ct. 1119; 10 L.Ed. 2d 323 (1963)

MR. CHIEF JUSTICE WARREN *delivered the opinion of the Court.*

The petitioners were convicted in the Recorder's Court of the City of Greenville, South Carolina, for violating the trespass statute of that state.* Each was sentenced to pay a fine of $100 or in lieu thereof to serve 30 days in jail. An appeal to the Greenville County Court was dismissed, and the Supreme Court of South Carolina affirmed. 239 S.C. 298, 122 S.E.2d 826. We granted *certiorari* to consider the substantial federal questions presented by the record. 370 U.S. 935, 82 S.Ct. 1577, 8 L.Ed.2d 806.

The 10 petitioners are Negro boys and girls who, on August 9, 1960, entered the S. H. Kress store in Greenville and seated themselves at the lunch counter for the purpose, as they testified, of being served. When the Kress manager observed the petitioners sitting at the counter, he "had one of [his] . . . employees call the Police Department and turn off the lights and state the lunch counter closed." A captain of police

and two other officers responded by proceeding to the store in a patrol car where they were met by other policemen and two state agents who had preceded them there. In the presence of the police and the state agents, the manager "announced that the lunch counter was being closed and would everyone leave" the area. The petitioners, who had been sitting at the counter for five minutes, remained seated and were promptly arrested. The boys were searched, and both boys and girls were taken to police headquarters.

The manager of the store did not request the police to arrest petitioners; he asked them to leave because integrated service was "contrary to local customs" of segregation at lunch counters and in violation of the following Greenville City ordinance requiring separation of the races in restaurants:

> "It shall be unlawful for any person owning, managing or controlling any hotel, restaurant, cafe, eating house, boarding house or similar establishment to furnish meals to

---

*S.C.Code, 1952 (Cum.Supp.1960), § 16–388:

"Entering premises after warned not to do so or failing to leave after requested.

"Any person:

"(1) Who without legal cause or good excuse enters into the dwelling house, place of business or on the premises of another person, after having been warned, within six months preceding, not to do so or

"(2) Who, having entered into the

dwelling house, place of business or on the premises of another person without having been warned within six months not to do so, and fails and refuses, without good cause or excuse, to leave immediately upon being ordered or requested to do so by the person in possession, or his agent or representative, Shall, on conviction, be fined not more than one hundred dollars, or be imprisoned for not more than thirty days."

white persons and colored persons in the same room, or at the same table, or at the same counter; provided, however, that meals may be served to white persons and colored persons in the same room where separate facilities are furnished. Separate facilities shall be interpreted to mean:

"(a) Separate eating utensils and separate dishes for the serving of food, all of which shall be distinctly marked by some appropriate color scheme or otherwise;

"(b) Separate tables, counters or booths;

"(c) A distance of at least thirty-five feet shall be maintained between the area where white and colored persons are served;

"(d) The area referred to in subsection (c) above shall not be vacant but shall be occupied by the usual display counters and merchandise found in a business concern of a similar nature;

"(e) A separate facility shall be maintained and used for the cleaning of eating utensils and dishes furnished the two races." Code of Greenville, 1953, as amended in 1958, § 31–8.

The manager and the police conceded that the petitioners were clean, well dressed, unoffensive in conduct, and that they sat quietly at the counter which was designed to accommodate 59 persons. The manager described his establishment as a national chain store of 15 or 20 departments, selling over 10,000 items. He stated that the general public was invited to do business at the store and that the patronage of Negroes was solicited in all departments of the store other than the lunch counter.

Petitioners maintain that South Carolina has denied them rights of free speech, both because their activity was protected by the First and Fourteenth Amendments and because the trespass statute did not require a showing that the Kress manager gave them notice of his authority when he asked them to leave. Petitioners also assert that they have been deprived of the equal protection of the laws secured to them against state action by the Fourteenth Amendment. We need decide only the last of the questions thus raised.

The evidence in this case establishes beyond doubt that the Kress management's decision to exclude petitioners from the lunch counter was made because they were Negroes. It cannot be disputed that under our decisions "[P]rivate conduct abridging individual rights does no violence to the Equal Protection Clause unless to some significant extent the State in any of its manifestations has been found to have become involved in it." . . .

It cannot be denied that here the City of Greenville, an agency of the State, has provided by its ordinance that the decision as to whether a restaurant facility is to be operated on a desegregated basis is to be reserved to it. When the State has commanded a particular result it has saved to itself the power to determine that result and thereby "to a significant extent" has "become involved" in, and in fact, has removed that decision from the sphere of private choice. It has thus effectively determined that a person owning, managing or controlling an eating place is left with no choice of his own but must segregate his white and Negro patrons. The Kress management, in deciding to exclude Negroes, did precisely what the city law required.

Consequently these convictions cannot stand, even assuming, as respondent contends, that the manager would have acted as he did independently of the existence of the ordinance. The State will not be heard to make this contention in support of the convictions. For the convictions had the effect, which the State cannot deny, of enforcing the ordinance passed by the City of Greenville, the agency of the State. When a state agency passes a law compelling persons to discriminate against other persons because of race, and the State's criminal processes are employed in a way which enforces the discrimination mandated by that law, such a palpable violation of the Fourteenth Amendment cannot be saved by attempting to separate the mental urges of the discriminators. *Reversed.*

SHUTTLESWORTH *v.* BIRMINGHAM

373 U.S. 262; 83 S. Ct. 1130; 10 L.Ed. 2d 335 (1963)

MR. CHIEF JUSTICE WARREN *delivered the opinion of the Court.*

The petitioners, both Negro ministers, were tried and convicted in the Birmingham, Alabama, Recorder's Court for aiding and abetting a violation of the city criminal trespass ordinance. The complaint filed with respect to Shuttlesworth charged:

"Comes the City of Birmingham, Alabama, a municipal corporation, and complains that F. L. Shuttlesworth, within twelve months before the beginning of this prosecution, and within the City of Birmingham or the police jurisdiction thereof, did incite or aid or abet in the violation of an ordinance of the City, to-wit, Section 1436[1] of the General City Code of Birmingham of 1944, in that F. L. Shuttlesworth did incite or aid or abet another person to go or remain on the premises of another after being warned not to do so, contrary to and in violation

1. Birmingham General City Code, 1944, § 1436 provides:

"*After Warning*—Any person who enters into the dwelling house, or goes or remains on the premises of another, after being warned not to do so, shall on conviction, be punished as provided in Section 4, provided, that this Section shall not apply to police officers in the discharge of official duties."

of Section 824[2] of the General City Code of Birmingham of 1944." (Footnotes added.)

An identical complaint was filed charging Billups.

On appeal to the Circuit Court petitioners received a trial *de novo* and were again convicted. Petitioner Shuttlesworth was sentenced to 180 days in jail at hard labor and a fine of $100. Petitioner Billups was sentenced to 30 days and a fine of $25. On further appeal to the Alabama Court of Appeals the convictions were affirmed. 41 Ala.App. 318, 319, 134 So.2d 213, 215. The Alabama Supreme Court denied writs of *certiorari.* 273 Ala. 704, 713, 134 So.2d 214, 215. Because of the grave constitutional questions involved, we granted *certiorari.* 370 U.S. 934, 82 S.Ct. 1580, 8 L.Ed.2d 805.

Though petitioners took separate appeals, they were jointly tried in the Circuit Court. The evidence is sketchy in character. Only one witness testified, a city detective who had listened to petitioners' trial in the Recorder's Court.[3] The detective testified to his recollection of the testimony of two college boys whom (among others) petitioners were alleged to have incited to commit the criminal trespass.

These two boys were James E. Gober and James Albert Davis. They were convicted for criminal trespass in a separate proceeding subsequent to petitioners' trial. In *Gober* v. *City of Birmingham*, 373 U.S. 374, 83 S.Ct. 1133, we hold on the authority of *Peterson* v. *City of Greenville*, 373 U.S. 244, 83 S.Ct. 1133, that the convictions of Gober and Davis are constitutionally invalid. The detective stated that in the Recorder's Court Gober and Davis had testified as follows:

James Gober and James Albert Davis, both Negro college students, went to the home of petitioner, Rev. Shuttlesworth, on March 30, 1960, where there were other college students. Petitioner, Rev. Billups, drove Davis there, and Billups was present when Shuttlesworth asked for volunteers to participate in "sit-down demonstrations." Gober "testified that in response to Rev. Shuttlesworth asking for volunteers to participate in the sit-down strikes that he volunteered to go to Pizitz at 10:30 and take part in the sit-down demonstrations." A list was made by someone, and Shuttlesworth announced he would get them out of jail. Gober and Davis participated in sit-down demonstrations on the following day as did others who were present.

This is the sole evidence upon which the petitioners were convicted. There was no evidence that any of the demonstrations which resulted from the meeting were disorderly or otherwise in violation of law.

Petitioners contend that there is

2. Birmingham General City Code, 1944, § 824 provides:

"It shall be unlawful for any person to incite, or aid or abet in, the violation of any law or ordinance of the city, or any

provision of state law, the violation of which is a misdemeanor."

3. Petitioners objected to all of this testimony as hearsay and on constitutional grounds, but these objections were overruled.

no evidence to show guilt of the charged offense. . . . We need not reach that question since there is a more compelling reason why these convictions cannot stand.

Petitioners were convicted for inciting, aiding, and abetting a violation of the city trespass ordinance. The trespass "violation" was that committed by the petitioners in *Gober* v. *City of Birmingham*, 373 U.S. 374, 83 S.Ct. 1133.[4] Since the

convictions in *Gober* have been set aside, it follows that the present petitioners did not incite or aid and abet any crime, and that therefore their own convictions must be set aside.

It is generally recognized that there can be no conviction for aiding and abetting someone to do an innocent act. . . .

Reversed.

---

4. The trial court stated, "[Y]ou have the ten students and the Court thinks they were misused and misled into a violation of a City Ordinance and has so ruled." As we understand the record, these convictions were based upon the inciting of the 10 students who are the petitioners in *Gober*.

LOMBARD v. LOUISIANA

373 U.S. 267; 83 S. Ct. 1122; 10 L.Ed. 2d 338 (1963)

MR. CHIEF JUSTICE WARREN *delivered the opinion of the Court.*

This case presents for review trespass convictions resulting from an attempt by Negroes to be served in a privately owned restaurant customarily patronized only by whites. However, unlike a number of the cases this day decided, no state statute or city ordinance here forbids desegregation of the races in all restaurant facilities. Nevertheless, we conclude that this case is governed by the principles announced in *Peterson* v. *City of Greenville*, 373 U.S. 244, 83 S.Ct. 1119, and that the convictions for this reason must be reversed.

Petitioners are three Negroes and one white, college students. On September 17, 1960, at about 10:30 in the morning they entered the McCrory Five and Ten Cent Store in New Orleans, Louisiana. They sat down at a refreshment counter at the back of the store and requested service which was refused. Although no sign so indicated, the management operated the counter on a segregated basis, serving only white patrons. The counter was designed to accommodate 24 persons. Negroes were welcome to shop in other areas of the store. The restaurant manager, believing that the "unusual circumstance" of Negroes sitting at the counter created an "emergency," asked petitioners to leave and, when they did not do so, ordered that the counter be closed. The restaurant manager then contacted the store manager and called the police. He frankly testified that the petitioners did not cause any disturbance, that they were orderly, and that he asked them to leave because they were Negroes. Presumably he asked the white petitioner to leave because he was in the company of Negroes.

A number of police officers, including a captain and major of police, arrived at the store shortly after they were called. Three of the officers had a conference with the store manager. The store manager then went behind the counter, faced petitioners, and in a loud voice asked them to leave. He also testified that the petitioners were merely sitting quietly at the counter throughout these happenings. When petitioners remained seated, the police major spoke to petitioner Goldfinch, and asked him what they were doing there. Mr. Goldfinch replied that petitioners "were going to sit there until they were going to be served." When petitioners still declined to leave, they were arrested by the police, led out of the store, and taken away in a patrol wagon. They were later tried and convicted for violation of the Louisiana criminal mischief statute.[1] This statute, in its application to this case, has all the elements of the usual trespass statute. Each petitioner was sentenced to serve 60 days in the Parish Prison and to pay a fine of $350. In default of payment of the fine each is to serve 60 additional days in prison. On appeal to the Supreme Court of Louisiana the judgments of conviction were affirmed. *State* v. *Goldfinch*, 241 La. 958, 132 So.2d 860. Because of the substantial federal questions presented, we granted *certiorari.* 370 U.S. 935, 82 S.Ct. 1579, 8 L.Ed.2d 805.

Prior to this occurrence New Orleans city officials, characterizing conduct such as petitioners were arrested for as "sit-in demonstrations," had determined that such attempts to secure desegregated service, though orderly and possibly inoffensive to local merchants, would not be permitted.

Exactly one week earlier, on September 10, 1960, a like occurrence had taken place in a Woolworth store in the same city. In immediate reaction thereto the Superintendent of Police issued a highly publicized statement which discussed the incident and stated that "We wish to urge the parents of both white and Negro students who participated in today's sit-in demonstration to urge upon these young people that such actions are not in the community interest. . . . [W]e want everyone to fully understand that the police de-

---

1. LSA—Rev.Stat., 1950 (Cum. Supp. 1960), § 14:59(6), provides in pertinent part:

"Criminal mischief is the intentional performance of any of the following acts:

. . .

"(6) Taking temporary possession of any part or parts of a place of business, or remaining in a place of business after the person in charge of such business or portion of such business has ordered such person to leave the premises and to desist from the temporary possession of any part or parts of such business."

partment and its personnel is ready and able to enforce the laws of the city of New Orleans and the state of Louisiana." On September 13, four days before petitioners' arrest, the Mayor of New Orleans issued an unequivocal statement condemning such conduct and demanding its cessation. This statement was also widely publicized; it read in part:

"I have today directed the Superintendent of Police that no additional sit-in demonstrations . . . will be permitted . . . regardless of the avowed purpose or intent of the participants. . . .

. . .

"It is my determination that the community interest, the public safety, and the economic welfare of this city require that such demonstrations cease and that henceforth they be prohibited by the police department."

Both statements were publicized in the *New Orleans Times-Picayune*. The Mayor and the Superintendent of Police both testified that, to their knowledge, no eating establishment in New Orleans operated desegregated eating facilities.

Both the restaurant manager and the store manager asked the petitioners to leave. Petitioners were charged with failing to leave at the request of the store manager. There was evidence to indicate that the restaurant manager asked petitioners to leave in obedience to the directive of the city officials. He told them that "I am not allowed to serve you here. . . . We *have* to sell to you at the rear of the store where we have a colored counter." (Emphasis supplied.) And he called the police "[a]s a matter of routine procedure." The petitioners testified that when they did not leave, the restaurant manager whistled and the employees removed the stools, turned off the lights, and put up a sign saying that the counter was closed. One petitioner stated that "it appeared to be a very efficient thing, everyone knew what to do." The store manager conceded that his decision to operate a segregated facility "conform[ed] to state policy and practice" as well as local custom. When asked whether "in the last 30 days to 60 days [he had] entered into any conference with other department store managers here in New Orleans relative to sit-in problems," the store manager stated: "[w]e have spoken of it." The above evidence all tended to indicate that the store officials' actions were coerced by the city. But the evidence of coercion was not fully developed because the trial judge forbade petitioners to ask questions directed to that very issue.

But we need not pursue this inquiry further. A State, or a city, may act as authoritatively through its executive as through its legislative body. . . . As we interpret the New Orleans city officials' statements, they here determined that the city would not permit Negroes to seek desegregated service in restaurants. Consequently, the city must be treated exactly as if it had an ordinance prohibiting such conduct. We have just held in *Peterson* v. *City of Greenville*, 373 U.S. 244, 83 S.Ct. 1119,

that where an ordinance makes it unlawful for owners or managers of restaurants to seat whites and Negroes together, a conviction under the State's criminal processes employed in a way which enforces the discrimination mandated by that ordinance cannot stand. Equally the State cannot achieve the same result by an official command which has at least as much coercive effect as an ordinance. The official command here was to direct continuance of segregated service in restaurants, and to prohibit any conduct directed toward its discontinuance; it was not restricted solely to preserve the public peace in a nondiscriminatory fashion in a situation where violence was present or imminent by reason of public demonstrations. Therefore here, as in *Peterson*, these convictions, commanded as they were by the voice of the State directing segregated service at the restaurant, cannot stand. . . .
Reversed.

MR. JUSTICE DOUGLAS, *concurring.*

While I join the opinion of the Court, I have concluded it necessary to state with more particularity why Louisiana has become involved to a "significant extent" . . . in denying equal protection of the laws to petitioners.

I.

The court below based its affirmance of these convictions on the ground that the decision to segregate this restaurant was a private choice, uninfluenced by the officers of the State. . . . If this were an intrusion of a man's home or yard or farm or garden, the property owner could seek and obtain the aid of the State against the intruder. For the Bill of Rights, as applied to the States through the Due Process Clause of the Fourteenth Amendment, casts its weight on the side of the privacy of homes. The Third Amendment with its ban on the quartering of soldiers in private homes radiates that philosophy. The Fourth Amendment, while concerned with official invasions of privacy through searches and seizures, is eloquent testimony of the sanctity of private premises. For even when the police enter private precincts they must, with rare exceptions, come armed with a warrant issued by a magistrate. A private person has no standing to obtain even limited access. The principle that a man's home is his castle is basic to our system of jurisprudence.

But a restaurant, like the other departments of this retail store where Negroes were served, though private property within the protection of the Fifth Amendment, has no aura of constitutionally protected privacy about it. Access by the public is the very reason for its existence.

> "Ownership does not always mean absolute dominion. The more an owner, for his advantage, opens up his property for use by the public in general, the more do his rights become circumscribed by the statutory and constitutional rights of those who use it." *Marsh* v. *Alaba-*

ma, 326 U.S. 501, 506, 66 S.Ct. 276, 278, 90 L.Ed. 265.

The line between a private business and a public one has been long and hotly contested. . . .

Some of the cases reflect creative attempts by judges to make innkeepers, common carriers, and the like perform the public function of taking care of all travelers. Others involve the power of the legislature to impose various kinds of restraints or conditions on business. As a result of the conjunction of various forces, judicial and legislative, it came to pass that "A large province of industrial activity is under the joint control of the market and the state."

The present case would be on all fours with the earlier ones holding that a business may be regulated when it renders a service which "has become a public interest" . . . if Louisiana had declared, as do some States, that a business may not refuse service to a customer on account of race and the proprietor of the restaurant were charged with violating this statute. We should not await legislative action before declaring that state courts cannot enforce this type of segregation. Common-law judges fashioned the rules governing innkeepers and carriers. . . .

Judges who fashioned those rules had no written constitution as a guide. There were, to be sure, criminal statutes that regulated the common callings. But the civil remedies were judge-made. We live under a constitution that proclaims equal protection of the laws. That standard is our guide. . . . And under that standard business serving the public

cannot seek the aid of the state police or the state courts or the state legislatures to foist racial segregation in public places under its ownership and control. The constitutional protection extends only to "state" action, not to personal action. But we have "state" action here, wholly apart from the activity of the Mayor and police, for Louisiana has interceded with its judiciary to put criminal sanctions behind racial discrimination in public places. She may not do so consistently with the Equal Protection Clause of the Fourteenth Amendment.

The criminal penalty (60 days in jail and a $350 fine) was imposed on these petitioners by Louisiana's judiciary. That action of the judiciary was state action. Such are the holdings in *Shelley* v. *Kraemer,* 334 U.S. 1, 68 S.Ct. 836, 92 L.Ed. 1161, and *Barrows* v. *Jackson,* 346 U.S. 249, 73 S.Ct. 1031, 97 L.Ed. 1586. Those cases involved restrictive covenants. *Shelley* v. *Kraemer* was a civil suit to enjoin violation of a restrictive covenant by a Negro purchaser. *Barrows* v. *Jackson* was a suit to collect damages for violating a restrictive covenant by selling residential property to a Negro. Those cases, like the present one, were "property" cases. In those cases, as in the present one, the line was drawn at dealing with Negroes. There, as here, no state legislature was involved, only the state judiciary. The Court said in *Shelley* v. *Kraemer:*

> "That the action of state courts and of judicial officers in their official capacities is to be regarded as action of the State within the

meaning of the Fourteenth Amendment, is a proposition which has long been established by decisions of this Court.". . .

The list of instances where action of the state judiciary is state action within the meaning of the Fourteenth Amendment is a long one. Many were noted in *Shelley* v. *Kraemer,* . . . Most state convictions in violation of the First, Fourth, or Fifth Amendment, as incorporated in the Due Process Clause of the Fourteenth Amendment, have indeed implicated not the state legislature but the state judiciary, or the state judiciary and the state prosecutor and the state police. *Shelley* v. *Kraemer* —and later *Barrows* v. *Jackson*— held that the state judiciary, acting alone to enforce private discrimination against Negroes who desired to buy private property in residential areas, violated the Equal Protection Clause of the Fourteenth Amendment.

Places of public accommodation such as retail stores, restaurants, and the like render a "service which has become a public interest" . . . in the manner of the innkeepers and common carriers of old. The substance of the old common-law rules has no direct bearing on the decision required in this case. Restaurateurs and owners of other places of amusement and resort have never been subjected to the same duties as innkeepers and common carriers. But, what is important is that this whole body of law was a response to the felt needs of the times that spawned it. In our time the interdependence of people has greatly increased; the days of

laissez faire have largely disappeared; men are more and more dependent on their neighbors for services as well as for housing and the other necessities of life. By enforcing this criminal mischief statute, invoked in the manner now before us, the Louisiana courts are denying some people access to the mainstream of our highly interdependent life solely because of their race. Yet, "If there is any one purpose of the Fourteenth Amendment that is wholly outside the realm of doubt, it is that the Amendment was designed to bar States from denying to some groups, on account of their race or color, any rights, privileges, and opportunities accorded to other groups." . . .

An innkeeper or common carrier has always been allowed to exclude drunks, criminals and diseased persons, but only because the public's interest in protecting his and his guests' health in providing accommodations for this small group of travelers. . . . But surely *Shelley* v. *Kraemer, supra,* and *Barrows* v. *Jackson, supra,* show that the day has passed when an innkeeper, carrier, housing developer, or retailer can draw a racial line, refuse service to some on account of color, and obtain the aid of a State in enforcing his personal bias by sending outlawed customers to prison or exacting fines from them.

Business, such as this restaurant, is still private property. Yet there is hardly any private enterprise that does not feel the pinch of some public regulation—from price control, to health and fire inspection, to zoning, to safety measures, to minimum wages and working conditions, to unemployment insurance. When the doors of a business are open to the public, they must be open to all regardless of race if *apartheid* is not to become engrained in our public places. It cannot by reason of the Equal Protection Clause become so engrained with the aid of state courts, state legislatures, or state police.

II.

There is even greater reason to bar a State through its judiciary from throwing its weight on the side of racial discrimination in the present case, because we deal here with a place of public accommodation under license from the State. . . .

The nexus between the State and the private enterprise may be control, as in the case of a state agency. . . . Or the nexus may be one of numerous other devices. "State support of segregated schools through any arrangement, management, funds, or property cannot be squared"

with the Equal Protection Clause. . . . A state-assisted enterprise serving the public does not escape its constitutional duty to serve all customers irrespective of race, even though its actual operation is in the hands of a lessee. . . . State licensing and surveillance of a business serving the public also brings its service into the public domain. This restaurant needs a permit from Louisiana to operate;[14] and during the existence of the license the State has broad powers of visitation and control. This restaurant is thus an instrumentality of the State since the State charges it with duties to the public and supervises its performance. The State's interest in and activity with regard to its restaurants extends far beyond any mere income-producing licensing requirement.

There is no constitutional way, as I see it, in which a State can license and supervise a business serving the public and endow it with the authority to manage that business on the basis of *apartheid* which is foreign to our Constitution.

---

14. Under the provisions of Article 7.02 of the Sanitary Code, promulgated by the State Board of Health pursuant to LSA—Rev.Stat. § 40:11, no person shall operate a public eating place of any kind in the State of Louisiana unless he has been issued a permit to operate by the local health officer; and permits shall be issued only to persons whose establishments comply with the requirements of the Sanitary Code.

MR. JUSTICE HARLAN'S opinions in
PETERSON v. GREENVILLE, S.C. supra;
SHUTTLESWORTH v. BIRMINGHAM, supra;
and LOMBARD v. LOUISIANA, supra.

MR. JUSTICE HARLAN, *concurring in the result in* No. 71, *and dissenting in whole or in part in* Nos. 58, ..., *and* 67.

These . . . racial discrimination cases, . . . were argued together. . . . Each of these convictions rests on state court findings, which in my opinion are supported by evidence, that the several petitioners had refused to move from "white" lunch counters situated on the premises of privately owned department stores after having been duly requested to do so by the management. The other case involves the conviction of two Negro ministers for inciting, aiding, or abetting criminal trespasses in Alabama (*Shuttlesworth*, 373 U.S. 262, 83 S.Ct. 1138).

In deciding these cases the Court does not question the long-established rule that the Fourteenth Amendment reaches only state action. *Civil Rights Cases*, 109 U.S. 3, 3 S.Ct. 18, 27 L.Ed. 835. And it does not suggest that such action, denying equal protection, may be found in the mere enforcement of trespass laws in relation to private business establishments from which the management, of its own free will, has

chosen to exclude persons of the Negro race.[2] Judicial enforcement is of course state action, but this is not the end of the inquiry. The ultimate substantive question is whether there has been "[S]tate action of a particular character" . . .—whether the character of the State's involvement in an arbitrary discrimination is such that it should be held *responsible* for the discrimination.

This limitation on the scope of the prohibitions of the Fourteenth Amendment serves several vital functions in our system. Underlying the cases involving an alleged denial of equal protection by ostensibly private action is a clash of competing constitutional claims of a high order: liberty and equality. Freedom of the individual to chose his associates or his neighbors, to use and dispose of his property as he sees fit, to be irrational, arbitrary, capricious, even unjust in his personal relations are things all entitled to a large measure of protection from governmental interference. This liberty would be overridden, in the name of equality, if the strictures of the Amendment were applied to governmental and private action without distinction. Also inherent in the concept of state

---

2. It is not nor could it well be suggested that general admission of Negroes to the stores prevented the management from excluding them from service at the white lunch counters.

action are values of federalism, a recognition that there are areas of private rights upon which federal power should not lay a heavy hand and which should properly be left to the more precise instruments of local authority.

My differences with the Court relate primarily to its treatment of the state action issue and to the broad strides with which it has proceeded in setting aside the convictions in all of these cases. In my opinion the cases call for discrete treatment and results.

I.

The Peterson Case (No. 71).

In this case, involving the S. H. Kress store in Greenville, South Carolina, the Court finds state action in violation of the Fourteenth Amendment in the circumstance that Greenville still has on its books an ordinance, 373 U.S. 244, 83 S.Ct. 1119, requiring segregated facilities for colored and white persons in public eating places. It holds that the *mere existence* of the ordinance rendered the State's enforcement of its trespass laws unconstitutional, quite irrespective of whether the Kress decision to exclude these petitioners from the white lunch counter was actually influenced by the ordinance. The rationale is that the State, having compelled restaurateurs to segregate their establishments through this city ordinance, cannot be heard to say, in enforcing its trespass statute, that Kress' decision to segregate was in fact but the product of its own un-

trammelled choice. This is said to follow because the ordinance removes the operation of segregated or desegregated eating facilities "from the sphere of private choice" and because "the State's criminal processes are employed in a way which enforces" the ordinance. . . .

This is an alluring but, in my view, a fallacious proposition. Clearly Kress might have preferred for reasons entirely of its own not to serve meals to Negroes along with whites, and the dispositive question on the issue of state action thus becomes whether such was the case, or whether the ordinance played some part in the Kress decision to segregate. That is a question of fact.

Preliminarily, I do not understand the Court to suggest that the ordinance's removal of the right to operate a segregated restaurant "from the sphere of private choice" renders the private restaurant owner the agent of the State, such that his operation of a segregated facility *ipso facto* becomes the act of the State. Such a theory might well carry the consequence that a private person so operating his restaurant would be subject to a Civil Rights Act suit on the part of an excluded Negro for unconstitutional action taken under color of state law . . . —an incongruous result which I would be loath to infer that the Court intends. Kress is of course a purely private enterprise. It is in no sense "the repository of state power,". . . and this segregation ordinance no more makes Kress the agent or delegate of the State than would any other prohibitory measure affecting the conduct of its business. The Court does not intimate anything to the contrary.

The majority's approach to the state action issue is in my opinion quite untenable. Although the right of a private restaurateur to operate, if he pleases, on a segregated basis is ostensibly left untouched, the Court in truth effectually deprives him of that right in any State where a law like this Greenville ordinance continues to exist. For a choice that can be enforced only by resort to "self-help" has certainly become a greatly diluted right, if it has not indeed been totally destroyed.

An individual's right to restrict the use of his property, however unregenerate a particular exercise of that right may be thought, lies beyond the reach of the Fourteenth Amendment. The dilution or virtual elimination of that right cannot well be justified either on the premise that it will hasten formal repeal of outworn segregation laws or on the ground that it will facilitate proof of state action in cases of this kind. Those laws have already found their just constitutional deserts in the decisions of this Court, and in many communities in which racial discrimination is no longer a universal or widespread practice such laws may have a purely formal existence and may indeed be totally unknown. Of course this is not to say that their existence on the books may never play a significant and even decisive role in private decision-making. But the question in each case, if the right of the individual to make his own decisions is to remain viable, must

be: was the discriminatory exclusion in fact influenced by the law? . . . The inexorable rule which the Court lays down reflects insufficient reckoning with the demands of history.

It is suggested that requiring proof of the effect of such laws in individual instances would involve "attempting to separate the mental urges of the discriminators", . . . But proof of state of mind is not a novel concept in the law of evidence, see 2 *Wigmore, Evidence* (3d ed. 1940), §§ 385–393, and such a requirement presents no special barriers in this situation. The mere showing of such an ordinance would, in my judgment, make out a *prima facie* case of invalid state action, casting on the State the burden of proving that the exclusion was in fact the product solely of private choice. In circumstances like these that burden is indeed a heavy one. This is the rule which, in my opinion, even-handed constitutional doctrine and recognized evidentiary rules dictate. Its application here calls for reversal of these convictions.

At the trial existence of the Greenville segregation ordinance was shown and the city adduced no rebutting evidence indicating that the Kress manager's decision to exclude these petitioners from the white lunch counter was wholly the product of private choice. All doubt on that score is indeed removed by the store manager's own testimony. Asked for the reasons for his action, he said: "It's contrary to local custom *and* it's also the ordinance that has been discussed" (quite evidently referring to the segregation ordinance). (Emphasis added.) This suffices to establish state action, and leads me to join in the judgment of the Court.

II.

The Lombard Case (No. 58).

In this case, involving "sit-ins" at the McCrory store in New Orleans, Louisiana, the Court carries its state action rule a step further. Neither Louisiana nor New Orleans has any statute or ordinance requiring segregated eating facilities. In this instance state action is found in the public announcements of the Superintendent of Police and the Mayor of New Orleans, set forth in the Court's opinion, 373 U.S. 267, 83 S.Ct. 1119, which were issued shortly after "sit-in" demonstrations had first begun in the city. Treating these announcements as the equivalent of a city ordinance, the Court holds that they served to make the State's employment of its "trespass" statute against these petitioners unconstitutional, again without regard to whether or not their exclusion by McCrory was in fact influenced in any way by these announcements.

In addition to what has already been said in criticism of the *Peterson* ruling, there are two further factors that make the Court's theory even more untenable in this case.

1. The announcements of the Police Superintendent and the Mayor cannot well be compared with a city ordinance commanding segregated eating facilities. Neither announcement was addressed to restaurateurs in particular, but to the citizenry generally. They did not press private proprietors to segregate eating facilities; rather they in effect simply urged Negroes and whites not to insist on nonsegregated service in places where segregated service obtained. In short, so far as this record shows, had the McCrory store chosen to serve these petitioners along with whites it could have done so free of any sanctions or official constraint.

2. The Court seems to take the two announcements as an attempt on the part of the Police Superintendent and the Mayor to perpetuate segregation in New Orleans. I think they are more properly read as an effort by these two officials to preserve the peace in what they might reasonably have regarded as a highly charged atmosphere. That seems to me the fair tenor of their exhortations.

If there were nothing more to this case, I would vote to affirm these convictions for want of a sufficient showing of state action denying equal protection. There is, however, some evidence in the record which might indicate advance collaboration between the police and McCrory with respect to these episodes. The trial judge refused to permit defense counsel to pursue inquiry along this line, although counsel had made it perfectly clear that his purpose was to establish official participation in the exclusion of his clients by the McCrory store. I think the shutting off of this line of inquiry was prejudicial error.

For this reason I would vacate the judgment of the state court and remand the case for a new trial so that the issue of state action may be properly explored.

.　　.　　.

V.

The Shuttlesworth Case (No. 67).

This last of these cases concerns the Alabama convictions of two Negro clergymen, Shuttlesworth and Billups, for inciting, aiding, or abetting alleged violations of the criminal trespass ordinance of the City of Birmingham.

On the premise that these two petitioners were charged with inciting, aiding, or abetting only the "sit-ins" involved in the *Gober* case, . . . the Court, relying on the unassailable proposition that "there can be no conviction for aiding and abetting someone to do an innocent act", . . . holds that these convictions must fall in consequence of its reversal of those in the *Gober* case. The difficulty with this holding is that it is based on an erroneous premise. Shuttlesworth and Billups were not charged *merely* with inciting the

Gober "sit-ins" but *generally* with inciting violations of the Birmingham trespass ordinance. And I do not think it can be said that the record lacks evidence of incitement of "sit-ins" other than those involved in *Gober*.[9] Hence the Court's reversal in *Gober* cannot well serve as the ground for reversal here.

There are, however, other reasons why, in my opinion, these convictions cannot stand. As to Billups, the record shows that he brought one of the students to Shuttlesworth's home and remained there while Shuttlesworth talked. But there is nothing to indicate Billups' purpose in bringing the student, what he said to him, or even whether he approved or disapproved of what Shuttlesworth urged the students to do. A conviction so lacking in evidence to support the offense charged must fall under the Fourteenth Amendment. . . .

On this score the situation is different with respect to Shuttlesworth. Given (1) the then current prevalence of "sit-in" demonstrations throughout the South, (2) the commonly understood use of the phrase "sit-in" or "sit-down" to designate

---

9. At the trial testimony was introduced showing that Gober and Davis (two of the 10 defendants in the *Gober* case), as well as "other persons" who "were present . . . in the Court room" when the defendants in the *Gober* case were tried for trespass, attended the meeting at Shuttlesworth's house. There was also testimony that "other boys who attended the meeting" participated in "sit-ins" in Birmingham on the same day that the *Gober* "sit-ins" occurred. The record does not reveal whether the *Gober* defendants were the *only* persons who participated in the "sit-ins," nor whether there were others who were incited by Shuttlesworth but who did not thereafter take part in "sit-in" demonstrations. The trial court's statement that "you have here the ten students and the Court thinks they were misused and misled into a violation of a City Ordinance" was made in the course of sentencing the *Gober* defendants, not Shuttlesworth or Billups (the trials of both of these groups of defendants having been conducted *seriatim* by the same judge, who reserved sentencing until all trials had been completed). It was in no sense a finding of fact with respect to the crimes with which Shuttlesworth and Billups had been charged.

a form of protest which typically resulted in arrest and conviction for criminal trespass or other similar offense, and (3) the evidence as to Shuttlesworth's calling for "sit-down" volunteers and his statement that he would get any who volunteered "out of jail," I cannot say that it was constitutionally impermissible for the State to find that Shuttlesworth had urged the volunteers to demonstrate on privately owned premises despite any objections by their owners, and thus to engage in criminal trespass.

Nevertheless this does not end the matter. The trespasses which Shuttlesworth was convicted of inciting may or may not have involved denials of equal protection, depending on the event of the "state action" issue. Certainly one may not be convicted for inciting conduct which is not itself constitutionally punishable. And dealing as we are in the realm of expression, I do not think a State may punish incitement of activity in circumstances where there is a substantial likelihood that such activity may be constitutionally protected.

. . . To ignore that factor would unduly inhibit freedom of expression, even though criminal liability for incitement does not ordinarily depend upon the event of the conduct incited.

Were I able to agree with the Court that the existence of the Birmingham segregation ordinance without more rendered all incited trespasses in Birmingham immune from prosecution, I think outright reversal of Shuttlesworth's conviction would be called for. But because of my different views as to the significance of such ordinances I believe that the bearing of this Birmingham ordinance on the issue of "substantiality" in Shuttlesworth's case, no less than its bearing on "state action" in the *Gober* case, involves questions of fact which must first be determined by the state courts. I would therefore vacate the judgment as to Shuttlesworth and remand his case for a new trial.

These then are the results in these cases which in my view sound legal principles require.

QUESTIONS

1. Why shouldn't a restaurant owner have the right to serve whomever he chooses in his restaurant? It's his property isn't it?

2. Can laws be successfully used to change the racial attitudes of people in the United States? Can the state legislate racial morality?

3. Is it the state's proper function to legislate racial morality?

4. How does Justice Douglas differentiate between private property, such as a home, and private property used as a restaurant?

5. If you are required by law to serve someone in your restaurant isn't that law requiring you to engage in "involuntary servitude" in violation of the Thirteenth Amendment? Why yes? Why no?

AMALGAMATED FOOD EMPLOYEES v. LOGAN VALLEY PLAZA

391 U.S. 308; 88 S. Ct. 1601; 20 L.Ed. 2d 603 (1968)

MR. JUSTICE MARSHALL *delivered the opinion of the Court.*

This case presents the question whether peaceful picketing of a business enterprise located within a shopping center can be enjoined on the ground that it constitutes an unconsented invasion of the property rights of the owners of the land on which the center is situated. We granted *certiorari* to consider petitioners' contentions that the decisions of the state courts enjoining their picketing as a trespass are violative of their rights under the First and Fourteenth Amendments of the United States Constitution. 389 U.S. 911, 88 S.Ct. 240, 19 L.Ed.2d 258 (1967). We reverse.

Logan Valley Plaza, Inc. (Logan), one of the two respondents herein, owns a large, newly developed shopping center complex, known as the Logan Valley Mall, located near the City of Altoona, Pennsylvania. The shopping center is situated at the intersection of Plank Road, which is on the east of the center, and Good's Lane, which is to the south. Plank Road, also known as U.S. Route 220, is a heavily traveled highway along which traffic moves at a fairly high rate of speed. There are five entrance roads into the center, three from Plank Road and two from Good's Lane. Aside from these five entrances, the shopping center is totally separated from the adjoining roads by earthen berms. The berms are 15 feet wide along Good's Lane and 12 feet wide along Plank Road.

At the time of the events in this case, Logan Valley Mall was occupied by two businesses, Weis Markets, Inc. (Weis), the other respondent herein, and Sears, Roebuck and Co. (Sears), although other enterprises were then expected and have since moved into the center. Weis operates a supermarket and Sears operates both a department store and an automobile service center. The Weis property consists of the enclosed supermarket building, an open but covered porch along the front of the building, and an approximately five-foot wide parcel pickup zone that runs 30 to 40 feet along the porch. The porch functions as a sidewalk in front of the building and the pickup zone is used as a temporary parking place for the loading of purchases into customers' cars by Weis employees.

Between the Weis building and the highway berms are extensive macadam parking lots with parking spaces and driveways lined off thereon. These areas, to which Logan retains title, provide common parking facilities for all the businesses in the shopping center. The distance across the parking lots to the Weis store from the entrances on Good's

Lane is approximately 350 feet and from the entrances on Plank Road approximately 400 to 500 feet. The entrance on Plank Road furthest from the Weis property is the main entrance to the shopping center as a whole and is regularly used by customers of Weis. The entrance on Plank Road nearest to Weis is almost exclusively used by patrons of the Sears automobile service station into which it leads directly.

On December 8, 1965, Weis opened for business, employing a wholly nonunion staff of employees. A few days after it opened for business, Weis posted a sign on the exterior of its building prohibiting trespassing or soliciting by anyone other than its employees on its porch or parking lot. On December 17, 1965, members of Amalgamated Food Employees Union, Local 590 began picketing Weis. They carried signs stating that the Weis market was nonunion and that its employees were not "receiving union wages or other benefits." The pickets did not include any employees of Weis, but rather were all employees of competitors of Weis. The picketing continued until December 27, during which time the number of picketers varied between four and 13 and averaged around six. The picketing was carried out almost entirely in the parcel pickup area and that portion of the parking lot immediately

adjacent thereto. Although some congestion of the parcel pickup area occurred, such congestion was sporadic and infrequent. The picketing was peaceful at all times and unaccompanied by either threats or violence.

On December 27, Weis and Logan instituted an action in equity in the Court of Common Pleas of Blair County, and that court immediately issued an *ex parte* order enjoining petitioners from, *inter alia*, "picketing and trespassing upon . . . the [Weis] storeroom, porch and parcel pick-up area . . . [and] the [Logan] parking area and entrances and exits leading to said parking area."[4] The effect of this order was to require that all picketing be carried on along the berms beside the public roads outside the shopping center. Picketing continued along the berms and, in addition, handbills asking the public not to patronize Weis because it was nonunion were distributed, while petitioners contested the validity of the *ex parte* injunction. After an evidentiary hearing, which resulted in the establishment of the facts set forth above, the Court of Common Pleas continued indefinitely its original *ex parte* injunction without modification.

That court explicitly rejected petitioners' claim under the First Amendment that they were entitled to picket within the confines of the

---

4. The court also enjoined petitioners from blocking access by anyone to respondents' premises, making any threats or using any violence against customers, employees, and suppliers of Weis, and physically interfering with the performance by Weis employees of their duties. Petitioners make no challenge to these parts of the order

and it appears conceded that there has been no subsequent picketing by petitioners in violation of these provisions. A portion of the order also directs that no more than "— pickets" be used at any one time, but no number has ever been inserted into the blank space and thus no limitation appears to have ever been imposed.

shopping center, and their contention that the suit was within the primary jurisdiction of the NLRB. The trial judge held that the injunction was justified both in order to protect respondents' property rights and because the picketing was unlawfully aimed at coercing Weis to compel its employees to join a union. On appeal the Pennsylvania Supreme Court, with three Justices dissenting, affirmed the issuance of the injunction on the sole ground that petitioners' conduct constituted a trespass on respondents' property.

We start from the premise that peaceful picketing carried on in a location open generally to the public is, absent other factors involving the purpose or manner of the picketing, protected by the First Amendment. . . . To be sure, this Court has noted that picketing involves elements of both speech and conduct, i.e., patrolling, and has indicated that because of this intermingling of protected and unprotected elements, picketing can be subjected to controls that would not be constitutionally permissible in the case of pure speech. . . . Nevertheless, no case decided by this Court can be found to support the proposition that the non-speech aspects of peaceful picketing are so great as to render the provisions of the First Amendment inapplicable to it altogether.

The majority of the cases from this Court relied on by respondents, in support of their contention that picketing can be subjected to a blanket prohibition in some instances by the States, involved picketing that was found either to have been directed at an illegal end, . . . or to have been directed to coercing a decision by an employer which, although in itself legal, could validly be required by the State to be left to the employer's free choice, . . .

Those cases are not applicable here because they all turned on the purpose for which the picketing was carried on, not its location. In this case the Pennsylvania Supreme Court specifically disavowed reliance on the finding of unlawful purpose on which the trial court alternatively based its issuance of the injunction. It did emphasize that the pickets were not employees of Weis and were discouraging the public from patronizing the Weis market. . . .

The case squarely presents, therefore, the question whether Pennsylvania's generally valid rules against trespass to private property can be applied in these circumstances to bar petitioners from the Weis and Logan premises. It is clear that if the shopping center premises were not privately owned but instead constituted the business area of a municipality, which they to a large extent resemble, petitioners could not be barred from exercising their First Amendment rights there on the sole ground that title to the property was in the municipality. *Lovell* v. *City of Griffin*, 303 U.S. 444, 58 S.Ct. 666, 82 L.Ed. 949 (1938); *Hague* v. *CIO*, 307 U.S. 496, 59 S.Ct. 954, 83 L.Ed. 1423 (1939); *Schneider* v. *State of New Jersey*, 308 U.S. 147, 60 S.Ct. 146, 84 L.Ed. 155 (1939); *Jamison* v. *State of Texas*, 318 U.S. 413, 63 S.Ct. 669, 87 L.Ed. 869 (1943). The essence of those opinions is that streets, sidewalks, parks, and other similar public places are so historically associated with the exercise of First Amendment rights that access to them for the purpose of exercising such rights cannot constitutionally be denied broadly and absolutely.

The fact that *Lovell, Schneider,* and *Jamison* were concerned with handbilling rather than picketing is immaterial so far as the question is solely one of right of access for the purpose of expression of views. Handbilling, like picketing, involves conduct other than speech, namely, the physical presence of the person distributing leaflets on municipal property. If title to municipal property is, standing alone, an insufficient basis for prohibiting all entry onto such property for the purpose of distributing printed matter, it is likewise an insufficient basis for prohibiting all entry for the purpose of carrying an informational placard. While the patrolling involved in picketing may in some cases constitute an interference with the use of public property greater than that produced by handbilling, it is clear that in other cases the converse may be true. Obviously, a few persons walking slowly back and forth holding placards can be less obstructive of, for example, a public sidewalk than numerous persons milling around handing out leaflets. That the manner in which handbilling, or picketing, is carried out may be regulated does not mean that either can be barred under all circumstances on publicly owned property simply by recourse to traditional concepts of property law concerning the incidents of ownership of real property.

This Court has also held, in *Marsh v. State of Alabama,* 326 U.S. 501,

66 S.Ct. 276, 90 L.Ed. 265 (1946), that under some circumstances property that is privately owned may, at least for First Amendment purposes, be treated as though it were publicly held. In *Marsh,* the appellant, a Jehovah's Witness, had undertaken to distribute religious literature on a sidewalk in the business district of Chickasaw, Alabama. Chickasaw, a so-called company town, was wholly owned by the Gulf Shipbuilding Corporation. "The property consists of residential buildings, streets, a system of sewers, a sewage disposal plant and a 'business block' on which business places are situated. . . . In short the town and its shopping district are accessible to and freely used by the public in general and there is nothing to distinguish them from any other town and shopping center except the fact that the title to the property belongs to a private corporation." . . .

.   .   .

The similarities between the business block in *Marsh* and the shopping center in the present case are striking. The perimeter of Logan Valley Mall is a little less than 1.1 miles. Inside the mall were situated, at the time of trial, two substantial commercial enterprises with numerous others soon to follow. . . . The general public has unrestricted access to the mall property. The shopping center here is clearly the functional equivalent to the business district of Chickasaw involved in *Marsh.*

It is true that, unlike the corporation in *Marsh* the respondents here do not own the surrounding residential property and do not provide municipal services therefore. Presumably, petitioners are free to canvass the neighborhood with their message about the nonunion status of Weis Market, just as they have been permitted by the state courts to picket on the berms outside the mall. Thus, unlike the situation in *Marsh*, there is no power on respondents' part to have petitioners totally denied access to the community for which the mall serves as a business district. This fact, however, is not determinative. In *Marsh* itself the precise issue presented was whether the appellant therein had the right, under the First Amendment, to pass out leaflets in the business district, since there was no showing made there that the corporate owner would have sought to prevent the distribution of leaflets in the residential areas of the town. . . .

We see no reason why access to a business district in a company town for the purpose of exercising First Amendment rights should be constitutionally required, while access for the same purpose to property functioning as a business district should be limited simply because the property surrounding the "business district" is not under the same ownership. . . . The shopping center premises are open to the public to the same extent as the commercial center of a normal town. So far as can be determined, the main distinction in practice between use by the public of the Logan Valley Mall and of any other business district, were the decisions of the state courts to stand, would be that those members of the general public who sought to use the mall premises in a manner

contrary to the wishes of the respondents could be prevented from so doing.

Such a power on the part of respondents would be, of course, part and parcel of the rights traditionally associated with ownership of private property. And it may well be that respondents' ownership of the property here in question gives them various rights, under the laws of Pennsylvania, to limit the use of that property by members of the public in a manner that would not be permissible were the property owned by a municipality. All we decide here is that because the shopping center serves as the community business block "and is freely accessible and open to the people in the area and those passing through," *Marsh* v. *State of Alabama*, 326 U.S., at 508, 66 S.Ct. at 279, the State may not delegate the power, through the use of its trespass laws, wholly to exclude those members of the public wishing to exercise their First Amendment rights on the premises in a manner and for a purpose generally consonant with the use to which the property is actually put.

We do not hold that respondents, and at their behest the State, are without power to make reasonable regulations governing the exercise of First Amendment rights on their property. Certainly their rights to make such regulations are at the very least co-extensive with the powers possessed by States and municipalities, and recognized in many opinions of this Court, to control the use of public property. Thus where property is not ordinarily open to the public, this Court has held that access to it for the purpose of exercising First Amendment rights may be denied altogether. . . . Even where municipal or state property is open to the public generally, the exercise of First Amendment rights may be regulated so as to prevent interference with the use to which the property is ordinarily put by the State. Thus we have upheld a statute prohibiting picketing "in such a manner as to obstruct or unreasonably to interfere with free ingress or egress to and from any . . . county . . . courthouses." . . . Likewise it has been indicated that persons could be constitutionally prohibited from picketing "in or near" a court "with the intent of interfering with, obstructing, or impeding the administration of justice." . . .

In addition, the exercise of First Amendment rights may be regulated where such exercise will unduly interfere with the normal use of the public property by other members of the public with an equal right of access to it. Thus it has been held that persons desiring to parade along city streets may be required to secure a permit in order that municipal authorities be able to limit the amount of interference with use of the sidewalks by other members of the public by regulating the time, place, and manner of the parade. . . .

. . . Respondents seek to defend the injunction they have obtained by characterizing the requirement that picketing to be carried on outside the Logan Mall premises as a regulation rather than a suppression of it. Accepting *arguendo* such a characterization, the question remains, under the First Amendment, whether it is a permissible regulation.

Petitioners' picketing was directed solely at one establishment within the shopping center. The berms surrounding the center are from 350 to 500 feet away from the Weis store. All entry onto the mall premises by customers of Weis, so far as appears, is by vehicle from the roads along which the berms run. Thus the placards bearing the message which petitioners seek to communicate to patrons of Weis must be read by those to whom they are directed either at a distance so great as to render them virtually indecipherable—where the Weis customers are already within the mall—or while the prospective reader is moving by car from the roads onto the mall parking areas via the entrance ways cut through the berms. In addition, the pickets are placed in some danger by being forced to walk along heavily traveled roads along which traffic moves constantly at rates of speed varying from moderate to high. Likewise, the task of distributing handbills to persons in moving automobiles is vastly greater (and more hazardous) than it would be were petitioners permitted to pass them out within the mall to pedestrians. Finally, the requirement that the picketing take place outside the shopping center renders it very difficult for petitioners to limit its effect to Weis only.

It is therefore clear that the restraints on picketing and trespassing approved by the Pennsylvania courts here substantially hinder the communication of the ideas which petitioners seek to express to the patrons of Weis. . . . As we observed earlier, the mere fact that speech is accompanied by conduct does not mean that the speech can be suppressed under the guise of prohibiting the conduct. Here it is perfectly clear that a prohibition against trespass on the mall operates to bar all speech within the shopping center to which respondents object. Yet this Court stated many years ago, "[O]ne is not to have the exercise of his liberty of expression in appropriate places abridged on the plea that it may be exercised in some other place." *Schneider* v. *State of New Jersey*, 308 U.S. 147, 163, 60 S.Ct. 146, 151 (1939).

The sole justification offered for the substantial interference with the effectiveness of petitioners' exercise of their First Amendment rights to promulgate their views through handbilling and picketing is respondents' claimed absolute right under state law to prohibit any use of their property by others without their consent. However, unlike a situation involving a person's home, no meaningful claim to protection of a right of privacy can be advanced by respondents here. Nor on the facts of the case can any significant claim to protection of the normal business operation of the property be raised. Naked title is essentially all that is at issue.

The economic development of the United States in the last 20 years reinforces our opinion of the correctness of the approach taken in *Marsh*. The large-scale movement of this country's population from the cities to the suburbs has been accompanied by the advent of the suburban shopping center, typically a cluster of individual retail units on a single large privately owned tract. It has been estimated that by the end of 1966 there were between 10,000 and 11,000 shopping centers in the United States and Canada, accounting for approximately 37% of the total retail sales in those two countries.

These figures illustrate the substantial consequences for workers seeking to challenge substandard working conditions, consumers protesting shoddy or overpriced merchandise, and minority groups seeking nondiscriminatory hiring policies that a contrary decision here would have. Business enterprises located in downtown areas would be subject to on-the-spot public criticism for their practices, but businesses situated in the suburbs could largely immunize themselves from similar criticism by creating a *cordon sanitaire* of parking lots around their stores. Neither precedent nor policy compels a result so at variance with the goal of free expression and communication that is the heart of the First Amendment.

Therefore, as to the sufficiency of respondents' ownership of the Logan Valley Mall premises as the sole support of the injunction issued against petitioners, we simply repeat what was said in *Marsh* v. *State of Alabama*, . . . "Ownership does not always mean absolute dominion. The more an owner, for his advantage, opens up his property for use by the public in general, the more do his rights become circumscribed by the statutory and constitutional rights of those who use it." Logan Valley Mall is the functional equivalent of a "business block" and for First Amendment purposes must be treated in substantially the same manner.

The judgment of the Supreme

Court of Pennsylvania is reversed and the case is remanded for further proceedings not inconsistent with this opinion. It is so ordered.

MR. JUSTICE DOUGLAS, *concurring.*

Picketing on the public walkways and parking area in respondents' shopping center presents a totally different question from an invasion of one's home or place of business. While Logan Valley Mall is not dedicated to public use to the degree of the "company town" in *Marsh* v. *State of Alabama*, . . . it is clear that respondents have opened the shopping center to public uses. They hold out the mall as "public" for purposes of attracting customers and facilitating delivery of merchandise. Picketing in regard to labor conditions at the Weis Supermarket is directly related to that shopping center business. Why should respondents be permitted to avoid this incidence of carrying on a public business in the name of "private property"? It is clear to me that they may not, when the public activity sought to be prohibited involves constitutionally protected expression respecting their business.

Picketing is free speech *plus*, the *plus* being physical activity that may implicate traffic and related matters. Hence the latter aspects of picketing may be regulated. . . . Thus, the provisions of the injunction in this case which prohibit the picketers from interfering with employees, deliv-

erymen, and customers are proper. It is said that the picketers may be banished to the publicly owned berms, several hundred feet from the target of their criticism. But that is to make "private property" a sanctuary from which some members of the public may be excluded merely because of the ideas they espouse. Logan Valley Mall covers several acres and the number of picketers at any time has been small. The courts of Pennsylvania are surely capable of fashioning a decree that will ensure noninterference with customers and employees, while enabling the union members to assemble sufficiently close to Weis' market to make effective the exercise of their First Amendment rights.

MR. JUSTICE BLACK, *dissenting.*

While I generally accept the factual background of this case presented in the Court's opinion, I think it is important to focus on just where this picketing, which was enjoined by the state courts, was actually taking place. The following extract is taken from the trial court's "Findings of Fact":[1]

"(7) . . .

"(a) small groups of men and women wearing placards . . . walked back and forth in front of the Weis supermarket, more particularly *in the pick-up zone* adjacent to the covered porch [emphasis added];

"(b) occasional picketing as

1. This appears in the opinion of the Court of Common Pleas of Blair County, Pennsylvania, dated February 14, 1966, and unreported.

above described has taken place *on the covered porch itself* [emphasis added]";

Respondent Weis Markets, Inc., the owner-occupant of the supermarket here being picketed, owns the real property on which it constructed its store, porch, and parcel pick-up zone. Respondent Logan Valley Plaza, Inc., owns the other property in the shopping center, including the large area which has been paved and marked off as a general parking lot for customers of the shopping center.

Anyone familiar with the operations of a modern-day supermarket knows the importance of the so-called "pick-up zone"—an area where the frequently numerous bags of groceries bought in the store can be loaded conveniently into the customers' cars. The phenomenon of the supermarket combined with widespread ownership of automobiles and refrigeration facilities has made the purchase of large quantities of groceries on a single shopping trip a common occurrence in this country. And in line with this trend the stores have had to furnish adequate loading areas and facilities including in many instances, such as here for example, extra employees to assist in loading customers' cars. . . .

It seems clear to me, in light of the customary way that supermarkets now must operate, that pick-up zones are as much a part of these stores as the inside counters where customers select their goods or the check-out and bagging sections where the goods are paid for. I cannot conceive how such a pick-up zone, even by the wildest stretching of *Marsh*

v. State of Alabama, . . . could ever be considered dedicated to the public or to pickets. The very first section of the injunction issued by the trial court in this case recognizes this fact and is aimed only at protecting this clearly private property from trespass by the pickets. Thus the order of the court separately enjoins petitioners from:

"(a) Picketing and trespassing upon the private property of the plaintiff Weis Markets, Inc., Store No. 40, located at Logan Valley Mall, Altoona, Pennsylvania, including as such private property the storeroom, porch and parcel pick-up area."

While there is language in the majority opinion which indicates that the state courts may still regulate picketing on respondent Weis' private property, this is not sufficient. I think that this Court should declare unequivocally that Section (a) of the lower court's injunction is valid under the First Amendment and that petitioners cannot, under the guise of exercising First Amendment rights, trespass on respondent Weis' private property for the purpose of picketing. It would be just as sensible for this Court to allow the pickets to stand on the check-out counters, thus interfering with customers who wish to pay for their goods, as it is to approve picketing in the pick-up zone which interferes with customers' loading of their cars. . . .

I would go further, however, and hold that the entire injunction is valid. With the exception of the

Weis property mentioned above, the land on which this shopping center (composed of only two stores at the time of trial and approximately 17 now) is located is owned by respondent Logan Valley Plaza, Inc. Logan has improved its property by putting shops and parking spaces thereon for the use of business customers. Now petitioners contend that they can come onto Logan's property for the purpose of picketing and refuse to leave when asked, and that Logan cannot use state trespass laws to keep them out. The majority of this Court affirms petitioners' contentions. But I cannot accept them, for I believe that whether this Court likes it or not the Constitution recognizes and supports the concept of private ownership of property. The Fifth Amendment provides that "no person shall . . . be deprived of life, liberty, or property, without due process of law; nor shall private property be taken for public use, without just compensation." This means to me that there is no right to picket on the private premises of another to try to convert the owner or others to the views of the pickets. It also means, I think, that if this Court is going to arrogate to itself the power to act as the Government's agent to take a part of Weis' property to give to the pickets for their use, the Court should also award Weis just compensation for the property taken.

In affirming petitioners' contentions the majority opinion relies on *Marsh* v. *State of Alabama, supra,* and holds that respondents' property has been transformed to some type of public property. But *Marsh* was never intended to apply to this kind of situation. *Marsh* dealt with the very special situation of a company-owned town, complete with streets, alleys, sewers, stores, residences, and everything else that goes to make a town. . . . Again toward the end of the opinion we emphasized that "the town of Chickasaw does not function differently from any other town." 326 U.S., at 508, 66 S.Ct. at 279. I think it is fair to say that the basis on which the *Marsh* decision rested was that the property involved encompassed an area that for all practical purposes had been turned into a town; the area had all the attributes of a town and was indistinguishable from any other town in Alabama. I can find very little resemblance between the shopping center involved in this case and Chickasaw, Alabama. There are no homes, there is no sewage disposal plant, there is not even a post office on this private property which the Court now considers the equivalent of a "town."[5] . . . All I can say is that this sounds like a very strange "town" to me.

. . .

In allowing the trespass here, the majority opinion indicates that Weis and Logan invited the public to the shopping center's parking lot. This statement is contrary to common sense. Of course there was an implicit invitation for customers of the ad-

---

5. In *Marsh* v. *State of Alabama, supra,* a deputy of the Mobile Sheriff, paid by the company, served as the town's police-man. We are not told whether the Logan Valley Plaza shopping center had its own policeman.

jacent stores to come and use the marked off places for cars. But the whole public was no more wanted there than they would be invited to park free at a pay parking lot. Is a store owner or several of them together less entitled to have a parking lot set aside for customers than other property owners? To hold that store owners are compelled by law to supply picketing areas for pickets to drive store customers away is to create a court-made law wholly disregarding the constitutional basis on which private ownership of property rests in this country. And of course picketing, that is patroling, is not free speech and not protected as such. . . . These pickets do have a constitutional right to speak about Weis' refusal to hire union labor, but they do not have a constitutional right to compel Weis to furnish them a place to do so on his property. . . .

For these reasons I respectfully dissent.*

MR. JUSTICE WHITE, *dissenting.*

The reason why labor unions may normally picket a place of business is that the picketing occurs on public streets which are available to all members of the public for a variety of purposes that include communication with other members of the public. The employer businessman cannot interfere with the pickets' communication because they have as much right to the sidewalk and street as he does and because the labor laws prevent such interference under various circumstances; the Government may not interfere on his behalf, absent obstruction, violence, or other

valid statutory justification, because the First Amendment forbids official abridgment of the right of free speech.

In *Marsh* v. *State of Alabama*, . . . the company town was found to have all of the attributes of a state-created municipality and the company was found effectively to be exercising official power as a delegate of the State. In the context of that case, the streets of the company town were as available and as dedicated to public purposes as the streets of an ordinary town. The company owner stood in the shoes of the State in attempting to prevent the streets from being used as public streets are normally used.

The situation here is starkly different. As MR. JUSTICE BLACK so clearly shows, Logan Valley Plaza is not a town but only a collection of stores. In no sense are any parts of the shopping center dedicated to the public for general purposes or the occupants of the Plaza exercising official powers. The public is invited to the premises but only in order to do business with those who maintain establishments there. The invitation is to shop for the products which are sold. There is no general invitation to use the parking lot, the pick-up zone, or the sidewalk except as an adjunct to shopping. No one is invited to use the parking lot as a place to park his car while he goes elsewhere to work. The driveways and lanes for auto traffic are not offered for use as general thoroughfares leading from one public street

*[Editor's Note: The dissenting opinion of MR. JUSTICE HARLAN is omitted.]

to another. Those driveways and parking spaces are not public streets and thus available for parades, public meetings, or other activities for which public streets are used. . . . Even if the Plaza has some aspects of "public" property, it is nevertheless true that some public property is available for some uses and not for others; some public property is neither designed nor dedicated for use by pickets or for other communicative activities. . . . The point is that whether Logan Valley Plaza is public or private property, it is a place for shopping and not a place for picketing.

The most that can be said is that here the public was invited to shop, that except for their location in the shopping center development the stores would have fronted on public streets and sidewalks, and that the shopping center occupied a large area. But on this premise the parking lot, sidewalks, and driveways would be available for all those activities which are usually permitted on public streets. . . .

. . .

It is not clear how the Court might draw a line between "shopping centers" and other business establishments which have sidewalks or parking on their own property. Any store invites the patronage of members of the public interested in its products. I am fearful that the Court's decision today will be a license for pickets to leave the public streets and carry out their activities on private property, as long as they are not obstructive. I do not agree that when the owner of private property invites the public to do business with him he impliedly dedicates his property for other uses as well. I do not think the First Amendment, which bars only official interferences with speech, has this reach. In *Marsh*, the company ran an entire town and the State was deemed to have devolved upon the company the task of carrying out municipal functions. But here the "streets" of Logan Valley Plaza are not like public streets; they are not used as thoroughfares for general travel from point to point, for general parking, for meetings, or for Easter parades.

If it were shown that Congress has thought it necessary to permit picketing on private property, either to further the national labor policy under the Commerce Clause or to implement and enforce the First Amendment, we would have quite a different case. But that is not the basis on which the Court proceeds, and I therefore dissent.

QUESTIONS

1. What justification can you advance for protecting one right (picketing) at the expense of another (private property)? Do you think the priorities of importance should be reversed? Why yes? Why no?

2. Using the majority opinion's reasoning, do you think the Court would uphold the right of the union employees to picket on the front lawn of the

manager's home? Why yes? Why not? Aren't both pieces of land privately owned?

3. What if a man has a shop in his home, do you think the majority would allow picketing by his employees on his front lawn as long as they did so peacefully and didn't block his movements? Should they allow it as part of free speech? Do you think this may frighten his little children ages 3 and 4?

4. What is Justice Black's concern about the "pick-up zone" of the store? How does he relate the importance of the "pick-up zone" to his Fifth Amendment argument?

5. What standards would you use as a justice to decide when "free speech" could be exercised in violation of somebody's property rights? Would these standards be useful in determining if a man could picket in your living room or use an amplifier to shout political slogans in your neighborhood at 3:00 A.M.?

glossary*

AD HOC —For this; for this special purpose.

AFFIRM —To ratify, make firm, confirm, establish, reassert (e.g., to affirm a judgment).

AMICAS CURIAE (pl. *AMICI*) —(Latin) A friend of the court.

APPEAL —The removal of a cause from a court of inferior to one of superior jurisdiction, for the purpose of obtaining a review and/or retrial.

APPELLANT —The party who takes an appeal from one court or jurisdiction to another.

APPELLATE COURT —A court having jurisdiction of appeal and review; a court to which causes are removable by appeal, *certiorari*, or error; a reviewing court, and except in special cases where original jurisdiction is conferred, not a court of first instance.

APPELLEE —The party in a case against whom an appeal is taken.

ARGUENDO —In arguing; in the course of the argument.

BRUTUM FULMEN —An empty noise; an empty threat.

CASE CITATION —(How to read one) *Illinois* v. *Allen*, 397 U.S. 337 (1970)—The case of *Illinois* v. *Allen* begins on p. 337 of the 397th volume of *United States* (U.S.) *Reports* and was announced by the Court in 1970; ergo 397 U.S. 337 (1970).

CERTIORARI, WRIT OF —(Latin) Name of a writ of review or inquiry. A writ directed only to an inferior tribunal. It brings into the superior tribunal the record of the administrative or judicial inferior tribunal. The writ is discretionary.

CONCURRING OPINION —An opinion which agrees with the disposition of the case by the majority opinion; it may even agree with the rationale of the majority opinion, but generally adds an additional point not mentioned in the court's opinion.

DE NOVO —Anew; afresh; a second time.

*Editor's note: This glossary has been prepared with extensive reliance on *Black's Law Dictionary* Rev. 4th ed. (St. Paul: West Publishing Co., 1968).

DECLARATORY JUDGMENT —One which simply declares the rights of the parties or expresses the opinion of the court on a question of law, without ordering anything to be done.

DICTUM (pl. *DICTA*) —(Latin) A statement, remark, or observation. The word is generally used as an abbreviated form of *obiter dictum*, "a remark by the way," not necessarily involved; not essential to determination of the case in hand.

DISSENTING OPINION —An opinion which disagrees with the disposition of a case, or its philosophy, or both.

EN BANC —(L. French) In the bench. (When judges of a court sit as a group to hear a case and make a determination without a jury.)

ENJOIN —To require; command; positively direct. To require a person, by writ of injunction from a court of equity, to perform, or to abstain or desist from, some act.

ET AL. —(Latin) An abbreviation for *et alii*, = "and others."

EX PARTE —(Latin) On one side only; by or for one party; done for, in behalf of, or on the application of, one party only. In its more usual sense *ex parte* means an application is made by one party in the absence of the other or without notice to the other.

EX REL. —(Abbr. *ex relatione*) Legal proceedings which are instituted by the attorney general in the name of or on behalf of the State, but on the information and at the instigation of an individual who has a private interest in the matter.

EX UI TERMINI —From or by the force of the term. From the very meaning of the expression used.

FACE, ON ITS —That which is shown by the mere language employed without any explanation, modification, or addition from extrinsic facts or evidence.

FEDERAL REPORTER and *FEDERAL REPORTER* 2d (cited as F. and F.2d) —These series of volumes contain the opinions of the Federal Circuit Courts of Appeal and some of the special federal courts.

FEDERAL SUPPLEMENT (cited as F. Supp.) —Contains the opinions of the federal district courts.

HABEAS CORPUS —(Latin) (You have the body.) The name given to a variety of writs having as their object to bring a party before a court or a judge. The sole function of the writ is to release from unlawful imprisonment or restraint.

INFORMATION, INDICTMENT BY —A criminal accusation in the nature of an indictment, from which it differs only in being presented by a competent public officer (usually a judge) instead of a grand jury.

INFRA —(Latin) Below, beneath, under, underneath. The opposite of *supra*, above.

INJUNCTION —A judicial writ requiring the person or persons to whom it is directed to do *or* refrain from doing a particular thing.

INTER ALIA   —Among other things.

IPSO FACTO   —(Latin) By the fact or act itself; by the very nature of the case.

JURISDICTION   —It is the authority by which courts and judicial officers take cognizance of and decide cases. It is power conferred by the Constitution or by law. It is the legal right by which judges and courts exercise their authority.

LAISSEZ FAIRE   —(French) non interference;—a phrase used in economics depreciating governmental intervention intended to reach some social end.

PER CURIAM OPINION   —(Latin) By the court. A phrase used in the reports to distinguish an opinion of the whole court, or the collective of judges in the majority, from an opinion written by any one judge.

PER SE   —(Latin) By himself or itself; in itself; taken alone; inherently; in isolation; unconnected with other matters.

PETITIONER   —One who initiates a legal proceeding by presenting the court with a request or action for relief.

PLAINTIFF   —A person who brings an action (suit); the party who complains or sues in a personal action.

PRIMA FACIE   —(Latin) At first sight; presumably; a fact presumed to be true unless disproved by some evidence to the contrary.

PRIOR RESTRAINT (PREVIOUS RESTRAINT)   —A prohibition placed upon an action before it has actually taken place. To previously restrain press would be to make illegal the publication and/or the distribution of the printed matter. It is distinguishable from punishment which takes place usually after publication and/or distribution. It is considered unconstitutional under the First Amendment *except in special circumstances.*

REMAND   —To send back. The sending back of a case to the same court out of which it came, for the purpose of having some action taken on it there (*e.g.,* reversed and remanded).

RESPONDENT   —In legal proceedings begun by petition, the person *against* whom action or relief is asked.

SERIATIM   —(Medieval Latin) In a series; serially.

STATUS QUO   —(Latin) The existing state of things at any given date; the state existing.

SUA SPONTE   —(Latin) Of his or its own will or motion; voluntarily; without prompting or suggestion.

SUPRA   —(Latin) Above.

UNITED STATES REPORTS   —*United States Reports* contains the complete official opinions of all U.S. Supreme Court decisions and are cited as U.S. (e.g., 103 U.S. 276).

VACATE —To annul; to set aside; to cancel or rescind (*e.g.*, to vacate a judgment).

VOIR DIRE —(L. French) To speak the truth.

WRIT —A mandatory order issuing from a court of justice. (There are many types of court writs depending upon the action desired to be taken or ended.)